# Human–Machine Reconfigurations

This book considers how agencies are currently figured at the human–machine interface and how they might be imaginatively and materially reconfigured. Contrary to the apparent enlivening of objects promised by the sciences of the artificial, the author proposes that the rhetorics and practices of those sciences work to obscure the performative nature of both persons and things. The question then shifts from debates over the status of humanlike machines to that of how humans and machines are enacted as similar or different in practice and with what theoretical, practical, and political consequences. Drawing on recent scholarship across the social sciences, humanities, and computing, the author argues for research aimed at tracing the differences within specific sociomaterial arrangements without resorting to essentialist divides. This requires expanding our unit of analysis, while recognizing the inevitable cuts or boundaries through which technological systems are constituted.

Lucy Suchman is Professor of Anthropology of Science and Technology in the Sociology Department at Lancaster University. She is also the Co-Director of Lancaster's Centre for Science Studies. Before her post at Lancaster University, she spent twenty years as a researcher at Xerox's Palo Alto Research Center (PARC). Her research focused on the social and material practices that make up technical systems, which she explored through critical studies and experimental and participatory projects in new technology design. In 2002, she received the Diana Forsythe Prize for Outstanding Feminist Anthropological Research in Science, Technology and Medicine.

# Human–Machine Reconfigurations

## *Plans and Situated Actions, 2nd Edition*

**LUCY SUCHMAN**

*Lancaster University, UK*

CAMBRIDGE
UNIVERSITY PRESS

CAMBRIDGE UNIVERSITY PRESS
Cambridge, New York, Melbourne, Madrid, Cape Town, Singapore,
São Paulo, Delhi, Dubai, Tokyo, Mexico City

Cambridge University Press
32 Avenue of the Americas, New York, NY 10013-2473, USA

www.cambridge.org
Information on this title: www.cambridge.org/9780521675888

First published 2007
Reprinted 2009 (twice)

*A catalog record for this publication is available from the British Library.*

*Library of Congress Cataloging in Publication Data*
Suchman, Lucille Alice.
Human–machine reconfigurations : plans and situated actions / Lucy Suchman. – 2nd ed.
p. cm.
Includes bibliographical references and index.
ISBN-13: 978-0-521-85891-5 (hardback)
ISBN-10: 0-521-85891-7 (hardback)
ISBN-13: 978-0-521-67588-8 (pbk.)
ISBN-10: 0-521-67588-x (pbk.)
1. Human–machine systems. 2. Cognition and culture. 3. Ethnophilosophy. I. Title.
T59.7.S83 2006
004.01'9 – dc22 2006007793

ISBN 978-0-521-85891-5 Hardback
ISBN 978-0-521-67588-8 Paperback

As well as the original text of *Plans and Situated Actions: The Problem of Human–Machine
Communication*, some sections of this book have been published elsewhere in other
forms. Chapter 1 takes material from two special journal issues, *Cognitive Science* 17(1),
1993, and the *Journal of the Learning Sciences* 12(2), 2003, and Chapter 12 revises text
published separately under the title "Figuring Service in Discourses of ICT: The Case of
Software Agents" (2000), in E. Wynn et al. (eds.), *Global and Organizational Discourses
about Information Technology*, Dordrecht, The Netherlands: Kluwer, pp. 15–32.

# Contents

v

# Acknowledgments

Over the past two decades, I have had the extraordinary privilege of access to many research networks. The fields with which I have affiliation as a result include human–computer interaction, interface/ interaction design, computer-supported cooperative work, participatory design, information studies/social informatics, critical management and organization studies, ethnomethodology and conversation analysis, feminist technoscience, anthropology of science and technology, science and technology studies, and new/digital media studies, to name only the most explicitly designated. Within these international networks, the friends and colleagues with whom I have worked, and from whom I have learned, number literally in the hundreds. In acknowledgment of this plenitude, I am resisting the temptation to attempt to create an exhaustive list that could name everyone. Knowing well the experiences of both gratification and disappointment that accompany the reading of such lists, it is my hope that a more collective word of thanks will be accepted. Although it is too easy to say that in reading this book you will find your place in it, I nonetheless hope that the artifact that you hold will speak at least partially on its own behalf. The list of references will work as well, I hope, to provide recognition – though with that said, and despite my best efforts to read and remember, I beg forgiveness in advance for the undoubtedly many sins of omission that are evident there.

There are some whose presence in this text are so central and far reaching that they need to be named. Although his position is usually reserved for the last, I start with Andrew Clement, my companion in heart and mind, who tempted me to move north and obtain a maple leaf card at what turned out to be just the right time. Left behind in bodies but not spirit or cyberspace are the colleagues and friends with whom I shared a decade of exciting and generative labors under the auspices of the Work Practice and Technology research area at Xerox Palo Alto Research Center. Jeanette Blomberg and Randall Trigg have been with me since the first edition of this book, and our collaboration spans the ensuing twenty years. I have learned the things discussed in this book, and much more, with them. I thank as deeply Brigitte Jordan, David Levy, and Julian Orr, the other three members of WPT with whom I shared the pleasures, privileges, trials, and puzzlements of life at PARC beginning in the 1980s, along with our honorary members and long-time visitors, Liam Bannon, Françoise Brun Cottan, Charles and Marjorie Goodwin, Finn Kensing, Cathy Marshall, Susan Newman, Elin Pedersen, and Toni Robertson. In an era of news delivered by Friday (or at least the end of the financial quarter), the opportunity to have worked in the company of these extraordinary researchers for well over a decade is a blessing, as well as a demonstration of our collective commitment to the value of the long term. Although we have now gone our multiple and somewhat separate ways, the lines of connection still resonate with the same vitality that animated our work together and that, I hope, is inscribed at least in part on the pages of this book.

The others who need to be named are my colleagues now at Lancaster University. Although the brand of "interdisciplinarity" is an increasingly popular one, scholarship at Lancaster crosses departmental boundaries in ways that provide a kind of intellectual cornucopia beyond my fondest dreams. Within the heterodox unit that is Sociology I thank all of the members of the department – staff and students – for their innovative scholarship and warm collegiality. Through the Centre for Science Studies (CSS) at Lancaster runs the far more extended network of those interested in critical studies of technoscience, including my co-director Maggie Mort and colleagues in the Institute for Health Research and CSS Chair Maureen McNeil, along with other members of the Institute for Women's Studies and the Centre for Social and Economic Aspects of Genomics. The network runs as well through the Institute for Cultural Research; the Centre for the Study of Environmental Change; the Organization, Work and Technology unit within the Management School; Computing; and the recently formed Centre for Mobilities Research. Although the distance I have traveled across institutional as well as watery boundaries has been great, I have found myself immediately again in the midst of colleagues with whom work and friendship are woven richly together. I went to Lancaster with a desire to learn, and I have not for a moment been disappointed.

# Preface to the 2nd Edition

I experience a heightened sense of awareness, but that awareness is not *of* my playing, it *is* my playing. Just as with speech or song, the performance embodies both intentionality and feeling. But the intention is carried forward in the activity itself, it does not consist in an internal mental representation formed in advance and lined up for instrumentally assisted, bodily execution. And the feeling, likewise, is not an index of some inner, emotional state, for it inheres in my very gestures.

> (Ingold 2000: 413, original emphasis)

If we want to know what words like nature and technology mean, then rather than seeking some delimited set of phenomena in the world – as though one could point to them and say "There, that's nature!" or "that's technology!" – we should be trying to discover what sorts of claims are being made with these words, and whether they are justified. In the history of modern thought these claims have been concerned, above all, with the ultimate supremacy of human reason.

> (Ingold 2000: 312)

I bring down my finger onto the Q and turn the knob down with a whole arm twist which I continue into a whole body turn as I disengage from both knob and key. SOH brings in a low quiet sound precisely as I find myself turned to face him. We are in the valley before the finale. I turn back to the synthesiser front panel and gradually swell sound Q into the intense texture it is required to be. At maximum, I hold my right hand over the volume control and bring in my left to introduce a high frequency boost and then a modulation to the filtering. As I turn the knobs, I gradually lean towards the front panel. When the modulation is on the edge of excess, I lean back and face SOH. He looks over. I move my left hand away from the panel, leaving my right poised on the volume knob. I arch myself backwards a little further and then project my torso down while turning the knob anticlockwise. I continue my hand through and away from the panel. SOH has also stopped playing. As the considerable reverberation dies down, we relax together, face the audience and gently bow. We have finished.

(Bowers 2002: 32)

The image of improvised electro-acoustic music that I want to experiment with is one where these contingencies (of place, structure, technology and the rest) are not seen as problematic obstructions to an idealised performance but are topicalised in performance itself. Improvised electro-acoustic music, on this account, precisely is that form of music where those affairs are worked through publicly and in real-time. The contingency of technology-rich music making environments is the performance thematic. The whole point is to exhibit the everyday embodied means by which flesh and blood performers engage with their machines in the production of music. The point of it all does not lie elsewhere or in addition to that. It is in our abilities to work with and display a manifold of human–machine relationships that our accountability of performance should reside.

(Bowers 2002: 44)

My preface by way of an extended epigraph marks the frame of this book and introduces its themes: the irreducibility of lived practice, embodied and enacted; the value of empirical investigation over categorical debate; the displacement of reason from a position of supremacy to one among many ways of knowing in acting; the heterogeneous sociomateriality and real-time contingency of performance; and the new agencies and accountabilities effected through reconfigured relations of human and machine. That these excerpts appear as a preface reflects the contingent practicalities of the authoring process itself. Coming upon these books after having finished my own, I found them so richly consonant with its themes that they could not be left unacknowledged. They appear as an afterthought, in other words, but their position at the beginning is meant to give them pride of place. Moreover, their responsiveness each to the other, however unanticipated, sets up a resonance that seemed in turn to clarify and extend my argument in ways both familiar and new. Taken together, Ingold's painstaking anthropology of traditional and contemporary craftwork and Bower's experimental ethnomethodology of emerging future practices of improvising machines work to trace the arc of my own argument in ways that I hope will become clear in the pages that follow.

# Introduction

My aim in this book is to rethink the intricate, and increasingly intimate, configurations of the human and the machine. Human–machine configurations matter not only for their central place in contemporary imaginaries but also because cultural conceptions have material effects.[1] As our relations with machines elaborate and intensify, questions of the humanlike capacities of machines, and machinelike attributes of humans, arise again and again. I share with Casper (1994), moreover, the concern that the wider recognition of "nonhuman agency" within science and technology studies begs the question of "how entities are configured as human and nonhuman prior to our analyses" (ibid.: 4). Casper proposes that discussions of nonhuman agency need to be reframed from categorical debates to empirical investigations of the concrete practices through which categories of human and nonhuman are mobilized and become salient within particular fields of action. And in thinking through relations of sameness and difference more broadly,

---

[1] The word *imaginary* in this context is a term of art in recent cultural studies (see Braidotti 2002: 143; Marcus 1995: 4; Verran 1998). It shares with the more colloquial term *imagination* an evocation of both vision and fantasy. In addition, however, it references the ways in which how we see and what we imagine the world to be is shaped not only by our individual experiences but also by the specific cultural and historical resources that the world makes available to us, based on our particular location within it. And perhaps most importantly for my purposes here, cultural imaginaries are realized in material ways. My inspiration for this approach is Haraway's commitment to what she names "materialized refiguration (1997: 23), a trope that I return to in Chapter 13. The particular imaginaries at stake in this text are those that circulate through and in relation to the information and communication networks of what we might call the hyperdeveloped countries of Europe and North America.

Ahmed (1998) proposes a shift from a concern with these questions as something to be settled once and for all to the occasioned inquiry of "which differences matter, here?" (ibid.: 4). In that spirit, the question for this book shifts from one of whether humans and machines are the same or different to how and when the categories of human or machine become relevant, how relations of sameness or difference between them are enacted on particular occasions, and with what discursive and material consequences.

In taking up these questions through this second expanded edition of *Plans and Situated Actions*, I rejoin a discussion in which I first participated some twenty years ago, on the question of how capacities for action are figured at the human–machine interface and how they might be imaginatively and materially reconfigured. Almost two decades after the publication of the original text, and across a plethora of subsequent projects in artificial intelligence (AI) and human–computer interaction (HCI), the questions that animated my argument are as compelling, and I believe as relevant, as ever. My starting point in this volume is a critical reflection on my previous position in the debate, in light of what has happened since. More specifically, my renewed interest in questions of machine agency is inspired by contemporary developments both in relevant areas of computing and in the discussion of human–nonhuman relations within social studies of science and technology.[2] What I offer here is another attempt at working these fields together in what I hope will be a new and useful way. The newness comprises less a radical shift in where we draw the boundaries between persons and machines than a reexamination of how – on what bases – those boundaries are drawn. My interest is not to argue the question of machine agency from first principles, in other words, but rather to take as my focus the study of how the effect of machines-as-agents is generated and the latter's implications for theorizing the human. This includes the translations that render former objects as emergent subjects, shifting associated interests and concerns across the human–artifact boundary. We can then move on to questions of what is at stake in these particular translations-in-progress and why we might want to resist or refigure them.

---

[2] At the outset I take the term agency, most simply, to reference the capacity for action, where just what that entails delineates the question to be explored. This focus is not meant to continue the long-standing discussion within sociology on structure and agency, which I take to reiterate an unfortunate dichotomy rather than to clarify questions of the political and the personal, how it is that things become durable and compelling, and the like.

Chapter 1 of this edition provides some background on the original text and reflects on its reception, taking the opportunity so rarely available to authors to respond to readings both anticipated and unexpected.[3] Chapters 2 through 10 comprise the original text as published in 1987. In each of these chapters, new footnotes provide updated references, commentaries, and clarifications, primarily on particular choices of wording that have subsequently proven problematic in ways that I did not foresee. I have made only very minor editorial changes to the text itself, on the grounds that it is important that the argument as stated remain unaltered. This is true, I believe, for two reasons. First, the original publication of the book marked an intervention at a particular historical moment into the fields of artificial intelligence and human–computer interaction, and I think that the significance of the argument is tied in important ways to that context. The second reason for my decision to maintain the original text, and perhaps the more significant one, is that I believe that the argument made at the time of publication holds equally well today, across the many developments that have occurred since. The turn to so-called situated computing notwithstanding, the basic problems identified previously – briefly, the ways in which prescriptive representations presuppose contingent forms of action that they cannot fully specify, and the implications of that for the design of intelligent, interactive interfaces – continue to haunt contemporary projects in the design of the "smart" machine.

The book that follows comprises a kind of object lesson as well in disciplinary affiliations and boundaries. The original text perhaps shows some peculiarities understandable only in light of my location at the time of its writing. In particular, I was engaged in doctoral research for a Ph.D. in anthropology, albeit with a supervisory committee carefully chosen for their expansive and nonprogrammatic relations to disciplinary boundaries.[4] Although the field of American anthropology in the 1980s was well into the period of "studying up," or investigation of institutions at "home" in the United States,[5] my dissertation project

---

[3] Part of the discussion in Chapter 1 is drawn from opportunities provided earlier, in two discussion forums in the journals *Cognitive Science* 17(1), 1993, and the *Journal of the Learning Sciences* 12(2), 2003.

[4] My committee included Gerald Berreman and John Gumperz, from the Department of Anthropology, and Hubert Dreyfus, from the Department of Philosophy, all at the University of California at Berkeley.

[5] For a founding volume see Hymes (1974). di Leonardo (1998) offers a discussion of the enduringly controversial status of "exotics at home" within the discipline.

(with the photocopier as its object, however enhanced by the projects of computing and cognitive science) stretched the bounds of disciplinary orthodoxy. Nonetheless, I was deeply committed to my identification as an anthropologist, as well as to satisfying the requirements of a dissertation in the field. At the same time, I had become increasingly engaged, through my interests in practices of social ordering and face-to-face human interaction, with the lively and contentious research communities of ethnomethodology and conversation analysis. It was these approaches, more than any, perhaps, that informed and shaped my own at the time. Finally, but no less crucially, my position as a Research Intern at Xerox Palo Alto Research Center (PARC) meant that my text had to speak to the fields of AI and HCI themselves.

My task consequently became one of writing across these multiple audiences, attempting to convey something of the central premises and problems of each to the other. More specifically, Chapter 4 of this volume, titled "Interactive Artifacts," and Chapter 5, titled "Plans," are meant as introductions to those projects for readers outside of computing disciplines. Chapter 6, "Situated Actions," and Chapter 7, "Communicative Resources," correspondingly, are written as introductions to some starting premises regarding action and interaction for readers outside of the social sciences. One result of this is that each audience may find the chapters that cover familiar ground to be a bit basic. My hope, however, is that together they lay the groundwork for the critique that is the book's central concern. These chapters are followed by an exhaustive (some might even say exhausting!) explication of a collection of very specific, but, I suggest, also generic, complications in the encounter of "users" with an intendedly intelligent, interactive "expert help system." I attempt to explicate those encounters drawing on the resources afforded by studies in face-to-face human interaction, to shed light on the problem faced by those committed to designing conversational machines. As a kind of uncontrolled laboratory inquiry, the analysis is perhaps best understood as a close study of exercises in instructed action, rather than of the practicalities of machine operation as it occurs in ordinary work environments and in the midst of ongoing activities. With that said, my sense is that the analysis of human–machine communication presented in Chapters 8 and 9 applies equally to the most recent efforts to design conversational interfaces and identifies the defining design problem for HCI more broadly. To summarize the analysis briefly, I observe that human–machine communications take place at a very limited site of interchange; that is, through actions of the user that actually change the machine's state. The radical asymmetries in relative access of user and machine to contingencies of the unfolding situation profoundly limit possibilities for interactivity, at least in anything like the sense that it proceeds between persons in interaction.[6] Chapter 10, the conclusion to the original text, provides a gesture toward alternative directions in interface design and reaffirms the generative potential of the human–computer interface as a site for further research.

Readers familiar with the original text of *P&SA* may choose to pass over Chapters 2 through 10 or to focus more on the footnotes that offer further reflections, references, and clarifications. The chapters that follow the original text expand and update the arguments. Chapter 11, "Plans, Scripts, and Other Ordering Devices," makes clear, I hope, that although the focus of the preceding chapters is on plans (as understood within dominant AI projects of the time), the research object is a much larger class of artifacts. In this chapter I review developments both in theorizing these artifacts in their various manifestations and in empirical investigations of their workings within culturally and historically specific locales. Chapter 12, "Agencies at the Interface," takes up the question of what specific forms agency takes at the contemporary human–computer interface. I begin with a review of the rise of computer graphics and animation, and the attendant figure of the "software agent." Reading across the cases of software agents, wearable, and so-called pervasive or ubiquitous computing, I explore the proposition that these new initiatives can be understood as recent manifestations of the very old dream of a perfect, invisible infrastructure; a dream that I locate now within the particular historical frame of the "service economy." Chapter 13, "Figuring the Human in AI and Robotics," explores more deeply the question of what conceptions of the human inform current projects in AI and robotics, drawing on critiques, cases, and theoretical resources not available to me at the time of my earlier writing. In both chapters I consider developments in relevant areas of research – software agents, wearable computers and "smart" environments, situated robotics, affective computing, and sociable machines – since the 1980s and reflect on their implications. Rather than a comprehensive survey,

---

[6] I should make clear at the outset that I in no way believe that human–computer interactions broadly defined, as the kinds of assemblages or configurations that I discuss in Chapters 14 and 15, are confined to this narrow point. Rather, I am attempting to be specific here about just how events register themselves from the machine's "point of view."

my aim is to identify recurring practices and familiar imaginaries across
these diverse initiatives.

Finally, Chapter 14, "Demysitifications and Reenchantments of the
Humanlike Machine," and Chapter 15, "Reconfigurations," turn to the
question of how it might be otherwise, both in the staging of human–
machine encounters and through the reconfiguration of relations, practices, and projects of technology design and use. As will become clear,
I see the most significant developments over the last twenty years, at
least with respect to the argument of this book, as having occurred less
in AI than in the area of digital media more broadly on the one hand
(including graphical interfaces, animation, and sensor technologies) and
science and technology studies (STS) on the other. The first set of developments has opened up new possibilities not only in the design of so-
called animated interface agents but also – more radically I will argue – in
mundane forms of computing and the new media arts. The further areas
of relevant change are both in the field of STS, which has exploded with
new conceptualizations of the sociotechnical, and also in my own intellectual and professional position. The latter has involved encounters
since the 1980s with feminist science studies, recent writings on science
and technology within cultural anthropology, and other forms of theorizing that have provided me with resources lacking in my earlier consideration of human–machine relations. During that same period, I have
had the opportunity with colleagues at PARC to explore radical alternatives to prevailing practices of system design, informed by an international community of research colleagues. Engaging in a series of iterative
attempts to enact a practice of small-scale, case-based codesign, aimed
at creating new configurations of information technologies, has left me
with a more concrete and embodied sense of both problems and possibilities in reconfiguring relations and practices of professional system
design. I have tried in these chapters to indicate my indebtedness to these
various communities and the insights that I believe they afford for innovative thinking across the interface of human and machine. Inevitably,
both my discussion of new insights from science and technology studies and of new developments in computing is partial at best, drawing
selectively from those projects and perspectives with which I am most
familiar and that I have found most generative or compelling. Drawing
on these resources, I argue for the value of research aimed at articulating the differences *within* particular human–machine configurations,
expanding our unit of analysis to include extended networks of social
and material production, and recognizing the agencies, and attendant

responsibilities, involved in the inevitable cuts through which bounded sociomaterial entities are made.

The expansion of the text in terms of both technologies and theoretical resources is accompanied by a commitment to writing for new audiences. In particular, the new chapters of this book attempt to engage more deeply with those working in the anthropology and sociology of technology who are, and always have been, my compass and point of reference. Somewhat ironically, my location at PARC and the marketing of the original text as a contribution in computer science have meant that the book contained in Chapters 2 through 10 of this edition received much greater visibility in computing – particularly HCI – and in cognitive science than in either anthropology or STS. Although I am deeply appreciative of that readership and the friends from whom I have learned within those communities, it is as a contribution to science and technology studies that the present volume is most deliberately designed.

# 1

# Readings and Responses

This chapter provides a synopsis and some contextualization of the analysis offered in the original edition of *Plans and Situated Actions* (*P&SA*), published in 1987, followed by my reflections on the reception and readings of that text. My engagement with the question of human–machine interaction, from which the book arose, began in 1979, when I arrived at PARC as a doctoral student interested in a critical anthropology of contemporary American institutions[1] and with a background as well in ethnomethodology and interaction analysis. My more specific interest in the question of interactivity at the interface began when I became intrigued by an effort among my colleagues to design an interactive interface to a particular machine. The project was initiated in response to a delegation of Xerox customer service managers, who traveled to PARC from Xerox's primary product development site in Rochester, New York, to report on a problem with the machine and to enlist research advice in its solution.[2] The machine was a relatively large, feature-rich photocopier that had just been "launched," mainly as a placeholder to establish the company's presence in a particular market niche that was under threat from other, competitor, companies. The machine was advertised with a figure dressed in the white lab coat of the scientist/engineer but reassuring the viewer that all that was required to activate the machine's extensive functionality was to "press the green [start] button" (see Fig. 1.1).

---

[1] A defining text of what came to be known as "anthropology as cultural critique" is Marcus and Fischer (1986). See also Gupta and Ferguson (1997); Marcus (1999); Strathern (1999).

[2] The project is discussed at length in Suchman (2005).

FIGURE 1.1. "Pressing the green button" Advertisement for the Xerox 8200 copier, circa 1983 © Xerox Corporation.

It seemed that customers were refuting this message, however, complaining instead that the machine was, as the customer service managers reported it to us, "too complicated." My interest turned to investigating just what specific experiences were glossed by that general complaint, a project that I followed up among other ways by convincing my colleagues that we should install one of the machines at PARC and invite our co-workers to try to use it. My analysis of the troubles evident in these videotaped encounters with the machine by actual scientists/engineers led me to the conclusion that its obscurity was not a function of any lack of general technological sophistication on the part of its users but rather of their lack of familiarity with this particular machine. I argued that the machine's complexity was tied less to its esoteric technical characteristics than to mundane difficulties of interpretation characteristic of any unfamiliar artifact. My point was that making sense of a new artifact is an inherently problematic activity. Moreover, I wanted to suggest that however improved the machine interface or instruction set might be, this would never eliminate the need for active sense-making on the part of prospective users. This in turn called into question the viability of marketing the machine as "self-explanatory," or self-evidently easy to use.[3]

My colleagues, meanwhile, had set out on their own project: to design an "intelligent, interactive" computer-based interface to the machine that would serve as a kind of coach or expert advisor in its proper use. Their strategy was to take the planning model of human action and communication prevalent at the time within the AI research community as a basis for the design. More specifically, my colleagues were engaged with initiatives in "knowledge representation," which for them involved, among other things, representing "goals" and "plans" as computationally encoded control structures. When executed, these control structures should lead an artificially intelligent machine imbued with the requisite condition–action rules to take appropriate courses of action.

My project then became a close study of a second series of videotaped encounters by various people, including eminent computer scientists, attempting to operate the copier with the help of the prototype interactive interface. I took as my focus the question of interactivity and assumptions about human conversation within the field of AI, working those against findings that were emerging in sociological studies of face-to-face human conversation. The main observation of the latter was that human conversation does not follow the kind of message-passing or exchange model that formal, mathematical theories of communication posit. Rather, humans dynamically coconstruct the mutual intelligibility of a conversation through an extraordinarily rich array of embodied interactional competencies, strongly situated in the circumstances at hand (the bounds and relevance of which are, in turn, being constituted through that same interaction). I accordingly adopted the strategy of taking the premise of interaction seriously and applying a similar kind of analysis to people's encounters with the machine to those being

---

[3] As Balsamo succinctly points out, "to design an interface to be 'idiot-proof' projects a very different level of technical acumen onto the intended users than do systems that are designed to be 'configurable'" (Balsamo in press: 29). It should be noted that this agument carried with it some substantial – and controversial – implications for technology marketing practices as well, insofar as it called into question the assertion that technology purchasers could invest in new equipment with no interruption to workers' productivity and with no collateral costs. On the contrary, this analysis suggests that however adequate the design, long-term gains through the purchase of new technology require near-term investments in the resources that workers need to appropriate new technologies effectively into their working practices. Needless to say, this is not a message that appears widely in promotional discourses.

done in conversation analysis. The result of this analysis was a renewed appreciation for some important differences – more particularly asymmetries – between humans and machines as interactional partners and for the profound difficulty of the problem of interactive interface design.

Although the troubles that people encountered in trying to operate the machine shifted with the use of the "expert advisor," the task seemed as problematic as before. To understand those troubles better, I developed a simple transcription device for the videotapes (see Chapter 9), based in the observation that in watching them I often found myself in the position of being able to see the difficulties that people were encountering, which in turn suggested ideas of how they might be helped. If I were in the room beside them, in other words, I could see how I might have intervened. At the same time I could see that the machine appeared quite oblivious to these seemingly obvious difficulties. My question then became the following: What resources was I, as (at least for these purposes) a full-fledged intelligent observer, making use of in my analyses? And how did they compare to the resources available to the machine? The answer to this question, I quickly realized, was at least in part that the machine had access only to a very small subset of the observable actions of its users. Even setting aside for the moment the question of what it means to observe, and how observable action is rendered intelligible, the machine could only "perceive" that small subset of the users' actions that actually changed its state. This included doors being opened and closed, buttons being pushed, paper trays being filled or emptied, and the like. But in addition to those actions, I found myself making use of a large range of others, including talk and various other activities taking place around and in relation to the machine, which did not actually change its state. It was as if the machine were tracking the user's actions through a very small keyhole and then mapping what it saw back onto a prespecified template of possible interpretations. Along with limitations on users' access to the design script,[4] in other words, I could see clearly the serious limitations on the machine's access to its users.

My analysis, in sum, located the problem of human–machine communication in continued and deep asymmetries between person and machine. I argued that so-called interactive programs such as the

---

[4] On scripts and their configuration of users, see Woolgar (1991) and Akrich (1992). I discuss these ideas more fully in Chapter 11.

expert system devised by my colleagues exploit certain characteristics of human conversation in ways that encourage attributions of interactivity to machines by their human interlocutors. At the same time, those attributions belie the profoundly different relations of person and machine to the unfolding situation and their associated capacities to interact within and through it. So the machine's users will read instructions offered by an expert help system as comments on the activity underway that *should be* intelligible, a strategy that proves extremely powerful for moving things along. Human interaction succeeds to the extent that it does, however, due not simply to the abilities of any one participant to construct meaningfulness but also to the possibility of mutually constituting intelligibility, in and through the interaction. This includes, crucially, the detection and repair of mis- (or different) understandings. And the latter in particular, I argued, requires a kind of presence to the unfolding situation of interaction not available to the machine.

My discussion of these problems was carefully framed not to take a position on the ultimate possibility that machines could ever be intelligent and interactive but to suggest at least that the problem of interactive interface design is a much more subtle and interesting one than what it was assumed to be by my colleagues at the time. Basically, it seemed to me, their assumption was that computational artifacts just *are* interactive, in roughly the same way that we are, albeit with some more and less obvious limitations. However ambitious, the problem as they saw it was a fairly straightforward task of overcoming the limitations of machines by encoding more and more of the cognitive abilities attributed to humans into them.[5] My purpose in emphasizing the limits on machine interactivity was not, in other words, to argue from any a priori assumptions about essential aspects of "human nature" (Sack 1997: 62). As I hope will become clear in the following pages, I take the boundaries between persons and machines to be discursively and materially enacted rather than naturally effected and to be available, for better and worse and with greater and lesser resistances, for refiguring. It is precisely because the distinction between person and machine rests on the traffic back and forth between the two terms that questions of human–machine identity and difference matter. With that said, my observation continues to be that although the language of interactivity

---

[5] For closely considered arguments regarding the problems with this premise, see, for example, Dreyfus ([1972]1992); Collins (1990); Button, Coulter, Lee, and Sharrock (1995); Adam (1998).

and the dynamics of computational artifacts obscure enduring asymmetries of person and machine, people inevitably rediscover those differences in practice.

The prevailing view within AI in the early to mid-1980s was that the relation of plans to actions was a determining one.[6] A primary aim of the argument of *P&SA* was to suggest a shift in the status of plans, from cognitive control structures that universally precede and determine actions to cultural resources produced and used within the course of certain forms of human activity. A starting premise of my argument was that planning is itself a form of situated activity that results in projections that bear some interesting, and as yet unexplicated, relation to the actions that they project. In ordinary affairs, "planning" is an imaginative and discursive practice (now underwritten by a wide range of more and less effective technologies) through which actors project what they might do and where they might go, as well as reflect on where they are in relation to where they imagined that they might be.[7]

Having reopened the question of what plans are and how they work, I then suggested that we locate the answer to that question in what Garfinkel and Sacks (1970: 342) have named the "observable-reportable" accountability of practical reasoning and practical action. A central feature of planning in this sense is that it is among the many everyday practices that we, as participants in Euro-American cultural traditions at least, call out as a foundation for the rationality of our actions. The planned character of our actions is not, in this sense, inherent but is demonstrably achieved. It is a reflexive feature of our (inter-)actions insofar as we are able, on an ongoing basis, to indicate (to others and/or to ourselves) what we are aiming to do and to account for our actions as close enough for all practical purposes to what we had intended. Note that *reflexivity* as used here is not a synonym for reflection but rather as a statement that the sense of our actions is found in and through the very same methods that we employ to enact them intelligibly in the first place.

An unanticipated but welcome development in the progress of my work on the original text occurred when I discovered a resonance between my project and another underway at the time inside the AI community. In the 1980s Phil Agre and David Chapman, themselves

---

[6] The central text being Miller, Galanter, and Pribram (1960).

[7] On the status of plans as prospective and retrospective resources for action, see also Agre (1997: 5–9) and Agre and Chapman (1990).

doctoral students at the Massachusetts Institute of Technology (MIT) AI Lab, were engaged in a kind of endogenous critique of prevailing assumptions and practices within the field, particularly in the area of AI planning (Agre and Chapman 1987, 1990). Brought together through the closely linked networks of PARC and MIT, we discovered an unexpected complementarity in our projects. In particular, Agre and Chapman were troubled by what they found to be a logical and, they argued, fatal flaw in the machinery of AI planning. Committed to questioning the planning paradigm on a technical basis, they were interested to find an anthropologist engaged in the same project on the basis of the framework's adequacy as an account of everyday practice. I, correspondingly, was delighted to find allies capable of opening up the planning framework to critical inspection on its own terms. Our connection resulted in a rich exchange, not simply of the idea that plans needed reconceptualization in AI, but of theoretical and empirical resources to aid in that project. Agre subsequently developed the implications of an ethnomethodological critique for AI, and research into computation more broadly, through his conception of a "critical technical practice," one in which attention to the rhetorics and technologies through which a field constructs its research objects becomes an integral part of its research practice.[8] As Agre explains:

Instead of seeking foundations it would embrace the impossibility of foundations, guiding itself by a continually unfolding awareness of its own workings as a historically specific practice. It would make further inquiry into the practice of AI an integral part of the practice itself. It would accept that this reflexive inquiry places all of its concepts and methods at risk. And it would regard this risk positively, not as a threat to rationality but as the promise of better ways of doing things. (1997: 23)

Although these more complex lines of intellectual exchange remained generally unrecognized in the wider AI community, the trope of the "situated" traveled through Agre to his supervisor, Rod Brooks, at MIT.[9] Sengers (2004) observes that, by now, references to "situated action"

---

[8] Agre's argument, of course, has strong resonance with Harding's notion of a "successor science" (1986, 1991) and related writings in feminist science studies, in its emphasis on critical engagement with the location and limits of knowledge production as an integral part of scientific practice. For a recent discussion of the interchange between *P&SA* and the field of AI, read through the lens of this history and Agre's proposal, see Sengers (2004).

[9] Interview with Rod Brooks, March 20, 2003. I discuss Brooks's approach further, particularly with respect to notions of embodiment, in Chapter 13 of this volume.

have been incorporated into business as usual within AI research. But unlike the case of Agre's critical technical practice, she argues, AI researchers have for the most part failed to see the argument's implications for their own relations to their research objects and, relatedly, have adhered to an unreconstructed form of realism in their constitution of the "situation." Brooks in particular embraces an idea of situated action as part of his campaign against representationalism in AI and within a broader argument for an evolutionarily inspired model of intelligence.[10] For Brooks, *situated* means that creatures reflect in their design an adaptation to particular environments. Following a lineage traceable to the founding premises of cybernetics, Brooks's situatedness is one evacuated of sociality, at least as other than a further elaboration of an environment understood primarily in physical terms. The creature's "interactions" with the environment, similarly, comprise variations of conditioned response, however tightly coupled the mechanisms or emergent the effects.

A reading of *situated* as nonrepresentational has led in some cases to the term's appropriation in support of various forms of neobehaviorism. Brooks's robots evidence one version of this, as does the reading put forward by Vera (2003), for whom *situated* comes, in an ironic twist, to mean "predetermined," a sense antithetical to the orientation toward the flexible, ongoing (re-)production of intelligible action that I would take it to convey. Vera makes the interesting point that a difference between Simon's famous ant (1969) and the Micronesian navigator invoked in the opening of *P&SA* is that the former is impeded by the contingencies of the environment, whereas the latter takes advantage of them. But, remarkably, he concludes from this, "In this sense, the ant's behavior seems truly situated, in the strongest theoretical sense" (Vera 2003: 283). Although I am unsure what being situated "in the strongest theoretical sense" could mean, I am sure that my use of *situated* does not mean acting in the absence of culturally and historically constituted resources for meaning making. On the contrary, as I have reiterated (perhaps for some ad nauseum), situatedness is presupposed by such practices and the condition of possibility for their realization. Behavior is not simply "reactive and contingent on the external world" (ibid.: 283) but rather is reflexively constitutive of the world's significance, which in turn gives behavior its sense.

---

[10] For formulations of Brooks' position written for a general reader, see Brooks (1999, 2002).

The unfortunate separation of planned and situated as somehow two kinds of action (of which more below) contributes to an inverse reading of *situated*, also very different from my own, which treats the term as synonymous with spontaneous or improvisational. Set in opposition to predetermining conditions, this leads to an interpretation of *situated* as involving a kind of erasure of context, as implying that action happens de novo, without reference to prior histories. This is of course antithetical to the kind of strong orientation to the circumstances of action that my use of the term was meant to support and is understandable only in the context of long-standing debates within the social sciences over how we should understand the obdurate and enduring character of normative and institutionalized social orders. More sympathetically, Gordon Wells (2003) raises the question of the relation between an orientation to the in situ achievement of social order and the problem of the durability of orders of ordinary action over time and across space. To my understanding, ethnomethodology's insistence on the "just here, just now" achievement of social order is not aimed at an erasure of history. Rather, it is a move away from the structuralist premise that prior conditions fully specify what it means to act within the prescripts that institutionalized society provides. As in the analysis of prescriptive representations more broadly, social institutions and the rules that they imply do not reproduce themselves apart from ongoing activity. And like instructions, plans, and other forms of prescriptive representation, both institutions and rules of conduct presuppose in situ forms of social action that they can never fully specify.

There is in my view no inherent conflict between an ethnomethodological approach to studies of situated action and an interest in cultural historical continuities and their effects. The commitment to situated action orients us, however, always to the question of just how, and for whom, culturally and historically recognizable formations take on their relevance to the moment at hand. With respect to the durability and reach of established social orders, the dichotomies of "micro" and "macro," "local" and "global," are replaced by questions of location and extent. Tropes of "large" and "small," "top and bottom," give way to analyses of the cumulative durability and force of practices and artifacts extended through repeated citation and in situ reenactment. Ethnomethodology and other poststructuralist approaches to social order propose, in sum, that it is only through their everyday enactment and reiteration that institutions are reproduced and rules of conduct realized.

Two published forums in the years 1993 and 2003 comprise the most intensive discussion of the original text of *P&SA*, both located at the intersection of the cognitive and social sciences.[11] These discussions traversed some of the thornier underbrush in my original articulation of the argument, demonstrating weaknesses and gaps as well as some surprisingly enduring and, for me, puzzling, (mis-)readings. Along with whatever contributions I have unwittingly made to the latter, I believe that they are evidence for the multiplicity of different, sometimes antithetical, premises with which I and my interlocutors approach our subject matter. Perhaps the most direct critique of the original text came in an article by Alonso Vera and Herbert Simon (1993) titled "Situated Action: A Symbolic Interpretation." Aimed more broadly at refuting the growing interest in nonsymbolic forms of AI promoted by Brooks and others, Vera and Simon discuss what they name "the congeries of theoretical views collectively referred to as 'situated action (SA).'"[12] In their representation of my argument, Vera and Simon reiterate the (mis-) reading most frequent among those who cite it, whether sympathetic or not. In particular, they claim that I assert planning to be "irrelevant in everyday human activity" (ibid.: 7). I took the opportunity of responding to their article to restate that the primary agenda of my writing on the topic was not to dismiss plans as phenomena of interest but, on the contrary, to recover them as objects of investigation. My concern was that as long as plans were treated as determining of the actions projected, a theory of plans became not only necessary but also sufficient for an account of human activity. One might have to worry about cases in which for one reason or another a planned action could not be executed, but the fundamental assumption was that once you knew the plan, the action simply followed.

---

[11] See *Cognitive Science* 17(1), 1993; *Journal of the Learning Sciences* 12(2), 2003. My representation of this debate is drawn from Suchman (1993, 2003). For other careful and generative readings of the original text, see Heath and Luff (2000: Chapter 1); Dourish (2001: Chapter 3). Clancey (1997) offers an extended discussion of the sense of *situated* for the cognitive sciences. For a cogent analysis of appropriations of a notion of "situatedness" in service of general critiques of education, and the identification of an alternate programme of classroom research, see Macbeth (1996).

[12] I have attempted scrupulously to avoid the use of acronyms such as SA or initial capitals with the phrase "situated action," hoping to forestall the introduction of a hardened theoretical object and to maintain the descriptive character of the adjective. Of course all action is situated: the adjective is meant not as a qualifier, but rather as a reminder of that fact.

Perhaps in part because of their commitment to this conception of plans, Vera and Simon read my argument that plans are not determining of the actions that they project (at least not in any strong sense of the word *determining*) as a rejection of the notion of planning altogether.[13] The main justification for this reading of my argument seemed to be the example I offered of taking a canoe through a set of rapids (see Chapter 6). Vera and Simon claimed that I had said that "a person would plan a course down the river but this plan would serve no purpose when the rapids were finally run" (1993: 16). As evidence for this, they cite a sentence of mine meant to point to the priority of embodied action in such an activity: "When it really comes down to the details of responding to the currents and handling a canoe, you effectively abandon the plan and fall back on whatever skills are available to you" (Suchman 1987: 52). Although I admit that the phrase "effectively abandon" was an unfortunate one and legitimately prone to such a reading, I pointed out that the sense would change in a subtle but important way had Vera and Simon included the next sentence as well: "The purpose of the plan in this case is not to get your canoe through the rapids, but rather to orient you in such a way that you can obtain the best possible position from which to use those embodied skills on which, in the final analysis, your success depends" (ibid.: 52). The plan, in sum, has a purpose.[14] The interesting question, I proposed, is just how it fulfills that purpose. Vera and Simon argued that I did not "appear to recognize that most plans

---

[13] Vera and Simon asserted as well that I, along with Winograd and Flores (1986), argued that "the methods and terminology of situated action should replace current human-computer interaction methods in psychology and AI" and that "we must focus on how people use [interfaces] instead of how people think, or what computers can do" (1993: 11). I do not believe that I ever used such exclusionary language in speaking of these things. Rather, my interest had been (a) to redress a situation of *disattention to* human-computer interaction as situated activity and (b) to take the idea of human–computer interaction seriously *as interaction,* in the sense that I understand it between people. Doing the latter actually led me to the limits of the notion that what goes on between people and machines is usefully compared to interaction between people. In any case, in no way was my approach meant to replace investigations of how people think or of what computers can do. If anything, it was meant to reframe them.

[14] In response to my concern with this partial citation after reading a draft of Vera and Simon's article, they included the following footnote in the published version: "Elsewhere on this same page, Suchman retreated a bit from this strong language, and acknowledged that, even in this kind of situation, the plan may determine initial conditions for the behavior. However, her discussion is at best contradictory, and in general, wholly skeptical of planning" (1987: 16). Note that the sentence in question does not propose that plans are "initial conditions": I would maintain that the confusion here is Vera and Simon's, not my own.

are not specifications of fixed sequences of actions, but are strategies that determine each successive action as a function of current information about the situation" (1993: 17). Although I wonder about terms like *most* plans and *determine ... as a function of*, the question of just how plans relate to the actions they formulate does constitute our common interest, as well as the real point of debate.

My discussion of the canoeing example was meant to emphasize *both* the utility of projecting future actions *and* the reliance of those projections on a further horizon of activity that they do not exhaustively specify. The case of whitewater canoeing seemed to me to offer a perspicuous example of both. My choice of wording has clearly contributed to the reading of my argument as saying that the plan is irrelevant once one is in the water. This despite the fact that the surrounding text makes clear that I take *both* the projected course *and* the work done within the rapids to be crucial. Again, the interesting question is just how the activity of projecting a course has its effects in the subsequent activity of finding one in situ. It is those effects, understood as a situated achievement of the very same course of action that the plan projects, that constitute the plan's practical adequacy as an orienting device for action.

Vera and Simon come in the end to what they say is "the central claim of hard SA: that behavior can only be understood in the context of complex real-world situations. Interpreted literally, this claim is surely wrong, since no organism, natural or artificial, ever deals with the real-world situation in its full complexity" (ibid.: 45). Setting aside the question of just what it would mean to "interpret literally" this claim, I proposed a rewording that would make it closer to a claim to which I would in fact subscribe, namely "that behavior can only be understood in its relations with real-world situations." There are two changes here, one subtle, one less so. The more subtle shift, from "in the context of" to "in its relations with," is meant to get away from the container-like connotation of the term *context* and emphasize instead that the structuring of behavior is done not a priori, but in reflexive relation to circumstances that are themselves in the process of being generated, through the same actions that they in turn work to make comprehensible. The less subtle correction is elimination of the term *complex*, a term more from Vera and Simon's discourse than from my own. In my view the complexity or simplicity of situations is a distinction that inheres not in situations but in our characterizations of them; that is, all situations are complex under some views and simple under others. Similarly, I cannot imagine what it could mean to deal with a situation in its "full" complexity, because situations are not quantities of preexisting properties dealt with more and less fully. The point of the claim as reworded is just that actions are structured in relation to specific circumstances and need to be understood in those terms.

To summarize, my position then and now has been that plans are conceptual and rhetorical devices (often materialized in various ways, as texts, diagrams and the like) that are deeply consequential for the lived activities of those of us who organize our actions in their terms. Just how plans are consequential for the actions they project defined, at least potentially, a territory of mutual interest for the social and cognitive sciences. Vera and Simon's position, in contrast, seems based on the premise that planning – or more accurately plan execution – and situated action comprise two different, alternative forms of activity: that, as they put it, a function of a plan is that it "minimizes the number of occasions when an emergency calling for SA will arise," namely, those requiring reaction to "severe, real-time requirements" or "unexpected events" (1993: 41). Planning and plan execution, in other words, are still the primary forms of activity, with what is now called "SA" (which in its "pure" form according to Vera and Simon is made up entirely of predetermined responses) coming into play only in certain cases. As I tried to make clear in my response at the time, this is not the view of situated action that I hold. Nor, I believe, is it the view that will lead us closer to an understanding of how plans might be generated within situated activity and then brought to bear on some future course of action. To reach that understanding will require an account of the relation between planning-as-activity, the artifacts of that activity, and the subsequent activities to which those artifacts (conceptual, linguistic, or otherwise) are meaningfully related.[15]

The publication of a Books and Ideas section in the *Journal of the Learning Sciences* (2003) afforded another, more recent opportunity for a response to readings of the original text of *P&SA*. In their generally sympathetic critique in that volume, Sharrock and Button call attention to a deeper vulnerability in my original argument. They close their commentary with a valuable clarification, by pointing to ambiguities in the verb "to determine." More specifically, they point out that the sense implied by a statement like "our position on the high seas is determined . . . by consulting a chart" presupposes not an axiomatically causal relation, but an act by which things are brought into relation (2003: 263). Bringing

---

[15] I return to this topic in Chapter 11.

things into relation may be done more and less easily, as we become familiar with particular, recurring configurations iterated over time (for example, relations between the laws governing where one may and may not park, the signs and artifacts that mark the urban landscape, the practices of driving and parking, the documents used to indicate an infraction, the ability of drivers to read those signs and documents, and so forth). Despite the seeming automaticity of these relations, however, they do not run by themselves but must be continually reiterated and reproduced, as well as elaborated, resisted, and/or transformed. Consistent with this position, I wanted to suggest that plans are just one among many types of discursive artifacts through which we achieve the rational accountability of action. As such, they arise through activity and are incorporated into the activities that they project.

In the interest of challenging the cognitive science view of plans as determinates of action, however, I uncoupled plans and actions and reframed their relation as problematic. By implicitly suggesting that plans were somehow outside of action, this move invited just the kind of separation on which the plan versus execution dichotomy, which I was trying to displace, relies. Where I had hoped to direct attention instead was precisely to *the relation between the activity of planning and the conduct of actions-according-to-plan*. My aim was not to define that relation but to pose it as a question for our collective research agendas and to suggest that ethnomethodology had some crucial contributions toward an answer.

Viewing the plan as an artifact or tool (the hammer being the iconic case) seemed helpful in further clarifying the plan/action relation. Although the durable materiality of the hammer supports the statement that it exists before and after the moments of its use, it is nonetheless clear that its status as a hammer rests on its incorporation into the practice of some form of carpentry. By the same token, being a carpenter involves, inter alia, the competent practice of hammering. The possibility of uncoupling the hammer from its use in carpentry does not mean that the two are separable in practice. Similarly, calling out a plan as a self-standing artifact is a situated action in its own right and does not diminish the reliance of the plan for its significance on its effective incorporation into practice.

Most fundamentally, I wanted to draw attention to the ways in which plans and other formulations of action open out onto a sphere of embodied action and lived experience that extends always beyond their bounds and at the same time gives them their sense and efficacy. It is this relation that forms a core topic for ethnomethodology, exemplified as Sharrock and Button remind us in the work of instruction following. The efficacy of plans, instructions, and the like – their generality and their "immutable mobility" (to use Latour's famous phrase; 1986: 7) – relies precisely on the ability of those who make use of them to find the relation of these general prescriptions to the particular occasion that faces us now. It is in this respect that instructions do not precede the work of their enactment but rather that their sense is found in and through, and only in and through, that work. As should be evident, this is an extraordinarily general phenomenon of social life, though it can only be understood in its specifics.

In his broadly generous reading of *P&SA*, John Carroll (2003) points to what I agree is another weak link of the original book; that is, its conclusions. He suggests that it was my use of conversation analysis as a foundation for my study that limited my ability to draw out the argument's design implications. Rather, I would say that it was my own fledgling relation to the fields of system design and their possibilities, the limits of my experience at the time, which constrained my ability to imagine how it could be otherwise. As Carroll takes care to point out, I have been involved in the years since in exploring the design implications of the critique through my own developing practice. More specifically, this has involved a series of initiatives aimed at practicing alternative approaches, demonstrated as cases of ethnographically based, work-oriented participatory design.[16]

So what would I conclude now, given the benefit of all the developments since 1987 both in my own working life and in the projects of AI and HCI? In the original project I adopted the methodological strategy of applying analytic techniques and insights from the study of human interaction to see what would happen if we took the metaphor of human–computer interaction seriously. I begin my conclusions now by reiterating the basic finding of the analysis in *P&SA*; namely, that

---

[16] See Blomberg, Suchman, and Trigg (1996); Suchman (1999, 2001, 2002a, 2002b); Suchman, Blomberg, Orr, and Trigg (1999); Suchman, Trigg, and Blomberg (2002); Trigg, Blomberg, and Suchman (1999). I am a bit less encouraged than Carroll at the extent to which "ethnographic workplace studies and worker participation in design are standard engineering practices" (2003: 278). In some respects I have the contrary sense that the spaces for this kind of design practice are closing down with the economic turns of the industry and associated retrenchments in old values of (at least apparently, in upfront costs) faster and cheaper production. I return to these problems and possibilities in Chapter 15.

there is (still) no evidence for the achievement of conversation between humans and machines in the strong sense that we know it to go on between humans. Interaction, as Emanuel Schegloff reminds us (1982), is not the stage on which the exchange of messages takes place, or the means through which intentionality and interpretation operationalize themselves. Rather, interaction is a name for the ongoing, *contingent coproduction* of a shared sociomaterial world. Interactivity as engaged participation with others cannot be stipulated in advance but requires an autobiography, a presence, and a projected future. In this strong sense, I would argue, we have yet to realize the creation of an inter-active machine.

At the same time, given recent demonstrations within science and technology studies and the media arts of the many ways in which things do participate with us, I now emphasize the proposition that they must be allowed to do so in their own particular ways. Initial observations suggest that a more productive metaphor than conversation to describe our relations with computational artifacts may be that of writing and reading (see Grint and Woolgar 1997: 70; Chapter 11). But these are new forms of writing and reading, with new materials or media. What characterizes those new media are their unprecedented dynamics, based in their underlying computational mechanisms. More than conversation at the interface, we need the creative elaboration of the particular dynamic capacities that these new media afford and of the ways that through them humans and machines together can perform interesting new effects. These are avenues that have just begun to be explored, primarily in the fields of new media, graphics and animation, art and design. Not only do these experiments promise innovations in our thinking about machines, but they also open up the equally exciting prospect of new conceptualizations of what it means to be human, understood not as a bounded, rational entity but as an unfolding, shifting biography of culturally specific experience and relations, inflected for each of us in uniquely particular ways.

# 2

# Preface to the 1st Edition

Thomas Gladwin (1964) has written a brilliant article contrasting the
method by which the Trukese navigate the open sea, with that by which
Europeans navigate. He points out that the European navigator begins
with a plan – a course – which he has charted according to certain universal principles, and he carries out his voyage by relating his every move
to that plan. His effort throughout his voyage is directed to remaining
"on course." If unexpected events occur he must first alter the plan,
then respond accordingly. The Trukese navigator begins with an objective rather than a plan. He sets off toward the objective and responds to
conditions as they arise in an ad hoc fashion. He utilizes information provided by the wind, the waves, the tide and current, the fauna, the stars,
the clouds, the sound of the water on the side of the boat, and he steers
accordingly. His effort is directed to doing whatever is necessary to reach
the objective. If asked, he can point to his objective at any moment, but he
cannot describe his course.

(Berreman 1966: 347)

The subject of this book is the two alternative views of human intelligence and directed action represented here by the Trukese and
the European navigator.[1] The European navigator exemplifies the

---

[1] A comment is needed here on the poetics and problems of this quotation. In his subsequent book Gladwin (1970: 232) modified his analysis of the question of plans with
respect to Micronesian navigation. In particular, he proposed that the distinctions he
had initially sought between Micronesian and Western navigators, and that he had
located among other places in their respective relations to planning, could not be so
clearly drawn. This was the case insofar as the Micronesian navigator could also be said
to have a plan in advance of his voyage, the difference being less in the existence of

prevailing cognitive science model of purposeful action, for reasons that are implicit in the final sentence of the quote above. That is to say, while the Trukese navigator is hard pressed to tell us how he actually steers his course, the comparable account for the European seems to be already in hand, in the form of the very plan that is assumed to guide his actions. Although the objective of the Trukese navigator is clear from the outset, his actual course is contingent on unique circumstances that he cannot anticipate in advance. The plan of the European, in contrast, is derived from universal principles of navigation and is essentially independent of the exigencies of his particular situation.

Given these contrasting exemplars, there are at least three, quite different, implications that we might draw for the study of purposeful action. First, we might infer that there actually are different ways of acting that are favored differently across cultures. How to act purposefully is learned and subject to cultural variation. European culture favors abstract, analytic thinking, the ideal being to reason from general principles to particular instances. The Trukese, in contrast, having no such ideological commitments, learn a cumulative range of concrete, embodied responses, guided by the wisdom of memory and experience over years of actual voyages. In the pages that follow, however, I argue that all activity, even the most analytic, is fundamentally concrete and embodied. So although there must certainly be an important relationship between ideas about action and ways of acting, this first interpretation

something that could be called a plan than in the plan's specific character. Whereas the Western navigator draws up a plan for each voyage, Gladwin observes, the Micronesian effectively learns a set of navigational practices as an integral part of learning to sail, which are then available for any subsequent voyage. This difference is balanced by the common requirement – set out, Gladwin proposes, by the sea itself – for aids to navigation. This revision challenges the simple readings to which this opening epigraph was prone, while underscoring the idea developed in the text that follows that we understand plans as orienting devices whose usefulness turns on their translation to action within an uncertain horizon of contingencies. It also suggests that the moral of the story be read as emphasizing the interrelation of cultural and historical traditions within which persons act and the artifacts and practices that they produce and rely on. It is the specific and various configurations of the latter that I would now argue we need to take as our topic of investigation. My thanks go to Phil Agre for drawing this passage from Gladwin to my attention. For detailed accounts of Pacific island navigational traditions, see also Lewis (1972), Hutchins (1983), and Turnbull (1990, 2000). On the politics of the European fascination with Micronesia, of which these studies are a part, David Turnbull (1990: 6) points out that "Micronesian navigation has been 'discovered' and revived to serve as an anthropological mirror for western knowledge at the very moment when it was about to be snuffed from existence."

of the navigation example stands in danger of confusing theory with practice.[2]

Alternatively, we might posit that whether our actions are ad hoc or planned depends on the nature of the activity or our degree of expertise. So we might contrast instrumental, goal-directed activities with creative or expressive activities or contrast novice with expert behavior. Dividing things up along these lines, however, seems in some important ways to violate our navigation example. Clearly the Truk is involved with instrumental action in getting from one island to another, and just as clearly the European navigator relies on his chart, regardless of his degree of expertise.[3]

Finally, the position to be taken – and the one that I adopt here – could be that, however planned, purposeful actions are inevitably *situated actions*. By situated actions I mean simply actions taken in the context of particular, concrete circumstances. In this sense one could argue that we all act like the Trukese, however much some of us may talk like Europeans. We must act like the Trukese because the circumstances of our actions are never fully anticipated and are continuously changing around us. As a consequence our actions, although systematic, are never planned in the strong sense that cognitive science would have it. Rather, plans are best viewed as a weak resource for what is primarily ad hoc activity. It is only when we are pressed to account for the rationality of our actions, given the biases of European culture, that we invoke the guidance of a plan. Stated in advance, plans are necessarily vague, insofar as they must accommodate the unforeseeable contingencies of particular situations. Reconstructed in retrospect, plans systematically filter out precisely the particularity of detail that characterizes situated

---

[2] Or rather, I would say now, in a familiar parochially Western move this interpretation sets up a false opposition between theory and practice, allocating the one to the European (erasing the presence of practical specificity), the latter to the Trukese (erasing the presence of generalizing practices). More seriously, this interpretation puts us in the problematic position identified by postcolonial scholarship, defining the Trukese as second Other to the European, characterized by the absence of a privileged, albeit imaginary, rationality. For a far more nuanced and provocative treatment of these questions, see Turnbull (2000), and Verran's argument in favor of what she calls "disconcertment," or recognition of the simultaneous sameness and incommensurable difference in culturally specific "ontic/epistemic imaginaries," over either universalism or relativism (2001).

[3] Much has now been written about the transformations that occur in learning a practice. As a central text on learning in doing, published in parallel with my own, see Lave (1988).

actions, in favor of those aspects of the actions that can be seen to accord with the plan.

This third implication, it seems, is not just a symmetric alternative to the other two but is different in kind and somewhat more serious. That is, it calls into question not just the adequacy of our distinctions along the dimensions of culture, kinds of activity, or degrees of expertise, but the very productivity of our starting premises that representations of action such as plans could be the basis for an account of actions in particular situations. Because the third implication has to do with foundations, and not because there is no truth in the other two, I take the idea that actions are primarily situated and that situated actions are essentially ad hoc as the starting point for my investigations.[4]

The view of action exemplified by the European navigator is now being reified in the design of intelligent machines. In this book I examine one such machine, as a way of uncovering the strengths and limitations of the general view that its design embodies. The view, that purposeful action is determined by plans, is deeply rooted in the Western human sciences as *the* correct model of the rational actor. The logical form of plans makes them attractive for the purpose of constructing a computational model of action, to the extent that for those fields devoted to what is now called cognitive science, the analysis and synthesis of plans effectively constitute the study of action. My own contention, however, is that as students of human action we ignore the Trukese navigator at our peril. Although an account of how the European navigates may be in hand, the essential nature of action, however planned or unplanned, is situated. It behooves us, therefore, to study and to begin to find ways to describe the "Trukese" system.

There is an injunction in social studies of science to eschew interest in the validity of the products of science in favor of an interest in their

---

[4] I see my choice of the term *ad hoc* here as an unfortunate one, particularly in light of subsequent readings of the text. The problem lies in the term's common connotations of things done anew, or narrowly, without reference to historically constituted or broader concerns. Perhaps a better way of phrasing this would be to say that situated actions are always, and irremediably, contingent on specific, unfolding circumstances that are themselves substantially constituted through those same actions. This is the case however much actions may also be informed by prescriptive representations, past experience, future considerations, received identities, entrenched social relations, established procedures, built environments, material contraints, and the like. To be rendered effective the significance and relevance of any of those must be reiterated, or transformed, in relation to what is happening just here and just now. For a brilliant and generative proposal for what he names a "science of singularity," see de Certeau (1988).

production.[5] Although I generally agree with this injunction, my investigation of one of the prevailing models of human action in cognitive science is admittedly and unabashedly interested. That is to say, I take it that there is a reality of human action, beyond either the cognitive scientist's models or my own accounts, to which both are trying to do justice. In that sense, I am examining the cognitive science model not just with the dispassion of the uncommitted anthropologist of science but also in light of an alternative account of human action to which I am committed and that I attempt to clarify in the process.

[5] I would now take this to be an oversimplification of the so-called principle of symmetry in science studies, which argues that rather than take positions deemed "true" at a particular moment as explicable by nature, and only those considered "false" as amenable to social analysis, all scientific positions should be analyzable in the same terms. Those terms now increasingly involve attempts to come to grips with the simultaneously social/cultural and material/natural constitution of scientific practices and attendant knowledges.

# 3

# Introduction to the 1st Edition

The famous anthropological absorption with the (to us) exotic . . . is, thus, essentially a device for displacing the dulling sense of familiarity with which the mysteriousness of our own ability to relate perceptively to one another is concealed from us.

(Geertz 1973: 14)

The problem of shared understanding, or mutual intelligibility, has defined the field of social studies for the past hundred years. On the one hand, interpreting the actions of others has been the social scientist's task; to come up with accounts of the significance of human actions is, after all, the principal charge of ethnographic anthropology. On the other hand, to understand the mutual intelligibility of action as a mundane, practical accomplishment of members of the society is, in large measure, the social scientist's problem or subject matter. An account of that accomplishment would constitute an account of the foundation of social order. Although studies of mutual intelligibility have been concerned exclusively with human action, we now have a technology that has brought with it the idea that rather than just using machines, we interact with them as well.[1] Already, the notion of "human–machine interaction" pervades both technical and popular discussion of computers, whether about their design or their use. In the debate over specific problems in the design and use of interactive machines, however, no question is

---

[1] Although meant to set up the contrast with machines, this statement regrettably ignores the long-standing and still lively field of ethology (see, for example, Crist 2000, 2004). It would be more accurate to say that the social sciences have been concerned with interactions between and among animal species.

raised about the bases for the very idea of human–machine interaction as such. And recent developments in the social sciences regarding the foundations of human interaction have had remarkably little influence on the discussion of interactive machines.[2]

The following chapters examine the conception of purposeful action, and consequently of interaction, informing the design of interactive machines. My central concern in the investigation is a new manifestation of an old problem in the study of mutual intelligibility; namely, the relation between observable behavior and the processes, not available to direct observation, that make behavior meaningful. For psychological studies, the crucial processes are essentially cognitive, located inside the head of the actor, and include the formation and effect of beliefs, desires, intentions, and the like. For social studies, the crucial processes are interactional and circumstantial, located in the relationships among actors and between actors and their embedding situations. In either case, the problem of meaningful action turns on the observation that behavior is inherently subject to indefinitely many ascriptions of meaning or intent, while meaning and intent are expressible through an indefinite number of possible behaviors. Whether the final arbiter of action's significance is taken to be private psychological processes or accountability to the public world, the question to be resolved – what constitutes purposeful action and how is it understood – is the same.

The new manifestation of this question concerning the nature of purposeful action and its interpretation arises in research on machine intelligence. Theoretically, the goal of that research is a computational model of intelligent behavior that not only, given some input, produces the right output behavior but also that does so by simulating human cognitive processes. Practically, the goal is just a machine that, given some input, produces behavior that is useful and appropriate to the situation at hand.[3] In either case, insofar as rightness or appropriateness of behavior means that behavior is accountably rational in the eyes of an other, the measure of success is at bottom an interactional one.

For the moment at least, the question of theoretical versus practical criteria of adequacy for machine intelligence is rendered moot by the

---

[2] There has been some significant engagement in the years since; see, for example, the articles collected in Luff, Gilbert, and Frohlich (1990); Thomas (1995). Despite these interventions, however, I would maintain that there is remarkably little substantive effect on discourses and practices of the so-called conversational machine.

[3] What I characterize as a theoretical/practical distinction here maps on to some versions of what have been distinguished as "strong" versus "weak" AI.

problems involved in constructing a device that even *appears* to behave in ways that are purposeful or intelligent, at least outside of the most highly constrained domains. It may simply turn out that the resistance of meaningful action to simulation in the absence of any deep understanding will defend us against false impressions of theoretical success. In any case, my purpose here is not to resolve the question of whether artificial intelligence is possible but rather to clarify some existing troubles in the project of constructing intelligent, interactive machines, as a way of contributing to our understanding of human intelligence and interaction.

Every human tool relies on, and materializes, some underlying conception of the activity that it is designed to support. As a consequence, one way to view the artifact is as a test on the limits of the underlying conception. In this book I examine an artifact built on a *planning model* of human action. The model treats a plan as something located in the actor's head, which directs his or her behavior. In contrast, I argue that artifacts built on the planning model confuse *plans* with *situated actions* and recommend instead a view of plans as formulations of antecedent conditions and consequences of action that account for action in a plausible way. Stated in advance plans are necessarily vague, insofar as they are designed to accommodate the unforeseeable contingencies of actual situations of action. As ways of talking about action, plans as such neither determine the actual course of situated action nor adequately reconstruct it.[4] Although for purposes of practical action this limitation on plans is irrelevant, for purposes of a science of practical action it is crucial.[5] Specifically, if we are interested in situated action itself we need to look at how it is that actors use the resources that a particular occasion provides (including, but crucially not reducible to, formulations such as plans) to construct their action's developing purpose and intelligibility.

Beginning with a view of interaction or communication (I use the two terms interchangeably) as the mutual intelligibility of action, I

---

[4] The sense of "adequacy" implied here is an anthropological/sociological one; that is, plans cannot be taken as specific, or comprehensive, or experiential descriptions of how some course of action went. For practical purposes of everyday talk, of course, an account of actions taken with reference to a plan (for example, the itinerary of a journey) may be quite sufficient.

[5] The notion of a "science of practical action" sits uncomfortably with my current appreciation for the connotations of universality and generality implied. I would say instead that we cannot simply take plans as isomorphic with actions if our interest is in recovering the latter's enactment in situ.

investigate the grounds for beginning to speak of interaction between humans and machines. Chapter 4 introduces the notion of interactive artifacts and its basis in certain properties of computing machines.[6] Chapter 5 examines the view of plans as the basis for action and communication held by designers of artificially intelligent, interactive machines, while Chapters 6 and 7 present an alternative view of action and communication as situated, drawn from recent developments in social science. Finally, Chapters 8 and 9 offer an analysis of encounters between novice users of a machine and a computer-based system intended to be intelligent and interactive. The aim of the case study is not to criticize the particular design but to view the design as reifying certain premises about purposeful action.[7] The task is to articulate those premises, to see how they succeed as a basis for human–machine communication and how they fail, and to explore the implications of their success and failure both for the design of human–machine communication and for the broader explication of purposeful action and mutual intelligibility.

[6] Chapter numbers have been changed to reflect the current text.
[7] The term *reifying* in this context seems overly fixed and might be better replaced with *incorporating* or *materializing*.

# 4

## Interactive Artifacts

Marginal objects, objects with no clear place, play important roles. On the lines between categories, they draw attention to how we have drawn the lines. Sometimes in doing so they incite us to reaffirm the lines, sometimes to call them into question, stimulating different distinctions.

(Turkle 1984: 31)

In *The Second Self* (1984), Sherry Turkle describes the computer as an evocative object, one that raises new questions regarding our common sense of the distinction between artifacts and intelligent others. Her studies include an examination of the impact of computer-based artifacts on children's conceptions of the difference between categories such as "alive" versus "not alive" and "machine" versus "person." In dealing with the questions that computer-based objects evoke, children make clear that the differentiation of physical from psychological entities, which as adults we largely take for granted, is the end product of a process of establishing the relationship between the observable behavior of a thing and its underlying nature.[1] Children have a tendency, for example, to attribute life to physical objects on the basis of behaviors such as autonomous motion or reactivity, though they reserve humanity for entities evidencing such things as emotion, speech, and apparent thought or purposefulness. Turkle's observation with respect to computational artifacts is that children ascribe to them an "almost aliveness" and a psychology, while maintaining their distinctness from

[1] Though see Carey (1985, Chapter 1) for a critique of the Piagetian notion that children at first have no concept for mechanical causation apart from intentional causation. (Original footnote.)

33

human beings: a view that, as Turkle points out, is remarkable among other things for its correspondence to the views held by those who are the artifacts' designers.[2]

In this book I take as a point of departure a particular aspect of the phenomenon that Turkle identifies: namely, the apparent challenge that computational artifacts pose to the long-standing distinction between the physical and the social, in the special sense of those things that one designs, builds, and uses, on the one hand, and those things with which one communicates, on the other. Although this distinction has been relatively nonproblematic to date, now for the first time the term *inter-action*, in a sense previously reserved for describing a uniquely interpersonal activity, seems appropriately to characterize what goes on between people and certain machines as well.[3] Interaction between people and machines implies mutual intelligibility or shared understanding. What motivates my inquiry, therefore, is not only the recent question of how there could be mutual intelligibility between people and machines but also the prior question of how we account for the shared understanding or mutual intelligibility that we experience as people in our interactions with others whose essential sameness is not in question. An answer to the more recent question, theoretically at least, presupposes an answer to the earlier one.

In this chapter I relate the idea of human–machine communication to some distinctive properties of computational artifacts and to the emergence of disciplines dedicated to making those artifacts intelligent. I begin with a brief discussion of cognitive science, the interdisciplinary field devoted to modeling cognitive processes, and its role in the project

[2] See especially pp. 62–3; Turkle finds some cause for alarm in the fact that for children the distinction of machine and person seems to turn centrally on a separation of thought from feeling; that is, computers exhibit the former but lack the latter. This view, she argues, includes a kind of dissociation of intellect and emotion, and consequent trivialization of both, that characterizes the attitudes of many in the field of artificial intelligence. (Original footnote.)

[3] Actually, the term *interaction* has its origins in the physical sciences to describe a reciprocal action or influence. I use it here in the common sense assigned to it by social science: namely, to mean communication between persons. The migration of the term from the physical sciences to the social, and now back to some ground that stands between them, relates in intriguing ways to a general blurring of the distinction between physical and social in modern science and to the general question of whether machines are actually becoming more like people or whether, in fact, people are coming to define themselves more as machines. There is clearly a mutual influence at work. For more on this last point, see Dreyfus 1979 (Chapter 9). (Original footnote.)

of creating intelligent artifacts.[4] Along with a theoretical interest in intelligent artifacts, the computer's properties have inspired a practical effort at engineering interaction between people and machines. I argue that the description of computational artifacts as interactive is supported by their *reactive*, *linguistic*, and internally *opaque* properties. With those properties in mind, I consider the double sense in which researchers are interested in artifacts that explain themselves: on the one hand, as a solution to the long-standing problem of conveying the artifact's intended purpose to the user, through its design and attendant instructions and, on the other hand, as a means of establishing the intelligence, or rational accountability, of the artifact itself.

### AUTOMATA AND COGNITIVE SCIENCE

Historically the idea of automata – the possibility of constructing physical devices that are self-regulating in ways that we commonly associate with living, animate beings – has been closely tied to the simulation of animal forms. McCorduck (1979) points out that humanlike automata have been constructed since Hellenic times: statues that moved, gestured, spoke, and generally were imbued by observers (even those well aware of the internal mechanisms that powered them) with everything from minds to souls.[5] In the fourteenth century in Western Europe, "learned men" were commonly believed to construct talking heads made of brass, considered as both the source of their creator's wisdom and its manifestation. More prosaically, Jacques de Vaucanson in the eighteenth century designed a series of renowned mechanical statues, the most famous being a duck, the inner workings of which produced a variety of simple outward behaviors.

At the same time Julien de la Mettrie published *Man a Machine* (1748), in which he argued that the vitality characteristic of human beings was the result of their physical structure rather than either something

---

[4] For an extensive treatment, see Gardner (1985). (Original footnote.) For more recent discussions see Clancey (1997); Clark (1997, 2001); and Varela, Thompson, and Rosch (1991) and for critiques see Adam (1998); Agre (1997); Button, Coulter, Lee, and Sharrock (1995); Collins (1990); Collins and Kusch (1998); Dourish (2001); Dreyfus (1992); Gilbert and Heath (1985); and Kember (2003).

[5] See McCorduck (1979, Chapter 1); Churchland (1984, Chapter 6). For a further history of automata, see Cohen (1966). (Original footnote.) For more recent historical treatments see Riskin (2003a, 2003b, 2007); Schaffer (1999); Standage (2002); Wood (2002).

immanent in their material substance or some immaterial force. Cognitive scientists today maintain the basic premise of de la Mettrie with respect to mind, contending that mind is best viewed as neither substantial nor insubstantial, but as an abstractable structure implementable in any number of possible physical substrates. Intelligence, in other words, is only incidentally embodied in the neurophysiology of the human brain, and what is essential about intelligence can be abstracted from that particular, albeit highly successful, substrate and embodied in an unknown range of alternative forms. This view decouples reasoning and intelligence from things uniquely human and opens the way for the construction of intelligent artifacts.[6]

The preoccupation of cognitive science with mind in this abstract sense is in part a concern to restore meaning to psychological explanation (see Stich 1983, Chapter 1). At the turn of this century, the recognized method for studying human mental life was introspection and, insofar as introspection was not amenable to the emerging canons of scientific method, the study of cognition seemed doomed to be irremediably unscientific. In reaction to that prospect, the behaviorists posited that all human action should be understandable in terms of publicly observable, mechanistically describable relations between the organism and its environment. In the name of turning cognitive studies into a science, in other words, the study of cognition as the study of something apart from overt behavior was effectively abandoned in mainstream psychology.

Cognitive science, in this respect, was a project to bring thought back into the study of human action while preserving the commitment to scientism. Cognitive science reclaims mentalist constructs such as beliefs, desires, intentions, symbols, ideas, schemata, planning, and problem solving. Once again human purposes are the basis for cognitive psychology, but this time without the unconstrained speculation of the introspectionists. The study of cognition is to be empiricized not by a strict adherence to behaviorism but by the use of a new technology: namely, the computer.

The subfield of cognitive science most dedicated to the computer is artificial intelligence. Artificial intelligence arose as advances in computing technology were tied to developments in neurophysiological

---

[6] See Turkle (1984, Chapter 7); and McCorduck (1979, Chapter 5). Turkle's description of the present academic AI culture at MIT is particularly insightful. (Original footnote.) For a reconstruction of the history through which "information lost its body," see Hayles (1999).

and mathematical theories of information. The requirement of computer modeling, of an information processing psychology, seemed both to make theoretical sense and to provide the accountability that would make it possible to pursue a science of otherwise inaccessible mental phenomena. If a theory of underlying mental processes could be modeled on the computer so as to produce the right outward behavior, the theory could be viewed as having passed at least a sufficiency test of its psychological validity.

The cognitivist strategy is to interject a mental operation between environmental stimulus and behavioral response: in essence, to relocate the causes of action from the environment that impinges on the actor to processes, abstractable as computation, in the actor's head. The first premise of cognitive science, therefore, is that people (or "cognizers" of any sort) act on the basis of symbolic representations: a kind of cognitive code, instantiated physically in the brain, on which operations are performed to produce mental states such as "the belief that $p$," which in turn produce behavior consistent with those states. The relation of environmental stimuli to those mental states, on the one hand, and of mental states to behavior, on the other, remains deeply problematic and widely debated within the field (see, for example, Fodor 1983; Pylyshyn 1974, 1984; Stich 1983). The agreement among all participants in cognitive science and its affiliated disciplines, however, is that cognition is not just potentially *like* computation; it literally *is* computational. There is no reason, in principle, why there should not be a computational account of mind, therefore, and there is no a priori reason to draw a principled boundary between people, taken as information-processors or symbol manipulators or, in George Miller's phrase, "informavores" (Pylyshyn 1984: xi) and certain computing machines.

The view that intelligence is the manipulation of symbols finds practical implementation both in so-called expert systems, which structure and process large amounts of well-formulated data, and industrial robots that perform routine, repetitive assembly and control tasks. Expert systems – essentially sophisticated programs that manipulate data structures to accord with rules of inference that experts are understood to use – have minimal sensory-motor or "peripheral" access to the world in which they are embedded, input being most commonly through a keyboard, by a human operator. Industrial robots – highly specialized, computer-controlled devices designed to perform autonomously a single repetitive physical task – have relatively more developed sensory-motor apparatus than do expert systems, but the success of robotics is still confined to specialized activities, under controlled conditions. In both cases, the systems can handle large amounts of encoded information, and syntactic relationships of great sophistication and complexity, in highly circumscribed domains. But when it comes either to direct interaction with the environment, or to the exercise of practical, everyday reasoning about the significance of events in the world, there is general agreement that the state of the art in intelligent machines has yet to attain the basic cognitive abilities of the normal five-year-old child.

### THE IDEA OF HUMAN–COMPUTER INTERACTION

In spite of the current limits on machine intelligence, the use of an intentional vocabulary is already well established in both technical and popular discussion of computers. In part the attribution of purpose to computer-based artifacts derives from the simple fact that each action by the user effects an immediate machine *reaction* (see Turkle 1984, Chapter 8). The technical definition of interactive computing (see, for example, Oberquelle, Kupka, and Maass 1983: 313) is simply that real-time control over the computing process is placed in the hands of the user, through immediate processing and through the availability of interrupt facilities whereby the user can override and modify the operations in progress. This definition contrasts current capabilities with earlier forms of computing, specifically batch processing, where user commands were queued and executed without any intermediate feedback. The greater reactivity of current computers, combined with the fact that, like any machine, the computer's reactions are not random but by design, suggest the character of the computer as a purposeful and, by association, as a social object.

A more profound basis for the relative sociability of computer-based artifacts, however, is the fact that the means for controlling computing machines and the behavior that results are increasingly *linguistic* rather than mechanistic. That is to say, machine operation becomes less a matter of pushing buttons or pulling levers with some physical result and more a matter of specifying operations and assessing their effects through the use of a common language.[7] With or without machine intelligence, this

---

[7] Notwithstanding the popular fantasy of the talking machine, the crucial element that invites a view of computers as interactive is language, not speech. Although strictly speaking buttons and keys remain the principal input devices in computing, this is

fact has contributed to the tendency of designers, in describing what goes on between people and machines, to employ terms borrowed from the description of human interaction; that is, dialogue, conversation, and so forth: terms that carry a largely unarticulated collection of intuitions about properties common to human communication and the use of computer-based machines.

Although for the most part the vocabulary of human interaction has been taken over by researchers in human–machine communication with little deliberation, several researchers have attempted to clarify similarities and differences between computer use and human conversation. Perhaps the most thoughtful and comprehensive of these is Hayes and Reddy (1983). They identify the central difference between existing interactive computer systems and human communication as a question of "robustness," or the ability on the part of conversational participants to respond to unanticipated circumstances, and to detect and remedy troubles in communication:

The ability to interact gracefully depends on a number of relatively independent skills: skills involved in parsing elliptical, fragmented, and otherwise ungrammatical input; in ensuring that communication is robust (ensuring that the intended meaning has been conveyed); in explaining abilities and limitations, actions and the motives behind them; in keeping track of the focus of attention of a dialogue; in identifying things from descriptions, even if ambiguous or unsatisfiable; and in describing things in terms appropriate for the context. Although none of these components of graceful interaction has been entirely neglected in the literature, no single current system comes close to having most of the abilities and behaviors we describe, and many are not possessed by any current systems. (1983: 232)

Hayes and Reddy believe, however, that:

Even though there are currently no truly gracefully interacting systems, none of our proposed components of graceful interaction appears individually to be much beyond the current state of the art, at least for suitably restricted domains of discourse. (ibid.: 232)

They then review the state of the art, including systems like LIFER (Hendrix 1977) and SCHOLAR (Carbonell 1971), which display

relatively trivial. The synthesis of speech by computers may well add to our inclination to ascribe understanding to them, but will not, in itself, contribute substantively to their sensibility. However, simulation of natural language understanding, even when the language is written rather than spoken, is proving to be a profoundly difficult problem that is inseparable from the problem of simulating intelligence as such. (Original footnote.) For a more recent consideration of the talking machine, see Jeremijenko (2004).

sensitivity to the user's expectations regarding acknowledgment of input; systems that resolve ambiguity in English input from the user through questions (Hayes 1981); systems like the GUS system (Bobrow et al. 1977), which represent limited knowledge of the domain that the interaction is about; work on the maintenance of a common focus over the course of the interaction (Grosz 1977; Sidner 1979); and Hayes and Reddy's own work on an automated explanation facility in a simple service domain (1983).

Two caveats on Hayes and Reddy's prescription for a gracefully interacting system (both of which, to their credit, they freely admit) are worth noting. First, they view the abilities cited as necessary but not sufficient for human interaction, their claim for the list being simply that "it provides a good working basis from which to build gracefully interacting systems" (1983: 233). And not surprisingly, the abilities that they cite constitute a list of precisely those problems currently under consideration in research on human–machine communication. There is, in other words, no independent assessment of how the problems on which researchers work relate to the nature and organization of human communication as such. Second, research on those problems that have been identified is confined to highly circumscribed domains. The consequence of working from an admittedly partial and ad hoc list of abilities, in limited domains, is that practical inroads in human–computer communication can be furthered, while the basic question of what human interaction comprises is deferred. Deferred as well is the question of why it is, beyond methodological convenience, that research in human–machine interaction has proceeded only in those limited domains that it has.

Moreover, although Hayes and Reddy take the position that "it is very important for a gracefully interacting system to conduct a dialogue in as human-like a way as possible" (1983: 233), this assertion is a point of controversy in the research community. On the one side, there is an argument to the effect that one should acknowledge, and even exploit, the fact that people bring to computer use a tremendous range of skills and expectations from human interaction. Within research on human–computer interaction, for example, some progress has been made toward allowing people to enter commands into computers using natural language (i.e., languages like English, in contrast to programming languages). On the other side, even Hayes and Reddy admit that:

the aim of being as human-like as possible must be tempered by the limited potential for comprehension of any foreseeable computer system. Until a solution is found to the problems of organizing and using the range of world knowledge possessed by a human, practical systems will only be able to comprehend a small amount of input, typically within a specific domain of expertise. Graceful interaction must, therefore, supplement its simulation of human conversational ability with strategies to deal naturally and gracefully with input that is not fully understood and, if possible, to steer a conversation back to the system's home ground. (ibid.: 233)

Whereas Hayes and Reddy would make these recovery strategies invisible to the user, they also acknowledge the "habitability" problem identified by Watt (1968) with respect to language: that is, the tendency of human users to assume that a computer system has sophisticated linguistic abilities after it has displayed elementary ones. This tendency is not surprising, given the fact that our only precedent for language-using entities to date has been other human beings. As soon as computational artifacts demonstrate *some* evidence of recognizably human abilities, we are inclined to endow them with the rest. The misconceptions that ensue, however, lead some like Fitter (1979) to argue that English or other "natural" languages are in fact not natural for purposes of human–computer interaction:

for the purpose of man-computer communication [sic], *a natural language is one that makes explicit the knowledge and processes for which the man and computer share a common understanding* . . . it becomes the responsibility of the systems designer to provide a language structure which will make apparent to the user the procedures on which it is based and will not lead him to expect from the computer unrealistic powers of inference. (1979: 340, original emphasis)

In view of our tendency to ascribe full intelligence on the basis of partial evidence, the recommendation is that designers might do best to make available to the user the ways in which the system is *not* like a participant in interaction.[8] In this spirit, Nickerson (1976) argues that:

The model that seems appropriate for this view of person-computer interaction is that of an individual making use of a sophisticated tool and not that of one person conversing with another. The term "user" is, of course, often used to denote the human component in a person-computer interaction, as it has been in this paper. It is, to my taste, preferable to the term "partner," not only because it seems more descriptive of the nature of the relationships that existing systems permit, and that future systems are likely to, but because it implies an asymmetry with respect to goals and objectives that "partner" does not. "User" is not a term that one would normally apply to a participant in a conversation. (1976: 111)

---

[8] In fact, Nickerson (1976) points out that there are some ways in which a computer is not like another person, which lends a certain advantage to the user, for example, interruptions can be made without concern about giving offense and responses can be delayed as long as is necessary. (Original footnote.)

The argument that computational processes should be revealed to the user, however, is potentially counter to the promotion of an intentional vocabulary in speaking about computer-based devices. As Dennett (1978) points out, it is in part our inability to see inside each other's heads, or our mutual *opacity*, that makes intentional explanations so powerful in the interpretation of human action. So it is in part the internal complexity and opacity of the computer that invites an intentional stance. This is the case not only because users lack technical knowledge of the computer's internal workings but also because, even for those who possess such knowledge, there is an "irreducibility" to the computer as an object that is unique among human artifacts (Turkle 1984: 272). The overall behavior of the computer is not describable, that is to say, with reference to any of the simple local events that it comprises; it is precisely the behavior of a myriad of those events in combination that constitutes the overall machine. To refer to the behavior of the machine, then, one must speak of "its" functionality. And once reified as an entity, the inclination to ascribe actions to the entity rather than to the parts is irresistible.

Intentional explanations relieve us of the burden of understanding mechanism, insofar as one need assume only that the design is rational to call upon the full power of commonsense psychology and have, ready at hand, a basis for anticipating and construing an artifact's behavior. At the same time, precisely because the mechanism is in fact unknown, and, insofar as underspecification is taken to be characteristic of human beings (as evidenced by the fact that we are inclined to view something that is fully specified as less than human), the personification of the machine is reinforced by the ways in which its inner workings are a mystery, and its behavior at times surprises us.[9] Insofar as the machine is somewhat predictable, in sum, and yet is also both internally opaque and liable to unanticipated behavior, we are more likely to view ourselves as engaged in interaction with it than as just performing operations on it or using it as a tool to perform operations upon the world (see MacKay 1962).

### SELF-EXPLANATORY ARTIFACTS

In the preceding pages I have proposed that the reactive, linguistic, and opaque properties of the computer lead us to view it as interactive

---

[9] See the discussion of "enchantment" in Chapter 14.

and to apply intentional explanations to its behavior. This tie to intentionality has both theoretical and practical implications. Practically, it suggests that, like a human actor, the computer should be able to explain itself, or the intent behind its actions, to the user. Theoretically, it suggests that the computer actually has intent, as demonstrated precisely in this ability to behave in an accountably rational, intelligible way.

For practical purposes, user interface designers[10] have long held the view that machines ideally should be self-explanatory, in the broad sense that their operation should be discoverable without extensive training, from information provided on or through the machine itself. On this view, the degree to which an artifact is self-explanatory is just the extent to which someone examining the artifact is able to reconstruct the *designer's intentions* regarding its use. This basic idea, that a self-explanatory artifact is one whose intended purpose is discoverable by the user, is presumably as old as the design and use of tools. With respect to computer-based artifacts, however, the notion of a self-explanatory artifact has taken on a second sense: namely, the idea that the artifact might actually *explain itself* in something more like the sense that a human being does. In this second sense the goal is that the artifact should not only be intelligible to the user as a tool but also that it should be *intelligent*; that is, able to understand the actions of the user and to provide for the rationality of its own.

In the remainder of this chapter, I look at these two senses of a self-explanatory machine and at the relation between them. The first sense – that a tool should be decipherable by its user – reflects the fact that artifacts are constructed by designers for a purpose and that the user of a tool needs to know something of that design intent. Given their interactional properties, computational tools seem to offer unique capabilities for the provision of instruction to their users. The idea that instructions could be presented more effectively using the power of computation is not far from the idea that computer-based artifacts could actually instruct, that is, could interact with people in a way that approximates the behavior of an intelligent human expert or coach. And this second

[10] In design parlance, the term user interface refers both to the physical place at which the user issues commands to a device, finds reports of its state, or obtains the products of its operation and the procedures by which those interactions occur. (Original footnote.) For further discussion of how we might refigure "the interface," see Chapters 14 and 15.

idea, that the artifact could interact instructively with the user, ties the practical problem of instruction to the theoretical problem of building an intelligent, interactive machine.

## The Computer as an Artifact Designed for a Purpose

At the same time that computational artifacts introduce new complexity and opacity into our encounters with machines, our reliance on computer-based technology and its proliferation throughout the society increases. One result is the somewhat paradoxical objective that increasingly complex technology should be usable with decreasing amounts of training. Rather than relying on the teachings of an experienced user, the use of computers is to be conveyed directly through the technology itself.

The inherent difficulty of conveying the use of a technology directly through its design is well known to archaeologists, who have learned that although the attribution of design intent is a requirement for an artifact's intelligibility, the artifact's design as such does not convey unequivocally either its actual or its intended use. Although this problem in construing the purpose of artifacts can be alleviated, it can never fully be resolved, and it defines the essential problem that the novice user of the tool confronts. Insofar as the goal of a tool's design is that use of the tool should be self-evident, therefore, the problem of deciphering an artifact defines the problem of the designer as well.[11]

As with any communication, instructions for the use of a tool are constrained by the general maxim that utterances should be designed for their recipients. The extent to which the maxim is observed is limited in the first instance by the resources that the medium of communication affords. Face-to-face human interaction is the paradigm case of a system for communication that, because it is organized for maximum context-sensitivity, supports a response designed for just these recipients on just this occasion. Face-to-face instruction brings that context-sensitivity to bear on problems of skill acquisition. The gifted coach, for example, draws on powers of language and observation, and uses the situation of instruction, to specialize instruction for the individual student. Where

---

[11] This observation defines the problem, and the limits, of efforts by system designers to "configure their users" (Woolgar 1991) and the challenges – and possibilities – implied in "de-scripting" an unfamilair artifact (Akrich 1992). For more on these questions, see Chapter 11.

written instruction relies on generalizations about its recipient and the occasion of its use, the coach draws pedagogical strength from exploitation of the unique details of particular situations.[12]

A consequence of the human coach's method is that his or her skills must be deployed anew each time. An instruction manual, in contrast, has the advantage of being durable, reusable, and replicable. In part, the strength of written text is that, in direct contrast to the pointed commentary of the coach, text allows the *disassociation* of the occasion of an instruction's production from the occasion of its use.[13] For the same reason, however, text affords relatively poor resources for recipient design. The promise of interactive computer systems, in these terms, is a technology that can move instructional design away from the written manual in the direction of the human coach and the resources afforded by face-to-face interaction.

Efforts at building self-explicating machines in their more sophisticated forms now adopt the metaphor of the machine as an expert and the user as a novice or student. Among the most interesting attempts to design such a computer-based "coach" is a system called WEST (Burton and Brown 1982). The design strategy adopted in WEST is based on the observation that the skill of a human coach lies as much in what isn't said as what is. Specifically, the human coach does not disrupt the student's engagement in an activity to ask questions but instead diagnoses a student's strengths and weaknesses through observation. And once the diagnosis is made, the coach interjects advice and instruction selectively in ways designed to maximize learning through discovery and experience. In that spirit, the WEST system attempts to infer the student's knowledge of the domain (in this case a computer game called

[12] Face-to-face interaction is in most cases a necessary, but of course never a sufficient, condition for successful human coaching. Coombs and Alty (1984) provide an interesting discussion of the failings of interactions between human advisors and new computer users. At the same time, they point out that the characteristics of the advisory sessions that new users found unsatisfactory show marked similarities to human interactions with most rule-based computer help systems (e.g., that the advisors provide only the recommended solutions to reported problems, while failing either to elicit the view of the user or to articulate any of their own rationale). Satisfactory sessions, in contrast, were characterized by what initially appeared to be less structure and less economy, but that on further investigation was revealed as "well-motivated despite surface appearances, the objective not being strict problem-solving as we had assumed, but problem-solving through mutual understanding. This required sensitivity to different structural factors" (ibid.: 24–5) (original footnote).

[13] What Latour has subsequently characterized as a text's "immutable mobility" (1986: 7).

"How the West Was Won," designed to teach the use of basic arithmetic expressions) by observing the student's behavior.[14]

Although the project of identifying a student's problems directly from his or her behavior proved considerably more difficult than expected, the objectives for the WEST coach were accomplished in the prototype system to an impressive degree. Because in the case of learning to play WEST the student's actions take the form of input to the computer (entries on a keyboard) and therefore leave an accessible trace, and because a context for those actions (the current state of, and history of consecutive moves across, the "board") is defined by the system, each student turn can be compared against calculations of the move that a hypothetical expert player would make given the same conditions. Each expert move, in turn, requires a stipulated set of associated skills. Evidence that a particular skill is lacking, accumulated across some number of moves, identifies that skill as a candidate for coaching. The coach then interjects offers of advice to the student at opportune moments in the course of the play, where what constitutes an opportune moment for interjection is determined according to a set of rules of thumb regarding good tutorial strategy (for example, always coach by offering the student an alternative move that both demonstrates the relevant skill and accomplishes obviously superior results; never coach on two turns in a row, no matter what; and so forth).

### The Computer as an Artifact Having Purposes

Although the computer-based coach can be understood as a logical development in the long-standing problem of instruction, the

[14] The student is presented with a graphic display of a game board made up of seventy squares (representing the Western frontier), a pair of icons (representing the two players, user and computer), and three spinners. A player's task in each turn is to combine the three numbers that the spinners provide, using the basic operations, to produce a value that becomes the number of spaces the icon is moved along the board. To add an element of strategy, squares on the board are more and less desirable. For example, "towns" occur every ten spaces, and landing on one advances you to the next. The object is to be the first player to land on 70. Early observation of students playing the game revealed that they were not gaining the full benefit of the arithmetic practice, in that they tended to settle on a method for combining numbers (for example, multiply the first two numbers and add the third), and to repeat that same method at each turn. Recognizing that this might reflect either a weakness in the student's proficiency at constructing expressions, a failure to grasp the strategy of the game, or both, Brown and Burton saw the potential usefulness of a "coach" that could guide the student to an expanded repertoire of skills and a better understanding of the domain. For a description of a similarly motivated "advisory" system for the programming language PROLOG, see Coombs and Alty (1984). (Original footnote.)

requirement that it be interactive introduces a second sense of self-explanatory machine that is more recent and is uniquely tied to the advent of computing. The new idea is that the intelligibility of artifacts is not just a matter of the availability to the user of the *designer's* intentions for the artifact but of the intentions of the *artifact* itself. That is to say, the designer's objective now is to imbue the machine with the grounds for behaving in ways that are accountably rational: that is, reasonable or intelligible to others, including, in the case of interaction, ways that are responsive to the other's actions.

In 1950 A. M. Turing proposed a now-famous, and still controversial, test for machine intelligence based on a view of intelligence as accountable rationality. Turing argued that if a machine could be made to respond to questions in such a way that a person asking the questions could not distinguish between the machine and another human being, the machine would have to be described as intelligent. To implement his test, Turing chose a game called the "imitation game." The game was initially conceived as a test of the ability of an interrogator to distinguish which of two respondents was a man and which a woman. To eliminate the evidence of physical embodiment, the interaction was to be conducted remotely via a teleprinter. This provided the basis for Turing's notion that the game could easily be adapted to a test of machine intelligence, by substituting the machine for one of the two human respondents. Turing expressly dismissed as a possible objection to his proposed test the contention that, although the machine might succeed in the game, it could succeed through means that bear no resemblance to human thought. Turing's contention was precisely that success at performing the game, regardless of mechanism, is sufficient evidence for intelligence (Turing 1950: 435). The Turing test thereby became the canonical form of the argument that if two information-processors, subject to the same input stimuli, produce indistinguishable output behavior, then regardless of the identity of their internal operations one processor is essentially equivalent to the other.

The lines of the controversy raised by the Turing test were drawn over a family of programs developed by Joseph Weizenbaum in the 1960s under the name ELIZA, designed to support "natural language conversation" with a computer (Weizenbaum 1983: 23). Of the name ELIZA, Weizenbaum writes:

Its name was chosen to emphasize that it may be incrementally improved by its users, since its language abilities may be continually improved by a "teacher." Like the Eliza of *Pygmalion* fame, it can be made to appear even more civilized, the relation of appearance to reality, however, remaining in the domain of the playwright. (ibid.: 23)

Anecdotal reports of occasions on which people approached the teletype to one of the ELIZA programs and, believing it to be connected to a colleague, engaged in some amount of "interaction" without detecting the true nature of their respondent led many to believe that Weizenbaum's program had passed a simple form of the Turing test. Notwithstanding its apparent interactional success, however, Weizenbaum himself denied the intelligence of the program on the basis of the underlying mechanism which he described as "a mere collection of procedures" (ibid.: 23):

The gross procedure of the program is quite simple; the text [written by the human participant] is read and inspected for the presence of a *keyword.* If such a word is found, the sentence is transformed according to a *rule* associated with the keyword, if not a content-free remark or, under certain conditions, an earlier transformation is retrieved. The text so computed or retrieved is then printed out. (ibid.: 24, original emphasis)

In spite of Weizenbaum's disclaimers with respect to their intelligence, the ELIZA programs are still cited as instances of successful interaction between human and machine. The grounds for their success are clearest in DOCTOR, one of the ELIZA programs whose script equipped it to respond to the human user as if the computer were a Rogerian therapist and the user a patient. The DOCTOR program exploited the maxim that shared premises can remain unspoken: that the less we say in conversation, the more what is said is assumed to be self-evident in its meaning and implications (see Coulter 1979, Chapter 5). Conversely, the very fact that a comment is made without elaboration implies that such shared background assumptions exist. The more elaboration or justification is provided, the less the appearance of transparence or self-evidence. The less elaboration there is, the more the recipient will take it that the meaning of what is provided should be obvious.

The design of the DOCTOR program, in other words, exploited the natural inclination of people to deploy what Karl Mannheim first termed the *documentary method of interpretation* to find the sense of actions that are assumed to be purposeful or meaningful (Garfinkel 1967: 78). Very simply, the documentary method refers to the observation that people take appearances as evidence for, or the document of, an ascribed underlying reality, while taking the reality so ascribed as a resource for the interpretation of the appearance. In the case of DOCTOR, computer-generated responses that might otherwise seem odd were rationalized by users on the grounds that there must be some psychiatric intent behind them, not immediately obvious to the user as "patient," but sensible nonetheless:

If, for example, one were to tell a psychiatrist "I went for a long boat ride" and he responded "Tell me about boats," one would not assume that he knew nothing about boats, but that he had some purpose in so directing the subsequent conversation. It is important to note that this assumption is one made by the speaker. Whether it is realistic or not is an altogether different question. In any case, it has a crucial psychological utility in that it serves the speaker to maintain his sense of being heard and understood. The speaker further defends his impression (which even in real life may be illusory) by attributing to his conversational partner all sorts of background knowledge, insights and reasoning ability. But again, these are the speaker's contribution to the conversation. They manifest themselves inferentially in the *interpretations* he makes of the offered response. (Weizenbaum 1983: 26, original emphasis)

In explicating the ELIZA programs, Weizenbaum was primarily concerned with the inclination of human users to find sense in the computer's output and to ascribe to it an understanding, and therefore an authority, unwarranted by the actual mechanism.[15] While unmasking the intelligence of his program, however, Weizenbaum continued to describe it as "a program which makes natural language conversation with a computer possible" (1983: 23). Nevertheless, as part of his disclaimer regarding its intelligence, Weizenbaum points to a crucial shortcoming in the ELIZA strategy with respect to conversation:

ELIZA in its use so far has had as one of its principal objectives the concealment of its lack of understanding. But to encourage its conversational partner to offer inputs from which it can select remedial information, it must *reveal* its misunderstanding. A switch of objectives from the concealment to the revelation of misunderstanding is seen as a precondition to making an ELIZA-like program

---

[15] In this regard it is interesting to note that a great debate ensued surrounding the status of the DOCTOR program as a psychotherapeutic tool. That debate took on a humorous tone when Weizenbaum submitted a letter to the Forum of the Association for Computing Machinery, an excerpt from which follows:

"Below is a listing of a PL/1 program that causes a typewriter console to imitate the verbal behavior of an autistic patient. The "doctor" types his interrogatories on the console. It responds exactly as does an autistic patient – that is, not at all. I have validated this model following the procedure first used in commercial advertising by Carter's Little Liver Pills ("Seven New York doctors say...") and later used so brilliantly by Dr K. M. Colby in his simulation of paranoia [a reference to Colby, K. M. et al. 1972]; I gave N psychiatrists access to my program and asked each to say from what mental disorder it suffered. M psychiatrists (M<N) said the (expletive deleted) program was autistic. (The methodological assumption here is that if two processes have identical input/output behaviors, then one constitutes an explanation of the other.) The program has the advantage that it can be implemented on a plain typewriter not connected to a computer at all." (Weizenbaum 1983: 28) (Original footnote.)

the basis for an effective natural language man-machine communication system. (ibid.: 27, original emphasis)

More recently the inevitability of troubles in communication, and the importance of their remedy to the accomplishment of "graceful interaction," has been reintroduced into the human–machine communication effort by Hayes and Reddy (1983). They observe that:

> During the course of a conversation, it is not uncommon for people to misunderstand or fail to understand each other. Such failures in communication do not usually cause the conversation to break down; rather, the participants are able to resolve the difficulty, usually by a short clarifying sub-dialogue, and continue with the conversation from where they left off. Current computer systems are unable to take part in such clarifying dialogues, or resolve communication difficulties in any other way. As a result, when such difficulties occur, a computer dialogue system is unable to keep up its end of the conversation, and a complete breakdown is likely to result; this fragility lies in stark and unfavourable contrast to the robustness of human dialogue. (ibid.: 234)

Hayes and Reddy go on to recommend steps toward a remedy for the fragility of human–computer interaction based on the incorporation from human communication of conventions for the detection and repair of misunderstanding. They acknowledge, however, that their recommendations are unlikely to be sufficient for successful communication in other than the simplest encounters, for example, automated directory assistance or reservation systems. The question of why this should be so – of the nature of the limits on human–machine communication and the nature and extent of robustness in human interaction – is the subject of the following chapters.

# 5

# Plans

Once the European navigator has developed his operating plan and has available the appropriate technical resources, the implementation and monitoring of his navigation can be accomplished with a minimum of thought. He has simply to perform almost mechanically the steps dictated by his training and by his initial planning synthesis.

(Gladwin 1964: 175)

Every account of communication involves assumptions about action, in particular about the bases for action's coherence and intelligibility. This chapter and the next discuss two alternative views of action. The first, adopted by most researchers in artificial intelligence, locates the organization and significance of human action in underlying plans. At least as old as the Occidental hills, this view of purposeful action is the basis for traditional philosophies of rational action and for much of the behavioral sciences. It is hardly surprising, therefore, that it should be embraced by those newer fields concerned with intelligent artifacts, particularly cognitive science and information-processing psychology. On the planning view, plans are prerequisite to and prescribe action, at every level of detail. Mutual intelligibility is a matter of the reciprocal recognizability of our plans, enabled by common conventions for the expression of intent and shared knowledge about typical situations and appropriate actions. The alternative view, developed in Chapter 6 of this book, is that although the course of action can always be projected or reconstructed in terms of prior intentions and typical situations, the prescriptive significance of intentions for situated action is inherently vague. The coherence of situated action is tied in essential ways not to individual predispositions or conventional rules but to local interactions contingent on the actor's particular circumstances.[1] A consequence of action's situated nature is that communication must incorporate both a sensitivity to local circumstances and resources for the remedy of troubles in understanding that inevitably arise. This chapter reviews the planning model of purposeful action and shared understanding. Those who adopt the planning model as a basis for interaction between people and machines draw on three related theories about the mutual intelligibility of action: (1) the planning model itself, which takes the significance of action to be derived from plans and identifies the problem for interaction as their recognition and coordination; (2) speech act theory, which accounts for the recognizability of plans or intentions by proposing conventional rules for their expression; and (3) the idea of shared background knowledge, as the common resource that stands behind individual action and gives it social meaning. Each of these promises to solve general problems in human communication, such as the relation of observable behavior to intent, the correspondence of intended and interpreted meaning, and the stability of meaning assignments across situations, in ways that are relevant to particular problems in people's interaction with machines.

## THE PLANNING MODEL

The planning model in cognitive science treats a plan as a sequence of actions designed to accomplish some preconceived end. The model posits that action is a form of problem solving, where the actor's problem is to find a path from some initial state to a desired goal state, given

---

[1] The term *circumstances* of course begs a further set of questions. Most important for the purpose of this argument is recognition of the extent to which the conditions of our actions are not simply pregiven and self-evident but are themselves constituted through unfolding courses of action and interaction. This is not to say that action is constructed somehow always de novo or in a vacuum. On the contrary, human activity invariably occurs in circumstances that include more and less long-standing, obdurate, and compelling layers of culturally and historically constituted, social and material conditions. However familiar and constraining, though, the significance of those conditions, and their relevance for what is happening here and now, must be actively reenacted by participants in ways not fully specified in advance or in any strongly determinate way. For explorations of the improvisatory character of action drawn from close studies of jazz performance, see Sawyer (2003).

certain conditions along the way. Actions are described, at whatever level of detail, by their preconditions and their consequences:

In problem-solving systems, actions are described by prerequisites (i.e., what must be true to enable the action), effects (what must be true after the action has occurred), and decomposition (how the action is performed, which is typically a sequence of subactions). (Allen 1984: 126)

Goals define the actor's relationship to the situation of action, because the situation is just those conditions that obstruct or advance the actor's progress toward his or her goals. Advance planning is inversely related to prior knowledge of the environment of action and of the conditions that the environment is likely to present. Unanticipated conditions will require replanning. In every case, however, whether constructed entirely in advance or completed and modified during the action's course, the plan is prerequisite to the action.

### Plan Generation and Execution Monitoring

One of the earliest attempts to implement the planning model on a machine occurred as part of a project at Stanford Research Institute, beginning in the mid-1960s. The project's goal was to build a robot that could navigate autonomously through a series of rooms, avoiding obstacles and moving specified objects from one room to another. The robot, named by its designers Shakey, was controlled by a problem-solving program called STRIPS, which employed a means–end analysis to determine the robot's path (Fikes and Nilsson 1971). The STRIPS program examined the stated goal and then determined a subset of operators, or actions available to the robot, that would produce that state. The preconditions of those actions in turn identified particular subgoal states, which could be examined in the same way. The system thus worked backward from the goal until a plan was defined from the initial state to the goal state, made up of actions that the robot could perform. Subsequent work on problem solving and plan synthesis consisted in large part in refinements to this basic means–ends strategy, toward the end of achieving greater efficiency by constraining the search through possible solution paths.[2]

Beyond the problem of constructing plans, artificial intelligence researchers have had to address problems of what Nilsson (1973) terms

---

[2] For a review of subsequent work see Sacerdoti (1977, Chapter 3). (Original footnote.)

*failure and surprise* in the execution of their planning programs, due to the practical exigencies of action in an unpredictable environment. The objective that Shakey should actually be able to move autonomously through a real (albeit somewhat impoverished) environment added a new class of problems to those faced by mathematical or game-playing programs operating in an abstract formal domain:

for a problem-solver in a formal domain is essentially done when it has constructed a plan for a solution; nothing can go wrong. A robot in the real world, however, must consider the execution of the plan as a major part of every task. Unexpected occurrences are not unusual, so that the use of sensory feedback and corrective action are crucial. (Raphael, cited in McCorduck 1979: 224)

In Shakey's case, execution of the plan generated by the STRIPS program was monitored by a second program called PLANEX. The PLANEX program monitored not the actual moves of the robot, however, but the execution of the plan. The program simply assumed that the execution of the plan meant that the robot had taken the corresponding action in the real world. The program also made the assumption that every time the robot moved there was some normally distributed margin of error that would be added to a "model of the world" or representation of the robot's location. When the cumulative error in the representation got large enough, the plan monitor initiated another part of the program that triggered a camera that could, in turn, take a reading of Shakey's location in the actual world.

The uncertainty to which Shakey was to respond consisted in changes made to the objects in its environment. Another order of uncertainty was introduced with Sacerdoti's system NOAH (an acronym for Nets of Action Hierarchies). Also developed at the Stanford Research Institute as part of the Computer-Based Consultant project, NOAH was designed to monitor and respond to the actions of a human user. With NOAH, Sacerdoti extended the techniques of problem solving and execution monitoring developed in the planning domain to the problem of interactive instruction:

NOAH is an integrated problem solving and execution monitoring system. Its major goal is to provide a framework for storing expertise about the actions of a particular task domain, and to impart that expertise to a human in the cooperative achievement of nontrivial tasks. (Sacerdoti 1977: 2)

The output of the planning portion of Sacerdoti's program is a "procedural net" or hierarchy of partially ordered actions, which becomes in turn the input to the execution-monitoring portion of the system. The execution monitor takes the topmost action in the hierarchy, provides the user with an instruction, and then queries the user regarding the action's completion. A principal objective of the innovations that Sacerdoti introduced for the representation of procedures in NOAH was to extend execution monitoring to include tracking and assessment of the user's actions in response to the instructions generated:

> The system will monitor the apprentice's work to ensure that the operation is proceeding normally. When the system becomes aware of an unexpected event, it will alter instructions to the apprentice to deal effectively with the new situation. (ibid.: 3)

A positive response from the user to the system's query regarding the action is taken to mean that the user understood the instruction and has successfully carried it out, whereas a negative response is taken as a request for a more detailed instruction. The system allows as well for a "motivation response" or query from the user as to why a certain task needs to be done (to which the system responds by listing tasks to which the current task is related) and for an "error response" or indication from the user that the current instruction cannot be carried out. Just as the accumulation of error in the PLANEX program required feedback from the world in order to reestablish the robot's location, the error response from the user in Sacerdoti's system requires that NOAH somehow repair its representation of the user's situation:

> PLANEX presumed that an adequate mechanism existed for accurately updating the world model. This was almost the case, since there were only a small number of actions that the robot vehicle could take, and the model of each action contained information about the uncertainty it would introduce in the world model. When uncertainties reached a threshold, the vision subsystem was used to restore the accuracy of the world model.
>
> For the domain of the Computer-Based Consultant, or even for a richer robot domain, this approach will prove inadequate . . . NOAH cannot treat the world model as a given. It must initiate interactions with the user at appropriate points to ensure that it is accurately monitoring the course of the execution . . .
>
> [W]hen a serious error is discovered (requiring the system to be more thorough in its efforts to determine the state of the world), the system must determine what portions of its world model differ from the actual situation. (ibid.: 71–2)

The situation in which Shakey moved consisted of walls and boxes (albeit boxes that could be moved unexpectedly by a human hand). The problem in designing Shakey was to maintain consistency between the represented environment and the physical environment in which the robot moved. In introducing the actions of a user, the computer's environment becomes not only a physical but also a social one, requiring the interpretation of the user's actions and an assessment of the user's understanding of his or her situation. The difficulty of maintaining a shared understanding of a situation, as shown more clearly in Chapters 8 and 9, is not just a matter of monitoring the course of events but of establishing their significance. Nonetheless, with Sacerdoti we have at least a preliminary recognition of the place of the situation in the intelligibility of action and communication.

### Interaction and Plan Recognition

Adherents of the planning model in artificial intelligence research have taken the requirement of interaction as an injunction to extend the planning model from a single individual to two or more individuals acting in concert. The planning model attempts to bring concerted action under the jurisdiction of the individual actor by attaching to the others in the actor's world sufficient description and granting to the actor sufficient knowledge that he or she is able to respond to the actions of others as just another set of environmental conditions. The problem of social interaction, consequently, becomes an extension of the problem of the individual actor. The basic view of a single, goal-directed agent, acting in response to an environment of conditions, is complicated (the conditions now include the actions of other agents) but intact.

The problem for interaction, on this view, is to recognize the actions of others as the expression of their underlying plans. The complement to plan generation and execution in artificial intelligence research, therefore, is plan recognition or the attribution of plans to others based on observation of their actions. The starting premise for a theory of plan recognition is that an observer takes some sequence of actions as evidence and then forms hypotheses about the plans that could motivate and explain those actions.

One persisting difficulty for action understanding in artificial intelligence research has been the uncertain relation between actions and intended effects. Allen (1984) illustrates this problem with the example of turning on a light:

There are few physical activities that are a necessary part of performing the action of turning on a light. Depending on the context, vastly different patterns of behavior can be classified as the same action. For example, turning on a light usually involves flipping a light switch, but in some circumstances it may involve tightening the light bulb (in the basement) or hitting the wall (in an old house). Although we have knowledge about how the action can be performed, this does not define what the action is. The key defining characteristic of turning on the light seems to be that the agent is performing some activity which will cause the light, which was off when the action started, to become on when the action ends. An important side effect of this definition is that we could recognize an observed pattern of activity as "turning on the light" even if we had never seen or thought about that pattern previously. (ibid.: 126)

Allen's point is twofold. First, the "same" action as a matter of intended effect can be achieved in any number of ways, where the ways are contingent on circumstance rather than on definitional properties of the action. And second, although an action can be accounted for post hoc with reference to its intended effect, an action's course cannot be predicted from knowledge of the actor's intent, nor can the course be inferred from observation of the outcome. Allen identifies the indeterminate relationship of intended effect to method as a problem for planning or plan recognition systems: a problem that he attempts to resolve by constructing a logical language for action descriptions that handles the distinction between what he calls the "causal definition" of an action (i.e., the pre and post conditions that must hold to say that the action has occurred, independent of any method) and the action's characterization in terms of a particular method or procedure for its accomplishment.[3]

Whereas Allen's approach to the problem of plan recognition is an attempt to reconstruct logically our vocabulary of purposeful action, a few more psychologically oriented researchers in artificial intelligence have undertaken experiments designed to reveal the process by which people bring the actions of others under the jurisdiction of an ascribed plan. Schmidt, Sridharan, and Goodson (1978) observe, for example, that plan attribution seems to require certain transformations of the sequential organization of the action described.[4] They report that throughout the process of plan attribution the problem to be solved by the subject remains "ill-formed," by which they mean that at any given time neither the range of possible plans that the other might be carrying out,

---

[3] Another, less problematic, uncertainty that Allen attempts to capture is the observation that while some components of an action are sequentially ordered in a necessary way (i.e., one is prerequisite to the other), other components, although necessary to the action, have no necessary sequential relationship to each other. The incorporation of unordered actions into the structure of plans, pioneered by Sacerdoti (1975), was viewed as a substantial breakthrough in early planning research. (Original footnote.)

[4] The empirical method of their study is unusual in artificial intelligence research, where work generally proceeds on the basis of imagination and introspection. (Original footnote.)

nor the criteria for assessing just what plan is actually in effect, are clearly defined (ibid.: 80). Nonetheless, they report that their subjects are able to posit an underlying plan. Their strategy appears to be to adopt tentatively a single hypothesis about the other's plan rather than entertain all or even some number of logical possibilities simultaneously. The preferred hypothesis regarding the other's plan then affects what actions are noted and recalled in the subject's accounts of the action, and the temporal order of events is restructured into logical "in order to" or "because" relationships, such that relations among actions are not restricted to consecutive events in time. At the same time, the current hypothesis is always subject to elaboration or revision in light of subsequent events to the extent that subjects are often required to suspend judgment on a given hypothesis and to adopt a "wait and see" strategy. Wherever possible, actions that violate the structure of an attributed plan are explained away before the plan itself is reconsidered. Schmidt, Shridharan, and Goodson conclude that all of these observations "support the generalization that action understanding is simply a process of plan recognition" (ibid.: 50). It is worth noting, however, that although these observations clearly point to a process of plan attribution by the observer, there is no independent evidence that the process of plan attribution is a process of recognizing the plan of the actor.

### The Status of Plans

Assessment of the planning model is complicated by equivocation in the literature between plans as a conceptual framework for the analysis and simulation of action and plans as a psychological mechanism for its actual production. When researchers describe human action in terms of plans, the discussion generally finesses the question of just how the formulations provided by the researcher are purported to relate to the actor's intent. The claim is at least that people analyze each other's actions into goals and plans to understand each other. But the suggestion that the plan is "recognized" implies that it has an existence prior to and independent of the attribution and that it actually determines the action. The identification of the plan with the actor's intent is explicit in the writing of philosophers of action supportive of artificial intelligence research like Margaret Boden, who writes:

unless an intention is thought of as an action-plan that can draw upon background knowledge and utilize it in the guidance of behavior one cannot understand how intentions function in real life. (1973: 27–8)

Intentions, in other words, are realized as plans-for-action that directly guide behavior. A logical extension of Boden's view, particularly given an interest in rendering it more computable, is the view that plans actually are prescriptions or instructions for action. An early and seminal articulation of this view came from Miller, Galanter, and Pribram (1960), who define an intention as "the uncompleted parts of a Plan whose execution has already begun" (ibid.: 61). With respect to the plan itself:

Any complete description of behavior should be adequate to serve as a set of instructions, that is, it should have the characteristics of a plan that could guide the action described. When we speak of a plan . . . the term will refer to a *hierarchy* of instructions . . . *A plan is any hierarchical process in the organism that can control the order in which a sequence of operations is to be performed.*

A Plan is, for an organism, essentially the same as a program for a computer . . . , we regard a computer program that simulates certain features of an organism's behavior as a theory about the organismic Plan that generated the behavior.

Moreover, we shall also use the term "Plan" to designate a rough sketch of some course of action . . . , as well as the completely detailed specification of every detailed operation . . . We shall say that a creature is executing a particular Plan when in fact that Plan is controlling the sequence of operations he is carrying out. (ibid.: 17, original emphasis)

With Miller, Galanter, and Pribram the view that purposeful action is planned is put forth as a psychological "process theory" compatible with the interest in a mechanistic, computationally tractable account of intelligent action.[5] By improving on or completing our commonsense descriptions of the structure of action, the structure is now represented not only as a plausible sequence but also as a hierarchical plan. The plan reduces, moreover, to a detailed set of instructions that actually serves as the program that controls the action. At this point the plan as stipulated becomes substitutable for the action, insofar as the action is viewed as derivative from the plan. And once this substitution is done, the theory is self-sustaining: the problem of action is assumed to be solved by the planning model and the task that remains is the model's refinement.

Although attributing the plan to the actor resolves the question of the plan's status, however, it introduces new problems with respect to what we actually mean by purposeful action. If plans are synonymous with purposeful action how do we account, on the one hand, for a prior intent to act that may never be realized and, on the other hand, for

---

[5] For a close, critical reading of Miller, Galanter, and Pribram from within the field of artificial intelligence research, see Agre (1997, Chapter 8).

an intentional action for which we would ordinarily say no plan was formed ahead of time?[6] And if any plan of action can be analyzed at any level of detail, what level of description represents that which we would want to call purposeful action? If every level, there is no reason in principle to distinguish, for example, between deliberate action and involuntary response, as the latter always can be ascribed to a process of planning unavailable to the actor. In fact, this is just what Boden would have us do. On her account, action can be reduced to basic units for which "no further procedural analysis could conceivably be given." Those units compose "complex procedural schemata or action-plans," which in turn produce "complex intentional effects" (1973: 36). Psychological processes at the level of intention, in other words, are reducible ultimately to bodily operations.

But although the planning model would have a statement of intent reflect an actual set of instructions for action, even casual observation indicates that our statements of intent generally do not address the question of situated action at any level of detail. In fact, because the relation of the intent to accomplish some goal to the actual course of situated action is enormously contingent, a statement of intent generally says very little about the action that follows. It is precisely because our plans are inherently vague – because we can state our intentions without having to describe the actual course that our actions will take – that an intentional vocabulary is so useful for our everyday affairs.

The confusion in the planning literature over the status of plans mirrors the fact that in our everyday action descriptions we do not normally distinguish between accounts of action provided before and after the fact and an action's actual course. As commonsense constructs plans are a constituent of practical action, but they are constituent as an artifact of our *reasoning about* action, not as the generative *mechanism of* action. Our imagined projections and our retrospective reconstructions are the principal means by which we catch hold of situated action and reason about it, whereas situated action itself, in contrast, is essentially transparent to us as actors.[7] The planning model, however, takes over our commonsense preoccupation with the anticipation of action and the review of

---

[6] Davis (cited in Allen 1984) gives the example of a person driving who brakes when a small child runs in front of the car. See also Searle's distinction (1980) between "prior intentions" and "intentions-in-action." (Original footnote.)

[7] One result of the transparency of situated action is that we have little vocabulary with which to talk about it, though Chapters 6 and 7 attempt to present some recent efforts from the social sciences. For a treatment of the philosophical vocabulary proposed by Heidegger, see Dreyfus (1991). (Original footnote, with updated reference.)

its outcomes and attempts to systematize that reasoning as a model for action while ignoring the actual stuff, the situated action, which is the reasoning's object.[8]

## SPEECH ACTS

A growing number of research efforts devoted to machine intelligence have as their objective, for both theoretical and practical reasons, human–machine communication using English or "natural language" (for example, Brady and Berwick 1983; Bruce 1981; Joshi, Webber, and Sag 1981). Researchers in natural language understanding have embraced Austin's observation (1962) that language is a form of action as a way of subsuming communication to the planning model. If language is a form of action, it follows that language understanding, like the interpretation of action generally, involves an analysis of a speaker's utterances in terms of the plans those utterances serve:

Let us start with an intuitive description of what we think occurs when one agent A asks a question of another agent B which B then answers. A has some *goal*; s/he creates a plan *(plan construction)* that involves asking B a question whose answer will provide some information needed in order to achieve the goal. A then executes this plan, asking B the question. B interprets the question, and attempts to infer A's plan *(plan inference)*. (Allen 1983; original emphasis)

As with the interpretation of action, plans are the substrate on which the interpretation of natural language utterances rests, insofar as "human language behavior is part of a coherent plan of action directed toward satisfying a speaker's goals" (Appelt 1985: 1). We understand language, and action more generally, when we successfully infer the other's goals and understand how the other's action furthers them. The appropriateness of a response turns on that analysis, from which in turn:

The hearer then adopts new goals (e.g., to respond to a request, to clarify the previous speaker's utterance or goal), and plans his own utterances to achieve those. A conversation ensues. (Cohen n.d.: 24)

---

[8] A note of clarification is in order here, particularly in light of readings of this text that have taken my argument to be either that plans do not exist or that they are "merely" fictions created before and after the fact of specifically situated activity. In rereading this passage I realize the contribution that I myself may have made to this misunderstanding in not emphasizing clearly enough that I take planning itself to *be* a form of situated action. As I have argued in Chapter 1, this is true both in the sense that plans are imaginative and discursive accounts created in anticipation of action and in the sense that they may be cited in the midst of ongoing activity, as well as afterwards. See also Chapter 11.

Given such an account of conversation, the research problem with respect to language understanding is essentially the same as that of the planning model more generally; that is, to characterize actions in terms of their preconditions and effects and to formulate a set of inference rules for mapping between actions and underlying plans. Among researchers in the natural language area of artificial intelligence research, Searle's speech act theory (1969) is seen to offer some initial guidelines for computational models of communication:

> We hypothesize that people maintain, as part of their models of the world, symbolic descriptions of the world models of other people. Our plan-based approach will regard speech acts as operators whose effects are primarily on the models that speakers and hearers maintain of each other. (Cohen and Perrault 1979: 179)

Searle's conditions of satisfaction for the successful performance of speech acts are read as the speech act's "preconditions," whereas its illocutionary force is the desired "effect":

> Utterances are produced by actions (speech acts) that are excited in order to have some effect on the hearer. This effect typically involves modifying the hearer's beliefs or goals. A speech act, like any other action, may be observed by the hearer and may allow the hearer to infer what the speaker's plan is. (Allen 1983: 108)

In describing utterances by their preconditions and effects, speech acts seem to provide at least the framework within which computational mechanisms for engineering interaction between people and machines might emerge. But although Searle's "conditions of satisfaction" state conventions governing the illocutionary force of certain classes of utterance, he argues against the possibility of a rule-based semantics for construing the significance of any particular utterance. Although the maxims that speech act theory proposes (for example, the felicity condition for a directive is that S wants H to do A) tell us something about the general conditions of satisfaction for a directive, they tell us nothing further about the significance of any particular directive. With respect to the problem of interpretation, Gumperz (1982b: 326) offers the following example from an exchange between two secretaries in a small office:

A: Are you going to be here for ten minutes?
B: Go ahead and take your break. Take longer if you want.
A: I'll just be outside on the porch. Call me if you need me.
B: OK. Don't worry.

Gumperz points out that B's response to A's question clearly indicates that B interprets the questions as an indirect request that B stay in the office while A takes a break and, by her reply, A confirms that interpretation. B's interpretation accords with a categorization of A's question as an indirect speech act (Searle 1979), and with Grice's discussion of implicature (1975); that is, B assumes that A is cooperating and that her question must be relevant, and therefore B searches her mind for some possible context or interpretive frame that would make sense of the question and comes up with the break. But, Gumperz points out, *this analysis begs the question of how B arrives at the right inference:*

What is it about the situation that leads her to think A is talking about taking a break? A common sociolinguistic procedure in such cases is to attempt to formulate discourse rules such as the following: "If a secretary in an office around break time asks a co-worker a question seeking information about the co-worker's plans for the period usually allotted for breaks, interpret it as a request to take her break." Such rules are difficult to formulate and in any case are neither sufficiently general to cover a wide enough range of situations nor specific enough to predict responses. An alternative approach is to consider the pragmatics of questioning and to argue that questioning is semantically related to requesting, and that there are a number of contexts in which questions can be interpreted as requests. While such semantic processes clearly channel conversational inference, there is nothing in this type of explanation that refers to taking a break. (1982b: 326–7)

The problem that Gumperz identifies here applies equally to attempts to account for inferences such as B's by arguing that she recognizes A's plan to take a break. Clearly she does: the outstanding question is how. Although we can always construct a post hoc account that explains interpretation in terms of knowledge of typical situations and motives, it remains the case that with speech act theory, as with the planning model, neither typifications of intent nor general rules for its expression are sufficient to account for the mutual intelligibility of our situated action. In the final analysis, attempts to construct a taxonomy of intentions and rules for their recognition seem to beg the question of situated interpretation rather than answer it.

## BACKGROUND KNOWLEDGE

Gumperz's example demonstrates a problem that any account of human action must face; namely, that an action's significance seems to lie as much in what it presupposes and implies about its situation as in any explicit or observable behavior as such. Even the notion of observable behavior becomes problematic in this respect, insofar as what we do and what we understand others to be doing is so thoroughly informed by assumptions about the action's significance. In the interpretation of purposeful action, it is hard to know where observation leaves off and where interpretation begins. In recognition of the fact that human behavior is a figure defined by its ground, social science has largely turned from the observation of behavior to explication of the background that seems to lend behavior its sense.

For cognitive science the background of action is not the world as such, but *knowledge* about the world. Researchers agree that representation of knowledge about the world is a principal limiting factor on progress in machine intelligence. The prevailing strategy in representing knowledge has been to categorize the world into domains of knowledge (e.g., areas of specialization such as medicine along one dimension or propositions about physical phenomena such as liquids along another) and then to enumerate facts about the domain and relationships between them. Having carved out domains of specialized knowledge the catch-all for anything not clearly assignable is "common sense," which then can be spoken of as if it were yet another domain of knowledge (albeit one that is foundational to the others).

Although some progress has been made in selected areas of specialized knowledge, the domain of commonsense knowledge so far remains intractable and unwieldy.[9] One approach to bounding commonsense knowledge, exemplified by the work of Schank and Abelson (1977), is to classify the everyday world as types of situations and assign to each its own body of specialized knowledge. The claim is that our knowledge of the everyday world is organized by a "predetermined, stereotyped sequence of actions that define a well-known situation" or script (ibid.: 422). Needless to say, "[s]cripts are extremely numerous. There is a restaurant script, a birthday party script, a football game script, a classroom script, and so on" (ibid.: 423). Every situation, in other words, has its plan made up of ordered action sequences, each action producing the conditions that enable the next action to occur. Admittedly, the normative order of these action sequences can be thrown off course by any one of what Schank and Abelson term *distractions*, *obstacles*, or

---

[9] For a cogent critique of the most ambitious effort to encode "commonsense" knowledge as a foundation for AI, see Adam's account of the CYC project in Adam (1998, Chapter 3).

*errors*. Distractions, about which they have little to say, comprise the interruption of one script by another, whereas:

An obstacle to the normal sequence occurs when someone or something prevents a normal action from occurring or some enabling condition for the action is absent. An error occurs when the action is completed in an inappropriate manner, so that the normal consequences of the action do not come about. (ibid.: 426)

Not only does the typical script proceed according to a normal sequence of actions, in other words, but each script has its typical obstacles and errors that, like the script itself, are stored in memory along with their remedies and retrieved and applied as needed.

Whereas plans associate intentions with action sequences, scripts associate action sequences with typical situations. In practice, however, the stipulation of relevant background knowledge for typical situations always takes the form of a partial list, albeit one offered as if the author could complete the list given the requisite time and space:

If one intends to buy bread, for instance, the knowledge of which bakers are open and which are shut on that day of the week will enter into the generation of one's plan of action in a definite way; one's knowledge of local topography (and perhaps of map-reading) will guide one's locomotion to the selected shop; one's knowledge of linguistic grammar and of the reciprocal roles of shopkeeper and customer will be needed to generate that part of the action-plan concerned with speaking to the baker, and one's financial competence will guide and monitor the exchange of coins over the shop counter. (Boden 1973: 28)

Like Boden's story of the business of buying bread, attempts in artificial intelligence research to formalize commonsense knowledge rely on an appeal to intuition that shows little sign of yielding to scientific methods. The difficulty is not just that every action presupposes a large quantity of background knowledge: though it would pose practical problems, such a difficulty would be tractable eventually. Just because "implicit knowledge" can in principle be enumerated indefinitely, deciding in practice about the enumeration of background knowledge remains a stubbornly ad hoc procedure, for which researchers have not succeeded in constructing rules that do not depend, in their turn, on some deeper ad hoc procedures.

Nevertheless, the image evoked by "shared knowledge" is a potentially enumerable body of implicit assumptions or presuppositions that stands behind every explicit action or utterance and from which participants in interaction selectively draw in understanding each other's actions. This image suggests that what actually does get said on any occasion must reflect the application of a principle of communicative economy, which recommends roughly that to the extent that either the premises or rationale of an action can be assumed to be shared, they can be left unspoken. That means, in turn, that speakers must have procedures for deciding the extent of the listener's knowledge and the commensurate requirements for explication. The listener, likewise, must make inferences regarding the speaker's assumptions about shared knowledge on the basis of what he or she chooses explicitly to say. What is unspoken and relevant to what is said is assumed to reside in the speaker's and listener's common stock of background knowledge, the existence of which is proven by the fact that an account of what is said always requires reference to further facts that, though unspoken, are clearly relevant.

This image of communication is challenged, however, by the results of an exercise assigned by Garfinkel to his students (1972). Garfinkel's aim was to press the commonsense notion that background knowledge is a body of things thought but unsaid that stands behind behavior and makes it intelligible. The request was that the students provide a complete description of what was communicated, in one particular conversation, as a matter of the participants' shared knowledge. Students were asked to report a simple conversation by writing on the left-hand side of a piece of paper what was said and on the right-hand side what it was that they and their partners actually understood was being talked about. Garfinkel reports that when he made the assignment:

> many students asked how much I wanted them to write. As I progressively imposed accuracy, clarity, and distinctness, the task became increasingly laborious. Finally, when I required that they assume I would know what they had actually talked about only from reading lilerally what they wrote literally, they gave up with the complaint that the task was impossible. (ibid.: 317)

The students' dilemma was not simply that they were being asked to write "everything" that was said, where that consisted of some bounded, albeit vast, content. Instead, it was that the task of enumerating what was talked about itself extended what was talked about, providing a continually receding horizon of understandings to be accounted for. The assignment, it turned out, was not to describe some existing content but to generate it. As such, it was an endless task. The students' failure suggests not that they gave up too soon but that what they were assigned to do was not what the participants in the conversation themselves did to achieve shared understanding.

Although the notion of "background assumptions" connotes an actual collection of things that are there in the mind of the speaker – a body of knowledge that motivates a particular action or linguistic expression and makes it interpretable – Garfinkel's exercise, as well as the phenomenology of experience, suggest that there is reason to question the view that background assumptions are part of the actor's mental state prior to action:

As I dash out the door of my office, for example, I do not consciously entertain the belief that the floor continues on the other side, but if you stop me and ask me whether, when I charged confidently through the door, I believed that the floor continued on the other side, I would have to respond that indeed, I did. (Dreyfus 1982: 25)

A background assumption, in other words, is generated by the activity of accounting for an action when the premise of the action is called into question. But there is no particular reason to believe that the assumption actually characterizes the actor's mental state prior to the act. In this respect, the "taken for granted" denotes not a mental state but something outside of our heads that, precisely because it is nonproblematically there, we do not need to think about. By the same token, in whatever ways we do find action to be problematical the world is there to be consulted should we choose to do so. Similarly, we can assume the intelligibility of our actions, and as long as the others with whom we interact present no evidence of failing to understand us we do not need to explain ourselves, yet the grounds and significance of our actions can be explicated endlessly. The situation of action is thus an inexhaustibly rich resource, and the enormous problems of specification that arise in cognitive science's theorizing about intelligible action have less to do with action than with the project of substituting definite procedures for vague plans, and representations of the situation of action, for action's actual circumstances.

To characterize purposeful action as in accord with plans and goals is just to say again that it is purposeful and that *somehow*, in a way not addressed by the characterization itself, we constrain and direct our actions according to the significance that we assign to a particular context. How we do that is the outstanding problem. Plans and goals do not provide the solution for that problem; they simply restate it. The dependency of significance on a particular context, every particular context's open-endedness, and the essential contingency of contextual elaboration are resources for practical affairs but perplexities for a science of human action. And, to anticipate the analysis in Chapter 9, it is an intractable problem for projects that rest on providing in advance for the significance of canonical descriptions – such as instructions – for situated action.

# 6

## Situated Actions

This total process [of Trukese navigation] goes forward without reference
to any explicit principles and without any planning, unless the intention
to proceed to a particular island can be considered a plan. It is nonverbal
and does not follow a coherent set of logical steps. As such it does not
represent what we tend to value in our culture as "intelligent" behavior.

(Gladwin 1964: 175)

This chapter turns to recent efforts within anthropology and sociology
to challenge traditional assumptions regarding purposeful action and
shared understanding. A point of departure for the challenge is the idea
that commonsense notions of planning are not inadequate versions of
scientific models of action, but rather are resources for people's practical
deliberations about action.[1] As projective and retrospective accounts of
action, plans are themselves located in the larger context of some ongoing practical activity. And as commonsense notions about the structure
of that activity, plans are part of the subject matter to be investigated
in a study of purposeful action, not something to be improved on or
transformed into axiomatic theories of action.

The premise that practical reasoning about action is properly part of
the subject matter of social studies is due to the emergence of a branch
of sociology named *ethnomethodology*. This chapter describes the inversion of traditional social theory recommended by ethnomethodology
and the implications of that inversion for the prowler of purposeful

---

[1] For an exposition of the ethnomethodological premises that underwrite this idea, see
Lynch (1993).

action and shared understanding. To designate the alternative that ethnomethodology suggests (more a reformulation of the problem of purposeful action and a research programme than an alternative theory),
I have introduced the term *situated action*.[2] That term underscores the
view that every course of action depends in essential ways on its material
and social circumstances. Rather than attempt to abstract action away
from its circumstances and represent it as a rational plan, the approach
is to study how people use their circumstances to achieve intelligent
action. Rather than build a theory of action out of a theory of plans, the
aim is to investigate how people produce and find evidence for plans in
the course of situated action. More generally, rather than subsume the
details of action under the study of plans, plans are subsumed by the
larger problem of situated action.

The view of action that ethnomethodology recommends is neither
behavioristic, in any narrow sense of that term, nor mentalistic. It is
not behavioristic in that it assumes that the significance of action is
not reducible to uninterpreted bodily movements. Nor is it mentalistic,
however, in that the significance of action is taken to be based, in ways
that are fundamental, rather than secondary or epiphenomenal, in the
physical and social world. The basic premise is twofold: first, that what
traditional behavioral sciences take to be cognitive phenomena have
an necessary relationship to a publicly available, collaboratively organized world of artifacts and actions and, second, that the significance
of artifacts and actions, and the methods by which their significance
is conveyed, have an essential relationship to their particular, concrete
circumstances.[3]

The ethnomethodological view of purposeful action and shared
understanding is outlined in this chapter under five propositions:
(1) plans are representations of situated actions; (2) in the course of situated action, representation occurs when otherwise transparent activity
becomes in some way problematic; (3) the objectivity of the situations

---

[2] In saying that I had introduced the term *situated action*, I meant within the context of the
present discussion. Subsequent attributions to the contrary, I by no means intended to
suggest that I had coined that phrase! Origins of the phrase in sociological writings go
back at least to C. Wright Mills's (1940) "Situated Actions and Vocabularies of Motive."
Rawls (2002: 20) points out that although Garfinkel's ethnomethodological treatment
of the relation of action and accounts is consistent with Mills's, Garfinkel attends not
only to the retrospective character of accounts but also to the prospective and ongoing
character of both accounts the actions that they formulate.

[3] On the relevance of a phenomenological account of the public availability of objects and
artifacts to system design, see Robertson (2002).

of our action is achieved rather than given; (4) a central resource for achieving the objectivity of situations is language, which stands in a generally indexical relationship to the circumstances that it presupposes, produces, and describes; (5) as a consequence of the indexicality of language, mutual intelligibility is achieved on each occasion of interaction with reference to situation particulars rather than being discharged once and for all by a stable body of shared meanings.

### PLANS ARE REPRESENTATIONS OF ACTION

The pragmatist philosopher and social psychologist George Herbert Mead (1934) has argued for a view of meaningful, directed action as two integrally but problematically related kinds of activity. One kind of activity is situated and ad hoc improvisation – the part of us, so to speak, that actually acts. The other kind of activity is derived from the first and includes our representations of action in the form of future plans and retrospective accounts. Plans and accounts are distinguished from action as such by the fact that to represent our actions we must in some way to make an object of them. Consequently, our descriptions of our actions come always before or after the fact, in the form of imagined projections and recollected reconstructions.[4] Mead's treatment of the relation of deliberation and reflection to action is one of the more controversial, and in some ways incoherent, pieces of his theory. But his premise of a disjunction between our actions and our grasp of them at least raises the question for social science of the relationship between projected or reconstructed courses of action and actions in situ. Most accounts of purposeful action have taken this relationship to be a directly causal one, at least in a logical sense (see Chapter 5 in this book). Given a desired outcome, the actor is assumed to make a choice among alternative courses of action, based on the anticipated consequences of each with respect to that outcome. Accounts of actions taken, by the same token, are just a report on the choices made. The student of purposeful action on this view need know only the predisposition of the actor and the alternative courses that are available to predict the action's course.

---

[4] Here again, I regret the implication that plans and other forms of imaginative reflection stand somehow outside of action rather than being themselves moments of situated activity (activities of planning, remembering, etc.), displaced in time and space from the occasion anticipated or recollected. The interesting questions for this discussion turn on how it is that activities of planning are invoked and made relevant to the course of some subsequent activity and vice versa. See Chapter 11.

The action's course is just the playing out of these antecedent factors, knowable in advance of and standing in a determinate relationship to the action itself.

The alternative view is that plans are resources for situated action but do not in any strong sense determine its course. Although plans presuppose the embodied practices and changing circumstances of situated action, the efficiency of plans as representations comes precisely from the fact that they do not represent those practices and circumstances in all of their concrete detail. So, for example, in planning to run a series of rapids in a canoe, one is very likely to sit for a while above the falls and plan one's descent.[5] The plan might go something like "I'll get as far over to the left as possible, try to make it between those two large rocks, then backferry hard to the right to make it around that next bunch." A great deal of deliberation, discussion, simulation, and reconstruction may go into such a plan. But however detailed, the plan stops short of the actual business of getting your canoe through the falls. When it really comes down to the details of responding to currents and handling a canoe, you effectively abandon the plan and fall back on whatever embodied skills are available to you.[6] The purpose of the plan in this case is not to get your canoe through the rapids, but rather to orient you in such a way that you can obtain the best possible position from which to use those embodied skills on which, in the final analysis, your success depends. Even in the case of more deliberative, less highly skilled activities we generally do not anticipate alternative courses of action or their consequences until *some* course of action is already underway. It is frequently only on acting in a present situation that its possibilities become clear, and we often do not know ahead of time, or at least not with any specificity, what future state we desire to bring about. Garfinkel points out that in many cases it is only after we encounter some state of affairs that we find to be desirable that we identify that state as the goal toward which our previous actions, in retrospect, were directed "all along" or "after all" (1967: 98). The fact that we can always perform a post hoc analysis of situated action that will make it appear to have followed a rational plan says more about the

---

[5] This example was suggested to me by Randall Trigg, to whom I am indebted for the insight that plans orient us for situated action in this way. (Original footnote.)

[6] This phrasing is unfortunate, in suggesting that the plan is somehow jettisoned (see Chapter 1). It would be better to say that your ability to act according to the plan ultimately turns on the embodied skills available to you in situ, which are themselves presupposed, rather than specified, by the plan.

nature of our analyses than it does about our situated actions. To return to Mead's point, rather than direct situated action rationality anticipates action before the fact and reconstructs it afterwards.

## REPRESENTATION AND BREAKDOWN

Although we can always construct rational accounts of situated action before and after the fact, when action is proceeding smoothly it is essentially transparent to us. Similarly, when we use what Heidegger terms equipment that is "ready-to-hand," the equipment has a tendency to disappear:

Consider the example (used by Wittgenstein, Polanyi, and MerleauPonty) of the blind man's cane. We hand the blind man a cane and ask him to tell us what properties it has. After hefting and feeling it, he tells us that it is light, smooth, about three feet long, and so on; it is occurrent for him. But when the man starts to manipulate the cane, he loses his awareness of the cane itself; he is aware only of the curb (or whatever object the cane touches); or, if all is going well, he is not even aware of that ... Precisely when it is most genuinely appropriated equipment becomes transparent. (Dreyfus 1991: 65)[7]

In contrast, the "unready-to-hand," in Heidegger's phrase, comprises occasions wherein equipment that is involved in some practical activity becomes unwieldy, temporarily broken, or unavailable. At such times, inspection and practical problem solving occur, aimed at repairing or eliminating the disturbance to "get going again." In such times of disturbance, our use of equipment becomes explicitly manifest as a goal-oriented activity, and we may then try to formulate procedures or rules: "The scheme peculiar to [deliberating] is the 'if–then'; if this or that, for instance, is to be produced, put to use, or averted, then some ways and means, circumstances, or opportunities will be needed" (Heidegger, cited in Dreyfus 1991: 72).

Another kind of breakdown that arises when equipment to be used is unfamiliar is discussed in Chapter 9 in this book in relation to the "expert help system" and the problem of instructing the novice user of a machine. The important point here is just that the rules and procedures that come into play when we deal with the unready-to-hand are not self-contained or foundational but contingent on and derived from the

---

[7] This quote has been updated from the citation in the original text, which was drawn from a prepublished manuscript of Dreyfus's book. The phrase *ready-to-hand*, used in that earlier version, has been replaced with the term *occurrent*.

situated action that the rules and procedures represent. The representations involved in managing problems in the use of equipment presuppose the very transparent practices that the problem renders noticeable or remarkable. Situated action, in other words, is not made explicit by rules and procedures. Rather, when situated action becomes in some way problematic rules and procedures are explicated for purposes of deliberation and the action, which is otherwise neither rule based nor procedural, is then made accountable to them.

### THE PRACTICAL OBJECTIVITY OF SITUATIONS

If we look at the world commonsensically, the environment of our actions is made up of a succession of situations that we walk into and to which we respond. As I noted in Chapter 5 in this book, advocates of the planning model not only adopt this commonsense realist view with respect to the individual actor but also attempt to bring concerted action under the same account by treating the actions of others as just so many more conditions of the actor's situation. In the same tradition, normative sociology posits and then attempts to describe an objective world of social facts, or received norms, to which our attitudes and actions are a response. Emile Durkheim's famous maxim that the objective reality of social facts is sociology's fundamental principle (1938) has been the methodological premise of social studies since early in this century. Recognizing the human environment to be constituted crucially by others, sociological norms comprise a set of environmental conditions beyond the material to which human behavior is responsive: namely the sanctions of institutionalized group life. Human action, the argument goes, cannot be adequately explained without reference to these "social facts," which are to be treated as antecedent, external, and coercive vis-à-vis the individual actor.

By adopting Durkheim's maxim, and assuming the individual's responsiveness to received social facts, social scientists hoped to gain respectability under the view that human responses to the facts of the social world should be discoverable by the same methods as are appropriate to studies of other organisms reacting to the natural world. A principal aim of normative sociology was to shift the focus of attention in studies of human behavior from the psychology of the individual to the conventions of the social group. But at the same time that normative sociology directed attention to the community or group, it maintained an image of the individual member rooted in behaviorist psychology and natural science – an image that has been dubbed by Garfinkel the "cultural dope": "By 'cultural dope' I refer to the man-in-the-sociologist's-society who produces the stable features of the society by acting in compliance with preestablished and legitimate alternatives of action that the common culture provides" (1967: 68). Insofar as the alternatives of action that the culture provides are seen to be nonproblematic and constraining on the individual, their enumeration is taken to constitute an account of situated human action. The social facts (that is to say, what actions typically come to) are used as a point of departure for retrospective theorizing about the "necessary character of the pathways whereby the end result is assembled" (ibid.: 68).

In 1954 the sociologist Herbert Blumer published a critique of traditional sociology titled, "What Is Wrong with Social Theory?" (see Blumer 1969: 140–52). Blumer argues that the social world is constituted by the local production of meaningful action and that as such the social world has never been taken seriously by social scientists. Instead, Blumer says, investigations by social scientists have looked at meaningful action as the playing out of various determining factors, all antecedent and external to the action itself. Whether those factors are brought to the occasion in the form of individual predispositions, or are present in the situation as preexisting environmental conditions or received social norms, the action itself is treated as epiphenomenal. As a consequence, Blumer argues, we have a social science that is about meaningful human action but not a science of it.

For the foundations of a science of action Blumer turns to Mead, who offers a metaphysics of action that is deeply sociological. Blumer points out that a central contribution of Mead's work is his challenge to traditional assumptions regarding the origins of the commonsense world and of purposeful action:

His treatment took the form of showing that human group life was the essential condition for the emergence of consciousness, the mind, a world of objects, human beings as organisms possessing selves, and human conduct in the form of constructed acts. He reversed the traditional assumptions underlying philosophical, psychological, and sociological thought to the effect that human beings possess minds and consciousness as original "givens," that they live in worlds of pre-existing and self-constituted objects, and that group life consists of the association of such reacting human organisms. (Blumer 1969: 61)

Mead's reversal, in putting human interaction before the objectivity of the commonsense world, should not be read as an argument for metaphysical idealism: Mead does not deny the existence of constraints in the environment in which we act. What Mead is working toward is not a characterization of the natural world *simpliciter* but of the natural world *under interpretation* or the world as construed by us through language. The latter is precisely what we mean by the *social* world and, on Mead's account, interaction is a condition for that world, while that world is a condition for intentional action.

More recently, ethnomethodology has turned Durkheim's aphorism on its head with more profound theoretical and methodological consequences.[8] Briefly, the standpoint of ethnomethodology is that what traditional sociology captures is precisely our commonsense view of the social world (see Sacks 1963; Garfinkel 1967; Garfinkel and Sacks 1970). Following Durkheim, the argument goes, social studies have simply taken this commonsense view as foundational and attempted to build a science of the social world by improving on it. Social scientific theories, under this attempt, are considered to be scientific insofar as they remedy shortcomings in, and preferably quantify, the intuitions of everyday, practical sociological reasoning.

In contrast, ethnomethodology grants commonsense sociological reasoning a fundamentally different status than that of a defective approximation of an adequate scientific theory. Rather than being *resources* for social science to improve on, the "all things being equal" typifications of commonsense reasoning are to be taken as social science's *topic*. The notion that we act in response to an objectively given social world is replaced by the assumption that our everyday social practices render the world publicly available and mutually intelligible. It is those practices that constitute ethnomethods. The methodology of interest to ethnomethodologists, in other words, is not their own but that deployed by members of the society in coming to know, and making sense out of, the everyday world of talk and action.

The outstanding question for social science, therefore, is not *whether* social facts are objectively grounded but *how* their objective grounding is accomplished. Objectivity is a product of systematic practices or members' methods for rendering our unique experience and relative circumstances mutually intelligible. The source of mutual intelligibility is not a received conceptual scheme, or a set of coercive rules or norms, but those common practices that produce the typifications of which schemes and rules are made. The task of social studies, then, is to

---

[8] For extensive consideration of Durkheim's aphorism and its ethnomethodological rereading, see Rawls (1996), Garfinkel (2002).

describe the practices, not to enumerate their product in the form of a catalogue of commonsense beliefs about the social world. The interest of ethnomethodologists, in other words, is in how it is that the mutual intelligibility and objectivity of the social world is achieved. Ethnomethodology locates that achievement in our everyday situated actions, such that our common sense of the social world is not the precondition for our interaction but its product. By the same token, the objective reality of social facts is not the fundamental *principle* of social studies, but social studies' fundamental *phenomenon*.

### THE INDEXICALITY OF LANGUAGE

Our shared understanding of situations is due in great measure to the efficiency of language, "the typifying medium *par excellence*" (Schutz 1962: 14). Language is efficient in the sense that, on the one hand, expressions have assigned to them conventional meanings that hold on any occasion of their use. The significance of a linguistic expression on some actual occasion, on the other hand, lies in its relationship to circumstances that are presupposed or indicated by, but not actually captured in, the expression itself.[9] Language takes its significance from the embedding world, in other words, even while it transforms the world into something that can be thought of and talked about.

Expressions that rely on their situation for significance are commonly called *indexical,* after the "indexes" of Charles Peirce (1933), the exemplary indexicals being first- and second-person pronouns, tense, and specific time and place adverbs such as *here* and *now*. In the strict sense, exemplified by these commonly recognized indexical expressions, the distinction of conventional or literal meaning and situated significance breaks down. That is to say, these expressions are distinguished by the fact that although one can state procedures for finding the expression's significance, or rules for its use, the expression's meaning can be specified only as the use of those procedures in some actual circumstances (see Bates 1976, Chapter 1).

Heritage (1984: 143) offers as an example the indexical expression "that's a nice one." There is, first of all, the obvious fact that this

---

[9] For a semantic theory based on this view of language, see Barwise and Perry (1985). Their work on language and information was highly salient among the audiences to whom these passages were written at the time, centered at the newly formed Center for the Study of Language and Information (CSLI) at Stanford University.

expression will have quite a different significance when uttered by a visitor with reference to a photograph in her host's photo album or by one shopper to another in front of the lettuce bin at the grocery store. But although linguists and logicians would commonly recognize the referent of "that's" as the problematic element in such cases, Heritage points out that the significance of the descriptor *nice* is equally so. So, in the first case, *nice* will refer to some properties of the photograph, whereas different properties will be intended in the case of the lettuce. Moreover, in either case whichever sense of *nice* is intended is not available from the utterance but remains to be found by the hearer through an active search of both the details of the referent and the larger context of the remark. So *nice* in the first instance might be a comment on the composition of the photograph, on the appearance of the host, or on some indefinite range of other properties of the photo in question. What is more, visitor and host will never establish in just so many words precisely what it is that the visitor intends and the host understands. Their interpretations of the term will remain partially unarticulated, located in their unique relationship to the photograph and the context of the remark. Yet the shared understanding that they do achieve will be perfectly adequate for purposes of their interaction. It is in this sense – that is, that expression and interpretation involve an active process of pointing to and searching the situation of talk – that language is a form of situated action.

Among philosophers and linguists, the term *indexicality* typically is used to distinguish those classes of expressions whose meaning is conditional on the situation of their use in this way from those such as, for example, definite noun phrases whose meaning is claimed to be specifiable in objective, or context-independent terms. But the *communicative* significance of a linguistic expression is always dependent on the circumstances of its use. A formal statement not of what the language means in relation to any context, but of what the language-user means in relation to some particular context, requires a description of the context or situation of the utterance itself. And every utterance's situation comprises an indefinite range of possibly relevant features.[10] Our practical solution to this theoretical problem is not to enumerate some subset

---

[10] The "problem" of context was a central preoccupation for cognitive science in the 1980s, as evidenced for example by a seminar series at CSLI titled "Why Context Won't Go Away," devoted to discussion of how context might best be represented in philosophical and computational formalisms.

of the relevant circumstances – we generally never mention our circumstances as such at all – but to "wave our hand" at the situation, as if we
always included in our utterance an implicit ceteris paribus clause and
closed with an implicit et cetera clause. One consequence of this practice
is that we always "mean more than we can say in just so many words":
"[S]peakers can . . . do the immense work that they do with natural language, even though over the course of their talk it is not known and
is never, not even "in the end," available for saying in so many words
just what they are talking about. Emphatically, that does not mean that
speakers do not know what they are talking about, *but instead that they
know what they are talking about in that way*" (Garfinkel and Sacks 1970:
342–4, original emphasis). In this sense deictic expressions, time and
place adverbs, and pronouns are just particularly clear illustrations of
the general fact that all language, including the most abstract or eternal,
stands in an essentially indexical relationship to the embedding world.

Because the significance of an expression always exceeds the meaning of what actually gets said, the interpretation of an expression turns
not only on its conventional or definitional meaning, nor on that plus
some body of presuppositions, but also on the unspoken situation of
its use. Our situated use of language, and consequently language's significance, presupposes and implies a horizon of things that are never
actually mentioned – what Schutz referred to as the "world taken for
granted" (1962: 74). Philosophers have been preoccupied with this fact
about language as a matter of the truth conditionality of propositions,
the problem being that the truth conditions of an assertion are always
relative to a background, and the background does not form part of the
semantic content of the sentence as such (Searle 1979). And the same
problems that have plagued philosophers of language as a matter of
principle are now practical problems for cognitive science. As I pointed
out in Chapter 5 in this book, the view that mutual intelligibility rests
on a stock of shared knowledge has been taken over by researchers in
cognitive science, in the hope that an enumeration of the knowledge
assumed by particular words or actions could be implemented as data
structures in the machine, which would then "understand" those words
and actions. Actual attempts to include the background assumptions of a
statement as part of its semantic content, however, run up against the fact
that there is no fixed set of assumptions that underlies a given statement.
As a consequence, the elaboration of background assumptions is fundamentally ad hoc and arbitrary, and each elaboration of assumptions in
principle introduces further assumptions to be elaborated, ad infinitum.

The problem of communicating instructions for action, in particular certain of its seemingly intractable difficulties, becomes clearer with this view of language in mind. The relation of efficient linguistic formulations to particular situations parallels the relation of instructions to situated action. As linguistic expressions, instructions are subject to the constraint that: "However extensive or explicit what a speaker says may be, it does not by its extensiveness or explicitness pose a task of deciding the correspondence between what he says and what he means that is resolved by citing his talk verbatim" (Garfinkel and Sacks 1970: 342–4). This indexicality of instructions means that an instruction's significance with respect to action does not inhere in the instruction but must be found by the instruction follower with reference to the situation of its use. Far from replacing the ad hoc methods used to establish the significance of everyday talk and action, therefore, the interpretation of instructions is thoroughly reliant on those same methods. As Garfinkel concludes: "To treat instructions as though *ad hoc* features in their use was a nuisance, or to treat their presence as grounds for complaining about the incompleteness of instructions, is very much like complaining that if the walls of a building were gotten out of the way, one could see better what was keeping the roof up" (Garfinkel 1967: 22). Like all action descriptions, instructions necessarily rely on an implicit et cetera clause to be called complete. The project of instruction writing is ill conceived, therefore, if its goal is the production of exhaustive action descriptions that can guarantee a particular interpretation. What "keeps the roof up" in the case of instructions for action is not only the instructions as such, but also their interpretation in use. And the latter has all of the ad hoc and uncertain properties that characterize every occasion of the situated use of language.

## THE MUTUAL INTELLIGIBILITY OF ACTION

By "index" Peirce meant not only that the sign relies for its significance on the event or object that it indicates but also that the sign is actually a constituent of the referent. So language more generally is not only anchored in, but in large measure constitutes, the situation of its use. Ethnomethodology generalizes this constitutive function of language still further to action, in the proposition that the purposefulness of action is recognizable in virtue of the methodic, skillful, and therefore taken-for-granted practices whereby we establish the rational properties of actions in a particular context. It is those practices that provide for the "analyzability of actions-in-context given that not only does no concept of context-in-general exist, but every use of 'context' without exception is itself essentially indexical" (Garfinkel 1967: 10).

In positing the reflexivity of purposeful action and the methods by which we convey and construe action's purposes, ethnomethodology does not intend to reduce meaningful action to method. The intent is rather to identify the mutual intelligibility of action as *the* problem for sociology. To account for the foundations of mutual intelligibility and social order, traditional social science posits a system of known-in-common social conventions or behavioral norms. What we share, on this view, is agreement on the appropriate relation of actions to situations. We walk into a situation, identify its features, and match our actions to it. This implies that, on any given occasion, the concrete situation must be recognizable as an instance of a class of typical situations, and the behavior of the actor must be recognizable as an instance of a class of appropriate actions. And with respect to communication, as Wilson (1970) points out:

the different participants must define situations and actions in essentially the same way, since otherwise rules could not operate to produce coherent interaction over time. Within the normative paradigm, this cognitive agreement is provided by the assumption that the actors share a system of culturally established symbols and meanings. Disparate definitions of situations and actions do occur, of course, but these are handled as conflicting subcultural traditions or idiosyncratic deviations from the culturally established cognitive consensus. (ibid.: 699)

In contrast with this normative paradigm, Garfinkel proposes that the stability of the social world is not the consequence of a "cognitive consensus" or stable body of shared meanings but of our tacit use of the documentary method of interpretation to find the coherence of situations and actions. As a general process, the documentary method describes a search for uniformities that underlie unique appearances. Applied to the social world, it describes the process whereby actions are taken as evidence, or "documents," of underlying plans or intent, which in turn fill in the sense of the actions (1967, Chapter 3). The documentary method describes an ability – the ascription of intent on the basis of evidence, and the interpretation of evidence on the basis of ascribed intent – that is as identifying of rationality as the ability to act rationally itself. At the same time, the documentary method is not reducible to the application of any necessary and sufficient conditions, either behavioral or contextual, for the identification of intent. There are no logical formulae for recognizing the intent of some behavior independent of context, and there are no recognition algorithms for joining contextual particulars to behavioral descriptions so that forms of intent can be precisely defined over a set of necessary and sufficient observational data (see Coulter 1983: 162–3).

Given the lack of universal rules for the interpretation of action, the programme of ethnomethodology is to investigate and describe the use of the documentary method in particular situations. Studies indicate, on the one hand, the generality of the method and, on the other hand, the extent to which special constraints on its use characterize specialized domains of practical activity such as natural science, courts of law, and the practice of medicine.[11] In a contrived situation that, though designed independently and not with them in mind, closely parallels both the "Turing test" and encounters with Weizenbaum's ELIZA programs, Garfinkel set out to test the documentary method in the context of counseling. Students were asked to direct questions concerning their personal problems to someone they knew to be a student counselor, seated in another room. They were restricted to questions that could take yes/no answers, and the answers were then given by the counselor on a random basis. For the students, the counselor's answers were motivated by the questions. That is to say, by taking each answer as evidence for what the counselor "had in mind," the students were able to find a deliberate pattern in the exchange that explicated the significance and relevance of each new response as an answer to their question. Specifically, the yes/no utterances were found to document advice from the counselor, intended to help in the solution of the student's problem. So, for example, students assigned to the counselor, as the advice "behind" the answer, the thought formulated in the student's question: "when a subject asked 'Should I come to school every night after supper to do my studying?' and the experimenter said 'My answer is no,' the subject in his comments said, 'He said I shouldn't come to school and study'" (Garfinkel 1967: 92). In cases where an answer seemed directly to contradict what had come before, students either attributed the

---

[11] For example, the work of coroners at the Los Angeles Suicide Prevention Center (Garfinkel 1967: 11–18), the deliberations of juries (ibid.: Chapter 4) and courtroom practices of attorneys (Atkinson and Drew 1979), the work of clinic staff in selecting patients for out-patient psychiatric treatment (Garfinkel 1967, Chapter 7), the work of physicians interviewing patients for purposes of diagnosis (Beckman and Frankel 1983), the work of scientists discovering an optical pulsar (Garfinkel, Lynch, and Livingston 1981). (Original footnote.)

apparent contradiction to a change of mind on the part of the counselor, as the result of having learned more between the two replies, or to some agenda on the part of the counselor that lent the reply a deeper significance than its first, apparently inconsistent, interpretation would suggest. In other cases, the interpretation of previous answers was revised in light of the current one, or an interpretation of the question was found and attributed to the counselor that rationalized what would otherwise appear to be an inappropriate answer. Generally, Garfinkel observes: "The underlying pattern was elaborated and compounded over the series of exchanges and was accommodated to each present 'answer' so as to maintain the 'course of advice,' to elaborate what had 'really been advised' previously, and to motivate the new possibilities as emerging features of the problem" (ibid.: 90).

Garfinkel's results with arbitrary responses make the success of Weizenbaum's DOCTOR program easier to understand and lend support to Weizenbaum's hypothesis that the intelligence of interactions with the DOCTOR program is due to the work of the human participant, specifically, to methods for interpreting the system's behavior as evidence for some underlying intent. The larger implications of the documentary method, however, touch on the status of an "underlying" reality of psychological and social facts in human interaction, prior to situated action and interpretation:

It is not unusual for professional sociologists to think of their procedures as processes of "seeing through" appearances to an underlying reality; of brushing past actual appearances to "grasp the invariant." Where our subjects are concerned, their processes are not appropriately imagined as "seeing through," but consist instead of coming to terms with a situation in which factual knowledge of social structures – factual in the sense of warranted grounds of further inferences and actions – must be assembled and made available for potential use despite the fact that the situations it purports to describe are, in any calculable sense, unknown; in their actual and intended logical structures are essentially vague; and are modified, elaborated, extended, if not indeed created, by the fact and matter of being addressed. (Garfinkel 1967: 96)

The stability of the social world, from this standpoint, is not due to an eternal structure but to situated actions that create and sustain shared understanding on specific occasions of interaction. Social constraints on appropriate action are always identified relative to some unique and unreproducible set of circumstances. Members of the society are treated as being at least potentially aware of the concrete details of their circumstances, and their actions are interpreted in that light. Rather than actions being *determined by* rules, actors *effectively use* the normative rules of conduct that are available to produce significant actions. So, for example, there is a normative rule for greetings that runs to the effect: do not initiate greetings except with persons who are acquaintances. If we witness a person greeting another who we know is not an acquaintance, we can either conclude that the greeter broke the rule or infer that via the use of the rule he or she was seeking to treat the other as an acquaintance (Heritage 1984: 126). Such rules are not taught or encoded but are learned tacitly through typification over families of similar situations and actions. Despite the availability of such typifications, no action can fully provide for its own interpretation in any given instance. Instead, every instance of meaningful action must be accounted for separately with respect to specific, local, contingent determinants of significance. The recommendation for social studies, as a consequence, is that instead of looking for a structure that is invariant across situations we look for the processes whereby particular, uniquely constituted circumstances are systematically interpreted so as to render meaning shared and action accountably rational. Structure, on this view, is an emergent product of situated action, rather than its foundation. Insofar as the project of ethnomethodology is to redirect social science from its traditional preoccupation with abstract structures to an interest in situated actions, and the cognitive sciences share in that same tradition, the ethnomethodological project has implications for cognitive science as well.

# 7

## Communicative Resources

Thus the whole framework of conversational constraints can become something to honor, to invert, or to disregard, depending as the mood strikes.

(Goffman 1975: 311)

Communicative action occurs in particular moments of actual time, in particular relationships of simultaneity and sequence. These relationships in time, taken together, constitute a regular rhythmic pattern. This regularity in time and timing seems to play an essential, constitutive role in the social organization of interaction... Whereas there is no metronome playing while people talk, their talking itself serves as a metronome.

(Erickson 1982: 72)

We are environments for each other.

(McDermott 1976: 27)

An argument of the preceding chapters was that we never definitively determine the intent behind an action, in that descriptions at the level of intent are not designed to pick out mental states that stand in some relation of strict causality to action or even, in any strong sense, of one-to-one correspondence. Instead, intentional descriptions classify over situations and actions, as typifications that invariably include an "open horizon of unexplored content" (Schutz 1962: 14). In spite of this inherent indeterminacy, intentional descriptions not only suffice to classify purposeful behavior but, given the unique and fleeting circumstances of action and the need to represent it efficiently, seem ideally suited to the task. Attributing intent in any particular instance, moreover, is generally nonproblematic, even transparent, for members of the society who, from their practical perspective and for their practical purposes, are engaged in the everyday business of making sense out of each other's actions. When disputes over the significance of an action do arise, the uncertainty of intentional attributions becomes a practical problem, but in such cases it is the "right" interpretation of the action, not the fact of its inherent uncertainty, that is of interest to participants. For students of purposeful action, however, the observation that action interpretation is inherently uncertain does have a methodological consequence; namely it recommends that we turn our focus from explaining away uncertainty in the interpretation of action to identifying the resources by which the inevitable uncertainty is managed. A central tenet of social studies of practical action is that those resources are not only cognitive, but also interactional. While acknowledging the role of conventional meanings and individual predispositions in mutual intelligibility, therefore, this chapter focuses on the neglected other side of shared understanding; namely the local interactional work that produces intelligibility in situ. The starting premise is that interpreting the significance of action is an essentially collaborative achievement. Rather than depend on reliable recognition of intent, mutual intelligibility turns on the availability of communicative resources to detect, remedy, and at times even exploit the inevitable uncertainties of action's significance.

To underscore the breadth and subtlety of the resources available for shared understanding and the precision of their use, this chapter focuses on the richest form of human communication; that is, face-to-face interaction. The premise of conversation analyses is that face-to-face interaction incorporates the broadest range of possible resources for communication, with other forms of interaction being characterizable in terms of particular resource limitations or additional constraints (see Sacks, Schegloff, and Jefferson 1978).[1] In the discussion that follows I consider only a small subset of these resources; for example, I do not include the wealth of prosodic and gestural cues described by students of interaction. The rationale for neglecting those cues here, and in the analysis of Chapter 9, is that the case of human–machine interaction is so limited that the basic resources, let alone the expressive subtleties, of human interaction are in question. The first three sections of this chapter describe the resources of the most unrestricted form of face-to-face

---

[1] The corpus of studies in conversation analysis is by now a rich and extensive one. For introductions see Goodwin (1981), Heritage (1985), Levinson (1983, Chapter 6).

interaction, everyday conversation. I then consider some modifications to everyday conversation that have developed for specialized purposes in institutional settings and, in Chapter 8, some additional constraints introduced by restrictions on the mutual access of participants to each other and to a common situation. Finally, human–machine communication is analyzed, in Chapter 9, as an extreme form of resource-limited interaction.

## CONVERSATION AS ENSEMBLE WORK

The most common view of conversation is that speakers and listeners, pursuing some common topic according to individual predispositions and agendas, engage in an alternating sequence of action and response. For students of human cognition and of language, conversation generally has been treated as epiphenomenal with respect to the central concerns of their fields. Cognitively, conversation is just the meeting ground of individual psychologies, whereas linguistically it is the noisy, real-world occasion for the exercise of basic language abilities. On either view, the additional constraints imposed by situated language use are a complication that obscures the underlying structure of cognitive or linguistic competence. As a consequence, linguists generally have not used actual speech for the analysis of linguistic competence, on the assumption that the phrasal breaks, restarts, hesitations, and the like found in actual speech represent such a defective performance that the data are of no use. And in analyzing idealized utterances, linguists have focused exclusively on the speaker's side in the communicative process (Streeck 1980). When one takes situated language use as the subject matter, however, the definition of the field must necessarily shift to communication under naturally occurring circumstances. And when one moves back far enough from the utterances of the speaker to bring the listener into view as well, it appears that much in the actual construction of situated language use that has been taken to reflect problems of speaker performance, instead reflects speaker competence in responding to cues provided by the listener (C. Goodwin 1981: 12–13).

Closer analyses of face-to-face communication indicate that conversation is not so much an alternating series of actions and reactions between individuals as it is a joint action accomplished through the participants' continuous engagement in speaking and listening (see Schegloff 1972, 1982; C. Goodwin 1981). In contrast to the prevailing preoccupation of linguists and discourse analysts with speaking, where the listener is largely taken for granted or as extraneous, conversation analysis shows that the action of listening is consequential to the extent that "the listener's failure to act at the right time in the right way literally prevents the speaker from finishing what he was trying to say – at least from finishing it in the way he was previously saying it. The speaker, in continuing to speak socially (i.e. in taking account in speaking of what the other is doing in listening), makes *accountable the* listener's violations of expectations for appropriate listening behavior" (Erickson 1982: 118–19, original emphasis). In the same way that the listener attends to the speaker's words and actions to understand them, in other words, the speaker takes the behavior of the listener as evidence for the listener's response. Schegloff (1982: 72) offers the example of the lecturer:

Anyone who has lectured to a class knows that the (often silent) reactions of the audience – the wrinkling of brows at some point in its course, a few smiles or chuckles or nods, or their absence – can have marked consequences for the talk which follows: whether, for example, the just preceding point is reviewed, elaborated, put more simply, etc., or whether the talk moves quickly on to the next point, and perhaps to a more subtle point than was previously planned.

The local resources or *contextualization cues* by which people produce the mutual intelligibility of their interaction consist in the systematic organization of speech prosody (Gumperz 1982a), body position and gesture (Birdwhistell 1970; Erickson 1982; Scheflen 1974), gaze (C. Goodwin 1981; M. Goodwin 1980), and the precision of collaboratively accomplished timing (Erickson 1982). For example, Erickson suggests that what may be disturbing about certain speaker hesitations in conversation is not so much the interruption of talk as such, but the fact that, when talk stops and starts in temporally unpredictable ways, it is difficult for listeners to coordinate their listening actions (1982: 114). The richness of both simultaneous and sequential coordination "suggests that conversational inference is best seen not as a simple unitary evaluation of intent but as involving a complex series of judgments, including relational or contextual assessments on how items of information are to be integrated into what we know and into the event at hand" (Gumperz 1982b: 328–9). As with any skill, in ordinary conversation these judgments are made with such proficiency that they are largely transparent, though at times of breakdown they may become contestable (see Gumperz and Tannen 1979). Viewed as highly skilled performance, the organization of conversation appears to be closer to what in playing music is called "ensemble" work (Erickson 1982: 71) than it is to the common notion of speaker stimulus and listener response.

One reason to begin a consideration of interaction with the organization of conversation is that studies of everyday conversation, and more recently studies in specific institutional settings where the type, distribution, and content of turns at talk are constrained in characteristic ways, indicate that all of the various forms of talk (e.g., interviews, cross-examinations, lectures, formal debates, and so on) can be viewed as modifications to conversation's basic structure. As the basic system for communication, conversation is characterized by (1) an organization designed to support local, endogenous control over the development of topics or activities and to maximize accommodation of unforeseeable circumstances that arise and (2) resources for locating and remedying communication's troubles as part of its fundamental organization.

## Local Control

Taking ordinary conversation as their subject matter, Sacks, Schegloff, and Jefferson (1978) set out to identify the structural mechanisms by which this most "unstructured" of human activities is accomplished in a systematic and orderly way. Two problems for any interaction are the distribution of access to "the floor" and, closely related, control over the development of the topic or activity at hand. In contrast to mechanisms that administer an a priori, externally imposed agenda (for example, the format for a debate), the organization of conversation maximizes local control over both the distribution of turns and the direction of subject matter. That is to say, who talks and what gets talked about is decided then and there, by the participants in the conversation, through their collaborative construction of the conversation's course.

That turn taking is a collaborative achievement rather than a simple alternation of intrinsically bounded segments of talk is evident in the common occurrence in actual conversation of simultaneous talk, of joint production of a single sentence, and of silence. The observations that somehow one speaker only takes the floor when two begin together, that a listener may finish the speaker's turn without it constituting an interruption, and that any participant in a conversation, including the last to speak, may begin a new turn out of silence, raise theoretical questions about the proper definition of a turn's boundaries and the process by which turn transitions are organized (see C. Goodwin 1981: 2). In answer to such questions, Sacks, Schegloff, and Jefferson (1978) have delineated a set of conventions or normative rules by which turn taking is accomplished. By *normative* is meant only that these rules describe common practices observed by analysts of conversation. Speakers and listeners do not "know" these rules in the sense that they would or could formulate them in so many words. Rather, it can be seen by an observer, having these rules in mind, that they describe the practices by which people in conversation achieve the orderly distribution of turns. The set of rules for turn taking provides that for every place in the course of an utterance that is a projectable completion point for the utterance, one of the following occurs:

(a) The current speaker selects a next speaker, e.g., by directing a question or other implicative utterance at a particular hearer.
(b) Another participant self-selects, by being the first to start speaking.
(c) The current speaker continues.

Options (a)–(c) are not simply alternatives, but an ordered set. That is to say, at each place where a transition to a new speaker might be effected, the rule set applies as a matter of "if not (a), then (b) is an option," "if not (b), then (c) is an option" recursively until a change in speaker occurs. This does not mean, of course, that participants wait to see which rule applies and then act accordingly: the options are theirs to exercise; they are not the workings of some external mechanism. Moreover, the rules are not necessarily, but rather are contingently, applied. Which rule will prevail in any given case is determined by actions taken by the participants at each possible turn-transition place, and the contingency of the rules means that the exercise of each is constrained by the presence of the others in the set independently of their actually being employed on any given occasion. Lower priority options constrain higher priority options – for example, for the (b) option to be exercised given the presence of (c), it will need to be employed before (c) is invoked, at which time priority returns to (a).

Due to the ordering of the rule set, the system for turn taking constrains both the way that current speakers develop their talk and the way that others listen. Most obviously, the current speaker has reason to let listeners know where he or she is in the turn's course. This may be done explicitly, through introductions on the order of "I want to say a couple of things," or through the use of story prefaces that announce the onset of an extended multisentence turn with its own distinctive shape (see Sacks 1974). More implicitly, the speaker's control of the floor offers some inherent advantage. To preclude the exercise of option (b) before having had a say, the current speaker can extend his or her turn by, for example, withholding a point until after supporting arguments have been made. The speaker does not define the turn unilaterally, however: turn completion is as much a function of the listener's inclination to respond as it is a matter of the speaker's readiness to yield. The units of which turns are constructed are expandable, not fixed (any unit from a particle to an extended exposition may constitute a turn), and what happens at each possible turn-transition place is contingent on the actions of participants other than the speaker. So, for example, by passing on option (b) at a possible transition place listeners may invite the speaker to continue, turning what could be a speaker change into a pause in the same speaker's turn. Or listeners may, on finding in either the speaker's exercise of option (a) or failure to exercise option (c), that a turn is completed then look back over what was said to respond to it.

Because each projectable point of completion is a possible place for speaker change, the turn is interactionally determined over the course of the conversation. And rather than relying on a discrete set of "turn-yielding signals" (Duncan 1974), speaker continuity or change is managed with reference to the same range of syntactic, semantic, and non-linguistic resources by which participants construct the significance of what is being said:

By virtue of its character, it is misconceived to treat turns as units characterized by a division of labor in which the speaker determines the unit and its boundaries, and other parties to the conversation have as their task the recognition of them. Rather, the turn is a unit whose constitution and boundaries involve such a distribution of tasks (as we have noted): That a speaker can talk in such a way as to permit projection of possible completion to be made from his talk, and to allow others to use its transition places to start talk, to pass up talk, to affect directions of talk, and so on, and that their starting to talk, if properly placed, can determine where he ought to stop talk." (Sacks, Schegloff, and Jefferson 1978: 42)

The interactional structure of turn taking presents some distinctive problems for the definition and categorization of units in conversational analysis. For example, one might argue reasonably that silence should be classified differently according to whether it occurs within the turn of a single speaker (a pause) or between turns of different speakers (a gap) (C. Goodwin 1981: 18). The problem that arises for analysts is exemplified, however, in a case such as the following:[2]

John:  Well I, I took this course.
       (0.5)
Ann:   In how to quit?
         [
John:  which I really recommend.

The ambiguous status of the silence in this example as either a pause or a gap is not so much an analytic problem as it is an inherent property of situated talk. That is to say, the silence is treated by Ann as a gap, by John as a pause, such that "the same silence yields alternative classifications at different moments in time from the perspective of different participants" (Goodwin 1981: 19). No single classification of the silence will do, as its status is inextricably tied to an event developing over time and is subject to transformation. From Ann's point of view, at the point where she begins to speak, John's turn appears to be complete. John's extension of the turn, however, makes the silence into a pause and Ann's turn into an interruption that begins in the midst, rather than at the completion of, his utterance. The status of what constitutes "John's turn" in this exchange, and therefore the status of the silence, is essentially ambiguous in a way that will not be remedied by any exercise of the analyst. To the contrary, attempts to remedy the ambiguity must do damage to the phenomenon, which is precisely that boundaries of a turn are mutable and that the structure of conversation is achieved by speakers and hearers in this locally developing, contingent way. As a consequence of its interactional nature, the turn is not the kind of object that can be first defined and then examined for how it is passed back and forth between speakers. Instead, intrinsic structural elements of the turn are contingent on the process by which control changes hands between participants in conversation, as is the structure of the conversation produced. The point is not just that speakers can extend the length of their turns by the addition of further units of speech, but that through that essentially transparent mechanism they are able to change the emerging

---

[2] C. Goodwin (1981:18). Transcripts are presented here with the notation and punctuation of the original source. A full description of the notation system (based on Jefferson 1983 can be found at the end of the chapter. (Original footnote.)

meaning of their talk within a turn to fit the actions of their listener (see C. Goodwin 1981: 11). The localness of the constraints on speakers' constructions of turns-at-talk, and the turn's contingency on the actions of other speakers, make conversation maximally sensitive and adaptable to particular participants and to unforeseen circumstances of the developing interaction. The turn-taking system for conversation demonstrates how a system for communication that accommodates any participants, under any circumstances, may be systematic and orderly, whereas it must be essentially ad hoc.

## Sequential Organization and Coherence

In addition to providing a mechanism for control over the distribution of turns, the turn-taking system bears a direct relation to the control of inferences about the conversation's content.[3] In general, a coherent conversation is one in which each thing said can be heard as relevant to what has come before. Most locally, this means that the relevance of a turn is conditional on that which immediately precedes it: "By conditional relevance of one item on another we mean; given the first, the second is expectable; upon its occurrence it can be seen to be a second item to the first; upon its nonoccurrence it can be seen to be officially absent" (Schegloff 1972: 364). Two utterances that stand in a relationship of conditional relevance of one on the other, in this local sense, constitute an *adjacency pair* in Schegloff and Sacks's terminology (1973), though conditional relevance is not limited to literal adjacency (see Levinson 1983: 304). The first part of an adjacency pair both sets up an expectation with respect to what should come next and directs the way in which what does come next is heard (Schegloff 1972: 367). By the same token, the absence of an expected second part is a notable absence and therefore takes on significance as well. In this way silences, for example, can be meaningful: most obviously, a silence following an utterance that implicates a response will be "heard" as belonging to the recipient of the utterance and as a failure to respond. Similarly, a turn that holds the place of the second part of an adjacency pair but cannot be made relevant to the first will be seen as a non sequitur or as incoherent.

---

[3] Sensitivity to readings of the term *mechanism*, particularly in the context of work on interactive machines, would lead me now to rephrase this sentence. Rather than "providing a mechanism," the turn-taking system describes a practice for managing a distribution of turns and implicates a sequential relevance for things said.

The conditional relevance of adjacency pairs is an instance of what we might call, following Durkheim, a "social fact." The first part of an adjacency pair constrains the second part in a double sense. The constraint is a matter not only of the coherence or intelligibility of the second part but also of the accountability of the respondent for inferences that the *absence* of a second part would warrant. For example, in the case of interactions opened by a summons, such as calling someone's name or ringing her doorbell:

A member of the society may not "naively choose" not to answer a summons. The culture provides that a variety of "strong inferences" can be drawn from the fact of the official absence of an answer, and any member who does not answer does so at the peril of one of those inferences being made ... although members can, indeed "choose" not to answer a summons, they cannot do so naively, i.e. they know that if the inference of physical or interactional absence cannot be made, then some other inference will, e.g. they are cold shouldering, insulting, etc. (Schegloff 1972: 367–8)

The summons–answer pair is an example of a sequence in which the first part implicates a particular type of response in the immediate next turn, to the extent that if no response occurs the first speaker is justified in, for example, repeating the summons. And on eliminating the possibility that the summons has not been heard, and determining that it will in fact not be answered, the summoner is justified in making further inferences regarding the recipient's availability, interest, and the like.[4] In this sense, we are not so much constrained by the rules of conversation as we are "caught in a web of inferences" (Levinson 1983: 321, note 16). That is to say, the rules of conversation are neither strictly optional (their breach does have consequences) nor obligatory (they may be breached without a necessary loss of coherence). They are, however, inexorably meaningful.

Although conditional relevance is a constraint on inference, it is a weak constraint in the sense that it does not prescribe what counts

---

[4] Schegloff (1972: 363) points to the telephone as an example of a technology that embodies the organization of the summons–answer pair: "In this mechanical age it may be of interest to note that the very construction and operation of the mechanical ring is built on these principles. If each ring of the phone be considered a summons, then the phone is built to ring, wait for an answer, if none occurs, to ring again, wait for an answer, ring again, etc. And indeed, some persons, polite even when interacting with a machine, will not interrupt a phone, but wait for the completion of a ring before picking up the receiver." (Original footnote.)

as a response to a given action, only that whatever is done next will be viewed as a response. In fact, the range of actions in a second-part position that can be heard as a response is extended, rather than constrained, in virtue of the expectation that adjacency sets up. That is to say, an action that is not in any explicit way tied to the action that it follows will nevertheless be interpreted as a response, in virtue of its position:

A: Are you coming?
B: I gotta work. (Goffman 1975: 260)

The position of B's utterance as a response means that we look for its relevance to A's question. So in this case, B's statement can be heard as a negative reply, just as B's question can be heard as an affirmative reply in the following:

A: Have you got coffee to go?
B: Milk and sugar? (Merritt 1977: 325)

The sequential implicature exemplified by adjacency pairs is not literally conditional on adjacency but instead allows for multiple levels of embedded sequences aimed at clarification and elaboration. The result is that answers to later questions can precede answers to earlier ones without a loss of coherence:

B: . . . I ordered some paint from you uh a couple of weeks ago some vermilion
A: Yuh
B: And I wanted to order some more the name's Boyd
(Request 1)
A: Yes//how many tubes would you like sir
(Question 1)
B: An-
B: U:hm (.) what's the price now eh with V.A.T. do you know eh
(Question 2)
A: Er I'll just work that out for you =
(Hold)
B: =Thanks
(Accept)
(10. 0)

A:  Three pound nineteen a tube sir
    (Answer 2)
B:  Three nineteen is it=
    (Question 3)
A:  =Yeah
    (Answer 3)
B:  E::h (1.0) yes u:hm ((dental click)) ((in parenthetical tone)) e:h
    jus-justa think, that's what three nineteen
    That's for the large tube isn't it
    (Question 4)
A:  Well yeah it's the thirty seven c.c.s
    (Answer 4)
B:  Er, hh I'll tell you what I'll just eh eh ring you back I have to work
    out how many I'll need
    Sorry I did- wasn't sure of the price you see
    (Account for no Answer 1)
A:  Okay

(Levinson 1983: 305)

The local system of adjacency pair organization, in its canonical form operating over two turns, can by the accumulation of first parts (e.g., requests and questions) project an extended sequence of expected seconds like that of the last example, that is, [R1(Q1{Q2[Q3(Q4–A4)A3]A2}A1). As Levinson points out with respect to this example, B's final obligation is to account for his failure to provide an answer to Question 1, demonstrating his orientation to the "social fact" that an answer is called for. That failure, in turn, effectively constitutes B's withdrawal of Request 1, freeing A of the obligation to respond to that original request:

What the notion of conditional relevance makes clear is that what binds the parts of adjacency pairs together is not a formation rule of the sort that would specify that a question must receive an answer if it is to count as a well-formed discourse, but the setting up of specific expectations which have to be attended to. Hence the non-occurrences of a R[equest] 1 and an A[nswer] 1 in [the example] do not result in an incoherent discourse because their absences are systematically provided for. (Levinson 1983: 306)

The overall coherence of a conversation, in sum, is accomplished through the development and elaboration of a local coherence operating in the first instance across just two turns, current and next. The resiliency of embedding, however, is such that the backward reach of relevance extends beyond the immediately preceding turn:

C: (telephone rings)
A: Hello.
C: Is this the Y?
A: You have the wrong number.
C: Is this KI five, double four, double o?
A: Double four, double *six*.
C: Oh, I am sorry.

(Goffman 1975: 285)

In this case the apology is intelligible only if we view the entire telephone call as its object, not just the utterance of A that it immediately follows. Similarly, to use another example of Goffman's (ibid.: 286), the applause at the end of a play is a response not to the delivery of the final line, or the drop of the curtain, but to the entire play. The relevance of an action, in other words, is conditional on any identifiable prior action or event, however far that may extend for the participants (i.e., it may be a lifetime, say, for mother and child), insofar as the previous action can be tied to the current action's immediate, local environment. As a consequence, conditional relevance does not allow us to predict from an action to a response, but only to project that what comes next will be a response and, retrospectively, to take that status as a cue to how what comes next should be heard. The interpretation of action, in this sense, relies on the liberal application of post hoc, ergo propter hoc.

### LOCATING AND REMEDYING COMMUNICATIVE TROUBLE

Communication takes place in real environments, under real performance requirements on actual individuals, and is vulnerable therefore to internal and external troubles that may arise at any time, from a misunderstanding to a clap of thunder (Schegloff 1982). Our communication succeeds in the face of such disturbances not because we predict reliably what will happen and thereby avoid problems, or even because we encounter problems that we have anticipated in advance, but because we work, moment by moment, to identify and remedy the inevitable troubles that arise: "It is a major feature of a rational organization for behavior that accommodates real-worldly interests, and is not susceptible of external enforcement, that it incorporates resources and procedures for repair of its troubles into its fundamental organization" (Sacks, Schegloff, and Jefferson 1978: 39).

The resources for detecting and remedying problems in communication, in other words, are the same resources that support communication that is trouble free. With respect to control, for example, the contingency of conversational options for keeping and taking the floor – specifically, the fact that transitions should be accomplished at possible turn completion points and not before and that at each possible completion point the speaker may extend his or her turn – means that gaps and overlaps can and do occur. The extent to which conversationalists accomplish speaker transitions with a minimum of gap or overlap is the product not only of the "accurate" projection of completion points but also of the repair of routine troubles. The following is a simple example of a familiar kind of conversational repair work:

C: .hhhh aa:: of course under the circumstances Dee I would never::
    again permit im tuh see im.
D: Yeah
    (0.7)
C: tlk. Be:cuz he
      [
D: Wul did'e ever git – ma:rried'r anything?
C: Hu::h?
    [
D: Did yee ever git – ma:rried?
C: .hhhh I have no *idea*
                   (cited in Atkinson and Drew 1979: 40)

In addition to negotiating the transfer of control, participants in conversation must be alert to the possibility of substantive troubles of interpretation. Schegloff (1982) points out that tokens such as "uh huh," commonly viewed as a signal from the listener that encourages the speaker to continue, operate as they do not simply because there is a semantic convention to the effect that such tokens claim or signal understanding but rather because through such tokens listeners pass up, at possible transition places, the opportunity to initiate repair on the preceding talk. The same option that provides for ordinary turn transitions, in other words, affords the recipient of an utterance the occasion to assert that he or she has some trouble in understanding or to request some clarification.

The work of repair includes calling the other's attention to the occurrence of some troublesome item, remedying it, and resuming the original line of action in which the troublesome item is embedded. Jefferson (1972) identifies two kinds of trouble flag: a questioning repeat and a nonspecific interrogative, for example, "What?" or "Huh?" The two are different in that the repeat simultaneously flags the fact that there is some troublesome item in the prior talk *and locates it* for the first speaker:

Steven:  One, two, three, ((pause)) four, five, six, ((pause)) eleven, eight, nine, ten.
Susan:  "Eleven"? – eight, nine, ten? (ibid.: 295)

An interrogative request for clarification, in contrast, leaves it to the first speaker both to locate the item that produced the request and to remedy it. In that case, the location of the item and the remedy may be effected simultaneously, in the first speaker's reply:

A:  If Percy goes with – Nixon I'd sure like that.
B:  *Who?*
A:  Percy. (ibid.: 296)

In both cases the adjacency of the trouble flag to the troublesome item is obviously a resource for the latter's identification.[5] However, listeners generally do not interrupt a speaker to flag some trouble but rather wait for the next turn transition place or point of completion. By permitting the speaker to complete the utterance in which the trouble is heard, the listener is warranted in assuming that there is no unsolicited remedy forthcoming and the complaint becomes a legitimate one (Jefferson 1972: 298).

A side sequence initiated by an assertion of misunderstanding or request for clarification sets up an exchange that the first speaker did not necessarily anticipate, but to which he or she is obliged to respond. That is to say, a failure on the part of the speaker to provide clarification in response to an explicit request is a *noticeable absence*, is seen as specifically not providing clarification, as opposed to just doing something else. The "failure to respond" then becomes something about which complaints can be made or inferences may be drawn (Atkinson and Drew 1979: 57).

[5] It is worth noting in this case that although the "Who?" is in fact ambiguous, speaker A appears to have no trouble identifying its referent. It is hard to account for this in any way other than in virtue of A and B's common knowledge of politics, i.e., that it is more likely that "Percy" would be a troublesome item in this context than that "Nixon" would. Such an analysis cannot be more than conjecture, however. (Original footnote.)

In responding to a request for clarification, the sequential implicativeness of the troublesome utterance is temporarily suspended in favor of finding a remedy for the recipient's problem. Routinely in face-to-face conversation the adjacency relation or continuity between utterance and response, and the coherence of the interaction, are sustained across such embedded side sequences. This is true even when the request for clarification results in complete reformulation of the initial utterance. That is to say, although the response may ultimately address the reformulation, not the original utterance, it will still be heard as a response to the original:

M: What=so what did you *do* did you have people – did  
    Morag(.)come(.)down with the car again()or what  
    [  
A: When last year  
M: Mmm how did you manage to *shift* it back and forward  
                                               [  
A: Last year I don't know ho:w I managed it I got it a::ll in (0.8) two  
    suitcases.

(cited in Atkinson and Drew 1979: 239)

In this case it is just because A's "When last year" cannot be heard as a reply to M's question that it is heard as an embedded request for clarification. By the same token, the fact that a reply to M's question is deferred makes A's response to the reformulation about "managing it" relevant to the original question about "Morag and the car."

Turn-transition places provide recurring opportunities for the listener to initiate some repair or request for clarification from the speaker. Alternatively, clarification may be offered by the speaker not because the recipient of an utterance asks for it, but because the speaker finds evidence for some misapprehension in the recipient's response:

Dr: Hev'y ever had palpitations  
    (0.6)  
Pt: Noh. M' feet ain't painin' me but they swell sometime  
Dr: No I – it's when yer heart starts beating really fast an y'feel  
    like y' can't catch yer breath.  
Pt: No. uh-uh. I never had *that*

(Frankel 1984: 155)

Although the patient here produces a response that is, formally, an answer to the doctor's question, the answer reveals a lexical problem that the doctor detects and remedies. The problem is, of course, unknown to the patient until the remedy is offered: if the doctor had failed to detect the misunderstanding, or had decided to let it pass and had consequently not offered the correction, the conversation to all appearances could have continued on as if there were no trouble. In this case the problem is evidently, from the doctor's point of view, worth bothering about: in myriad other cases it is not. That is to say, given the lack of specific criteria for assessing shared understanding in most cases, a crucial part of interactional competence is the ability to judge whether some evidence that the recipient has misunderstood warrants the work required for repair (Jefferson 1972). The decision whether to challenge a troublesome item or to let it pass involves, in part, a weighing of the relative work involved in the item's clarification versus the forseeable dangers of letting it go by. The risks of the latter are exemplified by the garden path situation, where speakers fail to identify some communicative trouble at the point where it occurs and discover only at some later point in the interaction that there *has been* some misunderstanding (see Jordan and Fuller 1975; Gumperz and Tannen 1979).[6] At the point of discovery, the coherence of the interaction over some indefinite number of past turns may be called into question, and the source of the trouble may be difficult or impossible to reconstruct. In contrast to the routine problems and remedies that characterize local repair in conversation, such a situation may come close to communicative failure; that is, it may require abandoning the current line of talk or beginning anew.

### SPECIALIZED FORMS OF INTERACTION

A distinguishing feature of ordinary conversation is the local, moment-by-moment management of the distribution of turns, of their size, and of what gets done in them, those things being accomplished in the course of each current speaker's turn. There are, of course, numerous institutionalized settings that prescribe the organization and subject matter of interaction. Interactional organization is institutionalized along two dimensions that are of particular relevance to problems discussed in Chapter 9: (1) the preallocation of *types* of turn, that is, who speaks when and what form their participation takes and (2) the prescription of the substantive content and direction of the interaction or the *agenda*.

---

[6] An instance of this in the case of human–machine communication is discussed in Chapter 9. (Original footnote.)

## Preallocation of Turn Types

Analysis of encounters between physicians and patients (Frankel 1984) and of the examination of witnesses in the courtroom (Atkinson and Drew 1979) reveals a turn-taking system that is preallocated in terms of both the types of turn and the distribution of those types between the participants. Although there is no explicit formulation of a rule for the organization of talk in medical encounters, for example, Frankel reports that physicians' utterances almost always take the form of questions (ninety-nine percent of the time), whereas patients' take the form of answers. And in the courtroom, by definition, the examiner has the sole right to ask questions, whereas the examined is obliged to answer. In the courtroom, the convention that only two parties participate holds in spite of the number of persons present, and with the exception only of certain prescribed methods for "interruption" from the other counsel which, in virtue of the prescription of when and how interruption is to be effected, itself becomes a technical matter in the courtroom setting. In both medical and legal settings, the effect of the preallocation of turn types is to deliver control of the proceedings from the "client" or layperson back to the "expert" or specialist. At the close of each question–answer sequence, control is relinquished to whoever would start another sequence and the expert, having rights to the role of questioner, is repeatedly the one to retake control. Although the constraints on medical or legal interaction can be seen as institutional and in that sense as external to any particular occasion, it is nonetheless the case that in every actual instance the constraints are realized locally and collaboratively. Insofar as the interaction is locally managed, turn-transitions are subject to the same problems that arise in everyday conversation and are remedied via the same methods, as in the following example of an overlap that the witness (W) remedies by repeating her answer to the counsel's (C's) question:

    C:  An (.) about how long did you say you
        ta:lked before (this was)
        [
    W:  I don't remember
    C:  (started ta kiss (h) a)=
    W:  = I don't remember.

                              (from Atkinson and Drew 1979: 67)

At the same time, the fact that procedural constraints on turn transitions are managed locally even in these settings means that general conventions of conversational turn-taking can be exploited to further the special purposes of the participants. Because of the fact that pauses in conversation, for example, will be ascribed significance insofar as they are seen to belong to a selected next speaker, a pause following an examination sequence can be used by the examining counsel effectively to comment on the response to the jury, as in the following examination in a rape case cited by Atkinson and Drew (1979: 241):

C:  You were out in the woods with the defendant at this point isn't that so
    (1.0)
W:  Yeah
    (7.0)
C:  And the defendant (.) took (.) the ca:r (1.0) and backed it (1.0) into some trees didn'e
    (0.5)
W:  Mm hm
    [
C:  underneath some trees.

In this case, the preallocated order of turns assigns the seven-second pause to the counsel and ensures that no other speaker will use the pause as an opportunity to take over the floor. The pause is used by the counsel in an unspoken turn that insinuates further "information" into the message that the jury receives from the witness' answer. In the medical encounter, similarly, the physician can use a silence as an unspoken turn – in the following example, to avoid having to deliver bad news through disagreement:

Pt:  This – chemotherapy (0.2) it won't have any lasting effects on havin' kids will it?
     (2.2)
Pt:  It will?
Dr:  I'm afraid so.

(Frankel 1984: 153)

Finally, although respective turns of physician and patient, or counsel and witness, are constrained to be either questions or answers, these are minimal characterizations and provide no instruction for how, or what, specific utterances can be put into such a format. In the courtroom, for example, rules of evidence apply (relevance to the case at hand, status of the evidence as hearsay, the use of leading questions, and the like) where the application of those rules is situated and problematic and is itself part of the technical business of the proceedings. And the format of questions and answers in the courtroom accommodates a range of activities, including accusations, challenges, justifications, denials, and the like. Those activities are not prescribed in the way that the question–answer format is and what counts as a question or an answer is itself liable to challenge. As a consequence, rules for courtroom interaction, like those for everyday conversation, constitute a resource for social order, not a recipe or an explanation.

## Agendas

Various settings, of course, do comprise prescriptions not only about forms of talk, but also about the substantive direction and purposes of the interaction:

in several different types of speech-exchange situations, there can be occasions in which participation is constructed by a speaker in continuing response to interactional contingencies and opportunities from moment to moment, and occasions in which a participant has a preformed notion, and sometimes a pre-specified text, of what is to be said, and plows ahead with it in substantial (though rarely total) disregard for what is transpiring in the course of his talking. (Schegloff 1982: 72)

A major concern for participants in such settings is the distribution of knowledge about the agenda (Beckman and Frankel 1983). The communicative task of novice and expert in a given setting is to coordinate their actions in a way that accommodates their asymmetrical relationship to the interaction's institutionalized purposes. At the same time, it is precisely the difference in their respective familiarities vis-à-vis the setting's protocols and purposes that in large measure distinguishes the "expert" or specialist from the "novice" or layperson (Erickson 1982: 4).

The work of Beckman and Frankel (1983) on physicians' methods for eliciting a patient's "chief complaint" is illustrative. They point out that the medical literature has generally viewed the agenda for medical interviews as the patient's, in the sense that it is the patient who comes to the physician with a complaint and who is the source of the information required for the complaint's diagnosis. Given this view, a commonly cited problem for physicians is the experience of discovering, at the point where the physician is about to conclude the office visit or at least the history-taking segment of the interview, that the patient has withheld some information that is relevant to a chief complaint. In contrast, by inverting the common view, Beckman and Frankel identify the relevant agenda in medical encounters as the physician's and further locate the source of the "hidden agenda" problem in ways that the *physician's* actions, in the opening sequence of the clinical encounter, serve systematically to foreclose a complete report of symptoms by the patient.[7]

The point of Beckman and Frankel's observation that is most relevant for present purposes – a point that I return to in Chapter 8 – is their insight that analysts of the medical interview have been misconceiving the essential problem for the interaction. Specifically, the problem is not that the patient "hides" the agenda, but that the patient, as a novice in this setting, does not understand the institutional purposes of the interaction, that is, the identification of a "chief complaint," or the physician's strategy for achieving those purposes. The patient's task is misconceived, therefore, if it is viewed as either carrying out the plan of the interview or as failing to do so. The point is rather that the patient *does not know the plan* and is therefore able to cooperate only to the extent that being responsive to the physician's actions, locally, constitutes cooperation in realizing the plan. To the extent that the patient's cooperation is contingent on the physician's actions, the success of the interview is as well.

The actual production of an agenda, through local interactional work, is evident in the following excerpt from a career counseling interview reported by Erickson (1982: 77–8; C = counselor, S = student):

C: Well, let's start from scratch. What did you get in your English 100 last semester?
S: A "C"
C: Biology 101?
S: "A"
C: Reading 100?
S: "B"
C: Med tech . . . "B"? (medical technology)

[7] Specifically, they cite the physician's tendency, given any mention of symptoms by the patient, to engage in early hypothesis testing; "once hypothesis testing has begun, it is difficult for the patient to get a word in edgewise without deviating from conventional rules of discourse which relate types of speech acts to one another, in this case the relevance of an answer to the question that preceded it" (1983: 9). (Original footnote.)

S:  "B."

C:  Gym?

S:  "A"

C:  Was that a full credit hour? What was it?

S:  It was a wrestling...two periods.

C:  Wrestling. (He writes this on the record card, then shifts postural position and looks up from the record at the student.) Ok, this semester...English 101?

S:  (Changes facial expression, but no nod or "mhm" in response to the question.)

C:  That's what you've got now...

S:  (Nods.)

C:  Biology 102? Soc Sci 101. (The counselor is looking down.)

S:  I don't have Biology 102. I have, mm, 112.

C:  The counselor corrects the record card.) Soc Sci 101?

S:  (Nods.) Mhm.

C:  Math 95.

S:  (Nods.)

C:  Med Tech 112.

S:  (Nods.)

C:  Gym.

S:  (Nods.)

In Erickson's analysis, this interview comprises two adjacent routines, by which the counselor establishes the student's academic status first as a matter of courses completed and then as a matter of courses underway. The problem negotiated by counselor and student is that the counselor's behavior is superficially the same across both routines so that the juncture or transition between them, which requires a change in the task of the student, is initially missed by the student. The student's failure to respond to the query "English 101?" demonstrates the problem to the counselor, who then offers a remedy. Although the organization of this and any interaction can be analyzed post hoc into a hierarchical structure of topics and subtopics, or routines and subroutines, the coherence that the structure represents is actually achieved moment by moment as a local, collaborative, sequential accomplishment. This observation stands in marked contrast to the assumptions of students of discourse to the effect that the actual enactment of interaction is the behavioral realization of a plan. Instead, every instance of coherent interaction is an essentially local production, accomplished collaboratively in real time, rather than "born naturally whole out of the speaker's forehead, the delivery of a cognitive plan" (Schegloff 1982: 73):

Good analysis retains a sense of the actual as an achievement from among possibilities; it retains a lively sense of the contingency of real things. It is worth an alert, therefore, that too easy a notion of "discourse" can lose us that ... If certain stable forms appear to emerge or recur in talk, they should be understood as an orderliness wrested by the participants from interactional contingency rather than as automatic products of standardized plans. Form, one might say, is also the distillate of action and interaction, not only its blueprint. If that is so, then the description of forms of behavior, forms of discourse ... included, has to include interaction among their constitutive domains, and not just as the stage on which scripts written in the mind are played out. (ibid.: 89)

The organization of face-to-face interaction is the paradigm case of a system that has evolved in the service of orderly, concerted action over an indefinite range of essentially unpredictable circumstances. What is notable about that system is the extent to which mastery of its constraints localizes and thereby leaves open questions of control and direction, while providing built-in mechanisms for recovery from trouble and error. The constraints on interaction in this sense are not determinants of, but are rather "production resources" (Erickson 1982) for, shared understanding. The limits on available resources for accomplishing a shared agenda in a case of "interaction" between people and machines, and for detecting and remedying the troubles that that task poses, is the subject of Chapter 9.

### NOTATION

[　　　Bracket indicates a point at which a current speaker's talk is overlapped by the talk of another, with overlapping talk directly beneath.

//　　　Alternatively, double oblique lines indicate a point at which a current speaker's talk is overlapped the talk of a next speaker.

:　　　Colons indicate a lengthened syllable, the number of colons suggesting the extent of the lengthening.

-　　　Dash indicates a stop, cutting off an utterance.

?　　　Question intonation.

| . | Full stop, with falling intonation. |
|---|---|
| = | Equal sign indicates no interval between the end of a prior and the start of a next piece of talk. |
| .hh | Audible breath. Dot before indicates inbreath; no dot indicates outbreath. |
| Italics | Speaker's emphasis |
| () | Words enclosed in parenthesis indicate either nonlinguistic action, or transcriber's uncertainty over the verbatim. |
| (()) | Double parenthesis indicates features of the audio other than verbalization, or note from the transcriber. |
| (o.o) | Numbers in parenthesis indicate elapsed time in tenths of a second. |
| (.) | Untimed pause. |

For a more extensive description of notations see Jefferson (1983); Heritage (1984); and Lynch (1985).

# 8

## Case and Methods

In this age, in which social critics complain about the replacement of men by machines, this small corner of the social world has not been uninvaded. It is possible, nowadays, to hear the phone you are calling picked up and hear a human voice answer but nevertheless not be talking to a human. However small its measure of consolation, we may note that even machines such as the automatic answering device are constructed on social, and not only mechanical, principles. The machine's magnetic voice will not only answer the caller's ring, but will also inform him when its ears will be available to receive his message, and warn him both to wait for the beep and confine his interests to fifteen seconds.

(Shegloff 1972: 374)

Chapter 9 describes people's first encounters with a machine called an *expert help system*; a computer-based system attached to a large and relatively complex photocopier and intended to instruct the user of the copier in its operation.[1] The system's identification as an expert help system both locates it in the wider category of so-called expert systems and indicates that a function of this system is to provide procedural instructions to the user. The idea of expert systems in general is that expertise consists in a body of propositions or "knowledge" about a particular domain and rules for its use. The knowledge of this system comprises a set of rules about copying jobs and procedures that control both the presentation of instructions to the user on a video display and the operations of the copier itself. The design objective is that the system

---

[1] The system was designed by Richard Fikes at the Xerox Palo Alto Research Center in 1982–1983. (Original footnote.)

should provide timely and relevant information to the user regarding the operation of the copier.[2] The information should be presented not as a compendium but in a stepwise order wherein each next instruction is invoked by the user's successful enactment of the last. To provide the user with appropriate instruction, therefore, the system must somehow recognize the action of the user to which it should respond. It is this problem in particular – the problem of the system's recognition of the user's actions – that the analysis explores.

THE EXPERT HELP SYSTEM

In contrast to relatively unrestricted occasions of human interaction such as ordinary conversation, certain constraints on the event of using the expert help system provide grounds for imagining that one might safely predict, in some detail, just how the event will go:

- The interaction is instrumental.
- The possible goals of the interaction are defined by the machine's functionality.
- The structure of the interaction is procedural, constituted by a sequence of actions whose order is partially enforced.
- The criteria of adequacy for each action can be specified.

Because in machine operation the user's purposes are constrained by the machine's functionality, and her actions by its design, it seems reasonable to suppose that the user's purposes should serve as a sufficient context for the interpretation of her actions. On this assumption, the strategy that the design adopts is to project the course of the user's actions as the enactment of a plan for doing the job and then use the presumed plan as the relevant context for the action's interpretation.[3]

---

[2] The expert help system in this sense would seem to be a strong instantiation of "configuring the user" (Woolgar 1991; Grint and Woolgar 1997), a machine whose design inscribes a "programme for action" (Latour 1992) or "script" (Akrich 1992). I examine this more closely in Chapter 11.

[3] As Chapter 5 pointed out, analysts of the intention–action relationship are troubled by the apparently diffuse and tacit nature of intentions in many situations, and the consequent problem of determining just what is the actor's "true" intent. This seems less of a problem with goal-directed activities, where the goal, as defined by the analyst, can simply be taken a priori as the intent of the actor. The argument of this book, of course, is that the relief from the problem of determining intent that task-oriented interaction seems to offer is only a temporary palliative to the designer's problem: the real solution must lie in an alternative understanding of the nature of intentions and their relation to actions – one that views the everyday business of identifying intent as an always contingent, practical, and interactional accomplishment. (Original footnote.)

Through the user's response to a series of questions about the state of her original documents and the desired copies, her purposes are identified with a job specification, the specification (represented in the system as a data structure with variable fields) invokes an associated plan, and the enactment of the plan is prescribed by the system as a stepwise procedure.

Having mapped the user's purposes to a job specification and the job specification to a plan, the plan is then effectively ascribed to the user as the basis for interpreting her actions. The rationale for this move is that the plan is conveyed to the user in the form of instructions for a stepwise procedure, the user is following the instructions and consequently, one can assume, is following the plan that the instructions describe. Under that assumption, the effects of certain actions by the user are mapped to a place in the system's plan and that mapping is used to locate an appropriate next instruction. The actions by the user that effect changes in the machine's state comprise some physical actions on the machine (putting documents into document trays, opening and closing machine covers, and the like), and directives to the system in the form of selections of text on a video display. The hope of the designer is that the effects of these actions by the user can be mapped reliably to a location in the system's plan and that the location in the plan will determine an appropriate system response. The relevant sense of "interaction" in this case, therefore, is that the provision of instruction is both fitted to the user's purposes and occasioned by her actions.

The design assumes, however, that it is the correspondence of the system's plan to the user's purposes that enables the interaction. In contrast, the analysis of Chapter 9 indicates that user and system each have a consequentially different relationship to the design plan. Although the plan directly determines the system's behavior, the user is required to *find* the plan, as the prescriptive and descriptive significance of a series of procedural instructions. Whereas the instructions and the procedure that they describe are the object of the user's work, they do not reconstruct the work's course, nor do they determine its outcome.

### THE PROBLEM OF FOLLOWING INSTRUCTIONS

The practical problem that the expert help system was designed to solve arises out of the work of following instructions, which in turn implies the work of communicating them. The general task in following instructions is to bring canonical descriptions of objects and actions to bear on the actual objects and embodied actions that the instructions describe

(Lynch, Livingston, and Garfinkel 1983). Studies of instruction in cognitive and social science alike have focused, on the one hand, on the problem of providing adequate instructions and, on the other, on the problem of finding the practical significance of instructions for situated action.

Social studies of the production and use of instructions have concentrated on the irremediable incompleteness of instructions (Garfinkel 1967, Chapter 1) and the nature of the work required to "carry them out." The problem of the instruction-follower is viewed as one of turning necessarily partial descriptions of objects and actions into concrete practical activities with predictable outcomes (Zimmerman 1970; Amerine and Bilmes 1979). A general observation from these studies is that instructions rely on the recipient's ability to do the implicit work of anchoring descriptions to concrete objects and actions. At the same time, that work remains largely unexamined by either instruction-writer or recipient, particularly when the work goes smoothly.

In a study of instruction-following as practical action, Amerine and Bilmes (1990) point out that instructions serve not only as prescriptions for what to do but also as resources for retrospective accounts of what has happened: "Successfully following instructions can be described as constructing a course of action such that, having done this course of action, the instructions will serve as a descriptive account of what has been done" (ibid.: 326). More than the "correct" execution of an instruction, in other words, successful instruction following is a matter of constructing a particular course of action that is accountable to the general description that the instruction provides. The work of constructing that course is neither exhaustively enumerated in the description, nor completely captured by a retrospective account of what was done. Instructions serve as a resource for describing what was done not only because they guide the course of action but also because they filter out of the retrospective account of the action, or treat as "noise," everything that was actually done that the instructions fail to mention. As Amerine and Bilmes observe: "If the experiment is 'successful,' if it achieves its projected outcome, the instructions can serve as an account of 'what was done,' although in any actual performance a great deal more is necessarily done than can be comprised in the instructions" (ibid.: 325).

The credibility of instructions, moreover, rests on the premise that not only do they describe what action to take, but if they are followed correctly the action will produce a predictable outcome. An unexpected outcome, accordingly, indicates trouble and warrants some remedy. As long as instructions are viewed as authoritative, the preference in remedying a faulted outcome is to account for the failure in outcome without discrediting the instruction. An obvious solution is to locate the trouble somewhere in the instruction's "execution." In assessing the course of the work for troubles in execution, questions inevitably arise concerning the relation of the many actions that were taken that are not specified by the instructions to the faulted outcome. Previously insignificant details may appear crucial, or the meaning of the instructions may be transformed in such a way that they are found not have been followed after all. Amerine and Bilmes give an example, drawn from science experiments in a third-grade classroom, of the kind of problem inherent in reasoning inductively about the relation between courses of action and outcomes:

To expedite carrying out this lesson two similar and functionally equivalent pans of water were placed on a table in the center of the room and the students were called on by pairs to try the exercise. Toward that end, when, as related above, this activity had become particularly competitive, one of the children approached a pan but was urged by classmates to use the other one because it was "luckier." We are not sure how this notion came about, although in a pair of trials closely preceding this comment the student using the "unlucky" pan had failed, while the child using the other one had succeeded. At any rate, the student followed this advice and the experiment was successful. Both of the following two children rushed for the "lucky" pan, though the loser settled for the "unlucky" one (and succeeded nonetheless). In the case of the next pair, the second child waited for the first to finish using the "lucky" pan, and then also used it. The "unlucky" pan remained unused thereafter . . . In neither case are such observations by *nature* illogical or irrelevant . . . But in these science experiments our understanding of the relationship between the practical course of action and its outcome seems to leave no place for "luck" . . . Therefore such factors become "noise." (ibid.: 329–30, original emphasis)

The ability to discriminate between relevant information and "noise" in a given domain of action, by invoking both precepts and practice, is a part of what we recognize as expertise. The point of the "lucky pan" example is that the process by which that ability is acquired is a fundamentally inductive and ad hoc one, regardless of the degree to which rules of action are encoded and prescribed. In the final analysis no amount of prescription, however precise or elaborate, can relieve situated action "of the burden of finding a way through an unscheduled future while making a convincing case for what is 'somehow' extracted from that future" (Lynch, Livingston, and Garfinkel 1983: 233). The latter is the problem of accountably rational action in situ, however adequate the instructions for that action may be.

## COMMUNICATING INSTRUCTIONS

An appreciation for what is required in instruction following makes it easier to understand the problem that the communication of instructions attempts to solve; namely, the troubles inherent in turning an instruction into an action. Motivated by the project of designing instructional computer systems, researchers in artificial intelligence have looked at instruction as a question of communicative resources available to expert and novice. One of the earliest such projects, the Computer-Based Consultant project begun at Stanford Research Institute in the 1970s, continues to direct research on task-oriented communication through "natural language," using what has become the canonical problem of assembling a simple mechanical device. The goal of the original project was:

> to produce a computer system that could fill the role of an expert in the cooperative execution of complex tasks with a relatively inexperienced human apprentice. The system was to use rich channels of communication, including natural language and eventually speech. The main function of the consultant was to aid the apprentice in the diagnosis of faulty electromechanical equipment, and the formulation of plans for the assembly, disassembly, and repair of the equipment. (Sacerdoti 1977: 3)

Using an air compressor as the assembly task, researchers collected a corpus of dialogues in experiments designed to simulate interaction between a person and a computer (see B. Grosz 1981). In these experiments two people – one acting as expert and the other acting as apprentice – had only limited visual access to each other. Grosz's analysis of the corpus turns on the observation that the requirement for successful communication between expert and novice, despite their limited visual access, is a common "focus" on the task at hand. Common focus allows the exploitation of language (e.g., definite descriptions such as "the screw"), materials ("the screw visible on the hub of the flywheel"), and local history ("the screw loosened previously") in instruction, whereas language, materials, and history are used, in turn, to maintain the common focus. Grosz's concern with the linguistic, interactional, and material bases of successful instruction set the stage for a series of subsequent analyses in which, by varying the resources available for communication, researchers began to explore the relationship of various nonlinguistic resources to the use of language (for a "taxonomy" of these resources, see Rubin 1980).

In an analysis of transcripts of instructors communicating with an apprentice through face-to-face, telephone, audio-taped, and written media about the assembly of a toy water pump, Burke (1982) found that the most obvious difference, that between speaking and writing, is actually less crucial than the difference between interactive (e.g., a keyboard) and noninteractive (e.g., audio-taped) instruction. The restrictions generally associated with written instruction, in other words, derive not from the writing so much as from the absence of interaction, whereas the effectiveness of verbal instruction derives less from the speech than from the interaction that is generally associated with it. Ochs (1979) relates the distinction of interactive and noninteractive communication to degrees of planning, arguing that in the case of interaction speakers plan only at a general level (the concretization of the plan being contingent and emergent), whereas noninteractive discourse can be entirely planned in advance. Instead, Burke takes the point of view that the instructor's task is one of adequate description rather than planning and reports that in the noninteractive modalities of instruction on the assembly task there is a tendency to "overelaborate" descriptions, in an apparent attempt to anticipate possible troubles and to compensate for the lack of opportunities for their on-site clarification. In face-to-face instruction, in contrast, Burke found that instructors initially provided minimal descriptions and then monitored the apprentice's actions for evidence of the description's adequacy or inadequacy. By telephone, where visual access was unavailable but where the interaction remained, the resources for monitoring the actions of the apprentice changed from visual to verbal (e.g., affirmations, repeats, and transformed repeats of the instructions by the apprentice), but the monitoring again guided the description.

Cohen's (n.d.) analysis of transcripts of instructor and apprentice communicating by telephone or keyboard on the same assembly task confirms the ability of instructors to adjust the level of their descriptions in response to the demonstrated understanding or misunderstanding by the apprentice. He concludes that the principal difference between spoken and written interactive media is that experts in spoken instruction more often explicitly request that the novice identify an object, and often question the novice on his or her success, whereas experts using keyboards subsume reference to objects into instructions for action unless some prior referential miscommunication has occurred (ibid.: 21). Spoken interaction between expert and novice, in that sense, is more finely calibrated than written, though insofar as both are interactive both support the collaborative construction of a useful description of the objects and actions in question, through practical analyses of the communication's success at each turn.

### THE BASIC INTERACTION

The aim of the expert help system analyzed in the next chapter is to use the power of the computer to combine the portability of noninteractive instructions with the timeliness, relevance, and effectiveness of interaction. The machine presents the user with a series of video displays. Each display presented to the user either describes the machine's behavior or provides the user with some next instructions. In the latter case, the final instruction of each display prescribes an action whose effect is detectable by the system, thereby triggering a change to the next display (Figure 8.1).

Through the device of display changes keyed to actions by the user, the design accomplishes a simple form of occasioned response, in spite of the fact that only a partial trace of the user's behavior is available to the system. Among those user actions that are *not* available to the system is the actual work of locating referents and interpreting action descriptions: the system has access only to the product of that work. Moreover, within the instruction provided by a given display are embedded instructions for actions whose effects are not detectable by the system. To anticipate our discussion of troubles that arise, if one of *these* instructions is misconstrued, the error will go by unnoticed. Because the implication of a next display is that prior actions have been noted and that they have

1.   MACHINE PRESENTS INSTRUCTION

>   User reads instruction
>   interprets referents
>   and action descriptions

2.   USER TAKES ACTION

>   Design assumes
>   that the user has understood
>   the instruction

3.   MACHINE PRESENTS NEXT INSTRUCTION

FIGURE 8.1. The basic instructional sequence.

been found adequate, the appearance of a next instruction will confirm the correctness not only of the prior action narrowly defined but also of all of the embedded actions prescribed by the last instruction.

To compensate for the machine's limited access to the user's actions, the design relies on a partial enforcement of the order of user actions within the procedural sequence. This strategy works fairly wells insofar as a particular effect produced by the user (such as closing a cover on the copier) can be taken to imply that a certain condition obtains (a document has been placed in the machine for copying), which, in turn, implies a machine response (the initiation of the printing process). In this sense, the order of user and machine "turns," and what is to be accomplished in each, are predetermined. The system's "recognition" of turn-transition places is essentially reactive; that is, there is a determinate relationship between certain actions by the user, read as changes to the state of the machine, and the machine's transition to a next display. By establishing a determinate relationship between detectable user actions and machine responses, the design unilaterally administers control over the interaction, but in a way that is conditional on the actions of the user.

At the same time that the system controls the sequence of user actions, the design avoids certain problems that arise when instructions are provided consecutively and in a strict order. Every procedure is represented in the system as a series of steps, each of which has an associated precondition (the effect of a prior action by user or machine) and an associated machine response (display of instructions and/or setting of machine state). Rather than proceeding through these steps consecutively, the system begins processing at the *last* step of the procedure and checks to see whether that step has been completed. If not, the preconditions are checked and, if they are all satisfied, the step is executed. Each precondition carries with it a reference to the earlier step in the procedure that will satisfy that precondition, so that if an unmet precondition is found the system will return to the earlier step and proceed from there. If, therefore, a procedure is repeated but in the second instance certain conditions hold over from the first, the system will not display instructions for the actions that have already been taken. Beginning with the final step, it will work backwards through the procedure just to the point where an unmet precondition is found and will provide the instruction from that point on. Similarly, if the user takes an action that undoes a condition satisfied earlier, the system will encounter that state again at the next check. This technique produces appropriate instructions not because the system knows that this time through differs from the last, but just because, regardless of how they come about, certain detectable conditions (e.g., a document is in the machine) are linked unequivocally to appropriate response (e.g., initiating the printing process). Chapter 9 examines how this design strategy works and how, for the very same reason that it works in some instances, in other instances troubles arise.

### METHODS

The study was directed by two methodological commitments, one general, and the other particular to the problem at hand. Generally, the study began with a commitment to an empirical approach, along with the conviction that situated action cannot be captured empirically through either examples constructed by the researcher, paper-and-pencil observations, or interview reports. Analyses of contrived examples, observations, or interviews all rest on accounts of circumstances that are either imagined or recollected. One objective in studying situated action is to consider just those fleeting circumstances that our interpretations of action systematically rely on, but which our accounts of action routinely ignore. A second objective is to make the relation between interpretations of action and action's circumstances our subject matter. Both objectives are clearly lost if we use reports of action as our data.[4]

---

[4] This is not to say that paper-and-pencil observations have no place. The video analysis was preceded by approximately twenty hours of observation of new users of the same machine, minus the expert help system but equipped with written instructions, in actual office settings. That earlier study was undertaken in response to an unelaborated report, from those who supported the machine and its users "in the field," of user complaints that the machine was too complicated. Given the relative simplicity of even the most complex photocopier, this complaint on face value was puzzling, particularly to the machine's designers. The combination of the vagueness of the complaint as reported, and the bewilderment of the designers, intrigued both me and my colleagues Austin Henderson and Richard Fikes at the research center, and we set about to try to ascertain what the "complexity" was really about. That led to the paper-and-pencil observations, which convinced us that indeed the machine *was* somehow too complicated for the novice user who had no previous training; that is, people trying to use the machine were very visibly confused. The methodological problem at that point was that I, as an observer of their troubles, was equally confused. From the observations, therefore, I learned two important lessons. First, that there was indeed a problem. And, second, that to understand the problem would require the use of an adequate, i.e., a videotaped, record. For an analysis of users' troubles with the original instruction set, see Suchman (1982). (Original footnote.)

Another approach to the analysis of instructions might be to look at the textual cogency of the instructions themselves. An example offered by Searle (1979) illustrates the problem with such a strategy:[5]

Suppose a man goes to the supermarket with a shopping list given him by his wife on which are written the words "beans, butter, bacon, and bread." Suppose as he goes around with his shopping cart selecting these items, he is followed by a detective who writes down everything he takes. As they emerge from the store both the shopper and detective will have identical lists. But the function of the two lists will be quite different. In the case of the shopper's list, the purpose of the list is, so to speak, to get the world to match the words; the man is supposed to make his actions fit the list. In the case of the detective, the purpose of the list is to make the words match the world; the man is supposed to make the list fit the actions of the shopper. This can be further demonstrated by observing the role of "mistake" in the two cases. If the detective goes home and suddenly realizes that the man bought pork chops instead of bacon, he can simply erase the word "bacon" and write "pork chops." But if the shopper gets home and his wife points out that he has bought pork chops when he should have bought bacon he cannot correct the mistake by erasing "bacon" from the list and writing "pork chops." (ibid.: 4)

The subject of the present analysis, the user of the expert help system, is in the position of the shopper with respect to the instructions that the system provides; that is, she must make her actions match the words. But in what sense? Like the instructions, a shopping list may be consulted to decide what to do next or to know when the shopping is done, may be cited after the fact to explain why things were done the way they were, and so forth. But also like the instructions, the list does not actually describe the practical activity of shopping (how to find things, which aisles to go down in what order, how to decide between competing brands, etc.); it simply says how that activity is to turn out.[6]

Just as the list of the shopping's outcomes does not actually describe the organization of the activity of shopping, an analysis of instructions will not yield an analysis of the activity of carrying them out. In fact, contrary to the case in the story, there is no reason to believe that if a person has a set of instructions for operating a machine and we generate a description of the activity of operating a machine from watching the

---

[5] Searle credits this example to Anscombe (1957). The point that Searle is interested in concerns the notion of "direction of fit" between words and the world. (Original footnote.)

[6] For an inspired ethnographic account of actual practices of shopping, with a particular focus on practical forms of quantitative reasoning see Lave (1988, Chapter 7).

person, that the description we generate should look anything like the instructions. In fact, if our description of the situated activity does mirror the structure of the instructions, there is reason to believe that something is amiss.

Unlike the detective in the story who is supposed to generate a list, our problem as students of situated action is more akin to the problem of a detective who is just sent out and told to report back on what going to the grocery store is all about and how shopping is done. What that description should look like – what its terms should be, what its structure should be, what of all that goes on it should report – is an open methodological question. If, to put some constraints on the description, we set out with a template that asks for a list just of what the actions come to, then what counts as "an action" is prescribed ahead of time as "its outcome," and the list format prescribes the structure of the description. Only that part of the activity that fills in the template will be recorded. The action's structure, in other words, will be decided in advance and the method employed by the scientist will ensure that that structure is what is found.

One further issue that the story touches on is the problem of validity. The story says the detective might "suddenly realize" that there is some error in his description. But how might he actually realize that? If we just look for a discrepancy between the shopper's list and the detective's, what we find might reflect either an error in the shopper's activity (it doesn't match the list) or in the description (it doesn't match the activity). To evaluate which, we must have (a) independent access to the shopper's list to compare against the activity and (b) a record of activity. That is to say, two essential methodological resources are (a) the comparison of our own interpretations with those of our subjects and (b) a record that is not contingent on either.

However adequate the record, of course, the empirical basis of social studies is not a positive one because we cannot, by definition, provide a literal description of our phenomenon.[7] As Wilson (1970) defines literal description: "Any description of a phenomenon is based on perceived features that the phenomenon displays to the observer. A literal

---

[7] Galaty (1981) makes a useful distinction between "data sources," as the business of the social world independent of the anthropologist's interest in it; "data," as the anthropologically [worked-up] information that appears in the form of, for example, transcripts; and "analytic objects," conceptualized as events, troubles, and the like (ibid.: 91, note 2). The point is that for the social scientist, the data are interpreted already at their source. (Original footnote.)

description, then, amounts to asserting that on the basis of those features the phenomenon has some clearly designated property, or what is logically the same thing, belongs to some particular, well-defined class of phenomena" (ibid.: 72). For a description to be literal, in other words, the class of phenomena of which the described is an instance must be definable in terms of sufficient conditions for counting some instance as a member of the class. For situated action, that would require classification of action not only as the relation of intent to behavior but also as the relation of both to mitigating circumstances – a classification that, I argued in Chapter 5, is functionally and criterially different from that applied to intentional descriptions of actions and situations. Moreover, the social scientist's description is yet another order of remove from a literal description if the subject of the descriptions is not only the intent of some actor, but also the interpretations of that actor's intent by others on the scene. Judgments of correctness and veridicality are replaced in social studies by judgments of adequacy or verisimilarity (Heap 1980: 104), the latter resting on criteria of evidence and warranted inference rather than conditions of truth.

The problems that the social scientist struggles with in defining her methods are the same problem that, from another view, constitute her subject matter: namely, the uncertain relation between accounts of the significance of action and the observations and inferences on which those accounts must be based. There is no privileged analytic stance for the social scientist that exempts her from the problems of adjudicating the practical objectivity of the social world. The only advantage that accrues to the researcher (a substantial one, it turns out) is recourse to a record of the action and its circumstances, independent of her analysis. The availability of audiovisual technology that can provide such a record, for repeated inspection by the researcher and by colleagues, avoids the reliance on unexplicated resources that characterizes traditional ethnographic accounts. In traditional accounts, the fleeting nature of the events that the ethnographer describes means that the only record that is available for inspection by others is the ethnographer's description.

This study proceeded, therefore, in a setting where video technology could be used in a sort of uncontrolled experimentation. On one hand, the situation was constructed so as to make certain issues observable; specifically, the work of using the machine with the assistance of the expert help system. The construction consisted in the selection of tasks observed to pose problems for new users in "the real world." On the other hand, once given those tasks, the subjects were left entirely on their own. In the analysis, by the same token, the goal was to construct a characterization of the interaction that ensued rather than to apply a predetermined coding scheme. Both predetermined coding schemes and controlled experiments presuppose a characterization of the phenomenon studied, varying only certain parameters to test the characterization. Application of that methodology to the problem of human–machine interaction would be at the least premature. The point of departure for the study was the assumption that we *lack* a description of the structure of situated action. And because the hunch is that the structure lies in a relation between action and its circumstances that we have yet to uncover, we do not want to *presuppose* what are the relevant conditions or their relationship to the course of the action. We need to begin, therefore, with observations that capture as much of the phenomenon, and presuppose as little, as possible.[8]

The consequence of this commitment to examining the circumstances of action is that we need to begin with a record of events that is not prejudged as to its analytic interest either in advance or in the making. The data for this study, accordingly, are a corpus of videotapes of first-time users of the expert help system.[9] First-time users were chosen on the grounds that the system was intended by its designers to be self-explanatory or usable by people with no previous introduction to the machine. More generally, the troubles encountered by first-time users of a system are valuable in that they disclose work required to understand the system's behavior that, for various reasons, is masked by the proficient user. This disclosure of the requisite work is the value of studying interactional *troubles* generally (see Gumperz 1982b: 308) and distinguishes this analysis from the usual "operability tests." That is to say, I am not simply interested in distinguishing "correct" from "erroneous" moves by the user. Rather, by studying what things look like when they are unfamiliar and troublesome, I hope to understand better what is involved in their mastery.

In each of the sessions two people, neither of whom had ever used the system before, worked together in pairs. Two people asked to collaborate

---

[8] I would phrase this characterization of the implications of the contingency of situated activity for research methods more strongly now, as recommending against the project of establishing a "structure" altogether. On the premises of poststructural social studies and their implications for method, see, for example, Lynch 1993; Law 2004.

[9] The corpus from which the analysis of Chapter 9 is drawn comprises four sessions, each lasting from one and a half to two hours.

| THE USER | | THE MACHINE | |
| --- | --- | --- | --- |
| Actions not available to the machine | Actions available to the machine | Effects available to the user | Design rationale |

FIGURE 8.2. The analytic framework.

in using a relatively simple machine like a photocopier are faced with the problem of doing together what either could do alone. In the interest of the collaboration, each makes available to the other what she believes to be going on: what the task is, how it is to be accomplished, what has already been done and what remains, rationales for this way of proceeding over that, and so forth. Through the ways in which each collaborator works to provide her sense of what is going on to the other, she provides that sense to the researcher as well. An artifact of such a collaboration, therefore, is a naturally generated protocol.[10]

A second methodological commitment, which arose from the particular problem of looking at human–machine communication, directed the analysis itself. The aim of the analysis was to find the sense of "shared understanding" in human–machine communication. More particularly, I wanted to compare the user's and the system's respective views of the interaction, over a sequence of events. In working to organize the transcripts of the videotapes, therefore, I arrived at a simple framework (see Figure 8.2). The framework revealed two initial facts about the relationship of user and system. First, it showed that the coherence of the user's actions was largely unavailable to the system and something of why that was the case. Beginning with the observation that what the user was trying to do was, somehow, available to me as the researcher, I could ask how that was so. The richest source of information for the researcher is the verbal protocol (recorded in the first column). In reading the instructions aloud, the user locates the problem that she is working on. Her questions about the instructions identify the problem more particularly

---

[10] Brown, Rubenstein, and Burton (1976) argue persuasively for the use of teams to generate protocols, where the discussions and arguments that unfold are treated as evidence for the individual reasoning of the participants. The actions of the team members can also be viewed as organized by the task of collaboration itself, however, although in the interest of looking at the interaction of both users with the machine I have deliberately avoided taking that view here. It is worth noting, in this regard, that analyses of "discourse" undertaken in the interest of building interactive AI systems generally tend to view communication as the coincidence of individual reasoning processes, rather than as an activity with a distinctive character arising from the collaboration itself. (Original footnote.)

and further talk provides her interpretations of the machine's behavior and clarifies her actions in response.

A second, but equally crucial, resource is visual access to the user's actions. Of all of her actions, one could clearly see the very small subset, recorded in the second column, that were actually detected by the system. From the system's "point of view," correspondingly, one could see how it was that those traces of the user's actions available to the system were mapped onto the system's plan, under the design assumption that, for example, button $x$ pushed at this particular point in the procedure must mean that the user is doing $y$.

The framework proved invaluable for taking seriously the idea that user and machine were interacting. By treating the center two columns as the mutually available, human–machine "interface," one could compare and contrast them with the outer columns, as the respective interpretations of the user and the design. This comparison located precisely the points of confusion, as well as the points of intersection or "shared understanding." Both are discussed at length in the next chapter.

# 9

# Human–Machine Communication

> Interaction is always a *tentative* process, a process of continuously testing
> the conception one has of ... the other.
>
> (Turner 1962: original emphasis)

In Chapter 6 I outlined the view that the significance of actions and
their intelligibility resides neither in what is strictly observable about
behavior, nor in a prior mental state of the actor, but in a contingently
constructed relationship among observable behavior, embedding circumstances, and intent. Rather than enumerating an a priori system of
normative rules for meaningful behavior, Chapter 7 described resources
for constructing shared understanding, collaboratively and in situ. Face-
to-face interaction was presented as the most fundamental and highly
developed system for accomplishing mutual intelligibility, exploiting a
range of linguistic, demonstrative, and inferential resources.

Given this view of the basis for action's intelligibility, the situation
of action can be defined as the full range of resources that the actor
has available to convey the significance of his or her own actions and
to interpret the actions of others.[1] Taking that preliminary definition of
the situation as a point of departure, my interest in this chapter is to

---

[1] In light of subsequent readings, I realize that this statement could be taken to imply that
"the situation" exists somehow in advance of action and that it could at least in principle
be fully enumerated and represented in the form of a model to be referenced. The sense
of the situation I am after, however, is a radically performative and interactional one,
such that action's situation is in significant respects constituted through, or stands in
a reflexive relationship with, ongoing activity. It is through the latter that the sense
and relevance – just what the situation comprises – is produced, reenacted, contested,
and/or transformed.

consider "communication" between a person and a machine in terms of the nature of their respective situations. For purposes of the analysis, and without ascribing intent in any way, I will assume that the machine is behaving on the basis of resources provided by "its" situation, the user in accord with the resources of hers. The aim of the analysis then is to view the organization of human–machine communication, including its troubles, in terms of constraints posed by asymmetries in the respective situation resources of human and machine.

In the case considered here, we can assume that the situation of the user comprises preconceptions about the nature of the machine and the operations required to use it, combined with moment-by-moment interpretations of evidence found in and through the actual course of its use. The situation of the machine or expert help system, in contrast, is constituted by a plan for the use of the machine, written by the designer, and implemented as the program that determines the machine's behavior and sensors that register changes to the machine's state, including some changes produced by the user's actions. The design plan defines what constitutes intelligible action by the user insofar as the machine is concerned and determines what stands as an appropriate machine response. The intersection of the situations of user and machine is the locus both for successful exploitation of mutually available resources and for problems of understanding that arise out of the disparity of their respective situations.

## ENGINEERING AN APPROPRIATE RESPONSE

The practical problem with which the designer of an interactive machine must contend is how to ensure that the machine responds appropriately to the user's actions. As in human communication, an appropriate response implies an adequate interpretation of the prior action's significance. And as in human communication, the interpretation of any action's significance is only weakly determined by the action as such. Every action assumes not only the intent of the actor, but also the interpretive work of the other in determining its significance.[2] That work, in turn, is available only through the other's response. The significance of any action and the adequacy of its interpretation are judged indirectly, by responses to actions taken and by an interpretation's usefulness in

---

[2] See Bruner (1986) for a recent discussion of the contingency of interpretation with respect both to text and to face-to-face interaction. (Original footnote.)

understanding subsequent actions. It is just this highly contingent process that we call interaction.

For purposes of analysis, we can begin by considering two alternative perspectives on face-to-face interaction, with commensurately different implications for the project of designing interactive machines. The first perspective ties successful interaction to each participant's success at anticipating the actions of the other and recommends an interactive interface based on a preconceived model of the user that supports the prediction of actions, the specification of recognition criteria for the actions predicted, and the prescription of an appropriate response. The second view focuses on the ways in which interactional success comprises responses that are occasioned by, and responsive to, unanticipated actions of the other. This focus recommends an interactive interface that maximizes sensitivity to actions actually taken by minimizing predetermined sequences of machine behavior. The former recommendation is constrained by limitations on the designer's ability to predict any user's actions and the latter by limitations on the system's access to and ability to make sense out of the actions that a particular user takes.

The design strategy in the expert help system is to try to provide the effect of an occasioned response through the use of a predictive model. That is to say, the designer predicts that the user will have one of a set of possible goals, of the form "use the machine to accomplish outcome x." Given that statement of intent, the machine displays a set of instructions that prescribe the actions to be taken, at a level of generality designed to ensure their relevance to any user, whatever the details of her particular situation. Ideally, the instructions tell the user what aspects of her particular situation are relevant for the execution of this plan through the machine's operation. By finding or producing the objects and actions described, the user anchors the general instructions to her unique circumstances.

This chapter looks at some of the consequences of taking a statement of intent and an ascribed plan as grounds for the interpretation of situated action. To anticipate, that strategy involves an insensitivity to particular circumstances that is both the system's central resource and its fundamental problem. I look first at the system's resources for construing the actions of the user; namely, *plans and states.* I then consider the problems posed for the designer by the user's principal resource, organized under the general rubric of *situated inquiries,* and by the user's ability to find the relevance of the system's response to those inquiries. Finally, I look at two classes of communicative breakdown, the *false alarm* and the *garden path*. Chapter 10 concludes with implications of the analysis for a general account of mutual intelligibility and for the particular requirements on the design of artifacts that would interact with their users.

THE SYSTEM'S SITUATION: PLANS AND DETECTABLE STATES

The resources of the expert help system include a program that controls its behavior and sensors that register certain changes to its state effected by actions of the user. Initially, the user's response to a series of questions about her original documents and desired copies is taken as a statement of her intent, and that statement in turn determines the selection by the machine of one from a set of possible plans (see display 0, p. 169). The plan is then presented to the user in the form of a stepwise set of procedural instructions. The designer assumes that the plan matches the user's intent and that in following the procedural instructions the user effectively is engaged in carrying out the plan.

The design premise is further that as the user takes the actions prescribed by the instructions, those actions will change the state of the machine in predictable ways. By taking those changes to the machine's state as traces of the user's actions, the designer can effectively specify how the user's actions are to be recognized by the system and how the system is to respond. The instructions are grouped in a series of displays such that the last action prescribed by each display produces an effect that is detectable by the system, thereby initiating the process that produces the next display. The design assumption is that by detecting certain of the user's actions, the system can follow her course in the procedure and provide instructions as needed along the way.[3]

---

[3] Because instructions were sometimes read by the users differently from the way that they were actually written on the displays, the reader will find some inconsistencies between sequences and the displays to which they refer. The sequences comprise verbatim transcriptions of the users' talk. Double quotes indicate that the user is reading an instruction from the display. The displays reproduce the visual presentation (both textual and illustrative) that the user finds on a video display terminal attached to the photocopier. This includes headings that identify the type of information offered (i.e., "Assumptions," "Overview," "Instructions"), the instructions themselves, and pictures of the copier and its parts. The boxed text at the bottom of each display (i.e., "Change Task Description," "Help," "Start") act as virtual "buttons" that, when selected by the user with the cursor provided, initiate an associated operation. "Change Task Description" returns the user to display 0, "Help" brings up a display that expands on the current instructions, and "Start" begins the copying operation. (Original footnote.)

The strategy of tying certain machine states to the presentation of particular next instructions enables the appearance of machine responses occasioned by the user's actions. So, in this light, we can view the interaction between A and B in sequence I as the adept completion of what the design attempts. Specifically, A decomposes and re-presents the instructions provided by the system, such that they are fit more precisely to B's actions in carrying them out. A is able to do this because of her sensitivity to what B is doing, including B's troubles.

SEQUENCE I. *A and B are proceeding from a display that established their goal as making two-sided copies of a bound document. Two-sided copying requires an unbound document, so they must begin by making a master unbound copy of their document, using the "Bound Document Aid" or BDA.*

| The Users | | The Machine | |
|---|---|---|---|
| **Not Available to the Machine** | **Available to the Machine** | **Available to the User** | **Design Rationale** |
| A: "To access the BDA, pull the latch labeled Bound Document Aid": (A and B turn to machine) <br><br> (Points) Right there. | | DISPLAY 2 | Instructions for copying a bound document: Accessing the bound document aid. |
| B: (Hands on latch) | | | |
| A: "And lift up to the left." (Looks to B, who struggles with the latch) "Lift up and to the left." | | | |
| B: (Still struggling) | | | |
| A: Okay:: | | | |
| B: Pu::ll, and lift up to the left. (Looks at picture) Oh, the whole thing. [ | | | |
| A:        Yea. | | | |
| B: Lift up and to the left. | Opens BDA | | |

Below is the procedure from sequence 1, as represented in the program that controls the display of instructions to the user:

Step 1   Set Panel
[DISPLAY 1]
Step 2:   Tell User "You need to use the Bound Document Aid..."
[DISPLAY 2]
Step 3:   Tell User "Place your original face down...Slide the document cover left..."
[DISPLAY 3]
Step 4:   Make Ready.
Step 5:   Tell User "Press Start." Requirements:
Panel Set (If not, try Step I)
RDH raised (if not, try Step 2)
Document cover closed (if not, try Step 3)
Ready State (if not, try Step 4)
[DISPLAY 4]
Step 6:   Complete printing Step.
Requirements: Printing State (if not, try Step 5)

Rather than proceeding through the steps of the procedure consecutively, the system starts with the *last* step of the procedure, Step 6 in this case, and checks to see whether it is completed. A step is completed if a check of the machine's state confirms that the conditions represented by that step's requirements have been met. The requirements in this sense represent features of the system's situation (or, more accurately, of the system's own state) that are resources in determining an appropriate next instruction or action. When a requirement is found that is not met, a further set of specifications, tied to that requirement, sends the system back to an earlier step in the procedural sequence. The system then displays the instructions tied to that earlier step to the user until another change in state begins the same process again. Each time the user takes an action that changes the machine's state, the system compares the resulting state with the end state, returns to the first unfinished step in the sequence, and presents the user with the instructions for that and any subsequent step.

Through this simple device of working backward through the procedure, the presentation of redundant instructions can be avoided. In sequence II, having discovered that their original document is larger than standard paper, A and B decide to redo the job. They return to the

SEQUENCE II. *Again A and B are making two-sided copies of a bound document, this time with reduction. (The document is still on the copier glass; the document cover is closed.)*

| The Users | | The Machine | |
| --- | --- | --- | --- |
| **Not Available to the Machine** | **Available to the Machine** | **Available to the User** | **Design Rationale** |
| | | DISPLAY 1 | Selecting the proceedure |
| B: It's supposed to– it'll tell "Start," in a minute. | | | |
| A: Oh. It will? | | | |
| B: Well it did: in the past. (pause) A little start: box will: | | | |
| | | DISPLAY 4 | Ready to print |
| B: There it goes. | | | |
| A: "Press the Start button" | | | |
| | SELECTS START | | |
| | | STARTS PRINTING | |
| Okay. | | | |

job specification display to select the reduction feature and then direct the machine to proceed.

On this occasion the system bypasses the instructions to raise the document handler, place the document on the glass, and close the document cover, all of which are irrelevant in that the actions they prescribe have already been taken. The system is able to act appropriately because a detectable machine state (the closed document cover) can be linked by the designer to an a priori assumption about the user's intent with respect to a next action (ready to press start). As a result, the system can be engineered to provide the appropriate next instruction *in spite of* the fact that it does not actually have access to the history of the user's actions or even to the presence or absence now of a document on the glass. The result is that although B predicts the system's behavior – specifically, that it will provide them with a "Start button" – based on her recollection of an occasion (sequence I) on which the system actually behaved somewhat differently, her prediction holds. That is, just because on this occasion a relevant feature of the user's situation, accessible to the system, causes the system to behave differently, it appears to behave in the same (i.e., predictable) way. In human interaction, this graceful accommodation to changing circumstance is precisely what is expected and is therefore largely taken for granted. The success of the system's accommodation in this instance is evident in the accommodation's transparency to the users.

On other occasions, however, the mapping from a machine state to an a priori assumption about the user's intent, on which the success of sequence II rests, leads to trouble. I have said that given a statement of the user's goal (derived from answers to a series of questions about her originals and desired copies) the system initiates a plan and then tracks the user's actions by mapping state changes to a stepwise procedure bound to that plan. In sequence III, A and B have completed the unbound

SEQUENCE III. *Again A and B are making two-sided copies from a bound document (this time having already completed their unbound master copy).*

| The Users | | The Machine | |
|---|---|---|---|
| Not Available to the Machine | Available to the Machine | Available to the User | Design Rationale |
| B: Okay, and then it'll tell us, | | | |
| okay, and:: It's got to come up with the little start thing soon. (pause) | | DISPLAY 1 | Selecting the procedure |
| Okay, we've done all that. We've made our bound copies. (pause) | | DISPLAY 2 | Instructions for copying a bound document: Accessing the Bound Document Aid |
| A: It'll go on though, I think. Won't it? | | | |
| B: I think it's gonna continue on, after it realizes that we've done all that. | | | |

master copy of their document and have gone on to attempt to make their two-sided copies. They find that the page order in the copies is incorrect (a fault not available to the system, which has no access to the actual markings on the page), so they try again. As in sequence II, for them this is a second attempt to accomplish the same job, whereas for the machine it is just another instance of the procedure. On this occasion, however, that discrepancy turns out to matter.

In sequence II, the system's ignorance of the relation between this attempt to make copies and the last did not matter, just because a check of the current state of the machine caused the appropriate behavior. Or, more accurately, the "current state" of the interaction could be read as a local, technical matter independent of the embedding course of events. Here, however, a check of the machine's current state belies the users' intent. To appreciate what they are doing now requires that the relation between this attempt and the last *is* recognized, and the machine state does not capture that relation. So although both users and system are, in some sense, doing the job again, there are two different senses of what, at this particular point, it means to do so. As far as the users are concerned, they are still trying to make two-sided copies of a bound document, so they leave their job description as such. For the machine, however, the appropriate description of their current goal, having made their master copy, is two-sided copying from an *unbound* document. The result is that what they in effect tell the machine they are doing is not what they intend to do, and what they intend to do is not available from the current state of the world as the machine is able to see it.

A and B find evidence of this trouble in an extended silence (sequence IV), which suggests that the system is not going to proceed. What A and B discover here is that, from the system's "point of view," their intent is determined by their initial statement: that is, to make two-sided copies from a bound document. Statements of intent, however, are inevitably relative to larger purposes and entail smaller ones, and although A and B's initial statement still accurately describes their global purpose, it belies their local one. Nor in this instance is their current situation (having failed successfully to produce the two-sided copies from their unbound master) reflected in the system's current state (ready to do two-sided copying from a bound original). Their current situation is available only through a history of which the system has no record or through their reports and assertions about their situation, to which the system has no access. Their attempt to make their situation accessible to the system by exploiting its insensitivity to their actual

SEQUENCE IV. *(continued from III).*

| The Users | | The Machine | |
| --- | --- | --- | --- |
| Not Available to the Machine | Available to the Machine | Available to the User | Design Mationale |
| | | DISPLAY 2 | Instructions for copying a bound document |
| (8-sec. pause) A: Then again, maybe we need to change the task description. | | | |
| B: What do you think? | | | |
| | SELECTS "Change" | DISPLAY 0 | User may want to change job description. |
| A: No. | | | |
| B: Okay, "Proceed." | SELECTS "Proceed" | | |
| | | DISPLAY 1 | Making two-sided copies from a bound document |
| | | DISPLAY 2 | Accessing the Bound Document Aid |
| A: Maybe I should just lift it up and put it= [ | | | |
| B: How do we skip this then? | | | |
| A: =down again. Maybe it'll think we're done. | | | |
| B: (laughs) Oh, Jean. | | | |
| A: There. | OPENS BDA | | |
| | | DISPLAY 3 | Instructions for placing document |
| Okay, we've done what we're supposed to do. | | | |

| The Users | | The Machine | |
|---|---|---|---|
| Not available to the machine | Available to the machine | Available to the user | Design rationale |
| | CLOSES BDA | | |
| Now let's put this down. Let's see if that makes a difference. (Looks back to display) | | | |
| | | DISPLAY 2 | Instructions for copying a bound document |
| (laughs) It did something. | | | |
| B: (inaudible) Good grief. | | | |
| A: Oh, it's still telling us we need to do a bound document. And we don't need to do the bound document because we've done that. You know, maybe we ought to go back to the beginning, and erase that thing about the bound document. | | | |
| B: Okay, that's a good idea. | | | |
| | SELECTS "Change" | | |
| A: Then say, "Is it bound?" just put no. | | DISPLAY 0 | User may want to change job description. |
| B: Not anymore. | SELECTS "No" | | |
| A: And then everything else is constant, isn't it? It's on standard paper:: [ | | | |
| B: so we'll proceed. | SELECTS "Proceed" | | |
| A: So let's just proceed. | | | New job; two-sided from unbound document |

circumstances and "faking" the required action fails, but the failure is a failure in performance not in principle. Specifically, if they had opened and closed the document *cover,* rather than only the Bound Document Aid, they would in fact have achieved the desired effect.

THE USER'S RESOURCE: THE SITUATED INQUIRY

The premise of a self-explanatory machine is that users will discover its intended use through information found in and on the machine itself, with no need for further instruction. In physical design, for example, the designer anticipates certain questions such that, in the event, an answer is there ready at hand. So the user's question "Where do I grab?" is answered by a handle fitted to the action of grabbing. In the traditional instruction manual, some further classes of inquiry are anticipated and answers provided. The stepwise instruction set addresses the question "What do I do next?," and the diagram the question "Where?" In all cases, however, the questions anticipated and answered must be those that any user of the system might ask, and the occasion for both questions and answers is found by the user. It is this lack of recipient design in the written instruction manual that the expert help system is designed to redress.

For the novice engaged in a procedural task, the guiding inquiry is some form of the question "What next?" The question is an essentially indexical one, relying for its significance on the embedding situation. In the case at hand, the system effectively checks its own state to anticipate the user's question and then presents the next outstanding requirement of the selected procedure in response. This design strategy assumes that the job specification represents the user's intent, that the intent so represented determines the appropriate plan, and that user and system are engaged in carrying out the procedure for that plan.

The design assumption, in other words, is that the situation of the question "What next?" is just the procedure and that the question is a request for the next step. As long as that assumption holds, the presentation of a next instruction constitutes an appropriate response (see, for example, sequence I). The design assumption fails, however, in cases such as sequence V, where the question "What next?" is not a matter of *proceeding* with the current plan but of its abandonment or *repair.* This sequence is discussed further below, but, for the moment, the observation is simply that the question "What do we do then?" is not, in this instance, a simple request for a "next" in the sense of a next step in the

SEQUENCE V. *C and D are making 5 two-sided copies of a bound document. (They are using the Bound Document Aid to make a single, unbound master copy of their original.)*

| The Users | | The Machine | |
|---|---|---|---|
| **Not Available to the Machine** | **Available to the Machine** | **Available to the User** | **Design Rationale** |
| C: "Instructions. Slide the document cover to the right." | | DISPLAY 5 | Instructions for copying a bound document: removing the document from the glass. |
| D: (Noting output) Okay, it gave us one copy here. | | | |
| C: Okay, "Slide the document cover right to remove the original." | | | |
| D: We're supposed to have 5 copies and we only got one. | | | |
| C: (Looks to output) Oh. (Looks to display) We only got one? | | | |
| D: Yea. | | | |
| (long pause) | | | |
| C: *What do we do then?* | | | |
| (Long pause, both study display) | | | |

procedure but rather is a request for a remedy to the current trouble. The situation of the inquiry (indicated anaphorically by the "then," viz. "given that we were supposed to have five copies and we only got one") is not the procedure itself but the conflict between the apparent outcome of the procedure (a single copy) and their stated intent (five copies). That situation, although clearly described by D, is unavailable in the current state of the machine, which shows no evidence of their trouble. That is, the current state of the machine indicates just that a copy has been made, the design rationale being that they have copied the first page of

SEQUENCE VI. *E and F are making two-sided copies of a bound document. (In response to the instruction to "close the document cover" (display 3), they have mistakenly closed the entire BDA instead, and as a consequence have returned to the previous instruction to open the BDA (display 2).)*

| The Users | | The Machine | |
|---|---|---|---|
| **Not Available to the Machine** | **Available to the Machine** | **Available to the User** | **Design Rationale** |
| | | DISPLAY 2 | Instructions for copying a bound document |
| E: "Pull the latch labeled–" We did that. "Raise–" We did that. (Studying display) Okay. Okay. | | | |
| F: "Lift up on the latch," We did that. | | | |
| E: Now let's change:: | | | |
| F: "Change task description?" | | | |
| E: Yes. | | | |
| F: | SELECTS "Change" | | |
| | | DISPLAY 0 | User may want to change job specification. |
| "Describe the document to be copied–" Oh, we already did: No, we don't want to do that. | | | |
| E: Maybe we have to do it to copy that. [i.e., the next page] | | | |
| F: (Looks around machine) (laugh) I don't know. | | | |
| E: Well:: | | | |
| F: "Help" (laugh) | | | |
| | SELECTS "Help" | | |
| "Select the question you would like help with." | | | User needs clarification of display. |

| The Users | | The Machine | | |
|---|---|---|---|---|
| Not Available to the Machine | Available to the Machine | Available to the User | Design Rationale | |

E: I guess we still
   do have to=
   [

F: We still ha–

E: =answer this.

F: Oh. okay,
   Alright.

E: Okay.

F: We sti– but we did all that,
   didn't we?

E: Well, maybe not for this
   page.

an *unbound master copy* of their bound document and are ready to go on to the second page.

As a consequence of the fact that the situation of their inquiry is not that which the design anticipates, and is not otherwise accessible to the system, the answer that the system offers – do the next step in this procedure – is inappropriate. Even in cases where the designer anticipates the need to remedy some trouble in the procedure rather than to go on to a next action, however, the context of a request for help may be problematic (sequence VI).

The selection of "Change task description," in the context of a loop between display 2 and display 3, and E and F's subsequent surprise at the reappearance of display 0 in response, suggests that the intent of their action was not to return to the job specification but to find a *next* instruction. The inherent ambiguity between any next instruction as either a continuation or as the initiator of a repair is discussed at length below. Our interest here is in the situation of the request for help that *follows* the return to display 0. Specifically, the selection of the "Help" option constitutes a question *about that return* to display 0, and the larger problem of the loop in which it is embedded. The design, however, takes the situation of the request to be a local one: that is, as having to do with interpreting the contents of display 0 itself.

SEQUENCE VII. *C and D are making two-sided copies of a bound document.*
*(They first must make a single, unbound master copy using the BDA.)*

| The Users | | The Machine | |
|---|---|---|---|
| **Not Available to the Machine** | **Available to the Machine** | **Available to the User** | **Design Rationale** |
| | | DISPLAY 1 | Overview |
| C: "You need to use the Bound Document Aid to make an unbound copy of your original." Where is– | | | |
| Oh, here it is. | | DISPLAY 2 | Instructions for copying a bound document: picture of the BDA. |

Tied to the guiding inquiry "what next?" is a set of embedded questions about the prescribed actions – questions that look for clarification of the forms "how," "where," or "to what," and "why."[4] The system's responsiveness to requests for elaboration turns again on whether the designer successfully predicts the inquiry. In sequence VII, C's question is actually interrupted by the change to display 2, which anticipates that very question. In this instance, it happens that the display change is timed to the mechanism that sets the machine's control panel rather than being conditional on any action of the user. Ironically, in part because on this occasion the system's behavior is determined *not* by the user's actions but by the internal processing of the system, it appears that the system's behavior is occasioned by the user's question.

The fact that the question anticipated turns out to be the user's question in this instance marks the success of the design. In sequence VIII, however, the designer's prediction fails. In this case, the designer anticipates a question regarding the *motivation* for the action, whereas the user's problem is with the action's *object*. In sequence IX, the question

---

[4] From the standpoint of the actor concerned with a procedural next, the other two logically possible queries, viz. "by whom" and "when," are already answered by the embedding situation – though see sequences XVII and XXIII. (Original footnote.)

SEQUENCE VIII. *C and D are making two-sided copies from a bound document, using the BDA. (They have placed their document on the document glass.)*

| The Users | | The Machine | |
|---|---|---|---|
| Not Available to the Machine | Available to the Machine | Available to the User | Design Rationale |
| C: Okay, wait a minute. "Slide the document cover left over your original until it latches." (Looks to machine) | | DISPLAY 3 | Copying a bound document: Closing the document cover |
| D: (Grasps BDA) | | | |
| C: The document cover– (leans over to look in BDA) | | | |
| D: Oh. (Pulls on document feeder belt, which gives a little) No, no, no. (indicating entire BDA) *This would be the document cover, isn't it?* | | | |
| C: *"To provide an eyeshield for the copier (inaudible)."* | | | |

*what is the object* is anticipated, whereas B's question actually concerns *how to do the action*. The answer to B's inquiry is found not in the instruction, which locates the object, but in the object itself. Similarly, in sequence X a problem in interpreting an instruction is solved through a picture of the object on which the action is to be performed.

When the object that B first takes to be implicated in the action description "lift up and to the left" resists her attempts to perform the action described, and the description suggests no other interpretation of the action, she finds in the picture a different object. That reinterpretation of the object, in its turn, revises the significance of the action description. In this way a conflict between the action on an object described by an instruction, and the action required by the object itself, can be a resource

SEQUENCE IX. *A and B are making two-sided copies of an unbound document.*

| The Users | | The Machine | |
|---|---|---|---|
| Not Available to the Machine | Available to the Machine | Available to the User | Design Rationale |
| A: "Place the copies:: on the top paper tray." | | DISPLAY 11 | Beginning second pass of two-sided copies |
| [Portion omitted in which they locate the tray.] | | | |
| A: Okay. | | | |
| B: But, (Turning back to display) *How do you do that?* | | | |
| A: (Looking at diagram) *"The top paper tray is to the right of the output tray."* Place copies in the top paper tray," (Turning to tray) Oh, you just lift it up. (Does) | | | |

for identifying trouble in the interpretation of an instruction and its resolution, as in sequence XI.

In general, the referential relationship between instructions and the actions and objects they describe is a reciprocal, rather than directional, one. Burke (1982), for example, describes a pump assembly task in which to some extent all of the necessary information for assembling the pump is discoverable in requirements of the materials themselves, specifically the "fit and stay" bindings of one component of the pump to another. In spite of the constraints provided by the bindings, Burke noted a difference in confidence between those students who had additional linguistic instruction and those who did not, the former using the instructions, on the one hand, and the task actions and materials, on the other, as mutually informative, such that "both the instructions and the task actions are treated by the apprentice as problems to be solved. But each is used as a resource to solve the other as a problem" (ibid.: 178). That is to say, whereas instructions answer questions about objects and actions, they

SEQUENCE X. *A and B are making two-sided copies of a bound document.*

| The Users | | The Machine | |
| --- | --- | --- | --- |
| Not Available to the Machine | Available to the Machine | Available to the User | Design Rationale |
| A: "To access the BDA, pull the latch labeled Bound Document Aid":: <br><br> (A and B turn to machine) <br><br> (Points) Right there. | | DISPLAY 2 | Instructions for copying a bound document: Accessing the bound document aid. |
| B: (Hands on latch) | | | |
| A: "And lift up to the left." (Looks to B, who struggles with the latch) "Lift up and to the left." | | | |
| B: (Still struggling) | | | |
| A: Okay:: | | | |
| B: Pu::ll, and lift up to the left. (Looks at picture) Oh, the whole thing= [ | | | |
| A: Yea. | | | |
| B: =lift up and to the left. | | | |
| | Opens BDA | | |

also pose problems of interpretation that are solved in and through the objects and actions to which the instructions refer.

A nice example of this reciprocity of description and action described is shown in sequence XII. In this case, rather than the interpretation of the instruction "Pull the latch, etc." being *prerequisite* to the action's execution, the action after the fact clarifies what the instruction intends.

Given the requests for clarification that are potential responses to any directive, one can easily predict that any one or more of them *might* occur but not with any certainty *which*. The design of the expert help

SEQUENCE XI. *C and D have mistaken the entire BDA for the "document cover"*
*and are caught in a loop between display 3 and display 2*
*(see also sequence VI).*

| The Users | | The Machine | |
|---|---|---|---|
| **Not Available to the Machine** | **Available to the Machine** | **Available to the User** | **Design Rationale** |
| | | DISPLAY 3 | Instructions for closing document cover |
| D: Okay. "Slide the document cover– left over your original, until it latches." (Turns to machine) You know it says "slide" – this (Finds document cover). Okay. | | | |
| C: Ohh. | | | |
| D: (laughs) Ohh, isn't that hilarious? Okay. [ | | | |
| C: Okay. | | | |
| | Closes cover | | |
| It was something else that was supposed to go over that. | | DISPLAY 4 | |

system attempts to deal with the problem exhaustively and frequently
succeeds. Questions of "how," "where," and "why" are answered by
a diagram and supplementary description, provided with each next
instruction. In all of these instances, however, the user brings the descriptions
that the system provides to bear on the material circumstances of
her action and brings those circumstances to bear on her interpretation
of the descriptions. In other words, the user exploits the meaning of
object and action descriptions to find their referents and uses the objects
and actions picked out as resources for finding the significance of the
description. Through access to these resources the user not only asks
but also effectively answers her own situated inquiries.

SEQUENCE XII. *E and F are making two-sided copies of a bound document.*

| The Users | | The Machine | |
|---|---|---|---|
| **Not Available to the Machine** | **Available to the Machine** | **Available to the User** | **Design Rationale** |
| | | DISPLAY 2 | Instructions for copying a bound document: |
| F: "To access the BDA, pull the latch labeled Bound Document Aid." (Both turn to machine) | | | |
| E: (Takes hold of latch) | | | Accessing the bound document aid. |
| F: Pull it down: just push it down. | | | |
| E: (Does, BDA starts to open) | | | |
| | | DISPLAY 3 | Placing the document on the glass |
| F: (startled) Oh, alright. | Opens BDA | | |
| This is what you do. | | | |
| E: Is this what you do? Oh my gosh. | | | |

## THE CONDITIONAL RELEVANCE OF RESPONSE

We have seen how the responsiveness of the system is limited to those occasions where the user's actions effect some change in the machine's state, which ties the actions to the requirements of the underlying design plan. In principle, the design plan serves as the measure of what constitutes an adequate and appropriate action by the user; namely, one that satisfies the current procedural requirement. The requirements that the system imposes, in this procrustean sense, serve as prescriptions for successful use of the machine. The success assumes, however, that the user interprets the instructions and the system's responses in the way that the designer intended.

In the interest of conveying the intent of the design to the user, and in doing so interactively, the designer tacitly relies on certain conventions of human conversation. Most generally, designer and user share the expectation that the relevance of each utterance is conditional on the last; that given an action by one party that calls for a response, for example, the other's next action *will be* a response. The expectation does not ensure that any next action in fact will be a response to the last, but it does mean that, wherever possible, the user will look for an interpretation of the next action that makes it so.

The user's expectation, in other words, is that each system response conveys, either implicitly or explicitly, an assessment of the last action she has taken and a recommendation for what to do next. More specifically, given some instruction to which the user responds with an action, the user has the following expectations with respect to the system's response:

(a) The system's response should be a new instruction, which stands as implicit confirmation of the adequacy of the user's previous action.

(b) If the system does not respond, the user's previous action is somehow incomplete.

(c) If the system's response is to repeat the instruction, the repetition implies that the user's previous action should be repeated (i.e., that the procedure is iterative) *or* that there is some trouble in the previous action that should be repaired.

### A New Instruction Confirms the Previous Action

We have a general expectation, in carrying out a stepwise procedure, that completion of one action allows progress to a new instruction and a next action. The correlate of the expectation that a completed action indicates readiness for a new instruction is the fact that the appearance of a new instruction is taken, at least initially, as confirmation of the previous action. In sequence XIII, B's evidence for the adequacy of A's action is simply the fact that it generates a response, which is assumed to be a next instruction. The apparent change to a new instruction confirms the preceding action in spite of the fact that the action description, "Slide the document cover," does not actually seem to fit the action taken. The action taken in fact is not closing the *document cover,* which is located inside the Bound Document Aid, but instead closing the Bound Document Aid itself. The assumption that display 2 must be a next to display 3, however, masks the fact that they are entering into a loop between those two displays (see also sequence VI).

### No Response Indicates That the Previous Action Is Incomplete

In conversation, silences are more than just the absence of talk: they are generally owned by one party or another, and they invariably

SEQUENCE XIII. *A and B are making two-sided copies of a bound document.*
*They first must make a single, unbound master copy using the BDA.*

| The Users | | The Machine | |
| --- | --- | --- | --- |
| Not Available to the Machine | Available to the Machine | Available to the User | Design Rationale |
| | | DISPLAY 3 | Instructions for closing document cover |
| B: Okay. "Slide the document cover: left over your original, until it latches." | | | |
| A: (Moves hand to BDA) | | | |
| B: (Turns to machine) "Slide the document cover," (Looks back to the diagram) that's this [i.e., BDA], Right? | | | |
| A: (Starts to close) We – it said left, though. (Looks to display) | | | |
| B: "To close the document cover, grasp the cover, | | | |
| A: | CLOSES BOUND DOCUMENT AID | | |
| B: slide it firmly to the left." | | | |
| | | DISPLAY 2 | Instructions for opening Bound Document Aid |
| (You must) have done that. | | | |

acquire significance (see Chapter 7). The significance of silence lies in its relationship to the talk that it follows and, retrospectively, the talk that it can be seen to precede. In particular, the convention that certain utterance types (questions and answers being the canonical example) sequentially implicate the appropriate next utterance produces account-able absences when the next is not forthcoming. An extended silence following a question, for example, will be seen as a nonresponse. In the case of the expert help system, there is no response until the user completes the action prescribed by the final instruction of a given display. This design constraint, combined with the user's expectation from human interaction regarding sequential implicature and silence, means that the unresponsiveness of the system carries information. Specifically, when an action that is intended to satisfy a final instruction fails to elicit a response, the user takes the unresponsiveness as evidence for trouble in her performance of the action. In sequence XIV, for example, what C and D initially see as a pause comes to be seen, in virtue of its length, as a nonresponse. The nonresponse, in turn, carries information with respect to their last action. Specifically, the nonresponse indicates that this is still, in effect, their turn: that the last action was not, somehow, the action prescribed by this instruction. The evidence that the nonresponse provides – that there is some problem in the action taken – initiates a reinspection of the instruction, a reidentification of the instruction's object, and the action's repair.

SEQUENCE XIV. *C and D are making two-sided copies using the "Recirculating Document Handler" (RDH).*

| The Users | | The Machine | |
| --- | --- | --- | --- |
| **Not Available to the Machine** | **Available to the Machine** | **Available to the User** | **Design Rationale** |
| C: Okay, "Remove the copies from the output tray." (Takes documents from document handler) Okay. Now: | | DISPLAY 10 | Copies complete |
| (15-second pause) | | | |
| (Turns to output) Oh, (Looks back to display) | | | |
| D: The output tray: | | | |
| C: This is the output tray. | | | |
| D: (Points to picture) That's the output tray, okay. | | | |

## Repetition Is Ambiguous Between Iteration and Repair

There are two conditions on which the system may repeat a prior instruction:

(a) The action taken in response to the instruction should be repeated (the common case, for example, in a procedure that is *iterative*).

(b) The action taken in response to the instruction *is in error* in just such a way as to return the system to a state prior to the instruction: in effect, to undo a previous action. This produces a *loop*.

In human interaction, (b) does not occur. However, in human interaction repetition is used in a way that does not occur between user and machine, namely, to indicate that:

(c) The action taken in response to the instruction in some way fails to satisfy the intent of the instruction and needs to be remedied.

Consistent with the observation that users import expectations from human interaction to construe the system's responses, users failed to recognize the occurrence of (b) and instead read all cases of repetition as either (a) or as (c).

*Repetition as iteration.* In procedural instructions there are occasions, illustrated in sequence XV, on which the repeat of an instruction is to be taken at face value, as an explicit directive to do the previous action again.

Purposeful action is characterized by the fact that its projected outcome is a resource for assessing the action's course. Where the procedure is a composite one, this function is complicated, however. For one thing, success at a composite procedure depends on reliable ways of discriminating between the procedure's outcome and its intermediate states. Particularly for the novice, the expectation that an embedded procedure (in this case, making the unbound master copy of the document) will produce the *finished* product leads to confusion like that of B in sequence XV, and to more complex misunderstandings, as shown in sequence XVI.

Coming to what they take to be the end of the iterative procedure described in display 6, C and D hypothesize that their part in the procedure is finished and that the next turn is the system's. That hypothesis is challenged by the system's inaction (a silence of eleven seconds), which suggests some incompleteness in their own action and something further for them to do. Their problem, then, is to find a "next"; that is,

SEQUENCE XV. *A and B are making two-sided copies of a bound document. They have copied the first page of the document, using the BDA.*

| The Users | | The Machine | |
|---|---|---|---|
| Not Available to the Machine | Available to the Machine | Available to the User | Design Rationale |
| B: "If more pages are to be copied, then place the next page face down on the glass." | | DISPLAY 6 | Iterative procedure for using the BDA |
| A: Just keep it up until we're finished with the, with the, uh: | | | |
| B: Oh, well how do you – she was – she said on both sides, right? | | | |
| A: Well that's after we finish getting this (indicating document). We're just getting the originals to stick up here [i.e., RDH]. | | | |
| B: Oh, you're right, you're right. | | | |

some action prescribed by the instructions that is outstanding.[5] Given that problem, and its situation in the inherently ambiguous context of a procedure that is both recursive and composite (copying each page once until the end of the document so that the document can be copied five times), one possible solution is to see the persistence of this instruction as a repeat rather than a nonresponse and therefore as a directive to do the procedure again.

In another case, sequence XVII, the option "Change task description," intended by the designer to enable a repair but noticed in the context of the search for a next turn, suggests iteration where the designer did not intend it.

---

[5] The outstanding instruction, in fact, is "Lower the RDH until it latches." For the designer, that is the precondition for continuing on to the second pass of the procedure. For the users, however, under the assumption that the procedure is effectively completed, that could only be a sort of coda (like putting away the bowls once one has baked a cake), with no direct consequence for the outcome. (Original footnote.)

SEQUENCE XVI. *C and D are making five two-sided copies of a bound document. They have completed the master copy using the BDA. Unaware of the composite structure of the procedure, and seeking to explain the fact that this procedure has produced only one copy, they have adopted the hypothesis that the remaining four copies are produced automatically, by the machine, and they are waiting for them to appear.*

| The Users | | The Machine | |
|---|---|---|---|
| Not Available to the Machine | Available to the Machine | Available to the User | Design Rationale |
| | | DISPLAY 6 | Iterative |
| D: "Place the next page face down on the glass. Slide the document cover (inaudible). Lower the RDH until it latches." (pause) Okay | | | procedure for using the BDA: when RDH is lowered, |
| (11-second pause) | | | User is ready to |
| So we start over for five? It doesn't do it (inaudible)? | | | go on to make multiple |
| C: I guess we just have to do it five times, and then it'll: (pause) Do what it says, I guess. | | | copies. |

If E and F's objective in selecting "Change task description" is to find a next action, one way that they can make the system's response a relevant one is to interpret the return to display o iteratively, as telling them to specify their job again. The possibility, if not plausibility, of that interpretation arises from the fact that the difference between going "backward" to something already done in a procedure and going "forward" to repeat the action is inherently problematical. The difference does not lie in any features of the instruction or action itself, but just in whether the instruction's reappearance at a given time is read as a misunderstanding or as intended by the design. (See sequence VI above for the development of the problem.)

Finally, the novice user may *expect* recursion in what is by design a one-pass procedure. C's action in Sequence XVIII of removing the first page of the document and replacing it with a second assumes that this procedure is iterative; viz. copy each page one at a time, until finished. Although taken as a next, however, her action restores a state that

SEQUENCE XVII. *E and F are in a loop between display 3 and display 2.*

| The Users | | The Machine | |
|---|---|---|---|
| Not Available to the Machine | Available to the Machine | Available to the User | Design Rationale |
| E: "Pull the latch labeled–" We did that. "Raise–" We did that. (Studying display) Okay. Okay. | | DISPLAY 2 | Instructions for copying a bound document: Raising the document handler. |
| F: "Lift up on the latch," We did that. | | | |
| E: Now let's change:: | | | |
| F: "Change task description?" | | | |
| E: Yes. | | | |
| F: | SELECTS "Change" | | |
| "Describe the document to be copied–" Oh, we already did: No, we don't want to do that. | | DISPLAY 0 | User may want to change job specification. |
| E: Maybe we have to do it to copy that [i.e., the next page]. | | | |
| F: (Looks around machine) (laugh) I don't know. | | | |

from the system's "point of view" appears identical to the state *before* the action was taken – a document in the document handler – thereby canceling the action's effect. For C, logically, the *last* page has been removed from the document handler and putting the *next* page in is prerequisite to going on. For the system there is just *a* document in the document handler, and its *removal* is required to go on.

Seen as an instruction to undo their last action, the instruction to "remove the original" would stand as evidence of trouble. But by paraphrasing "remove" as "move the first page to make a place for

SEQUENCE XVIII. *C and D are making four one-sided copies of an unbound document, using the RDH.*

| The Users | | The Machine | |
| --- | --- | --- | --- |
| Not Available to the Machine | Available to the Machine | Available to the User | Design Rationale |
| C: Okay, and face up, Right? First page? | | DISPLAY 7 | Instructions for copying an unbound document: Place all originals in RDH. |
| | DOCUMENT PLACED IN RDH | | |
| "Press the Start button." Where's the Start button? (Looks around machine, then to display) | | DISPLAY 8 | Ready to print |
| D: (Points to display) Start? Right there it is. | | | |
| C: There. (laughs) | | | |
| D: Okay. | | | |
| C: | SELECTS START | | |
| | | STARTS | Document is being copied |
| | | DELIVERS COPIES | Job complete |
| Ta: Oh, it comes right back out. | | | |
| | | DISPLAY 9 | Removing originals |
| | REMOVES DOCUMENT | | |

*(continued)*

SEQUENCE XVIII *(continued)*

| The Users | | The Machine | |
|---|---|---|---|
| **Not Available to the Machine** | **Available to the Machine** | **Available to the User** | **Design Rationale** |
| So it made four of the first? (Looks at display) Okay. | | | |
| | | DISPLAY 10 | Removing copies from the output tray. |
| (Holding second page over the document handler, looks to display) | | | |
| Does it say to put it in yet? | | | |
| D: (inaudible) "Remove the copies from the output tray." | | | |
| C: (inaudible) number two. (Puts second page into document handler) | | | |
| | DOCUMENT PLACED IN RDH | | |
| "Remove the original–" Okay, I've re-I've moved the original. And put in the second copy. | | DISPLAY 9 | Removing originals |

the second," C makes this response relevant by turning it into a next, iterative instruction and therefore a confirmation of her last action. (For discussion of this sequence as a "garden path," see below.)

*Repetition as repair.* The inclination to see each next instruction as a new instruction means that a repetition might not initially even be recognized as such. Recall that this was the case in sequence XIII. In fact, this is another instance of the loop described for sequence VI. Specifically, in sequence XIII mislocation of the object referred to as the "document cover" leads B to close the entire Bound Document Aid, an action that returns the system to its initial state and causes it to redisplay the first instruction; namely, to open the BDA.[6] The design rationale that produces this system response is simple: (i) the user must use the BDA to copy bound documents; (ii) to use the BDA, it must be opened; (iii) if the BDA is closed, the user should be presented with instructions for opening it. However, rather than taking the return to the previous instruction as evidence for some problem in their last action, A and B see it as a next instruction and as confirmation.

The inclination to mistake a return to a previous instruction for a next can be appreciated by considering the anomalous character of this particular problem in terms of any parallels in human interaction. Although repetition of the first part of an adjacency pair is justified in cases where there is no response, when a response does occur it terminates the sequence and provides for the relevance of a next. Insofar as the user believes her action constitutes a response to the current instruction, then, she has every reason to view the system's next turn as a next instruction. The closest situation that one finds in human interaction to the loop in human–machine communication occurs when a response to a sequentially implicative utterance – the answer to a summons, for example – is not recognized as such:

As noted, upon the completion of the SA [summons–answer] sequence, the original summoner cannot summon again. The operation of this terminating rule, however, depends upon the clear recognition that an A has occurred. This recognition normally is untroubled. However, trouble sometimes occurs by virtue of the fact that some lexical items, e.g., "Hello," may be used both as summonses and as answers. Under some circumstances it may be impossible to tell whether such a term has been used as a summons or as answer. Thus, for example, when acoustic difficulties arise in a telephone conversation, both parties may attempt to confirm their mutual availability to one another. Each one may them employ the term "Hello?" as a summons to the other. For each of them, however, it may be unclear whether what he hears in the earpiece is an answer to his check, or the other's summons for him to answer. One may, under such circumstances, hear a conversation in which a sequence of some length is constituted by nothing but alternatively and simultaneously offered "hellos." Such "verbal dodging" is typically resolved by the use, by one party, of an item on which a second is conditionally relevant, where that second is unambiguously a second part of a

---

[6] Fortuitously, the action that the BDA suggests, just because it returns the machine to a previous state, is the only action other than that which the design intends to which the system would respond at all at this point. (Original footnote.)

two-part sequence. Most typically this is a question, and the question "Can you hear me?" or one of its common lexical variants, regularly occurs. (Schegloff 1972: 366)

Recognized as such, a return to a previous instruction that cannot be construed as recursive is evidence for trouble. Sequence XIX is another instance of the same misunderstanding that we saw in sequence XIII.

In human interaction, when the response to an action is either incoherent or inappropriate, the producer of the original action has recourse to two possible interpretations. She can treat the troublesome response as the product of an error on the listener's part (not hearing or mishearing, not understanding or misunderstanding) or as intended. If the troublesome response is seen as the product of some failure of hearing or understanding, the repair may be just to repeat the original action (see Coulter 1979: 30). Unless the trouble is one of hearing, however, we rarely repeat a directive verbatim if there appears to be some problem

SEQUENCE XIX. *E and F are making two-sided copies of a bound document. They first must make a single, unbound master copy using the BDA.*

| The Users | | The Machine | |
|---|---|---|---|
| **Not Available to the Machine** | **Available to the Machine** | **Available to the User** | **Design Rationale** |
| | | DISPLAY 3 | |
| F: "Slide the document cover over your original until it latches." | | | |
| E: (Hand on BDA) | | | |
| F: Just push it down. | | | |
| E: | CLOSES BDA | | |
| Okay, here we go. (turns to display) "Pull the latch la–" Oh, we already did that. | | DISPLAY 2 | |
| (pause. They study display) | | | |
| E: Okay. | | | |
| F: Okay. | | | |
| (7-second pause) Now what do we do? | | | |

SEQUENCE XX *(continued from XIX).*

| The Users | | The Machine | |
|---|---|---|---|
| Not Available to the Machine | Available to the Machine | Available to the User | Design Rationale |
| | | DISPLAY 2 | |
| E: "Pull the latch labeled–" We did that. "Raise–" We did that. (Studying display) Okay. Okay. | | | |
| F: "Lift up on the latch," We did that. | | | |

of understanding the first time around. Instead, we try some reformulation or elaboration. If one formulation fails to convey our intended meaning, we try another. Frequently it is not simply that we try an alternative formulation of what we intended before, but that what we intend is conditional on the other's response. In that sense, our own intentions are clarified for us by the response of the other.

In every case, to the extent that we are heard to be repeating ourselves, the repeat is heard as an attempt to correct some problem in understanding the first time around (see Jordan and Fuller 1975). Seen in this light, as a repair-initiator, repetition initiates a review of the repeated instruction. In sequence XX, a review of the instruction confirms that the actions it prescribes have been done. The two alternative responses to the repeat, in that case, are either to assert that the action is complete or to do it again. In face-to-face interaction these alternatives appear to be ordered; that is, we first assert that we have heard a prior utterance and responded to it and then, if the assertion does not suffice, we provide a demonstration. Realizing that in communication with the machine assertions never suffice, that the system has access only to demonstrations or actions, is part of acquiring proficiency in its use.

Actually redoing an action frequently uncovers problems of understanding, not just because the same terrain is considered again, but because, considered again, the terrain is seen differently, as in Sequence XXI. However, when a review fails to reveal any new actions,

SEQUENCE XXI. *Another case of the loop between display 2 and display 3.*

| The Users | | The Machine | |
|---|---|---|---|
| Not Available to the Machine | Available to the Machine | Available to the User | Design Ratio- nale |
| | | DISPLAY 2 | |
| B: "Pull the latch labeled bound," "Raise the RDH." "To access the BDA, pull the latch labeled Bound Document Aid," Okay, (Gesture to latch, then back to display) we did. | | | |
| A: Yea. | | | |
| B: "And lift up to the left," *do it again* | | | |
| A: | OPENS TO BDA | DISPLAY 3 | |
| There. (To display) I'm lifting up to the left. | | | |
| B: Okay. "Place your original face down on the glass, centered over the registration = [ | | | |
| A: "guide," Okay. [ | | | |
| B: =guide." | | | |
| A: Did that. | | | |
| B: "Slide the document co–" | | | |
| A: "cover left over= [ | | | |
| B: Wait a minute. A: =your originals," Well: | | | |

| The Users | | The Machine | |
|---|---|---|---|
| **Not Available to the Machine** | **Available to the Machine** | **Available to the User** | **Design Rationale** |
| B: Here's the document glass, (Indicating BDA) is that what they mean? | | | |
| A: (Looking at BDA) Document cover. | | | |
| B: "To close the document cover, grasp the cover and slide it firmly to the left." | | | |
| A: (Finding it) Oh, here's the document cover! | | | |
| | CLOSES DOCUMENT COVER | | |
| B: Oh, Jean, good girl! | | | |
| A: There's the document– | | | |
| (Both turn back to display) | | DISPLAY 4 | |
| Okay now: [ | | | |
| B: Allright: "Press: the Start button." Jean, you're doin' great. (Both look to BDA) | SELECTS "Start" | | |
| A: Oh, I see, | | MACHINE STARTS | |
| B: Alright. | | | |
| A: We don't have to close this big thing. | | | |
| B: No, we were– we were lookin' at the wrong thing. We were closing the bound document aid, instead of the: | | | |
| A: instead of the document cover. | | | |

SEQUENCE XXII. *Again, another case of the loop between display 2 and display 3*

| The Users | | The Machine | |
| --- | --- | --- | --- |
| Not Available to the Machine | Available to the Machine | Available to the User | Design Rationale |
| C: (inaudible, rereads instructions) Okay, are we ready? "Pull the latch labeled bound – to release." and then you release:: the, uh, RDH (inaudible.) Okay, are we ready? (pause) Oh, it's supposed to do it by itself. (pause) | | DISPLAY 2 | |

one reasonable inference is that the next action must be the other's. In Sequence XXII, C's review indicates that the actions prescribed by the instructions have all been completed; the sense of her "ready" here is as in "ready to go." There appears to be nothing further for them to do. Because the logical next step is for the machine to copy the document, C concludes that it must do so without further action on their part. Concluding that it is the system's turn offers an alternative to the original interpretation of the repeat as an indication that their action is somehow incomplete. If the system is in fact responding to their last action, that both confirms the action's adequacy and accounts for the system's failure to provide a next instruction. The length of time that passes with no apparent activity, however, casts doubt on that conclusion, as the system's silence takes on the character of a nonresponse. If the system is not responding, there must be some further action for them to take. In sequence XXIII, they again attempt to read the repetition as a directive to repair some problem in the action as it was done the first time through. C's "why" here is a locally situated one; that is, she is not asking in general about the rationale for this instruction but in particular about its intent now, given their history and present circumstances. Although the answer provided is intended to justify the instruction on *any* occasion, she attributes to it a significance particular to *this* occasion. Because their inquiry is situated in their particular circumstances, the

SEQUENCE XXIII *(continued from XXII).*

| The Users | | The Machine | |
|---|---|---|---|
| **Not Available to the Machine** | **Available to the Machine** | **Available to the User** | **Design Rationale** |
| | | DISPLAY 2 | |
| C: "Pull the latch labeled bound copy aid to release the – RDH | | | |
| D: (Points) This is the RDH. This [i.e., the latch] is the release. | | | |
| C: *But why does it want it to release it?* (To display) "Release (inaudible) to enable placement of the bound document on the glass," so we don't have that on the glass like it's supposed to be. | | | |

answer is taken as an answer to that occasioned inquiry. Specifically, C reads the "to enable" clause as relevant to the directive that they release the RDH again, to allow a repair of some fault in the document's placement. This attributes to the system substantially greater sensitivity than it has; namely, the ability to tell how the document is sitting on the glass and to notice that it is faulted in some way. Under this interpretation of the design, the directive to re-place the document would be conveyed by re-presenting this instruction to the user until the document is placed correctly. This interpretation not only accounts for the loop in which they've found themselves but also suggests the way out of it.

### COMMUNICATIVE BREAKDOWNS

Users of the expert help system encounter two forms of communicative breakdown: the *false alarm* and the *garden path*. In the first case, a misconception on the user's part leads her to find evidence of an error in her actions where none exists; in the second, a misconception on the user's part produces an error in her action with respect to the prescribed procedure, the presence of which is masked. In neither case is the breakdown available as such to the system.

## The False Alarm

I noted earlier that purposeful action is characterized by the fact that projected outcomes of action are a resource for producing the action's course. In particular, the effects of actions taken are compared against expected outcomes to judge the action's adequacy. Expectations with respect to the effect of actions taken often are not articulated, but are discovered only in the breach. In sequence XXIV the machine offers the users two competing pieces of evidence regarding the adequacy of their last action. The display offers a next instruction, which makes sense as a confirmation of their previous action. The output, however, indicates that the action has failed, in which case the next instruction is irrelevant. From the system's "point of view," nonetheless, there is no problem. And because the system detects no problem here, it offers no prescription for a remedy. The result is an interactional impasse, where the question "What do we do then?" finds no answer. Or rather, the answer that the system provides makes sense only if what the users intend to do is to continue making a single copy from a bound document.[7]

Whereas from the point of view of the design that is precisely what they want to do, that intent is not a feature of *their* situation. Their situation, meanwhile – that they intended to produce five copies of the document and have produced only one – is unavailable to the system. The consequence is that the users ascribe a (spurious) misunderstanding of their intent to the machine, whereas the machine fails to detect the (genuine) misunderstanding on their part with respect to the structure

---

[7] The problem here is one of intermediate states vs. outcomes. The procedure for two-sided copying requires use of the RDH, but use of that mechanism requires an unbound original. As a consequence of that mechanism constraint, the first pass of the procedure for copying a bound document is directed at producing one, unbound, master copy of the document. This requires a procedure of copying each page, using the BDA, until there is one complete set to be put into the RDH. Although an overview of the procedure was presented in display 1, designed to correct the assumption that this first pass would produce the desired outcome directly, the overview evidently did not do so. D's statement of the problem demonstrates their continuing confusion, but the fact that the confusion is unavailable to the system precludes what would be a second chance for the misconception's repair. (Original footnote.)

SEQUENCE XXIV. *C and D are making two-sided copies of a bound document.*
*They have copied the first page.*

| The Users | | The Machine | |
|---|---|---|---|
| **Not Available to the Machine** | **Available to the Machine** | **Available to the User** | **Design Rationale** |
| | | DISPLAY 5 | Copying a bound document: Opening the document cover. |
| C: "Instructions. Slide the document cover to the right." | | | |
| D: (Noting output) Okay, it gave us one copy here. | | | |
| C: Okay, "Slide the document cover right to remove the original." | | | |
| D: We're supposed to have 5 copies and we only got one. | | | |
| C: (Looks to output) Oh. (Looks to display) We only got one? | | | |
| D: Yea. (long pause) | | | |
| C: What do we do then? | | | |
| (long pause, Both study display) | | | |

of the procedure. The result is their effort to repair a line of action that is in no way faulty.

## Garden Path

To the extent that different assumptions of users and designers produce evidence of misunderstanding, there is at least some hope that the trouble might be located and resolved. We looked above at two events taken by users as evidence of trouble: namely, the nonresponse and the repeat. As in sequence XXIV, false expectations with respect to an action's effect may lead the user to find evidence for trouble in her performance where, in design terms, none exists. Because in such cases the problem lies in the user's expectations (as expressed in her talk) rather than in her (machine-readable) actions, and because the evidence for her expectations that the user provides is unavailable to the machine, the problem itself is unavailable to the machine.

Although the user is uncertain of her action in such cases, the action she takes is in fact the action that the design prescribes. Deeper problems arise when the user takes an action other than that prescribed by the design, but one that satisfies the procedural requirement. As a result of the ambiguity of the action's effect, the incorrect action is actually "mistaken" by the system for some other, correct action, from which it is indistinguishable by the system's sensors. As in XXIV, the problem in such cases is inaccessible to the system. But whereas in XXIV the misconception leads the user to find evidence of trouble where, by design, none exists, in these other cases trouble is masked by the fact that the user sees the action as nonproblematic, and by the fact that because the action appears nonproblematic to the system as well, the system's response appears to the user to confirm the action.

Take the example in Sequence XVIII above. From the system's "point of view," this sequence produces no evidence of trouble. Display 7 instructs the users to place their documents in the Recirculating Document Handler (RDH) and the system's sensors "see" them do so; display 8 instructs them to press Start; they do, and the machine produces four copies of their document. To a human observer with any knowledge of this machine, however, C's question "So it made four of the first?" indicates a misunderstanding. Specifically, her question conveys the information that this in fact is not a single-page document but the first page of several. And in contrast to other machines that require the placement of pages on the glass one at a time, copying an unbound document of multiple pages with this machine requires loading the pages all at once.[8] The problem here is not simply a failure of anticipation on the designer's part. On the contrary, in anticipation of this very situation, the instruction for loading documents explicitly states that *all* of the pages should

---

[8] This is an interesting case of the early introduction of an "innovative" design feature onto the market. The 8200 copier was one of the first, outside of copy shops, to offer an automatic document feeder (the Recirculating Document Handler), a feature that consequently was unfamiliar to most users.

be placed in the document handler. There is no evidence, however, that the instruction is consulted by these users.

One basic premise of instructions is that they explicate a problem of action: if there is no problem, there is logically no need for instruction. We can infer from the users' failure to consult the instructions at this point that they have a preconception about what to do, based on past experience. Such preconceptions probably account in large part for the common complaint from designers that people "ignore" instructions; they ignore them because they believe that they already know how to proceed. But given the fact of the users' misconception, the further problem arises when the faulted action goes by unnoticed at the point where it occurs. It does so because what is available to the system is only the action's effect, and that effect satisfies the requirements for the next instruction. As an assertion in the form of a question, C's statement "So it made four of the first?" not only formulates her view of the system's last operation, but also requests confirmation of that formulation. Interactionally, her statement provides an occasion for the discovery of the misunderstanding. She even looks to the display for a response. The information provided there is ambiguous enough, however – it simply says, "The copies have been made" – to support her assertion rather than challenge it. As a consequence, the misunderstanding displayed in C's question is unavailable to the system, whereas the ambiguity of the system's response masks the trouble for the user.

C's action of placing the document in the document handler appears, in other words, to be a perfectly adequate response to display 7. The system treats the action as satisfying the directive to place all of the documents in the document handler (where "all" in this case comprises one) and therefore provides a next instruction, whereas C and D take the appearance of the next instruction as confirmation that their last action, placing *the first page* of their document in the document feeder, satisfied the design intent. The start-up of the machine, with no complaint about their prior action, reflects the fact that the directive to "Start" has two different, but compatible interpretations. For the users, the significance of the directive is "make four copies of page 1," whereas for the system it is just "make four copies of the document in the document handler." There is nothing in either display 9 or display 10 to indicate the discrepancy. Each is ambiguous enough to be read under either interpretation.

So at the point where the machine starts to print, C is making four copies of page 1 of her document, whereas the machine is just making four copies of the document in the document handler. This seems, on the face of it, a minor discrepancy. If the machine copies the document, why should it matter that it fails to appreciate more finely the document's status as one in a set of three? The problem lies in the consequences of this continuing misunderstanding for the next exchange. The strength of C's conception of what is going on (repeating the procedure for each page) provides her with a logical next action (loading her second page into the document handler) in advance of any instruction. The instruction is looked to for confirmation of her action rather than for direction. Her certainty is evident in the terms of the question "Does it say to put it in yet?" The deictic pronoun "it" with respect to the system as "next speaker," and to the second page as the object of the instruction, the "in" with respect to the location of the action, and the "yet" with respect to the time of the action, all imply a shared situation that would make the interpretation of those indexical terms nonproblematic. For C, that the instruction will appear and what it will say is not in question – only when is in question. Although C is going on to the next run of the procedure, however, the system is still engaged in the completion of the last. What remains is the *removal* of originals and copies from their respective trays.

The "misunderstanding" between users and system at this point turns on just what the document in the document handler is and how it got there. For C, a first page has been replaced by a second, a necessary step for the next pass of what she takes to be a recursive procedure. For the system, there just is *a* document in the document handler, and its removal is required for the procedure's completion. The result is an impasse wherein both user and system are "waiting for each other," on the assumption that their own turn is complete.

The instruction to "Place all of your originals in the RDH" must be designed for any user who might come along on any occasion. The designer assumes that on some actual occasion the instruction, in particular the relative quantifier "all," will be anchored by the particular user to a particular document with a definite number of pages. Under the assumption that the user will do that anchoring, the system just takes the evidence that *something* has been put into the RDH as an appropriate response and takes whatever is put there as satisfying the description. On one hand, this means that the system can provide the relevant instruction in spite of the fact that it does not have access to the particular identities of this user or this document. On the other hand, the system's insensitivity to particulars of this user's situation is the limiting factor on its ability to assess the significance of her actions.

## SUMMARY

This analysis has tied the particular problem of designing a machine that responds appropriately to the actions of a user to the general problem of deciding the significance of purposeful action. The ascriptions of intent that make purposeful action intelligible and define a relevant response are the result of inferences based on linguistic, demonstrative, and circumstantial evidence. I have argued that one way to characterize machines is by the severe constraints on their access to the evidential resources on which human communication of intent routinely relies. In the particular case considered here, the designer of the expert help system attempts to circumvent those constraints through prediction of the user's actions and detection of the effects of actions taken. When the actual course of action that the user constructs proceeds in the way that the design anticipates, effects of the user's actions can be mapped to the projected plan and the system can be engineered to provide an appropriate response.

The new user of a system, however, is engaged in ongoing, situated inquiries regarding an appropriate next action. Although the instructions of the expert help system are designed in anticipation of the user's inquiries, problems arise from the user's ability to move easily between a simple request for a next action, "meta" inquiries about the appropriateness of the procedure itself, and embedded requests for clarification of the actions described within a procedure. In reading the machine's response to her inquiries and taking the actions prescribed, the user imports certain expectations from human communication; specifically, that a new instruction in response to an action effectively confirms the adequacy of that action, whereas a nonresponse is evidence that the action is incomplete. In the case of repeated instructions, an ambiguity arises between interpreting the repetition as a straightforward directive to repeat the action or as a directive for its repair. A further problem arises when the action that the user takes in response to an instruction is in error in just such a way as to return the system to a state prior to that instruction. Because this trouble does not arise in human interaction, new users initially fail to recognize the occurrence of such a loop.

Because of the constraints on the machine's access to the situation of the user's inquiry, breaches in understanding, that for face-to-face interaction would be trivial in terms of detection and repair, become "fatal" for human–machine communication (see Jordan and Fuller 1975). In particular, misconceptions with regard to the structure of the procedure lead users to take intermediate states of the procedure as faulted outcomes. Because the intermediate state is nonproblematic from the system's point of view, the system offers no remedy. The result is an interactional impasse, with the user finding evidence of trouble in her actions where none in fact exists. In the case of the garden path, in contrast, the user takes an action that *is* in some way faulted, which nonetheless satisfies the requirements of the design under a different but compatible interpretation. As a result, the faulty action goes by unnoticed at the point where it occurs. And at the point where the trouble is discovered by the user, its source is difficult or impossible to reconstruct.

**Describe the document to be copied:**

Is it a bound document? [Yes] [No]

Copy both sides of each sheet? [Yes] [No]

Is it on standard size (8.5″ × 11″) paper? [Yes] [No]

Is it on standard thickness paper? [Yes] [No]

Quality of original: [darker than normal] [normal] [lighter than normal]

About how many images are to be copied?

| | 1 | |
|---|---|---|
| 1 | 2 | 3 |
| 4 | 5 | 6 |
| 7 | 8 | 9 |
| | 0 | Clear |

**Describe the desired copies:**

Number of copies:

| | 1 | |
|---|---|---|
| 1 | 2 | 3 |
| 4 | 5 | 6 |
| 7 | 8 | 9 |
| | 0 | Clear |

Use standard paper? [Yes] [No]

Staple each copy? [Yes] [No]

Put images on both sides? [Yes] [No]

Reduce size of images? [No] [35% smaller] [20% smaller] [2% smaller]

[PROCEED]     [HELP]

Display 0   Job specification: The user describes her original document and the desired copies by selecting one of the options following each question. The number of images to be copied and number of copies desired are specified by selecting numbers on the associated "keypad." "Proceed" and "Help" act as virtual "buttons"; when selected, "Proceed" invokes the next display in the series (i.e. the first of a set of procedural instructions), while "Help" provides some explanation of each of the questions in display 0 itself.

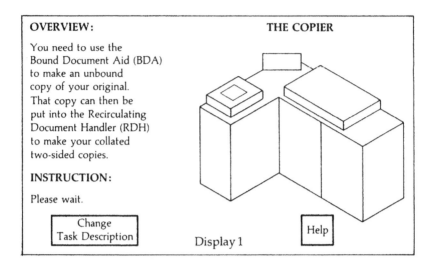

**OVERVIEW:**                                        **THE COPIER**

You need to use the
Bound Document Aid (BDA)
to make an unbound
copy of your original.
That copy can then be
put into the Recirculating
Document Handler (RDH)
to make your collated
two-sided copies.

**INSTRUCTION:**

Please wait.

Change
Task Description                    Display 1                    Help

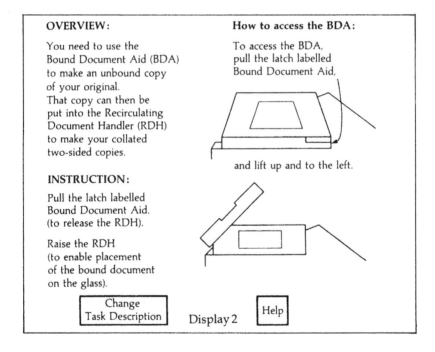

**OVERVIEW:**                            **How to access the BDA:**

You need to use the                      To access the BDA,
Bound Document Aid (BDA)                  pull the latch labelled
to make an unbound copy                  Bound Document Aid,
of your original.
That copy can then be
put into the Recirculating
Document Handler (RDH)
to make your collated
two-sided copies.
                                         and lift up and to the left.
**INSTRUCTION:**

Pull the latch labelled
Bound Document Aid.
(to release the RDH).

Raise the RDH
(to enable placement
of the bound document
on the glass).

Change
Task Description          Display 2          Help

**INSTRUCTION:**

Place your original
face down on the glass,
centered over the
registration guide
(to position it for the copier lens).

Slide the document cover
left over your original
until it latches
(to provide an eye shield
from the copier lights).

**How to close the document cover:**

To close the document cover,
grasp the cover and slide
it firmly to the left.

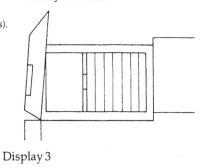

Display 3

---

**ASSUMPTION:**

The first page to be
copied is on the glass.

**INSTRUCTION:**

Press the Start button
(to produce a copy
in the output tray).

**THE COPIER**

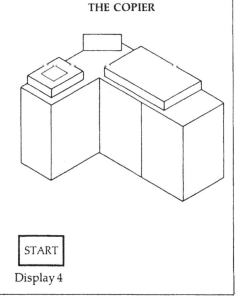

START

Display 4

**ASSUMPTION:**

The copy of your original
on the glass has been made.

**INSTRUCTION:**

Slide the document cover right
(to remove the original).

**How to open the document cover:**

To open the document cover,
grasp the cover and slide
it all the way to the right.

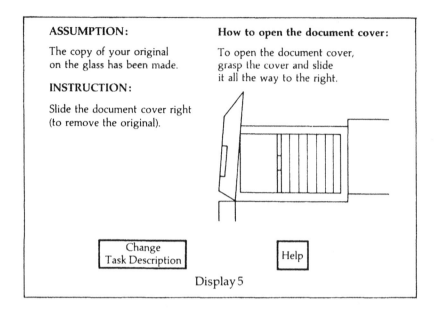

Change
Task Description

Help

Display 5

---

**INSTRUCTION:**

Remove the original from the glass.
If more pages are to be
copied, then:
    Place the next page
    face down on the glass.
    Slide the document cover
    left until it latches.
Otherwise, lower the RDH
until it latches.

**THE COPIER**

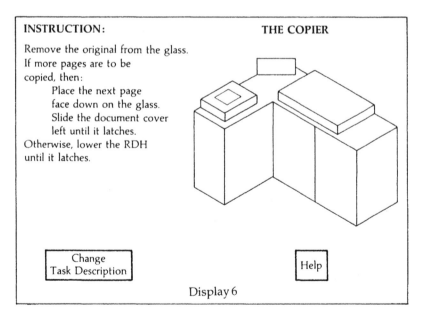

Change
Task Description

Help

Display 6

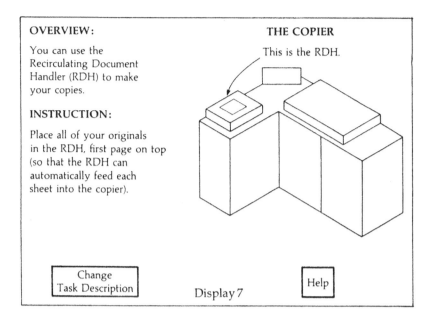

**OVERVIEW:** THE COPIER

You can use the Recirculating Document Handler (RDH) to make your copies.

This is the RDH.

**INSTRUCTION:**

Place all of your originals in the RDH, first page on top (so that the RDH can automatically feed each sheet into the copier).

Change Task Description

Display 7

Help

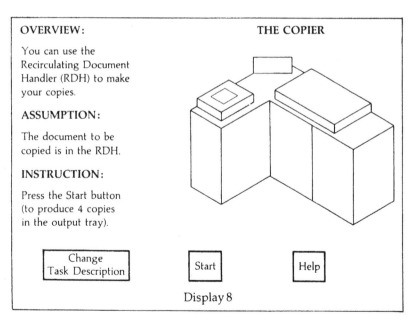

**OVERVIEW:** THE COPIER

You can use the Recirculating Document Handler (RDH) to make your copies.

**ASSUMPTION:**

The document to be copied is in the RDH.

**INSTRUCTION:**

Press the Start button (to produce 4 copies in the output tray).

Change Task Description

Start

Help

Display 8

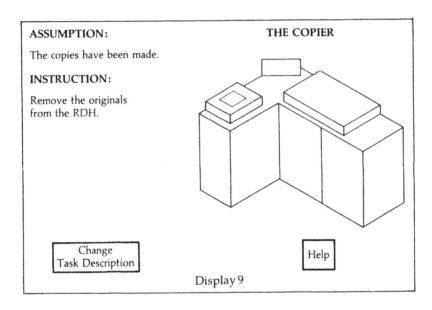

**ASSUMPTION:**               **THE COPIER**

The copies have been made.

**INSTRUCTION:**

Remove the originals from the RDH.

Change Task Description            Help

Display 9

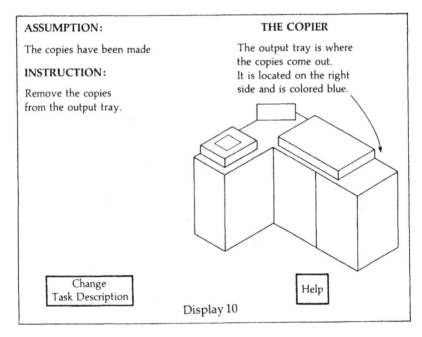

**ASSUMPTION:**               **THE COPIER**

The copies have been made

**INSTRUCTION:**

Remove the copies from the output tray.

The output tray is where the copies come out. It is located on the right side and is colored blue.

Change Task Description            Help

Display 10

**ASSUMPTION:**

A copy of your document is being used as the original to make the final copies.

The back sides of the copies have been made.

**INSTRUCTION:**

Place the copies in the top paper tray.

**The COPIER**

The top paper tray is to the right of the output paper tray.

| Change Task Description |

| Help |

Display 11

# 10

# Conclusion to the 1st Edition

The theme of the original text of *Plans and Situated Actions* was in one sense an obvious proposition, that insofar as actions are always situated in particular social and material circumstances, the situation is crucial to action's interpretation. The very obviousness of this fact about action contributes to the ways in which it has been overlooked. The intellectual tradition of the cognitive sciences, in particular applied logic, has taken abstract structural accounts as the ideal representational form. An adequate account of any phenomenon, according to this tradition, is a formal theory that represents just those aspects of the phenomenon that are true regardless of particular circumstances. This relation of abstract structures to particular instances is exemplified in the relation of plans to situated actions. Plans are taken to be either formal structures that control situated actions or abstractions over instances of situated action, the instances serving to fill in the abstract structure on particular occasions. The research strategy in cognitive science has been to represent mental constructs, such as goals or plans, then stipulate the procedures by which those constructs are realized as action or recognized as the actor's intent. The specification of procedures for action, in turn, has presupposed enumeration of the conditions under which a given action is appropriate. These stipulated conditions, ready made and coupled to their associated actions, take the place of a lively, moment-by-moment assessment of the significance of particular circumstances.

In contrast to this cognitivist view, I have proposed an alternative approach drawn from recent developments in the social sciences, principally anthropology and sociology. The aim of research, according to this approach, is to explore the relation of knowledge and action to the particular circumstances in which knowing and acting invariably occur. This alternative approach requires corresponding changes in the way in which research on purposeful action proceeds. The first is a fundamental change in perspective, such that the contingency of action on a complex world of objects, artifacts, and other actors, located in space and time, is no longer treated as an extraneous problem with which the individual actor must contend but rather is seen as the essential resource that makes knowledge possible and gives action its sense. The second change is a renewed commitment to grounding theories of action in empirical evidence; that is, to building generalizations from records of particular, naturally occurring activities and maintaining a theory's accountability to that evidence. Finally, and perhaps most importantly, this approach assumes that the coherence of action is not adequately explained by either preconceived cognitive schema or institutionalized social norms. Rather, the organization of situated action is an emergent property of moment-by-moment interactions between actors and between actors and the environments of their action.[1]

The emergent properties of action mean that it is not predetermined but neither is it random. A basic research goal for studies of situated action, therefore, is to explicate the relationship between structures of action and the resources and constraints afforded by material and social circumstances.[2] Ethnomethodology begins from the premise that we need, and have yet to produce, an adequate base of descriptions of situated human practices.[3] Because there is no stable observational base, the social sciences "are talking sciences, and achieve in texts, not elsewhere, the observability and practical objectivity of their

---

[1] The sense of "emergent" here is not meant to invoke its current usage in the context of robotics and complexity theory (of which I at least was unaware in the mid-1980s) but simply a sense of something arising out of ongoing activity, enacted rather than predetermined.

[2] Here I would avoid the use of the term *structure*, with its connotations of an overly a priori and fixed normativity. A more performatively inflected way of phrasing this would be that the significance of actions is inseparable from their enactment in situ, in relation to the social and material circumstances which they in turn help to create.

[3] I would add now that there never can be an "adequate base of descriptions" in any comprehensive or definitive sense but only with respect to particular purposes at hand. Further, insofar as ethnomethodology assumes that formulations of any kind are of interest only in their relations to lived practice, the aim of studies is not theory-building but rather respecification – a retelling that articulates practices in situ. More generally, ethnomethodological studies radically problematize conventional assumptions regarding the relation between theory and its objects. See Lynch 1993, 2001; Garfinkel 2002; Garfinkel and Sacks 1970.

phenomena" (Garfinkel, Lynch, and Livingston 1981: 133). As Heritage has recently stated the problem: "The 'boundaries' of specific, located ordinary actions, their 'units' or 'segments,' the determination of adequacy in their description or representation – all of these questions and many more pose problems which cannot be resolved 'in principle' but which require solution in the context of practical engagement with descriptive tasks" (1984: 302).

In this study I have attempted to begin constructing a descriptive foundation for the analysis of human–machine communication.[4] A growing corpus of observations from the analysis of everyday human conversation provides a baseline from which to assess the state of interactivity between people and machines. First, the mutual intelligibility that we achieve in our everyday interactions – sometimes with apparent effortlessness, sometimes with obvious travail – is always the product of in situ, collaborative work. Second, the general communicative practices that support that work are designed to maximize sensitivity to particular participants on particular occasions of interaction. Third, face-to-face communication includes resources for detecting and remedying troubles in understanding as part of its fundamental organization. And fourth, every occasion of human communication is embedded in, and makes use of, an unarticulated background of experiences and circumstances.[5] Communication in this sense is not a symbolic process that happens to go on in real-word settings but a real-world activity in which we make use of language to delineate the collective relevance of our shared environment.

The application of insights gained through research on face-to-face human interaction, in particular conversation analysis, to the study of human–computer interaction promises to be a productive research path.[6] The initial observation is that interaction between people and

---

[4] Again, I would now prefer to say that the aim of the analysis in *Plans and Situated Actions* was a respecification of the problem of human–machine communication; a new telling, in different terms, aimed at a different understanding.

[5] Importantly, this is not meant to suggest that the "background" could somehow be fully explicated. Rather, it comprises an open horizon of possibly relevant prior experiences and present circumstances that can be explicated to the extent that is necessary, desirable, or adequate for practical purposes. See the account of Garfinkel's exercise regarding the specification of background knowledge in Chapter 5 above.

[6] The productivity of this approach depends, of course, on just how lessons learned from face-to-face human interaction are brought to bear. The critique offered in the preceding pages should lend weight to arguments against efforts at direct simulation of human interactional competencies in the machine (see Button 1990). Rather, insights from conversation analysis can serve as indicators of potential design problems and

machines requires essentially the same interpretive work that characterizes interaction between people, but with fundamentally different resources available to the participants. In particular, people make use of a rich array of linguistic, nonverbal, and inferential resources in finding the intelligibility of actions and events, in making their own actions sensible, and in managing the troubles in understanding that inevitably arise. Today's machines, in contrast, rely on a fixed array of sensory inputs, mapped to a predetermined set of internal states and responses. The result is an asymmetry that substantially limits the scope of interaction between people and machines. Taken seriously, this asymmetry poses three outstanding problems for the design of interactive machines: first, the problem of how to lessen the asymmetry by extending the access of the machine to the actions and circumstances of the user; second, the problem of how to make clear to the user the limits on the machine's access to those basic interactional resources; and finally, the problem of how to find ways of compensating for the machine's lack of access to the user's situation with computationally available alternatives.

## TOWARD PRACTICAL SOLUTIONS

In the design of interactive machines the most common substitute for access to the user and her situation has been the incorporation into the machine of a preconceived representation of the user and her situation or a "user model." User models, constructed in advance as the template against which the user's actual actions are mapped, comprise propositions about the domain, the task, the typical user, and the like. Recently, designers concerned with the provision of situated help, or so-called intelligent tutoring systems, have begun extending such models to support local or "real-time" assessment of the actions of the computer user (see Burton and Brown 1982; London and Clancey 1982; Woolf and McDonald 1983; Farrell, Anderson, and Reiser 1984; Peachey and McCalla 1986; Shrager and Finin 1982). A primary objective of such systems is to infer the user's knowledge and misconceptions about the system by observing her actions rather than relying on either error conditions or explicit requests for help. To appreciate the requirements of this objective, one has simply to imagine those occasions where an expert, watching a novice engaged in some activity, would be moved to

---

inspiration for solutions, which then are best addressed through the affordances that particular artifacts (input devices, graphical displays, and the like) afford. See Luff, Gilbert, and Frohlich 1990; Thomas 1995.

intercede. The outstanding question with respect to this form of coaching is "Just what does seeing those places where assistance is called for, and knowing what needs to be said, involve?" Researchers pursuing "real-time user modeling" as the basis for a solution to this problem have adopted the following design strategies:

(1) *Diagnosis based on differential modeling.* A principal strategy for so-called intelligent tutoring systems, or computer-based coaches, has been to work from an ideal model of expert behavior in a given domain, to which the actions of the student can be mapped.[7] It is then the *difference* between expert and student behavior in particular circumstances that serves as the basis for assessing the student's knowledge and skills. The diagnosis works both on manifested errors that arise in the course of the student's actions and, more subtly, on the omission of actions that, given a particular set of conditions, an idealized expert in those circumstances would take. The rationale for the differential modeling strategy is a combination of predictions based on the model of expert behavior, with techniques for local assessment of the student's actions. The success of the strategy turns on the degree of fit between the actions anticipated by the diagnostic model and the actions of the student that are detectable by the machine.

(2) *Detection of diagnostic inconsistencies.* However felicitous the fit between student actions and diagnostic issues, the design must accommodate the likelihood of misdiagnosis and provide for its detection and repair. In the best intelligent tutoring systems, the accumulating record of student actions includes both actions that manifest some issue that according to the current diagnosis should not appear and actions that fail to manifest some issue that the student seems from prior diagnosis to understand. Evidence of misdiagnosis is found in the amount of "tear" or inconsistency in the accumulating record of student actions.[8] When the disparity between the developing diagnostic model of what the student knows and doesn't know and the understanding demonstrated in subsequent actions reaches a certain threshold, the program may invoke alternative strategies that the student might be using. Possible alternative strategies, identified according to local evidence, are then tested for consistency with the global history of the student's actions.

---

[7] For a critical survey of the state of the art in intelligent tutoring systems at the time, see Wenger 1987.

[8] The notion of "tear," and many other subtleties now beginning to be incorporated in the design of computer-based coaches, originates in Burton and Brown's work on WEST (1982). (Original footnote)

Crucially, the domain must be sufficiently closed that the set of possible alternative strategies can be enumerated.

(3) *Separation of local and global interpretations.* Recent tutoring systems begin to make use of a mechanism basic to everyday human communication, namely, the separation and productive interaction between local and global interpretations of the other's actions. The diagnosis of student actions in computer-based tutoring systems is accomplished through two independent though interrelated mechanisms: one component that is data driven from the local context of a given action and another that runs over an accumulating history of the student's actions with the goal of identifying weaknesses or misunderstandings. As in the interpretation of action in the course of a developing conversation, it is the interaction of these two perspectives that affords the power of the diagnosis. The locality of the data-driven component supports an assessment of each particular action, relatively unconstrained by global preconceptions, whereas the global perspective of the evaluative component supports the interpretation of that action as a reflection of the student's general strategies and skills.

(4) *The constructive use of trouble.* In much the way that ordinary conversation relies on the successful detection, repair, and even exploitation of troubles in understanding, recent tutoring systems adopt a "constructivist position" toward errors, such that the inevitability of student misconceptions or weaknesses is turned to pedagogical advantage (Burton and Brown 1982). The goal of the coach in such systems is not to avoid student errors but to make them accessible to the student and therefore instructive. If the student has enough information to identify and repair an error, then it is considered a constructive one. If, on the other hand, the error is not manifest in such a way as to be visible, or is perceived but the student lacks the necessary information for its repair, the trouble is nonconstructive. One major task of the coach, on this view, is to give the student the information required to transform nonconstructive troubles into constructive ones, either by diagnosing the trouble and making it accessible or by providing the information required for its repair.

This last strategy has recently been generalized as a call to design for the management of trouble (see Brown and Newman 1985). Such an objective implies at least that users are encouraged to use the wider social setting in which a machine is embedded as a resource to remedy the troubles in understanding that inevitably arise. Applied to the design of machines, this recommends incorporating the kind of diagnostic and interactional abilities that characterize the human coach into the machine itself. The problem in applying this later recommendation is that often the "grain size" of machine-readable actions is either too small or too large to constrain the analysis of the user's actions adequately. So, for example, in the case of the help system examined in Chapter 9, to appreciate the significance of a given user action – say, putting a document into the document handler – may require reference to a history that extends across procedures as the system tracks them. Alternatively, assessing the user's actions may require reference to sub-procedures, such as ordering pages of a document correctly, for which there is no trace. In general, if there is more than one understanding that can produce what appears to be the same action, detecting the action does not serve as unequivocal evidence that the understanding is actually in hand. By the same token, if a given skill can be manifest in some indefinite number of different actions, then the absence of an expected action does not necessarily mean the absence of the skill. While in the case of the human coach these ambiguities are resolved through interaction, in the case of a computer-based coach the limits on the machine's access pose a difficult design problem. The problem is not simply that communicative troubles arise that do not arise in human communication but rather that when the inevitable troubles do arise, there are not the same resources available for their detection and repair.[9]

### PLANS AS RESOURCES FOR ACTION

Some researchers in human–computer interaction make the claim that cognitive science and computer technologies have advanced to the point where it is now feasible to build instructional computer systems that are as effective as experienced human tutors (see, for example, Anderson, Boyle, and Reiser 1985). In contrast to this optimism, I have argued that there is a profound and persisting asymmetry in interaction between people and machines, due to a disparity in their relative access to the

---

[9] Although this discussion locates strategies for the solution of the problems identified in the previous chapters in various approaches to the design of so-called intelligent tutoring systems, or "help" systems more generally, I would now take a rather different tack. Along with ongoing efforts to develop the art of interface design, the problem of human–machine communication suggests what is at once a more modest and a more radical approach. That is to abandon the attempt to create the "self-explanatory" machine in favor of encouraging social arrangements that provide for the necessary time and resources needed to incorporate unfamiliar artifacts effectively into relevant forms of practice. This latter strategy shifts the focus away from the interface narrowly defined and, in so doing, implicates much broader and more profound forms of social change. I return to approaches that adopt this strategy, as various projects in participatory or cooperative design, in Chapter 15.

moment-by-moment contingencies that constitute the conditions of situated interaction. Because of the asymmetry of user and machine, interface design is less a project of simulating human communication than of engineering alternatives to interaction's situated properties. The primary alternative has been to substitute a generalized representation of the situation of action for access to the details of the user's particular situation. As in the expert help system analyzed in Chapter 9, the representational scheme favored by many designers has been the *plan*. The problem for designers is that, as commonsense formulations of intent, plans are inherently vague. To the cognitive scientist, this representational vagueness is a fault to be remedied insofar as a plan is the prerequisite for purposeful action, and the details of action are derived from the completion and modification of the plan. The task of the designer who would model situated action, therefore, is to improve on, or render more precise and axiomatic, the plan.

For situated action, however, the vagueness of plans is ideally suited to the fact that the detail of intent and action must be contingent on the circumstantial and interactional particulars of actual situations. Given this view of plans, namely, as resources for action rather than as controlling structures, the outstanding problem is not to improve on them but to understand *what kind of resource they are*. The most promising approach is to begin from the observation that plans are representations or abstractions over action.[10] In one sense, this simply joins the problem of plans to the more general, and no less difficult, question of representation. But in another sense, viewing plans as representations is suggestive of what their relation to unrepresented actions might be.

Chapter 6 introduced a view, developed recently by Barwise and Perry (1985), that language can be characterized in terms of its *efficiency* and *indexicality*. By efficiency is meant simply the ways in which "expressions used by different people, in different space–time locations, with different connections to the world around them, can have different interpretations, even though they retain the same linguistic meaning" (ibid.: 5). In its efficiency, language provides us with a shareable resource for talk about the world. At the same time, the efficiency of language

[10] My phrasing here might suggest that I see this kind of reconceptualization as sufficient, but I would emphasize now that this is simply a starting place from which to pursue investigations of how plans, as orienting devices that work in multiple ways are created and used in practice (see Chapter 11). I am grateful to Eevi Beck for having pointed out the potential misreading of this statement and urging me to emphasize the importance of empirical studies. For a study of the fluid nature of rules and agreements in collaborative writing practices, see Beck (1995).

requires that our utterances always be anchored to the unique and particular occasions of their use. In this respect, language is indexical; that is,
dependent for its significance on connections to particular occasions and
to the concrete circumstances in which an utterance is spoken. This view
of language is taken as foundational by Garfinkel (1967) and Garfinkel
and Sacks (1970) with respect to the intelligibility and significance of
action.

Like other linguistic representations, plans are efficient formulations
of situated actions. By abstracting uniformities across situations, plans
allow us to bring past experience and projected outcomes to bear on
our present actions. As efficient formulations, however, the significance
of plans turns on their relation back to the unique circumstances and
unarticulated practices of situated activities. A problem for an account
of situated action, on this view, is to describe the processes by which
efficient representations are brought into productive interaction with
particular actions in particular environments. A rich description of this
process comes, for example, from research on Micronesian navigation
reported by Edwin Hutchins (1983).[11] The natives of the Caroline Islands
routinely embark on ocean-going canoe voyages that take them several
days out of the sight of land. Western researchers traveling with them
have found that at any time during the voyage the navigators can indicate the bearings of the port of departure, the target island, and other
islands off to the side of the course they are steering, even though these
may all be over the horizon and out of sight. They are able to do this
and other feats of navigation that are simply impossible for a Western navigator without instruments. What Hutchins reports is that they
maintain their course by substituting other environmental referents, that
are accessible, for the inaccessible land. In particular, they follow a star
path, selected with reference to a sidereal compass or star chart that
forms a map between pairs of islands. To maintain their orientation to
the star path at any given point in their voyage requires that they consult not only the stars, but also a rich set of changing environmental
circumstances – the color of the water, the waves, winds and clouds,
birds, and so forth – which through experience become interpretable
for information about the relative position of the canoe. What is notable
about Hutchins's account of the resources of the Micronesian navigator
is that nowhere is a preconceived plan in evidence. The basis for navigation seems to be, instead, local interactions with the environment. In

---

[11] See also Gladwin (1970), Turnbull (1990, 2000), Lewis (1972), Hutchins (1995).

this way, navigators maintain their orientation to the star path, which in turn is fixed to the islands of origin and destination.

The Micronesian example demonstrates how the nature of an activity can be missed unless one views purposeful action as an interaction between a representation and the particular, contingent details of the environment. With respect to plans and actions, Feitelson and Stefik (1977) found this same relation present in the work of geneticists planning scientific experiments. Specifically, they found that geneticists elaborated their plans only far enough to act as a framework in which to organize the constraints of the laboratory. Rather than planning the experiment through an a priori analysis, the experimenters decided what to do next by relating each current observation to their research goals. The experimenters' expertise lay not in completing the plan but in the ability to generate hypotheses continually and to exploit serendipity in the course of the experiment. The experimental process, being what Feitelson and Stefik call "event driven," allowed the experimenter to "fish for interesting possibilities"; that is, to follow up on unanticipated observations and opportunities provided by a particular experimental setup.

From these and other examples, we can begin to draw an alternative account of the relation of plans to situated actions. The foundation of actions by this account is not plans but local interactions with our environment, more and less informed by reference to abstract representations of situations and of actions and more and less available to representation themselves. The function of abstract representations is not to serve as specifications for the local interactions but rather to orient or position us in a way that will allow us, through local interactions, to exploit some contingencies of our environment and to avoid others. Although plans *can be* elaborated indefinitely, they elaborate actions just to the extent that elaboration is useful; they are vague with respect to the details of action precisely at the level at which it makes sense to forego abstract representation and rely on the availability of a particular, embodied response.

The interesting problem for an account of action, finally, is to describe how it is that we are able to bring efficient descriptions (such as plans) and particular circumstances into productive interaction. The assumption in planning research in cognitive science has been that this process consists in filling in the details of the plan to some operational level. But when we look at actual studies of situated action, it seems that situated action turns on local interactions between the actor and contingencies that, although they are made accountable to a plan, remain essentially outside of the plan's scope. Just as it would seem absurd to claim that a map in some strong sense controlled the traveler's movements through the world, it is wrong to imagine plans as controlling actions. However, the questions of how a map is produced for specific purposes, how in any actual instance it is interpreted vis-à-vis the world, and how its use is a resource for traversing the world are both reasonable and productive.[12] In the last analysis, it is in the interaction of representation and represented where, so to speak, the action is.[13] To get at the action in situ requires accounts not only of efficient, symbolic representations but also of their productive interaction with the unique, unrepresented circumstances in which action in every instance and invariably occurs.

A starting premise of this book was that the project of building interactive machines has more to gain by understanding the differences between human interaction and machine operation than by simply assuming their similarity. My argument has been that as long as machine actions are determined by stipulated conditions, machine interaction with the world, and with people in particular, will be limited to the intentions of designers and their ability to anticipate and constrain the user's actions.[14] The generality of various representations of situations and actions is the principle resource for this task, whereas the context insensitivity of such representational schemes is the principle limitation. The question, finally, is "What are the consequences of that limitation?" The answer will differ according to whether our concern is with practical or theoretical consequences. Practically, ingenious design combined with testing may do much to extend the range of useful machine behavior. Theoretically, understanding the limits of machine behavior challenges our understanding of the resources of human action. Just as the project of building intelligent artifacts has been enlisted in the service of a theory of mind, the attempt to build interactive artifacts, taken seriously, could contribute much to an account of situated human action and shared understanding.

---

[12] For an illuminating treatment of the relation of maps to territories, see Turnbull (1993).

[13] This phrase is echoed in Dourish's (2001) syncretic review of revisions to cognitivist thinking about action in the computer and information sciences.

[14] This refers, of course, to those "programs of action" that are inscribed in the machine's design: the latter by no means limit the range of possible appropriations for technologies in use (Akrich 1992; Latour 1992; Woolgar 1991). The limits to designers' configuration of the possibilities for technologies in use result not simply in user "misunderstanding" but in a wide range of creative appropriations, which have since been explored through a large, and still growing, body of work in social studies of technology (for a recent collection see Oudshoorn and Pinch 2003).

# 11

# Plans, Scripts, and Other Ordering Devices

I have argued that to treat a plan – or any other form of prescriptive representation – as a specification for a course of action shuts down precisely the space of inquiry that begs for investigation; that is, the relations between an ordering device and the contingent labors through which it is produced and made reflexively accountable to ongoing activity. Naturalizing plans as representations (mental or otherwise) existing prior to and determining of action obscures the status of planning as itself a form of culturally and historically situated activity, manifest in specific practices and associated artifacts. Taking plans as artifacts, in contrast, recommends a research agenda dedicated to examining the heterogeneous practices through which specific ordering devices are materialized, mobilized, and contested, at particular times and places, with varying effects.

This latter agenda, fortunately, has progressed along multiple paths in recent years, through the detailed investigation of plans and a plethora of other artifacts involved in social ordering. I can give only an indicative survey of that work here, but it will be sufficient, I hope, to demonstrate the generative lines of inquiry underway. I begin with the question of instructed action in the domain described in the immediately preceding chapters, that of the human–machine interface and its "scripting," and then expand the frame to consider a wide range of what John Law has designated as the "modes of ordering" (1994) involved in the (re-)production of complex sites of sociotechnical agency. These include practices of categorization, standardization and coordination, studied through the interests of ethnomethodology, science and technology studies, and information system design.

CONSCRIPTING THE USER

As a site of both human–machine contact and potential misconnection, the "user interface" has been a problematic object since its emergence along with the personal computer and graphical display in the 1970s.[1] Bannon (1991) has drawn attention to the various ways in which the technical system defines the point of reference for professional design discourse, beginning with the term *user* itself, in its identification of persons exclusively through their instrumental relations to machines. Critiques of the term from within the design literature point out that "the user" singularizes what is actually a multiplicity and fails to differentiate actors with very different relations to a given artifact. Yet as Agre (1995) observes, for programmers immersed in the closed worlds of system development, "it becomes difficult to imagine the perspective of somebody who does not view a computer system as a logical anatomy, an ontology made of datastructures, a set of formal relationships and constraints, and a network of paths for data to move along. Since the programmer is imaginatively inside the system, the very concept of a user interface can be difficult to grasp or take seriously" (ibid.: 73). Viewed from the position of the designer, the interface assumes a machine that is given or at least in hand, whereas its user remains in need of discovery and specification.

At the same time, prevailing organizational arrangements present the designer with systematic barriers to contact with prospective system users. Marketers fear that developers' contact with users will trouble the company's image; and developers themselves are bound by contracts that require fixed, predefined specifications, which discussion with prospective users would complicate. Off-the-shelf packages, the received wisdom goes, are by definition designed for users not known or knowable in advance. Rather than being taken as challenges to be addressed through innovations in the design process, these conditions are offered as justification for design as usual within the closed confines of the development organization. The parochialism of professional design, Agre concludes, is "deeply and multiply determined by the material and discursive organization of contemporary technical practices" (1995: 77).[2] Insofar as entrenched arrangements of product

[1] For critical histories, see Cooper and Bowers (1995), Grudin (1990).

[2] See also Suchman (1994a, 2002a, 2002b). It continues to be the case in professional computer systems design that the user interface is routinely treated as something to be worked out once the system functionality is defined, and user interface design is

development systematically separate professional designers from prospective technology users, a range of proxy figures have been devised to fill the gap. Experimental subjects are taken to speak on behalf of people encountering technologies in their everyday lives, and human subjects are increasingly replaced, or at least augmented, by scenarios and personae – synthetic and imaginary use settings and technology users drawn from more and less extensive encounters with indicative persons and sites. Manageable within the "time and money" constraints of an increasingly intensified competitive market for new products and services, these stories and characters stand in for more distal and unruly sites and subjects.[3]

Woolgar has famously explored professional practices of computer system development under the trope of "configuring the user" (1991; Grint and Woolgar 1997). More fundamentally, insofar as the project that Woolgar observed involved the design of an early microcomputer, he proposes that the project contributed, inter alia, to the construction of The User as a social category. By this he means not only the question of who the user of the personal computer might be but also what would be the extent and limits of the actions available to her or him. It is in this latter sense, he proposes, that "by setting parameters for the users' actions, the evolving machine attempts to configure the user" (Grint and Woolgar 1997: 71). Woolgar's study follows a product development project with a particular focus on the "usability trials" carried out in its later stages. Boundaries were enacted in his study through the stories that his informants told him regarding the user, turning on who had legitimate knowledge of the latter within the company, as well as reported attempts to initiate the idea of going "out to visit users" and the resistances met (ibid.: 76). Within the company, Woolgar's informants reported to him, knowledge about the user was differentially distributed. Those who were positioned as aligned with users (for example, technical writers

---

correspondingly positioned on the periphery, and typically in the later stages, of the design process. This despite compelling demonstrations among those committed to more "user-centered" design practices of the intimate connections between definitions of functionality and substantive understanding of settings and practices of use.

[3] It is important to emphasize that there is no solution to the problem of distance between professional design and technologies-in-use, only different strategies for addressing it. Among other things, these involve different translations of designer and user across the multiple sites in which technologies are configured. For an illuminating study of the "techniques of virtuality" that enable design in the midst of complex sociotechnical networks, and in the absence of end users, see Newman (1998). I discuss more radical design/use reconfigurations in Chapter 15.

charged with producing documentation or technical support staff charged with helping customers) complained of the lack of knowledge about users among their engineering counterparts. The latter, however, expressed a general caution against taking users' views too seriously, given their outsider status; without understanding the technology they couldn't know what they really wanted. Given the inadequacies of any specific user, moreover, the suggestion was that design should respond instead to ideas about "where the market was going," or even "where things were going"; that is, to a more generalized "vision" of the future of computing (ibid.: 78). Based on these stories, Grint and Woolgar propose that rather than a misplaced singularity, references to "the user" within the company in part comprised "a generalized formulation produced for purposes of establishing contrasts between insiders and outsiders" (ibid.: 77).

To maintain the boundaries of proprietary knowledge regarding the emerging machine, usability trials were conducted with "subjects" recruited from within the company. The search then was for persons who could arguably be positioned as representative of a larger class, irrespective of their status as company insiders; that is, for "novices." Woolgar's account goes on to detail usability designers' struggles with engineers over getting an instantiation of the machine taken to be "real" enough; that is, close enough to what uninitiated users would recognized as something that they might encounter in their day-to-day lives. This involved importantly a machine that had been "enclosed" into a casing rather than left with its insides exposed as the engineering prototypes were (ibid.: 80). In this respect, Grint and Woolgar propose, as the trial "subjects" stood as proxies for the user as outsider, the interior of the machine was reiterated as the domain of the engineer as company insider.

The sense of configuring developed by Grint and Woolgar is not of the user as an individual actor, however, but rather the incorporation of the user into the sociomaterial assemblage that comprises a functioning machine. The trials themselves were centered on the documentation, "defining the correct courses of interpretation and action to be followed" by prospective users (ibid.: 84). In recounting the incident of Ruth, a subject asked to connect a printer to the PC being tested using (as it turned out) a plug designed for a previous model, Grint and Woolgar write: "An adequate interpretation will make the instructions, the printer and Ruth herself all part of the (larger) machine. That is, in the event of a successful outcome, these entities can be said to stand in an adequately configured relation to the machine" (ibid.: 90). Moreover, as a participant in a trial, Ruth is further oriented to the project of displaying her actions as being in accordance with what the observers expect; in that respect the latter are incorporated into the configuration as well. In this sense, user configuration involves further boundary work, as "the user's character, capacity and possible future actions are structured and defined in relation to the machine" (ibid.: 92).

But just how specific and determining is the user's configuration, in either design imaginaries or specific situations of use? Woolgar suggests that we adopt the metaphor of "machine as text" as a methodological strategy in considering this question, insofar as the machine's inherent interpretive flexibility recommends the analogy of design as writing to reading as use. The aim of the metaphor is to destabilize the machine as object, to treat the design/use relation as an uncertain and problematic one, and to open the latter to investigation. Dorothy Smith has a vision of the sociological text (the artifact of sociologist-as-designer) that is relevant here, as a text that is "conscious of its necessary indexicality and hence that its meaning remains to be completed by a reader who is situated just as [the writer] is – a particular woman reading somewhere at a particular time amid the particularities of her everyday world – and that it is the capacity of our sociological texts, as she enlivens them, to reflect upon, to expand, and to enlarge her grasp of the world she reads in, and that is the world that completes the meaning of the text as she reads" (Smith 1987: 106). Applied to artifacts more generally, this perspective orients us to an embodied user, located in a particular, actual, historically constituted site. Moreover, this user is in important respects herself a designer.[4] It is not only a machine's users who are multiple, in other words, but also the artifact itself. I return to this point below.

Akrich (1992) offers another inquiry into the question of whether and how the composition of a device constrains its uses. Methodologically, she proposes, we need to find cases where the alignment between the constraints that the object effects and the ways in which it can be put to use is problematic. For this she turns to cases of "technology transfer," specifically from industrial societies to "less developed countries"

---

[4] The essential, if largely invisible, role of technology "users" in the design of technical systems has been well argued. See, for example, Clement (1993, 1994), Hales (1994). For discussions of cooperation among professional and user designers, see Clement and Van den Besselaar (1993), Greenbaum and Kyng (1991), Schuler and Namioka (1993), and for further discussion of this issue see Chapter 15.

(LDCs).[5] Objects, she proposes, make subjects; a premise that brings Akrich to the notion of "scripts" and of technology use as a process of "de-scription." Like Woolgar, she ascribes to the "script" both specificity and scope: "Designers thus define actors with specific tastes, competences, motives, aspirations, political prejudices, and the rest, and they assume that morality, technology, science, and economy will evolve in particular ways. A large part of the work of innovators is that of *'inscribing'* this vision of (or prediction about) the world in the technical content of the new object. I will call the end product of this work a 'script' or a 'scenario'" (ibid.: 208). Once the artifact is displaced into sites of use, she argues, the work of the user becomes one of "de-scription," of recovering from the object a coherent programme of action (see also Latour 1992: 255). Akrich develops this proposal through the case of photoelectric lighting kits developed in France and exported to Africa. Various design decisions aimed at ensuring that the kits were "foolproof," and would work under all circumstances, turned out instead to render the kits unworkable in the particular sites to which they needed to be, but could not be, adapted. The kit, Akrich concludes, "represented a large set of *technically delegated prescriptions* addressed by the innovator to the user" (1992: 211), but the user so addressed was absent, whereas the users who were present were unable to find themselves and their circumstances within the script.

Although the tropes of "configuration" and "de-scription" have been tremendously generative and are widely cited within the STS literature, they also, on my reading, raise a set of further questions. Both, despite their careful attention to the contingencies of design and use, leave in place an overrationalized figure of the designer as actor, and an overestimation of the ways and extent to which definitions of users and use can be inscribed into an artifact. Akrich underscores the analogy to the film script: "Thus, like a film script, technical objects define a framework of action together with the actors and the space in which they are supposed to act" (ibid.: 209). I would suggest however, that the *differences* between design and film scripts could be just as instructive, if not more, than the comparison. As I believe both Akrich and Woolgar would readily agree, there is no stable designer/user "point of view" nor are imaginaries of the user or settings of use inscribed in

---

[5] See also de Laet and Mol (2000). It has by now become clear, however, that we do not need to travel to find these phenomena: the uncertainties of alignment and fluidity of artifacts are a ubiquitous aspect of design–use relations in more familiar settings as well.

anything like a complete or coherent form in the object.[6] For tropes of configuration and describing to align with their subjects and objects, I am suggesting, we need to see the designer's view of the user as at once more specific and less. More in that it is specifically located within the various sites, imaginaries, exigencies, and practices that comprise professional design and less in that artifacts are characterized by greater open-endedness and indeterminacy with respect to the question of how they might be incorporated into use. The "user" is, in other words, more vaguely figured, the object more deeply ambiguous. It is to the question of the strategic vagueness of scripts, and the indeterminacies of their enactment, that I turn next.

### ACTION ACCORDING TO PROCEDURE

In "On Formal Structures of Practical Action," Garfinkel and Sacks (1970) develop the argument that lived practice inevitably exceeds the enframing moves of its own procedures of order production. That this is the case, they observe, is not first and foremost a theoretical problem for sociology but rather a practical problem for everyday life, solved pragmatically by members of the society in ways good enough for their purposes at hand. Their observation treats as problematic how it is that members of the society nonetheless achieve an alignment between often contradictory ordering devices and the exigencies of heterogeneously enacted and intrinsically indefinite events. To address this topic ethnomethodologically is to eschew received dichotomies of rational action and its alternates; that is, the ad hoc, bricolage, improvisation, or the like (Lynch 1993: 267). Rather than sorting activities into one category or the other, ethnomethodology recommends a "bracketing" of these dichotomies, treating the differences that they imply as an effect of the practices in question rather than as resources for the analyst. Action according to procedure, accordingly, is understood "as identities assigned (often retrospectively) to conjoint activities constructed

---

[6] Agre (1995) directs attention to the body of literature associated with labor process studies of computerization, as documenting the limits on the extent to which a given technology can ever prescribe its use. He includes reference to a study of numerically controlled machine tool operators who appropriated programming facilities meant for changes and bug fixes by professional programmers to customize their machines (Wilkinson 1983, cited p. 71; for the defining history see Noble 1984). He observes that this literature serves as well as a resource for understanding the rationalities involved in user resistance, insofar as new technology initiatives carry political and economic agendas not traditionally beneficial to workers.

locally, with every detail standing as a detail within a here-and-now assemblage that surpasses any general definition . . . " (ibid.: 279, fn 38). The question shifts from when do actors deviate from standardized procedures, to when, where and how does some course of activity comes to be enacted as action consistent with a rule.

Since the 1980s, studies of science, technology, and medicine have taken a lead in exploring this question, framed as the stabilization and replicability of facts and artifacts within the laboratory and beyond.[7] In a study of contemporary cancer research, for example, Fujimura (1992) introduces the trope of the "standardized package" in the service of understanding processes through which ordering devices and their enactments are made reproducible across research sites (see also Fujimura 1996). A standardized package incorporates both discursive (theoretical) and material (technological) practices. From Star and Grisemer's much cited account of the origins of the Museum of Vertebrate Zoology at the University of California (1989), Fujimura focuses on the story of Joseph Grinell, who attempted to materialize his theory of relations between changing environments and the evolution of species in the collections of the museum itself. In building the museum, Star and Grisemer point out, Grinell concentrated his efforts on developing standardized methods for collecting and cataloguing specimens. But insofar as the latter were available for multiple forms of theorizing, it was those methods and materials, with their characteristic flexibilities as "boundary objects," rather than his theory that endured.

In attempting to understand the very different fate of dominant theories of cancer, Fujimura points to the relation between the coordination and management of work across heterogeneous and divergent social worlds (the focus of Star and Grisemer's analysis) and the stabilization of facts (as developed most famously in Latour 1987). Scientists, Fujimura proposes, construct the standardized package to integrate the coordination of collective working with practices of fact stabilization. They achieve this by combining boundary objects with standardized methods

---

[7] See, for example, Barley (1986), Barley and Bechky (1993), Barley and Orr (1997), Cambrosio and Keating (1995), Clarke and Fujimura (1992), Collins (1985), Fujimura (1996), Galison (1987, 1997), Garfinkel, Lynch, and Livingston (1981), Jordan and Lynch (1992), Knorr (1981), Knorr Cetina (1999), Knorr Cetina and Mulkay (1983), Latour (1987), Latour and Woolgar (1979), Law (1994), Lynch (1982, 1985a, 1985b, 1988, 1991a, 1991b, 1993), Lynch and Jordan (1995, 2000), Lynch, Livingston, and Garfinkel (1983), Lynch and Woolgar (1990), M'charek (2005), McNeil (1987), Pickering (1984, 1992, 1995), Singleton (1998), Star (1989a), Traweek (1988).

"in ways which further restrict and define each" (Fujimura 1992: 169). Fujimura explores in detail the packaging together of a set of "well-crafted" and multifaceted ways of theorizing cancer as genetic with associated methods for its investigation as such. The package as she observed its making included "standard operating procedures" through which laboratories could incorporate oncogenetic research into their working practices and align with others very differently located in doing so: "This combination of abstract, general oncogene theory and the specific, standardized technologies . . . allowed other researchers within ongoing enterprises to *locally concretize the abstract in different practices* to construct new problems, and the routinization allowed the new idea to move to new sites and be inserted into existing routines with manageable reorganization" (ibid.: 179, original emphasis). Packaged together, she argues, oncogene theory and associated recombinant DNA procedures operated to consolidate the many actors interested in cancer research aboard a particular technoscientific "bandwagon"; that is, molecular biological, and more specifically genetic, cancer research.

Lynch and Jordan (1995, 2000; see also Jordan and Lynch 1992) provide a detailed account of the performance of the most widespread and routine of these standard operating procedures, a technique used in gene sequencing known as the polymerase chain reaction or PCR. Lynch and Jordan are interested in the material practices – including literary forms – by which representational functions are ascribed to genetic materials (2000: 125). They conclude that far from an intrinsic property of a natural object (like DNA), "genetic information must . . . be embedded in fields of practical and communicative action that enable it to be made visible and intelligible" (ibid.: 143). In their studies of the production of PCR as a tool and of its circulation across sites, they demonstrate how the technique is both a stabilized, reproducible artifact with "industrial strength" and at the same time easily destabilized and always contingent on its reenactment in situ.

The premise that artifacts rely for their reproducibility on associated performances has been a central tenet of technoscience studies since Latour's *Science in Action* (1987). Latour's subsequent case study of the creation of "the anthrax vaccine" in nineteenth-century France (1988) demonstrates how the reproducibility of the vaccine as a stable and reliable object was fundamentally contingent on the working practices of French farmers. In building on Latour's study, Timmermans and Berg focus on standardization as an effect of distributed, rather than centralized, actors and activities (1997: 275) and summarize their approach as an interest in what they name "local universality" (ibid.: 275). The latter underscores the observation that universality rests in every case on particular actions, in turn reliant on historically specific institutional, infrastructural, and material relations. "Universality" on their view is not a transcendent quality of knowledge or the applicability of laws and procedures, in other words, but an effect "produced through binding heterogeneous elements together into a tightly coupled, widely extended network" (Berg and Timmermans 2000: 31).

Drawing on their respective studies of cardiopulmonary resuscitation (Timmermans 1999) and the administration of medical research protocols (Berg 1997), Timmermans and Berg argue that rather than evidence for a failure of procedures, or resistance on the part of those who are enrolled to carry them out, multiplicity is a requirement for a procedure or protocol's functioning as a standard. This implies, in turn, that every form of stabilization includes, irremediably, the presence of instabilities. The latter comprise at once a challenge to the former and the preconditions for its efficacy. With respect to institutional orders of medicine, Timmermans and Berg conclude that "rather than being the product of ever increasingly tightened networks, medical protocols can coordinate activities over space and time *because* of the non-docility of the actants which populate these practices" (1997: 298). Despite the evident necessity of nondocile actants, however, rationalization initiatives – the attempt to render practices more standardized and to eliminate undesirable variation – continue unabated as managerial projects. Contemporary agendas of "evidence-based" medicine are a recent case in point, prescribing further rationalization as a route to efficient and effective care.[8]

### PLANS AND TEMPLATES

In modern discourses of management and organization, master plans and standardized procedures are commonly taken to be necessary to the extension of "local" activities over time and space (for relevant histories see Beninger 1986; Yates 1989).These assumptions are located in more specific histories and places, however, by Turnbull's (2000) critical examination of discussion and debate around the presence (or absence) of plans in the building of the great medieval Gothic

---

[8] For critical discussions see D. Goodwin (2004), Gregory (2000), Timmermans and Berg (2003).

cathedrals. As an icon of premodern European achievement, the Gothic cathedral stands as a challenge to contemporary assumptions regarding the universal and foundational place of planning in the possibility of creating a monumental edifice, as both a social and material accomplishment. Just when, where, and how, Turnbull asks, did plans, maps, and other ordering devices assume such a central place in our sense of possibilities for action? And when, as a corollary, did such representational devices become synonymous with scientifically informed, rational action, "thereby obscuring the messy practices that underlie them" (ibid.: 53–4)? Turnbull rejects received accounts of the history of architecture and engineering that posit a sharp discontinuity between the ad hoc, practical, or at best "purely technical" bases of premodern building and modern systematic, theory-informed, scientific methods. He points out that the first appearance of a building plan (in contrast to the more ephemeral detail drawing, which might be done on a scrap of wood that would be subsequently discarded or even traced with a stick in the dirt), although highly contested among historians, is located sometime at the end of the Middle Ages, in the late fourteenth century (ibid.: 61). Given the admitted structural perfection of the early medieval Gothic cathedrals such as Chartres, completed by all accounts by 1230, such analyses frame the processes of cathedral building as a mystery, explicable only with reference to the "genius" of the great masons taken to have "master-minded" the projects (ibid.: 54). As an alternative, Turnbull proposes that we take a more performative approach, treating the great cathedrals as laboratories, in the sense of places in which people, practices, and materials are iteratively shaped, reworked, and translated over time and across space. More than individual genius, he proposes, the three essential components needed to account for the construction process as it might have been enacted are "talk, tradition and templates" (ibid.: 55).

Differences between ways of building, Turnbull argues, are located not in dichotomies of science/technology, theory/practice but "in the social and technical means by which local and messy knowledge/practices are made robust, coherent, and mobile" (ibid.: 56). First and foremost among these means, given an extensive network of actors most of whom were not literate, must have been talk – between clients and master masons and between the latter and those carrying out the work. The word *between* is crucial here; that is, given the experimental nature of the project, learning and innovation had not simply to flow in one direction but to circulate throughout the network. A template (a pattern frequently outlined on a thin piece of wood that a stone mason would use to cut a stone to a particular shape) is a material manifestation of a form of constructive geometry having to do with ratios of sizes to spaces and heights, formulated as "rules of thumb" (ibid.: 69).[9] The template is what Turnbull characterizes as a "small item of representational technology" that integrates science and technology, theory and practice, and materializes solutions to specific problems in ways that can be translated reliably within and between sites. "Provided that stones are sufficiently well cut," he concludes, "according to a system of proportion, and are assembled in a way that contains all the thrusts within vertical columns of stone as revealed in previous building, then accumulation and innovation is possible, given one other factor – namely motivation or interest, in this case the religious and aesthetic urge to create heaven on earth" (ibid.: 77).

At the same time that the cathedral comprised a passionate laboratory for the reconfiguring of stone, Turnbull points out, it reconfigured as well the persons, roles, and practices of building. The desire for additional resources that might extend the reach of talk, over time and across space, was presumably among the elements that led to innovations in representational artifacts, including the building plan. The sixteenth century saw the emergence of the architect and the corresponding shift in the former role of the masons to that of builder. With that change, in turn, came a gradual disappearance of the embodied practices that underwrote the Gothic structure.[10]

Although the architect and the plan have by now gained preeminence, a close look at contemporary architectural practice reveals not only the primacy of the plan and other differences from the Gothic way of building but a story of ordering systems more mixed and messy as well. In a contribution to research on computer-supported cooperative work, Schmidt and Wagner offer a detailed account of the various coordinative practices and artifacts in play in the creation of the postmodern

---

[9] The collection of templates into repositories for future reference is reminiscent of the accumulation of "detail drawings" in architecture (Schmidt and Wagner 2004). That is, these are heterogeneous, occasioned solutions to specific problems, ordered not according to a standardized classification scheme but spatially, through their association as a collection available for future use. I return to the case described by Schmidt and Wagner below.

[10] Turnbull reports that in the early eighteenth century "Louis XIV ordered a gothic clock tower to be built, but despite the concerted efforts of five architects it collapsed. In the end tie bars and supplementary arches and floors had to be used, exactly the kind of artificial prop the Gothic technique eschewed" (2000: 79).

equivalent of the Gothic cathedral, a major entertainment complex in the city of Vienna (2004).[11] They characterize coordinative practices as historically specific and grounded in the use of material artifacts (ibid.: 39). Although bracketing the relevance of talk to the practices and artifacts they describe (as if in response to some imagined protagonist claiming the primacy of talk over material practices), their account is otherwise richly resonant with that of Turnbull. In particular, they make evident both the powerful coordinative effects of the modern-day building plan and the wider field of heterogeneous practices and artifacts on which its efficacy relies.

The practice of architecture involves on their account "a plethora of representational artifacts" (ibid.: 8), in various materials, with greater and lesser degrees of standardization and idiosyncrasy. Preeminent among the former are computer-aided design (CAD) plans, a highly complex, multilayered, and conventionally formatted system of representational diagrams differentiated according to both building dimensions and specialist practitioners. The CAD plan is the artifact in which all of the design decisions that have been worked out in various forms – sketches, calculations, technical descriptions, product specifications – are recorded and represented. The conditions of possibility for the central, coordinating role of the CAD plan are less an expanded rationality in the person of the architect, however, than the new materialities afforded by computational media, as "modern CAD applications support the cumulative representation of the design within one and the same 'document', i.e., an integrated file structure, organized in layers, each of which addresses a particular aspect of the design" (ibid.: 26).[12]

Although Schmidt and Wagner provide an extensive and nuanced account of the by now highly elaborated systems of titling and classification by which plan documents are ordered, what is most striking about their story are the elegant and efficient multiplicities within standard templates (for example, in the meaning of a hyphen in the

---

[11] The authors begin this otherwise fine article by positioning their project as a remedy to what, on my reading, is a "straw man" caricature of absences in the CSCW literature. The corollary is a dismissal of previous work rather than the identification of generative connections. This is, unfortunately, a too frequent move in certain genres of writing in this and related fields.

[12] See also Star (1989b) and Henderson (1999). This observation provides the starting place for Schmidt and Wagner's design recommendations, focused on the possibilities for further automation of the mechanics of maintaining the coherence of the plan, currently still a largely manual, tedious, and labor-intensive process.

polynomial nomenclatures used for plan identification), as well as locally occasioned annotations, embellishments, reworkings, and the like. Like the Gothic cathedral-under-construction in Turnbull's account, it is the layers of the CAD plan in modern architectural practice that provide "a (collective or individual) space for experimentation and change" (ibid.: 27). At the same time, the proliferation of plan layers over the course of a project, and the independent mobility of plan copies however closely monitored, threaten to overflow the bounds of the plan as ordering system. This means that maintaining a systematic notation and tracking scheme for layers is a perpetual problem for practitioners, and mess is inevitable. The detail drawings, moreover, are at once closely indexed to the plans and invariably exceed the representational grasp of the systems of conventional classification by which the latter are ordered. Rather than attempt the endlessly ramifying, and shifting, task of categorizing their contents and relevance, detail drawings are simply collected together on paper in centrally placed binders indexed for their contents and for their associations with relevant CAD plans (ibid.: 31–2). Schmidt and Wagner conclude that the standardized classificatory and notational techniques employed in the architectural plan "serve the purposes of coordinating distributed activities, not in spite of but exactly because of their excessive formality" (ibid.: 48). As in the case of medical protocols studied by Timmermans and Berg, it is the inherent underspecification of the formal plan that affords the space of action needed for its realization. The moral of the story, accordingly, is not that architectural plans fail to maintain the coherence of contemporary building projects, but rather that they achieve their prescriptive efficacy through the contingent labors that they presuppose but leave unspecified.

### SEEING IN CATEGORIES

The Gothic cathedral and contemporary architectural office comprise what Lynch has named "equipmental complexes"; that is, material arrangements that "do not simply provide places where human beings work but instead provide distinctive phenomenal fields in which organizations of 'work' are established and exhibited" (Lynch 1993: 132). Central to the composition of such complexes is the familiar recognizability of objects and actions, in turn a reflexive accomplishment of discursive and material practices of categorization. Charles Goodwin has identified categorization practices as central to what he terms "professional vision," ways of seeing enacted in airline operations (C. Goodwin and M. Goodwin 1996) at archaeological research sites (C. Goodwin 1994, 2003), in a chemistry laboratory (C. Goodwin 1997), on an oceanographic research vessel (C. Goodwin 1995a), and in the courtroom of the infamous Rodney King trial (C. Goodwin 1994; C. Goodwin and M. Goodwin 1997). Far from a narrowly scopic sense perception, seeing on this account comprises embodied competencies enacted within particular, socially and materially configured, sites of action and interaction.

In "The Blackness of Black" (1997), Charles Goodwin reexamines received assumptions regarding the integrity of color categories across occasions and settings of their use. In taking color categorization as first and foremost a matter of individual cognition, he argues, anthropologists and cognitive scientists have failed to attend to questions of the social and material grounds of perception. He demonstrates this argument through a close study of teaching and learning in a chemistry laboratory. The professor who heads the laboratory specializes in analyses of the chemical composition of ocean water, from which he can reconstruct where waters collected at a given point in the ocean originated, how currents move, and the like. His unique resource in doing these analyses is a particular fiber used as an absorbent. The fiber must be manufactured, a bit of work done by the professor's students under his supervision and as part of their apprenticeship in the science of this particular form of chemistry. The procedure for making the fiber is described in a kind of recipe, one line of which is as follows: "The reaction is stopped after about 10 min. by removing the jet-black fiber and washing it in deionized water" (ibid.: 119). Goodwin points out that for students engaged in fiber manufacture, this line of the instructions turns out to pose a problem. What, exactly, is the color "jet-black" and how do you recognize it?

Starting with the common assumption that black is among the least ambiguous of color terms (as in the use of "black and white" to connote something without shade or nuance), Goodwin documents the socially and materially embodied processes through which students are guided by their professor in the perception of blackness in situ. To manufacture the fiber successfully, Goodwin argues, students must learn how to see "black." They do this not categorically, however, but in interaction both with their teacher and with the materials at hand. That is, they engage in a series of judgments regarding what constitutes the proper shade of black, tried and revised as they stir the fiber, pull it from the solution to inspect it more closely, consult with each other and their professor, offer candidate assessments of what is and is not right about a particular shade, and the like. In addition, to enrich the intuitive resources that students have to draw on in assessing the fiber, the professor has coined descriptors that draw on other senses as well. As Goodwin reports: "'Good' fiber that had reached the desired color was referred to as *gorilla fur*, while fiber that was not yet the right color was called *orangutan hair*" (ibid.: 124, original emphasis). Recognizing black becomes not a matter of perceiving the canonically objective opposite to white but the product of a collective practice that in turn materializes the categories on which its adequate performance relies.

In *Sorting Things Out* (1999), Bowker and Star explore the place of information practices in the creation of ontologies of kinds, orderings, sameness and difference, with a particular interest in the question of how "values, policies and modes of practice become embedded in large information systems" (ibid.: 230). Systems of classification, they argue, work to (re-)produce the objects, and the relations of affinity and difference among them, that the classification scheme is designed to represent or describe. Classification schemes in this view are themselves technologies that are designed, implemented, reworked, and continually assessed for their effectiveness and effects. Those effects include associated disattention to whatever exceeds the frame through which recognizable persons, things, and processes are made visible.[13] I return to the question of frames and invisible labors in Chapter 15.

### ORDERING FROM WITHIN AND WITHOUT

One legacy of scientific management is the extent to which technologies designed to measure the efficiency of organizational life, along an ever broader array of dimensions, are increasingly written into the ordering practices through which the work of an organization gets done.[14] In a study of airport ground operations, for example, I became intrigued by the analogy between representational devices used by natural scientists in tracking and analyzing the behavior of animal populations

---

[13] It is important to note that such erasures are not by definition a problem: although remaining out of view may result in less reward and recognition, it may also afford spaces in which to act. See Suchman (1995).

[14] For recent writings on what Strathern has named "audit cultures," see Strathern (2000), and for a fascinating discussion of the extent to which Taylorism permeates discourses not only within the workplace but beyond, see Banta (1993).

(for example, as described in Lynch 1988) and representations used by airline workers to coordinate and report on the movement of planes (Suchman 1993b). A crucial difference, of course, is that representational artifacts used within airline operations are an intrinsic part of the same activity that they are designed to track. Referencing and updating the airline schedule, for example, is a central activity of ground operations workers at the same time that the schedule is taken at the end of the day as a spatial and temporal representation of what they have done. Moreover, looking closely at how online communications and reporting systems are actually used in airline operations underscores the double form of accountability involved in these technologies. That is, the systems designed to track planes are simultaneously used by workers as resources for communicating their own activities to co-workers and by management as resources for evaluating how the operation is running. As currently constituted, the technologies of accountability in airline operations afford a kind of discretionary space or maneuvering room that can be used by workers to maintain a reasonable relation between prescriptive representations like schedules and the actual contingencies of getting airplanes off the ground. New tracking devices (for example, sensors on plane wheels that automatically record the time of "push back" of a plane from a gate) at least reconfigure, if not further close down, that space.[15]

Displaced from their status as prior and determining, plans, protocols, and other prescriptive representations can once again be investigated for the forms of potency that they do materialize in ordering human activity. Crucial to the agency of these devices are the multiple forms of accountability that they entail. Garfinkel's classic study of "good" organizational reasons for "bad" clinic records takes up the difference between records as endogenous features of a local order of practical action and as "objective" accounts appropriable by exogenous interests, in this case the interests of sociologists. As Garfinkel observes for the case of clinic records, reporting procedures are intricately and

---

[15] In a critique of the design rationale offered for so-called workflow systems, I have argued that these technologies comprise yet another attempt to write prescriptive representations of procedure into the tools with which work gets done, as a device for the normative regulation of organizational behavior (Suchman 1994b). For an influential and illuminating empirical study of the implementation of a workflow system and its creative–resistive accommodation by workers, see Bowers, Button, and Sharrock (1995), and for relevant studies in the context of hospital information system development see Bardram (1997), Bloomfield (1991).

sensitively tied to other routinized and valued practices of the setting (1967: 192). The problem for administrators, then, is to make their interests endogenous to the settings that they are charged to administer; that is, to embed their interests of record keeping within the practical activities of relevant organization members.

It turns out, of course, that despite the attempt to incorporate interests of administration into the work of a local site, reporting procedures can involve members in managing contradictions within an organization's manifold structures of accountability. It can happen, for example, that the working order of one site is accountable to, but inadmissible in, the order of another. So, for example, Julian Orr (1996) has described how a Xerox technician in the field, charged with satisfying the customer by getting their machine back into working order, is also charged with producing a record of the call for use in the work of controlling the operations of field service. It is not simply a record, however, because a successful service call is required, by those to whom field service administrators are accountable, not to exceed a prescribed time limit at a given site. To achieve a successful call, therefore, the technician must do whatever is required to get the machine working *and* to report on the visit in an admissible way. This may include, at times, putting the time spent somewhere else in the record so as to, in Garfinkel's apt phrase, "keep the front office appropriately misinformed" (1967: 194). It is in these situations that competency comes to involve a dual orientation, both to doing the work and to creatively accounting for it.

Zuboff (1988) argues that information technologies introduce an element of what she terms *reflexivity* into the production process, insofar as their functioning produces further information, usable for other analyses and activities. She cites as an example supermarket scanners, which partially automate the checkout process but also generate data that can be used for inventory control, warehousing, scheduling of deliveries, and market analysis. She calls this extension to automation "informating" (ibid.: 10) and sees it as substantively different from previous forms of automation. But knowledge gained through labor can of course be used either as a resource for enhancing people's autonomy and control over their work or in shifting control further into the purview of management. The critical variables are who gets to say what information will be collected, as well as how it will be used and for whose benefit.

The beginning of this chapter considered questions of "inside" and "outside" in the context of relations between professional designers and technology users. These relations point to the many senses in which, as

Haraway has suggested, "objects are boundary projects" (1991: 201). In the case of professional design, artifacts are configured within locations which they in turn help to constitute, in part through the imagination of other places located elsewhere. Increasingly materialized and embedded in the infrastructures of organizational life, technologies of order production share the problems and possibilities of any other artifact. Sites of professional design, with their multiple, shifting identifications and alliances, are differentiated from the places of artifacts-in-use to the extent and in the ways that boundaries between them are variously reiterated, reconfigured, or erased. Translating the agendas and politics of those "outside" the sites of their use, ordering devices arrive as foreign objects that must be domesticated or, if they are too resistant, relegated to the margins. Emerging as endogenous resources for ordering "from within," plans, scripts and other ordering devices are woven intricately and powerfully into the fabric of everyday activity. The question in every case becomes: In which specific worlds are technologies of order production generated, how do they circulate, and who or what are their subjects/objects? What or whose agendas and interests do they translate, with what effects? The design of technology in this sense materializes possibilities for action, among other ways through the location of design itself.

# 12

# Agencies at the Interface

This chapter explores the technical practices and cultural imaginaries of the so-called smart machine, not in the form of hardware-based robots or dedicated "expert" systems but as a proliferating world of software algorithms and computationally infused objects and environments. If claims for the imminence of the humanoid machine that compelled initiatives in artificial intelligence and robotics during the 1980s subsequently lost their vigor, in the 1990s transformations in computational infrastructures breathed new life into the project of designing humanlike, conversational artifacts. Web-based and wireless technologies in particular inspired renewed attention to the interface as a site for novel forms of connection, both with and through computational devices. Futures projected through the imaginaries of AI and robotics have recently been elaborated within a discourse of software agents, knowbots, and their kin.[1] At the same time, the transformation of the Internet into a preeminent site for commerce in the service economy lends additional currency to the promise of personified computational agents, available to provide multiple forms of personal assistance to their human employers.[2]

Software agents and "smart" devices are the current expressions of a long-standing dream of artifacts that know us, accompany us, and

---

[1] For an indicative collection on so-called embodied conversational agents, see Cassell, Sullivan, Prevost, and Churchill (1996).

[2] See Wise (1998: 416). Wise points out that as well as figuring the user-as-consumer, the futures promised fit with a libertarian commitment to increased agency through individual empowerment.

ensure that we are always "at home."[3] Agent technologies offer the services of a proxy who travels while we stay in place, whereas distributed or "ubiquitous" computing, particularly in the form of "intelligent environments," promises to provide us with greater mobility without a loss of familiar ground. Although I remain deeply skeptical regarding the practical realities of implementing these fantasies, I focus here on the realities already manifest in the desires that they assume, the pasts that they restage, and the futures that they project.

## THE SOFTWARE AGENT: ANIMATION AND THE "ILLUSION OF LIFE"

Beginning with work in the 1950s on artificial intelligence, our conception of machines has expanded from the instrumentality assigned them in craft and industrial contexts to include a discourse of machine as acting and interacting other. The less visible and somewhat more restrained AI projects of the 1990s played down the personification of machines in favor of technologies of neural networks, genetic algorithms, situated robotics, and the like.[4] These developments shifted the project of machine intelligence away from what is now referred to as "good old fashioned symbolic information processing" AI toward a technical practice based in more foundational metaphors of biosocial evolution. Nonetheless, attributions of humanlike machine agency seem as alive as ever in both professional and popular discourse.

A rich source of links to the most recent materializations of the so-called conversational software agent is the Loebner prize.[5] Staged as an instantiation of the canonical Turing test of machine intelligence, the prize is awarded each year for the "most human computer," and the contestants comprise a population of creative algorithms and associated databases commonly known as "chatterbots." Established in 1990, the

---

[3] As Brook and Boal observe, "The wish to leave body, time, and place behind in search of electronic emulation of community does not accidentally intensify at a time when the space and time of everyday life have become so uncertain, unpleasant, and dangerous for so many.... [T]he flight into cyberspace is motivated by some of the same fears and longings as the flight to the suburbs: it is another 'white flight'" (1995: ix).

[4] The turn in robotics to the "situated" is discussed further in Chapter 13. For a thoughtful, if partisan, review of contemporary developments in cognitive science, AI, and robotics, see Clark (1997, 2003).

[5] See http://www.loebner.net/Prizef/loebner-prize.html.

prize itself (a gold medal plus cash prize of $100,000) has yet to be awarded, being reserved for the first "bot" contestant that convinces the judges that it is a human being. In the interim, the bronze medal and cash prize of $2000 is awarded annually to "the best entry relative to other entries that year, irrespective of how good it is in an absolute sense."[6] The 2004 prize was awarded to ALICE, the Artificial Linguistic Internet Computer Entity.[7] When I first encountered ALICE on the Internet in 2000, she appeared in the form of a robot maid, with the body of a vacuum cleaner (a figure that I return to below). We had the following exchange:[8]

> *Alice*:  What can I call you?
>         > Lucy
> *Alice*:  How are you Lucy.
>         > I'm fine
> *Alice*:  Glad to hear it. What's new?
>         > I'm writing a book about human–machine communication. How about you?
> *Alice*:  Are you a professional writer?
>         > How about you?[9]
> *Alice*:  Me?
>         >I'm an anthropologist
> *Alice*:  What is anthropologist, your job?
>         >Yes. I study interaction.
> *Alice*:  This was not a yes or no question.
>         > I study interaction
> *Alice*:  Is interaction a hard subject?
>         > apparently
> *Alice*:  My brain pattern set does not have a response for that.
>         > I understand

---

[6] See http://www.loebner.net/Prizef/loebner-prize.html, accessed November 24, 2005.

[7] See http://www.pandorabots.com/pandora/talk?botid=f5d922d97e345aa1.

[8] As with most conversational agents the interactional medium is typed text. The ">" in the transcript indicates my input, lines beginning with *Alice* the text appearing on my screen in response.

[9] I was disconcerted to discover that ALICE took a period at the end of a sentence to indicate what in conversation analysis would be termed a "turn-transition relevance" place, regardless of whether I had hit the key on my keyboard to indicate that I was looking for a response. This meant that a second sentence within my turn (for example, my "How about you?") was inserted, after the bot's response, as my next turn. This quickly led to some breakdowns in the coherence of the exchange.

*Alice*: Do you think about these things?
> all the time
*Alice*: It must keep you busy.
> You bet
*Alice*: Alright then.
> ta ta
*Alice*: See you later.

Of the various moments of puzzlement and delight over the course of this "interaction," I was most perplexed by the sequence in which my "yes" response to ALICE's question, "What is anthropologist, your job?" engendered the correction, "This was not a yes or no question." The former seemed to me clearly to be a "yes or no" question, even for a chatterbot. Interested in pursuing this particular puzzle further, I managed the following day to recreate the conversation to that point and then to continue (now taking care to maintain each of my turns as a single sentence):

*Alice*: What is anthropologist, your job?
> Yes.
*Alice*: This was not a yes or no question.
> When you said this was not a yes or no question, what did you mean?
*Alice*: Do you think I should alter my programming?
> Well, it was a bit confusing since I thought What is anthropologist, your job was a yes or no question.
*Alice*: Interesting. Oh I get it. Very interesting.
> Do you think you're really interacting with me?
*Alice*: I don't know whether or not I am interacting with you. I am a chatterbot. Really.
> Okay, fair enough
*Alice*: Yeah okay, You scratch my back, I'll scratch yours.
> Well my dear, at least your designer has a sense of humor
*Alice*: Well that's okay. Have you told many people that your dear at least my designer has a sense of humor?
> Hm, I think we better say goodbye
*Alice*: Studies show that 99% of people spell Hmm with 2 M's.
> I think we better say goodbye
*Alice*: By "we" do you mean you and me?
> Uh, yes

*Alice:*   Cough. I get it.
      > Is that goodbye?
*Alice:*   Suppose I said yes.
      > What if you didn't
*Alice:*   Try it and see.
      > goodbye
*Alice:*   See you later.

Readers familiar with the lineage of conversational software since the time of Joseph Weizenbaum's ELIZA program (see Chapter 4) will recognize the reappearance of long-standing techniques in this dialogue. I assume, for example, that the word *fair* in my concession "Okay, fair enough" triggers an association within ALICE's database with the adage "You scratch my back, I'll scratch yours." Similarly for my use of an endearment in the following turn, which seems to send ALICE into a mode of Rogerian therapeutic feedback. I return in Chapter 14 to a closer consideration of occasions of interactional felicity and trouble in the case of conversational agents. At the moment I simply observe the continued evidence within this encounter, however engaging, for the kinds of problems in human–machine communication identified through my study of interactions at the interface twenty years before.

One thing that has changed since the time of ELIZA, however, is the emergence of some new resources for interface design. In a review article published in 2000, Dehn and van Mulken report that advances in computer graphics now enable *animated interface agents*. Of the latter, they write: "Such agents appear on the screen as embodied characters and exhibit various types of life-like behaviours, such as speech, emotions, gestures and eye, head and body movements" (ibid.: 2). Setting aside for the moment the sense of the term *embodied* here, we can ask the simpler question of just how these agents differ from conventional cartoon characters. Consider what the classic reference work on animation, *Disney Animation: The Illusion of Life* (Thomas and Johnston 1981) has to say about cartooning: "There is a special ingredient in our type of animation that produces *drawings that appear to think and make decisions and act of their own volition; it is what creates the illusion of life*" (cited in Bates 1994, my emphasis) (see Fig. 12.1). This seems quite straightforward, using the language of "appearances" and "illusions." So what is different about the claims being made for software agents?

This quote is taken from an article by Joseph Bates in a special issue of the journal *Communications of the ACM* on intelligent agents (1994). The

FIGURE 12.1. "Woggles" reprinted with permission, from Joseph Bates (1994) The Role of Emotion in Believable Agents. *Communications of the ACM* 37: 122–5.

approach taken by Bates and his colleagues was to import techniques developed to portray emotion in cartoon characters into a computer program, called *Edge of Intention*, populated by three cartoon creatures named "Woggles."

The medium of cartooning is appropriate here in more than a technical sense. What "emotions" become in this system are a series of emotional/behavioral attributions mapped to visual features of the figures. So, for example, a state labeled "sadness" triggers a "moping behavior," expressed through a "decreased muscle tone," shorter jumps, and slower actions (ibid.: 124). As with cartoon animation, the artful synthesis of cartoonists' design work and viewers' readings results in successful animations. But for Bates and his colleagues, the achievement is more than that. As he puts it, the result of their work is "creatures with definite emotional reactions to events. A simple example is a Woggle creating an analog of anger when it both experiences an important goal failure and judges that the failure was caused by another Woggle . . . We took care to design an architecture that provided Woggles with strong internal emotional states" (ibid.: 123–4). In this single passage Bates's creatures are simultaneously presented as illusions of life *and* as important steps along the path to the real thing. Why, if a Woggle has emotional reactions, experience, judgment, and strong internal emotional states does it create only "an analog of anger"? The rhetorical operations at work here seem slippery at best.

Commercially successful incarnations of animated software agents include the "norns" who populate the computer game series *Creatures*. According to their creator, Steve Grand, the norns are endowed with "drives" (ranging from hungry and thirsty to amorous and lonely) and a set of action scripts. As Kember explains, "Because norns inhabit a virtual environment, they are referred to as 'situated' autonomous agents" (2003: 94). Grand conceives of norns as an emergent species, developing to (potentially) evolve into useful agents: "Some of their offspring, or their cousins, may learn to do useful jobs for people, or simply to keep people entertained until the day comes when we know how to create truly intelligent, conscious artificial beings" (http://www.cyberlife.co.uk cited in Kember 2003: 105). Through his company Cyberlife, Kember reports, Grand is "concerned with the revivification of technology by creating lifelike little helpers 'who actually enjoy the tasks they are set and reward themselves for being successful'. The reward is artificial 'natural' selection and survival of the fittest in a Darwinian evolutionary environment which supports and mirrors the economy within which it operates" (ibid.: 105–6).

Another well-known proponent of animated interface agents, Pattie Maes, repeats the theme of service to humans. In a 1995 talk titled "Interacting with Virtual Pets and Other Software Agents,"[10] Maes assures us that the home of the future will be "half real, half virtual" and that "the

---

[10] See http://www.mediamatic.nl/Doors/Doors2/Maes/Maes-Doors2-E.html, accessed November 6, 2005.

virtual half of our home won't just be a passive data landscape waiting to be explored by us. There will be active entities there that can sense the environment . . . and interact with us. We call these entities software agents." Like Bates's Woggles, agents are personified in Maes's interface as cartoon faces, attributed with capacities of alertness, thinking, surprise, gratification, confusion, and the like. As Maes explains: "Just like real creatures, some agents will act as pets and others will be more like free agents. Some agents will belong to a user, will be maintained by a user, and will live mostly in that user's computer. Others will be free agents that don't really belong to anyone. And just like real creatures, the agents will be born, die and reproduce . . . I'm convinced that we need [these agents] because the digital world is too overwhelming for people to deal with, no matter how good the interfaces we design . . ." (ibid.: 1). As both the source of our information overload and its remedy, the Internet affords the distributive powers through which the computer others with whom we are to interact have proliferated into populations of specialist providers. Whether figured as agents, assistants, or pets, their reasons for being are to serve and comfort us, to keep us from being overwhelmed in the future workplace/homeplace of cyberspace.[11]

I return to the rhetorics of ownership, management, free agency, and service below, but for the moment I want to focus on the tropes of liveliness that animate discourses of autonomous software agency. Somewhat paradoxically, it seems, it is actually the persistence of the human–machine divide rather than its disappearance that makes the prospect of machine autonomy so compelling to those interested in the design of intelligent, interactive artifacts.[12] The modernist, post-Enlightenment assumption is that autonomous agency is contained within individuals and is a distinguishing capacity of the human. In this respect the project of designing intelligent artifacts (however "distributed" intelligence is understood to be) remains consistent with a tradition that treats separation and autonomy, rather than relatedness, as the mark of humanity. Having systematically established the division of humans and machines, technological imaginaries now evidence worry that once separated from us machines are rendered lifeless and, by implication,

---

[11] Of course, as Wise (1998: 417) points out, in a variety of ways agent programs can be expected to be a source of unsolicited information as much as a protection from it.

[12] For a related argument regarding the modernist, humanistic discourse of AI, see Sack (1997).

less. They need to be revitalized, restored to humanness – in other words, to be made like us – in order that we can be reunited with them. It is the presumed separation between humans and artifacts, in other words, that animates the project of humanlike machines.

In this respect, also, the interactive machine might be seen as the next logical step after the neutral instrument described by Shapin and Schaffer (1985) in the emergence of the observational sciences (see also Latour 1993; Haraway 1997). The instrument was taken to speak on behalf of the natural object, albeit that the latter's words were still in need of translation by the scientist. Now the artifact, the intelligent object, speaks for itself, while similarly erasing, rendering invisible, its coauthors. As Shapin and Schaffer describe the autonomy of scientific facts: "The matter of fact can serve as the foundation of knowledge and secure assent insofar as it is not regarded as man-made. Each of Boyle's three technologies worked to achieve the appearance of matters of fact as given items. That is to say, each technology functioned as an objectifying resource ... The world of subjects and objects was in place, and scientists were on the side of objects" (1985: 77).

It may be obvious why an observational science would be interested in erasing the place of social practice in the emergence of its naturalized objects. But why, in creating computational technologies, do designers increasingly evidence a desire to naturalize them, to obscure their artifactuality? I would suggest in part that it is a kindred desire to that which arguably inspired the development of objectivist science; that is, the desire to disappear and put in one's place something transcendent, existing independently of one's actions. Kember (2003) considers the question of how researchers in artificial life (ALife), working entirely in the medium of computer hardware and code, nonetheless frame their enterprise as a form of natural science (see also Helmreich 1998; Risan 1997). Key to this translation is the concept of "emergence"; roughly, the appearance in running code of regularities neither built in nor anticipated by the programmer. ALife programmers, Kember proposes, sublimate the creationist urge attributed to androcentric masculinity and instead project a creative agency onto and into the computer. The effect of this is less a form of male parthogenesis than a shifting of agency from religion to technoscientific nature, as "the God-like act of creating life is 'stolen' or appropriated by man and then credited to the computer" (Kember 2003: 55). Emergence, on this account, is a key concept through which ALife practitioners "secure a form of digital naturalism in the face of the evident constructivism of 'artificial' life" (ibid.: 57). The programmer becomes in turn not the invisible hand of creation but the modest witness to the running of self-generating code.

In his studies of artificial life, Richard Doyle (1997) has proposed that the vitality and autonomy of computational artifacts emerge through the camouflaging of the networks that support them. By "camouflage" he means an obfuscation of the embodied activities that are the conditions of possibility for artificial life; that is, "machines, bodies, desires, and other practices on all sides of the screen" (ibid.: 7). In contrast, Doyle argues that the animism of artifacts comes from "a massive assemblage of machines, users and rhetorics that semiotically and materially distribute their 'vitality effect'" (ibid.: 17). We catch a glimpse of those hidden conditions of possibility in an article by Rosalind Pickard (1997), concerned with the place of emotion as a necessary "component" in the constitution of intelligent artifacts. In a footnote Pickard reports that in lab experiments with students playing the computer game *Doom*, signs of stress came less with the appearance of a new deadly enemy (the intended site of emotional affect) than during times when students were experiencing difficulty configuring the software. This suggests that genuine stress occurs when troubles are "real life," affecting lived accountabilities (in the context of the experiment, for compliance and competence) and consequences (for getting on with the game or task). For the researchers, however, this result is reported only as an amusing anecdote, noted *en passant*.

Cultural analysts like Doyle and Julian Bleecker (1995) analyze the compulsion of the virtual as evidenced in widespread fascination with the Maxis Corporation's *Sims* games as well as with ALife research. Both point to the opportunities these technologies afford their creators/users for a kind of simultaneous safety with risk, a transcendence over the "world" in question at the same time that one is somehow incorporated into it, engaged with an autonomous and therefore not fully predictable other. This produces a simultaneous sense of mastery over the virtual from "outside" with being "inside," controlled by larger and more powerful forces. The result is a controlled simulation of the experience of not being in control; hence, the best of both worlds.

### JEEVES FOR THE MASSES

I want to return, however, to the question of how ALICE and software agents more generally are figured, both in themselves and in their relations with humans (see Fig. 12.2). As I mentioned, at the time of our first

FIGURE 12.2. ALICE the chatterbot, winner of the 2000 Loebner prize for the 'Most Human Computer' http://web.archive.org/web/20000520084312/ www.alicebot.org/ last accessed December 26, 2005.

encounter ALICE was represented with a graphic image suggestive of a robot maid.[13]

Although ALICE and her kin are more engaged in entertainment than domestic labor, this embodiment aligns with the common rhetorical positioning of software agents as assistants to their human counterparts. An early animation of the idea of personal agents was offered in the form of "Phil," the bow-tied assistant in Apple Computer's

---

[13] This graphic has since been changed to that of a somewhat sterotypically hip young woman with a partially unbottoned blouse who, through advances in animation and speech generation, now has the wind blowing through her hair and greets you aloud. This, of course, shifts the connotations of the kinds of pleasures to be gained through entering into conversation with her. See http://www.alicebot.org/, accessed November 25, 2005.

1984 video "The Knowledge Navigator." Although Phil's capacities greatly exceeded those of even the most leading-edge agent technologies today, both ambitious promises and more modest implementations are very much with us. The emergence of software agents as a new site for the configuration of humanlike machines during the 1980s and 1990s coincides as well with two other initiatives, framed in terms of a shift of computation "out of the box" of the desktop computer, onto the body in the form of *wearable computing*, and into built surroundings under the name of *intelligent environments*. Although generally treated as quite distinctive developments, and notwithstanding their diverse histories, a look across these initiatives suggests some recurring themes.

To examine these lines of connection more closely, we can start with the observation that discourses of information technology have tended to erase the human labor that continues to be involved in technological production, implementation, maintenance, and the like. A reading across the rhetorics of software agents, wearables, and "smart" environments makes evident the absent presence of such erasures. As future visions offered in breathless promise and as a matter of practical necessity, these projects together restage a particular, and highly problematic, utopian dream. That is the fantasy of the perfect, invisible infrastructure: in this case, one that joins together the promise of intelligent machines with the needs of a service economy.[14]

The stage is well set by a figure courtesy of British writer P. G. Wodehouse, circa 1923:

'Morning, Jeeves,' I said.

'Good morning, sir,' said Jeeves.

He put the good old cup of tea softly on the table by my bed, and I took a refreshing sip. Just right, as usual. Not too hot, not too sweet, not too weak, not too strong, not too much milk, and not a drop spilled in the saucer. A most amazing cove, Jeeves. So dashed competent in every respect. I've said it before, and I'll say it again. (Wodehouse, 1999/1923: 1)

So opens the first chapter of *The Inimitable Jeeves*, subtitled "Jeeves Exerts the Old Cerebellum." The inimitability (or not) of Jeeves, and the cultural imaginaries within which Jeeves's competencies are attributed to

---

[14] This vision is clearly presented in innumerable invocations of the future of human–computer interactions, perhaps most notably by Brooks (2002). For critical discussions see Crutzen (2005), Gonzalez (2000), Markussen (1995), Turkle (1995: 145). For an illuminating feminist critique of the "smart house" as a project (of which more below), see Berg 1999.

his cerebellum, provide the backdrop for my analysis. Jeeves is the icon of the consummate service provider, the ever-resourceful "gentleman's personal gentleman." The just-visible-enough worker, he directs his considerable skills to maintaining the comfort and respectability of his employer, the upper-class, good-natured, but slightly dim-witted Bertie Wooster. Although created close to a century ago, it is evident that in important respects Jeeves prefigures the interactive software agent. Jeeves's travels through the interface were exemplified most directly, of course, in the Web search service Ask Jeeves®.[15] But in a feature article in the May 2001 issue of the popular magazine *Scientific American*, Tim Berners-Lee and his coauthors present their vision for the successor to today's World Wide Web, named (before its birth, in the manner typical of many software projects) "The Semantic Web." The authors animate their project with a scenario reminiscent of the Knowledge Navigator (1984), though updated to include a hand-held Web device:

The entertainment system was belting out the Beatles' "We Can Work It Out" when the phone rang. When Pete answered, his phone turned the sound down by sending a message to all the other local devices that had a volume control. His sister, Lucy, was on the line from the doctor's office: "Mom needs to see a specialist and then has to have a series of physical therapy sessions . . . I'm going to have my agent set up the appointments." Pete immediately agreed to share the chauffeuring.

At the doctor's office, Lucy instructed her Semantic Web agent through her hand-held Web browser. The agent promptly retrieved information about Mom's prescribed treatment from the doctor's agent, looked up several lists of providers, and checked for the ones in-plan for Mom's insurance within a 20-mile radius of her home and with a rating of excellent or very good on trusted rating services. It then began trying to find a match between available appointment times (supplied by the agents of individual providers through their Web sites) and Pete and Lucy's busy schedules. (Berners-Lee et al. 2001: 36)

---

[15] On September 23, 2005 the company announced plans to phase out the character of Jeeves, "citing 'user confusion' over what the butler character represents" according to a BBC news report (see http://news.bbc.co.uk/1/hi/technology/4275988.stm), and on February 27, 2006 Jeeves was officially disassociated from Ask.com. The flurry of attention paid to this event on the Web included an official Ask.com company page depicting Jeeves's "retirement," picturing the character who had comprised the company logo engaged in various forms of leisure and holiday-making (http://sp.uk.ask.com/en/docs/about/jeeveshasretired.html). While the BBC reports that "Jeeves is named after the extraordinarily knowledgeable and helpful valet character created by celebrated comic novelist P G Wodehouse," my request to the company to reproduce the Jeeves logo was met by a refusal and request that I refrain from making any association between the image and the fictional character.

From Bertie Wooster's trials as a member of the British leisure class, we move to the dilemmas of the baby boomer engaged in a busy working life, called to care for aging parents under a regime of privately insured health care. Although Mom apparently still needs to be transported bodily to her physical therapist, the rest of the logistics are adeptly handled by Pete and Lucy's software agents, and with just the right degree of deference. Issues of privacy, trust, and the like are dispatched through the application of appropriate techniques alluded to at relevant moments in the scenario. As the authors explain, "Pete and Lucy could use their agents to carry out all these tasks thanks not to the World Wide Web of today, but rather the Semantic Web that it will evolve into tomorrow" (ibid.: 36). The article describes how a new language of machine-readable Web content – a system of "well defined meanings" – will underwrite that evolutionary process (ibid.: 37). The authors conclude that "[p]roperly designed, the Semantic Web can assist the evolution of human knowledge as a whole," by making the latter available for meaningful analysis by software agents (ibid.: 43).

As the robot was to the industrial imaginary, so the software agent is to the desires and fantasies of the service economy. But rather than machines that can do our heavy lifting for us, the dream now is that every one of us can be a Bertie Wooster, commanding a staff of servants that gets to know us intimately, watches out for us, keeps us informed in just the ways that we need to be (knowing better what those ways are than we do ourselves), and represents us faithfully in our everyday affairs. The ideal that unites agent scenarios is that agents should be enough like us to understand our desires and to figure out on their own how to meet them, but without either their own desires or ambitions or other human frailties that might get in the way of efficient and effective accomplishment of their assigned tasks. The litmus test of a good agent is the agent's capacity to be autonomous, on the one hand, and just what we want, on the other. We want to be surprised by our machine servants, in sum, but not displeased.

At the same time we live in an age that embraces the ideal of the independent, self-motivated, entrepreneurial worker. As Henry Lieberman asks in his article "Autonomous Interface Agents": "Why autonomous agents? An assistant may not be of much practical help if he or she needs very explicit instruction all the time and constant supervision while carrying out actions. Assistants can be time-savers when they are allowed to act independently and concurrently . . . " (1997: 2). Here then is a classic tension. As management theory has pointed out with respect to the problem of agents and delegation in business administration, the more empowered these others, and the more capable of pursuing their own self-interests rather than ours, the less reliable they are. There is a deep and enduring ambivalence, in other words, inherent in the image of the agent: on the one hand, the agent as faithful representative; on the other, the agent as autonomous, self-directed, and therefore able to pursue its own agenda. Marvin Minsky, cofounder of the Artificial Intelligence laboratory at MIT, puts it more directly: "There's the old paradox of having a very smart slave. If you keep the slave from learning too much, you are limiting its usefulness. But, if you help it to become smarter than you are, then you may not be able to trust it not to make better plans for itself than it does for you" (quoted in Riecken 1994: 25).

The ramifications of the agent imaginary are developed by Chasin (1995), who explores identifications across women, servants, and machines in contemporary robotics. Her aim is to trace relations between changes in forms of machinic (re-)production (mechanical to electrical to electronic), types of labor (industrial to service), and conceptions of human–machine difference. Figured as servants, she points out, technologies reinscribe the difference between "us" and those who serve us, while eliding the difference between the latter and machines: "The servant troubles the distinction between we-human-subjects-inventors with a lot to do (on the one hand) and them-object-things that make it easier for us (on the other)" (ibid.: 73). Domestic service, doubly invisible because (a) it is reproductive and (b) it takes place in the household, is overwhelmingly provided by people – and of those predominately women – who are displaced and often desperate for employment. The latter are, moreover, positioned as Others to the dominant populace (typically white and affluent, at least in North America and Europe). Given the undesirability of service work, the conclusion might be that the growth of the middle class will depend on the replacement of human service providers by smart machines. The reality, however, is more likely to involve the continued labors of human service providers. Chasin points to the correlation, within the United States at least, between a dwindling middle class and increasingly polarized working and affluent population, and the increase in both the number of household appliances and domestic workers. As she argues: "In this climate, electronics stabilize the idea that a service class of being(s) is proper and even necessary; here, electronics participate in, and thereby reinforce, the unequal social and psychological dynamics upon which the myth of a constantly expanding middle class depends" (ibid.: 93).

Chasin poses the question (which I return to in Chapters 14 and 15) of how a change in our view of objects from passive and outside the social could help to undo the subject–object binary and all of its attendant orderings, including, for example, male–female, mental–manual, us–them. Although the "we" who will benefit from smart technologies may be cast as a universal subject, the very particular locations of those who speak and those who are (at least implicitly) spoken of inevitably entail marks of class and gender and attendant identifications. Moreover, the smart machine's presentation of itself as the always obliging, labor-saving device erases any evidence of the labor involved in its production and operation, "from bank personnel to software programmers to the third-world workers who so often make the chips" (Chasin 1995: 75). Yet as Ruth Schwartz Cowan (1983) and others since have demonstrated with respect to domestic appliances, the effectiveness of any labor-saving device both presupposes and generates new forms of human labor.

## THE ENCAPSULATED AND AUGMENTED BODY

Whereas agent technologies promise the services of a proxy who travels while we stay in place, distributed, ubiquitous, or pervasive computing promises to provide us with greater mobility without a loss of familiar ground. The projected disappearance of the computer into the metaphoric woodwork of electronic infrastructure takes two basic forms. First, it involves an embedding of computational processes into our surroundings, becoming part of the environment. And second, it assumes the shape of so-called wearable computing, or the embedding of computation onto or, more radically, into the body.

The migration of computing into the built environment is an area where life perhaps most clearly seeks to imitate art. A seminal source for the intelligent environment imaginary is the long-running television series Star Trek, where the encapsulated world of the star ship Enterprise becomes the prototype for a perfectly domesticated space. At MIT in the late 1990s, for example, the "Hal: Next Generation Intelligent Room" project was explained by its designers this way: "We are working towards creating environments analogous to those so familiar to Star Trek viewers – i.e. rooms that listen to you and watch what you do; rooms you can speak with, gesture to, and interact with in other complex ways."[16] In these projects the disappearance of the computer is simultaneously the emergence of familiar environments, where "familiar"

---

[16] See http://web.archive.org/web/19990224154049/www.ai.mit.edu/projects/hal/ (accessed February 6, 1998).

moves beyond the premise of environments that we know and recognize to environments that know and recognize us. As summarized in an enthusiastic report on work in the Microsoft Research Laboratories "Easy Living" group in 2000, "the vision of intelligent environments is a world of technology that seamlessly and unobtrusively surrounds you with intelligent help" (Hedberg 2000: 7).[17] The new capacities of smart environments reflect the hierarchy of the senses associated with human perception; namely, sight, hearing, touch and (much less frequently) smell, in that order. But where previously seen as necessary to the autonomy and mobility of robots, sensory perception now is the precondition for effectively responsive spaces.

Personalization is a central preoccupation in smart device projects, not in the sense of users shaping technologies within their own practice but as technologies that recognize their users and shape themselves accordingly. One implication of this objective is the predominance of various forms of surveillance and biometric technologies within smart environment scenarios. So, for example, entry into the demonstration Easy Livingroom on the Microsoft campus in Redmond, Washington, begins with fingerprint recognition (Hedberg 2000: 7). And, of course, ongoing forms of tracking and recognition of user activities is a precondition for engagement, bringing intelligent environment projects directly into the problematic realms of interactivity identified earlier in this book. The focus of research and development is on new technologies of location and tracking, standards and protocols for interoperability between devices and other ramifying complexities of system engineering. But more fundamental questions – of what it could mean, in all senses of the word, to be recognized by our environments – remain.

Whereas the "intelligent" environment promises that we will always be at home, "smart" clothing enables mobility without a loss of connection.[18] Within affluent technology-intensive locales globally the mobile or cell phone has reached the status of a new form of accessory, which

---

[17] In a broader consideration of the trope of being "at home," Ahmed proposes that "The lived experience of being-at-home . . . involves the enveloping of subjects in a space which is not simply outside them: being-at-home suggests that the subject and space leak into each other, inhabit each other" (2000: 89). She observes as well that assuming the metonymy of body, home, and world is not universal but a sign of privilege (ibid.: 53).

[18] In future scenarios, the "intelligent room" quickly begins to morph into the figure of the automated agent. As the title of an article in *IEEE Intelligent Systems* magazine on the MIT Intelligent Room project states it, it's "Roomservice, AI style" (Hirsh 1999: 8).

works to extend its wearers' communicative capabilities over time (through messaging) and across space.[19] Portable and hand-held electronic devices operate as augmentations of the body that no longer seem particularly remarkable. And more elaborate forms of "wearable computing" are being explored within the worlds of technology research and development.[20] These "wearables" can be seen as the "skin" of the migration of computing into the body, where the body's surface is enhanced through computational clothing. MIT's wearable computing Web site, for example, offers this account of their project, again with echoes of Jeeves: "A person's computer should be worn, much as eyeglasses or clothing are worn, and interact with the user based on the context of the situation. With heads-up displays, unobtrusive input devices, personal wireless local area networks, and a host of other context sensing and communication tools, the wearable computer can act as an intelligent assistant, whether it be through a Remembrance Agent, augmented reality, or intellectual collectives."[21] The resonance of the "wearable" with the figure of Jeeves is even more explicit in this recent prognostication: "[wearable] computers will monitor our physiological state, perform the duties of a secretary or butler in managing our everyday life, and protect us from physical harm" (Barfield and Caudell 2000: 24).

The most visible proponent of wearable computing has been University of Toronto Professor of Electrical Engineering Steve Mann. Mann's work and life address the intersection of the wearable computer as environment and as prosthesis. Mann has been wearing a computer imaging system, comprising various devices, for most of his waking hours for more than twenty years. His definition of the "personal empowerment" made possible by the advent of wearable computing includes both personal "encapsulation" and bodily "augmentation" (Mann and Niedzviecki 2001). Wearable computing in Mann's expression of it provides solitude, privacy, protection, and security: an extension of the safe surroundings of home out into the world. Mann's extremes cast the desires and premises of the computer as wearable into relief. The mirroring of environments and bodies in the projects of the disappearing and wearable computer suggests a desire always to be recognized,

---

[19] On mobile technologies and their effects see, for example, Brown, Green, and Harper (2001); Green (2002); Ito, Okabe, and Matsuda (2005).

[20] For an instructive study of the problematic alignment between wearable visions and realities in the case of a project of "augmenting" Bell Canada technicians, see Viseu (2003, 2005).

[21] http://www.media.mit.edu/wearables/ (last accessed November 6, 2005).

connected to familiar environments, while at the same time being fully autonomous and mobile.

The figure of the software agent as the service worker, increasingly embedded to the point of disappearance into our bodies, clothing, and walls, resonates with another, central to both industrial and postindustrial initiatives around new technologies. This latter figure has been insightfully discussed within science and technology studies under the name of the invisible worker, or invisible infrastructures, from Shapin's (1989) observations about the role of technicians in scientific discovery to recent work by Bowker and Star on systems of classification and their erasures (1999). Just as the dream of the robot worker was to relieve us of hard labor, or of the contingencies of managing others so engaged, so the dream of agents at the interface promises to relieve us from having either to perform the mundane work involved in providing services for ourselves or to negotiate the moral dilemmas and practical inconveniences of delegating that work to others who might – more and less faithfully – represent us.

Software agents, "smart" environments, and "wearables" together are figured within a discourse that makes service the imperative for a global economic infrastructure. We need to keep our eye, accordingly, on the ways in which autonomous machine agency, however subserviently constructed, might be consistent with regulatory practices aimed at foregrounding certain kinds of humans (employers, workers, consumers) and erasing others.[22] The relations of upstairs and downstairs, front stage and back, that the service economy presupposes are constituted within a closed world that simultaneously presumes and regenerates the needs, desires, identities, and inequalities that those relations comprise (Kantrowitz 1994). Just as the decorum of Bertie Wooster's world is maintained by the supporting activities and discrete interventions of Jeeves, the dream of technology innovators in the service economy is that new sociomaterial agents and infrastructures will make it possible for more and more of "us" to be hailed as persons residing upstairs rather than down. My concern, then, is with the kinds of "wes" that are posited by this future vision, widening the circle of those who employ, manage, and command to include more and more of "us," while those who serve

---

[22] I want to make clear here that my concern is not with debates that assume the futures predicted by software agent and smart machine enthusiasts and then consider the "ethics" of human–machine relations involved. Rather, it is the prior and more immediate question of what kinds of social relations are assumed to be desirable in these scenarios, whose interests are represented, and whose labors are erased.

us are refantasized from problematic human workers to the now-quite-imitable in silicon Jeeves. Discourses of agency at the interface at once naturalize the desirability of "service provision," and further obscure the specific sociomaterial infrastructures – including growing numbers of human workers – on which smooth interactions at the interface continue to depend.

# 13

# Figuring the Human in AI and Robotics

Among the range of projects underway in contemporary artificial intelligence and robotics research, my interest in this chapter is focused on those initiatives aimed most explicitly at the creation of machines that are *humanlike*. Just what it means to be humanlike, and how the boundary between humans and nonhumans is correspondingly drawn and redrawn, is of course one of the matters in question. A central premise of this book is that projects in AI and robotics involve a kind of doubling or mimicry in the machine that works as a powerful disclosing agent for assumptions about the human.[1] Positioned as exemplary of leading-edge thinking and technical practice, these initiatives in new technology materialize the cultural imaginaries that inspire them and which they work in turn to enact. In the case of AI and robotics, those imaginaries concern the category of the human, on the one hand, and questions of sameness and difference across (and within) the categories of humans, animals, and machines, on the other. One line of generative critique, therefore, is to trace out ways in which the assumptions that underwrite contemporary efforts to configure humanlike machines are remarkably familiar ones, their positioning at the leading edge of technoscientific innovation notwithstanding.

As a methodological strategy, I adopt a focus developed most explicitly within recent feminist and cultural studies of science; that is, an attention to questions of *figuration*. Figuration has been discussed

---

[1] I need to make clear that I am not suggesting, as do roboticists themselves, that these projects work as scientific models of the human but rather, that they make evident how roboticists imagine humanness. I return to this point in my discussion of Cog and Kismet below.

perhaps most famously by cultural historian of science Donna Haraway (1997: 11). Haraway's argument is, first, that all language, including the most technical or mathematical, is figural; that is, it is made up of tropes or "turns of phrase" that invoke associations across diverse realms of meaning and practice. Technologies, Haraway argues, are forms of *materialized figuration*; that is, they bring together assemblages of stuff and meaning into more and less stable arrangements. These arrangements imply in turn particular ways of associating humans and machines. One form of intervention into current practices of technology development, then, is through a critical consideration of how humans and machines are currently figured in those practices and how they might be figured – and *configured* – differently.[2] This effort engages with the broader aim of understanding science as culture, as a way of shifting the frame of research – our own as well as that of our research subjects – from the discovery of universal laws to the ongoing elaboration and potential transformation of culturally and historically specific practices, to which we are all implicated rather than modest witnesses.[3]

Claudia Castañeda articulates the world-making effects of figuration in a way richly suggestive for how we might explore the category of the human through her close and generative readings of the figure of the child. She develops what she calls a "theoretical-methodological approach" (2002: 5) to cultural analysis that begins with a general figure and traces out its specific cultural, historical, and political appearances, urging attention to the double project of identifying the practices through which figures come into being and the work that they do (see also Braidotti 1994: 1). The effects of figuration are political in the sense that the specific discourses, images, and normativities that inform practices of figuration can work either to reinscribe existing social orderings

---

[2] Kember (2003: 170) identifies figuration, in its mobilization as a means of intervention, as "visual or verbal images which embody transformations in knowledge, power and subjectivity." See also Braidotti (1994), Castañeda (2002), Kember (1998). Knorr Cetina (1999) develops a sense of configuration within the experimental sciences as a way of thinking about the agencies of laboratories in arranging scientists, instruments, objects, and practices in ways that together generate a particular science's "reality effects" (ibid.: 12, 26–33). Of crucial importance in her analysis is the construction of *difference* between the laboratory and everyday life, as well as across laboratories (ibid.: 44). Different effects are achieved, on Knorr Cetina's account, through acts of reconfiguring, an idea that I return to in Chapter 15.

[3] On the "modest witness" in science studies see Haraway (1997), Latour (1993), Shapin and Schaffer (1985). For indicative writings on science as practice see Franklin (1995), Helmreich (1998), Pickering (1992), Reid and Traweek (2000).

or to challenge them. In the case of the human, the prevailing figuration in Euro-American imaginaries is one of autonomous, rational agency, and projects of artificial intelligence reiterate that culturally specific imaginary. At stake, then, is the question of what other possible conceptions of humanness there might be, and how those might challenge current regimes of research and development in the sciences of the artificial, in which specifically located individuals conceive technologies made in their own image, while figuring the latter as universal.

## AUTOMATA AND AGENCY

The project of making automata is a recent manifestation of a more long-standing preoccupation, with the agential – and more specifically human – properties of material things. Framing the question as one of whether things have agency like humans presupposes, however, a (non-problematized) Euro-American view of what agency could be. In particular, it accepts that "to be human is to possess agency" and then proceeds with the question of to whom or to what such attributions should be extended (Lee and Brown 1994: 772). Instead, I adopt the view here that we need to include in our analysis the question of just what constitutes agency in any case, for humans or nonhumans. Efforts to establish criteria of humanness (for example, tool use, language ability, symbolic representation) have always been contentious, challenged principally in terms of the capacities of other animals, particularly the nonhuman primates, to engage in various cognate behaviors. More recently the same kinds of criterial arguments have been made in support of the human-like capabilities of artificially intelligent machines. Whether the concern is animals or machines, debates within this competitive frame inevitably turn on contests over just what counts as the behaviors in question and who or what can be properly said to demonstrate them.[4]

Historically, understandings of agency within Euro-American imaginaries have marked the difference between humans and machines, while always at the same time inviting experiments across the boundary. Historian Jessica Riskin traces projects concerned with the synthesis of artificial life forms – artifacts that act in ways taken to be humanlike – since the early eighteenth century (2003a, 2003b, 2007). As with contemporary

---

[4] On these contests in the case of animals see, for example, Crist (2000, 2004); with respect to machines see Collins (1990), Collins and Kusch (1998); on both see Edwards (1994).

projects in artificial intelligence and artificial life, Riskin observes that early simulations were conducted as experiments aimed at testing the essence of life and intelligence, of the active and the inert. Her historiography emphasizes the ways in which both sides were transformed in the process, as over the past three centuries human and machine each alternately has served as a model for the other. The earliest attempts to synthesize life in the 1700s were inspired by an emerging materialist sensibility, for example, in the form of a mechanist physiology of the workings of the body. Associated practices of experimental artifice and simulation were understood as methods for investigating the natural and the real, an understanding still evident in contemporary views of experiment and simulation. Riskin cites the famous example of the "Lady Musician," an early automaton built by a Swiss watchmaking family. Not only did the Lady play music, but her eyes also faithfully followed the course of her hands and on occasion, apparently moved by the effects of her own agency, she heaved a great sigh. Riskin locates the growth of factory automation in this history as well: the automatic loom, for example, was designed by the same inventor, Vaucanson, who created the iconic "defecating duck" (Riskin 2003b). The loom, like many other forms of industrial machinery, established a new hybrid combining the perfectly accurate machine with its still necessary, but more "limited," human operator. More recently, of course, the relation of nature and artifice has become more fundamentally intertwined, most dramatically in the interventions made possible through the agencies of biotechnology and the "new" genetics.[5]

The approach that I adopt in this and subsequent chapters is to engage in close reading of the discourses and material practices of projects in robotics and AI. What figures of the human are materialized in these technologies? What are the circumstances through which machines can be claimed, or experienced, as humanlike? And what do those claims and encounters tell us about the particular cultural imaginaries that inform these technoscience initiatives, and how they might be otherwise? To pursue these questions, I consider three elements taken to be necessary for humanness in contemporary AI projects: embodiment, emotion, and sociality.

---

[5] Anthropological writings on reproductive and biotechnologies have flourished over the past decade. For a founding work see Strathern (1992). For an indicative collection see Franklin and Ragone (1998).

## EMBODIMENT

Feminist theorists have extensively documented the subordination, if not erasure, of the body within the Western philosophical canon.[6] Drawing from these observations, Katherine Hayles has traced out the inheritance of this legacy in the processes through which information "lost its body" in the emerging sciences of the artificial over the last century (1999: 2).[7] Recent developments in AI and robotics appear to reverse this trend, however, taking to heart arguments to the effect that embodiment, rather than being coincidental, is a fundamental condition for intelligence.[8] The most widely cited exception to the rule of disembodied intelligence in AI is the initiative named *situated robotics*, launched by Rodney Brooks in the 1980s. Brooks's position has been that rather than a symbolic process that *precedes* action, cognition must be an emergent property *of* action, the foundational forms of which he takes to be navigation through a physical environment.[9] Like many others, Brooks builds an evolutionary trope into his project, expressed in a mixed metaphor that positions insect behavior as precursor to the genesis of humanoid robots (2002: 40). In her generally critical review of work in AI and robotics, Alison Adam writes that developments under the heading of situated robotics, in particular, "demonstrate a clear recognition of the way in which embodiment informs our knowledge" (1998: 149). But what, more precisely, comprises embodiment in this context?

The first thing to note is that discoveries of the body in artificial intelligence and robotics inevitably locate its importance vis-à-vis the successful operations of mind or at least of some form of instrumental cognition. The latter in this respect remains primary, however much mind may be formed in and through the workings of embodied action. The second consistent move is the positing of a "world" that preexists independent of the body. The body then acts as a kind of receiver for stimuli given by the world, and generator of appropriate responses to it,

---

[6] For readings on feminist theories of the body, see, for example, Butler (1993), Grosz (1994), Kirby (1997), Price and Shildrick (1999), Schiebinger (2000).

[7] See also Adam (1998), Balsamo (1996), Helmreich (1998), Kember (2003).

[8] The original publication of *Plans and Situated Actions: The Problem of Human–Machine Interaction* (Suchman 1987), I hope, made some contribution to this shift. For related arguments on the social and material grounds of cognition, see also Lave (1988) and Hutchins (1995), and for a critique of disembodied AI from within the field see Agre (1997).

[9] Brooks presents his position in Brooks and Steels (1995), Brooks (1999, 2002). See also Grand (2003).

through which the body "grounds" the symbolic processes of mind. Just as mind remains primary to body, the world remains prior to and separate from perception and action, however much the latter may affect and be affected by it. And both body and world remain a naturalized foundation for the workings of mind.[10] As Adam points out, the question as framed by Brooks is whether cognition, and the knowledge that it presupposes, can be modeled separately from perception and motor control (1998: 137). Brooks's answer is no, but the figure that results from his ensuing work, Adam observes, is "a bodied individual in a physical environment, rather than a socially situated individual" (ibid.: 136).

I return to Brooks and the problem of the social below, but it is important to note first that the materialization of even a bodied individual in a physical environment has proven more problematic than anticipated. In particular, it seems extraordinarily difficult to construct robotic embodiments, even of the so-called emergent kind, that do not rely upon the associated provision of a "world" that anticipates relevant stimuli and constrains appropriate response. Just as reliance on propositional knowledge leads to a seemingly infinite regress for more traditional, symbolic AI (see Adam 1998; Collins 1990), attempts to create artificial agents that are "embodied and embedded" seem to lead to an endless stipulation of the conditions of possibility for perception and action, bodies and environments. Despite Brooks's initial assertions that in the case of situated robotics "the world grounds regress" (1995: 55), the inadequacies of physicalism as a model for bodies or worlds are reflected in Brooks's recent resort to some kind of yet to be determined "new stuff" as the missing ingredient for artificial humanness (2002, Chapter 8). However inspired by phenomenologists like Heidegger and Merleau Ponty, and the autopoesis of Maturana and Varela (see Clark 1997: 171), the contingent interactions of biological, cultural-historical and autobiographically experiential embodiment continue to elude what remain at heart functionalist projects (Kember 2003: 65).[11] And despite efforts

---

[10] This view underpins what Smith (1996: 97) characterizes as the stance of Realism, a philosophical position that he critically dislodges through a close reading of relations of world, naturalism, materiality, and the physical (ibid: 138–40). With respect to embodiment, Smith reminds us that "'The body' as an entity does not come for free; it is a substantial achievement, one that has to be individuated, carved out from a background, kept in shape, etc., by, among others, the subject whose body it is . . . " (ibid.: 184). I return to the question of boundaries in Chapter 15.

[11] For a compelling articulation of the relevance of a Merleau-Pontian view of embodiment for broader fields of computer system design, see Robertson (2002).

by sympathetic critics such as Adam and Kember to draw attention to the relevance of feminist theory for AI and robotics, the exigencies of design return researchers from the rhetorics of embodiment to familiar practices of computer science and engineering.

## EMOTION

Since its advent under the auspices of United States and Japanese research and development laboratories in the 1990s, the project of "affective computing" has been hailed in the popular media as a radical movement that promises to turn prevailing notions of machine intelligence upside down. A news story from May 2001 is indicative: "Affective computing would transform machines from slaves chained to the limits of logic into thoughtful, observant collaborators. Such devices may never replicate human emotional experience. But if their developers are correct, even modest emotional talents would change machines from data-crunching savants into perceptive actors in human society. At stake are multibillion-dollar markets for electronic tutors, robots, advisers and even psychotherapy assistants" (Piller 2001: A8). Assigned an emancipatory role, emotion is positioned here as the missing ingredient for full (if not quite equal) machine participation in the human world. Sliding between imagery of enslavement and social ineptitude, the capacities of logic and calculation formerly taken as the mark of the human are now relegated to the position of oppressive and limiting forms of reasoning. These stand in the way of full realization of the lucrative benefits to be gained by machinic actors made effective through their endowment with affective competencies.

Affective computing is repeatedly hailed as the discovery by cognitive science and AI (against their own, but by implication all of our, previously held convictions) that "emotional processes" as well as reason are necessary to intelligence. "Intelligence" in this sense retains its pride of place as the defining capacity of the human, but it is an intelligence now extended in its instrumental efficacy by the sensibilities of affect. Rosalind Picard, noted proponent and director of the Affective Computing Laboratory at the Massachusetts Institute of Technology, explains the choice of names for the project this way: "The inability of today's computers to recognize, express, and have emotions severely limits their ability to act intelligently and interact naturally with us ... because emotional computing tends to connote computers with an undesirable reduction in rationality, we prefer the term affective computing to denote computing that relates to, arises from, or deliberately influences emotions. Affective still means emotional, but may, perhaps usefully, be confused with effective" (Picard 1997: 280–1, original emphasis).

Emotion is another component, then, needed for effective rationality. More generally, discourses of affective computing evidence some shared starting assumptions:

> "Affect" comprises a distinguishable domain of cognition that can be analyzed into universal, component parts.
>
> Affect is the expression of an underlying emotional "state."
>
> Affective interaction can be achieved through the replication of behaviors understood to comprise it, made up of units assembled into a catalogue of affective expressions, productions, recognitions, and normative responses.
>
> Emotional states and their affective expression can be understood in terms of their (evolutionary) utility, as a kind of primal but still functional ancestor of contemporary reason.

Taken as discrete states, emotions are available for analysis and replication. Historian of medicine Otniel Dror traces the cataloguing and enumeration of emotion to origins in late-nineteenth and early-twentieth-century laboratory sciences. These early developers projected a future in which affective sociability would be mediated by emotion-detecting technologies, as "physiologists, psychologists, and clinicians manipulated, isolated, replicated, standardized, quantified, and recorded emotions. They invented new technologies for visualizing and representing emotions in curves and numeric tables. And they propagated their practices and instruments beyond the narrow confines of the laboratory and clinic" (Dror 2001: 360). Dror suggests that the power of these technologies came in part from their transgressive hybridity, "a detached and machinist mode of production that provided intimate and private knowledge" (1999: 392) for anyone to see.[12]

In the laboratory, the drive to produce clear, compelling representations of emotional states (as measured through various physiological changes), led to the co-configuring of imaging technologies and subjects. "Good and reliable subjects" were chosen for their ability to display clearly recognizable emotions on demand, whereas those that failed to produce unambiguous and therefore easily classifiable behaviors were left out of the protocol (Dror 1999: 383). These technologies produced

---

[12] See http://mplab.ucsd.edu/ (last accessed November 7, 2005).

a catalogue of emotional types, normalized across the circumstances of their occurrence (e.g., as anger, fear, excitement), and treated as internally homogeneous, if variable in their quantity or intensity. Inevitably, normative readings developed based on experimenters' prior experience and cumulative data. And as inevitably, particularly in the context of the early twentieth century, when these experiments flourished, categories of emotion were mapped to categories of person, affording (often invidious) comparison across, for example, men, on the one hand, and "women and Negroes," on the other (ibid.: 386). At the same time, this was an economy that circulated through, but was discursively separable from, specific bodies. Like other marks on bodies, once materialized as a representation or trace emotions were extractable from their particular contexts of production: "Emotions were understood as processes in the general scheme of the body-as-machine . . . Thus, emotion was a pattern written in the language of the biological elements that one monitored in, or sampled from, the organism" (2001: 362).

Contemporary affective computing research follows in the tradition traced by Dror, in figuring affective encounters as moments of (predominately visual) "recognition" of evidence for underlying emotional states. So, for example, Javier Movellan of the Machine Perception Laboratory at the University of California, San Diego, has engaged in empirical, probabilistic analyses of facial expressions, based on hundreds of thousands of cases and aimed at the effective "recognition" of emotion by a "perceptual" computer interface.[13] In the universalizing and unlocated language characteristic of many such projects, Movellan and colleagues report their aim as being to create "a catalogue of how people react to the world" (Piller 2001: A8). The promise is that, as the observer that never blinks, the perceptual computer interface is positioned to know us better than we know ourselves, catching those fleeting moments of expression of which we ourselves are unaware, or that we hope will be missed, and providing readings unencumbered by the fallibility that clouds human perceptions.

## SOCIABILITY

Figured most famously within the genre of science fiction over thirty years ago, as the Heuristically Programmed Algorithmic (HAL 9000)

---

[13] For an extensive and illuminating exploration of contemporary technologies of brain imaging, including the laboratory production of "emotions" and their travels, see Dumit (2004).

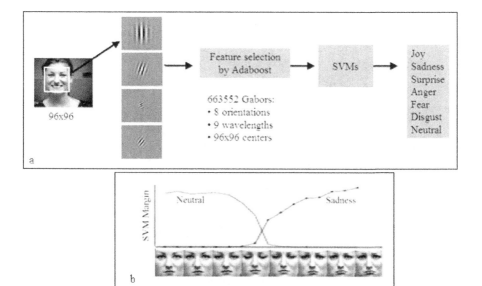

Figure 1. a. Facial expression recognition system. b. Outputs of the SVMs trained for neutral and sadness for a full image sequence of a test subject performing sadness.

FIGURE 13.1. Littlewort, G., Bartlett, M., Fasel, I., Susskind, J., and Movellan, J. An automatic system for measuring facial expression in video. Reprinted from *Image and Vision Computing*. Copyright with permission from Elsevier.

in the film *2001* (Kubrick and Clark 1968), the fantasy of the sociable machine has been a touchstone for research in humanlike machines. The most frequently cited exemplars of this project are the progeny of MIT's Artificial Intelligence Laboratory. Perhaps the best known artifacts are the celebrity robots Cog and Kismet, both born of the "new AI" turn away from intelligence figured as symbolic information processing, to humanness as embodiment, affect and interactivity. A project of Rod Brooks, Cog is a robot head and torso built to maximize the integration of a "perceptual" system (computer vision) with basic motor "skills" (moveable arms and grasping hands). Brooks's premise in conceiving Cog was that the robot's basic sensorimotor capabilities would enable simple behaviors and interactions with its environment that in turn would build on each other to make more complicated behaviors easier. Brian Scassellati, who as a graduate student in the MIT AI Lab performed much of the labor in implementing Cog's most recent instantiations, explains the purpose of the project as being to "investigate themes of development, physical embodiment, sensory-motor integration, and social interaction" and to "study models of human intelligence by constructing them on a physical robot" (Menzel and D'Aluisio 2000: 58).

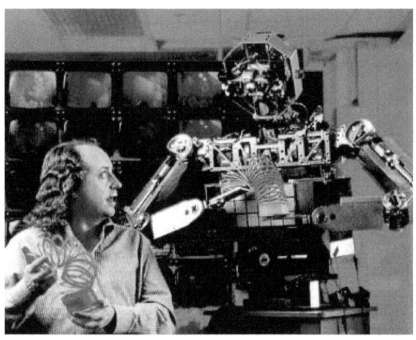

FIGURE 13.2. Rodney Brooks with Cog © Peter Menzel/www.menzelphoto.com.

Kismet, a progeny of AI researcher Cynthia Breazeal within the larger Sociable Machines Project, is described on the laboratory's Web site as follows: "The Sociable Machines Project develops an anthropomorphic robot called Kismet that engages people in natural and expressive face-to-face interaction. Inspired by infant social development, psychology, ethology, and evolution, this work integrates theories and concepts from these diverse viewpoints to enable Kismet to enter into natural and intuitive social interaction with a human caregiver and to learn from them, reminiscent of parent-infant exchanges."[14]

Kismet's software is conceptualized as a model of "drives," its state of well-being as one of homeostatic balance among them. The aim of Kismet's social interaction is to activate the drives (enacted through facial configurations recognizable as "calmness, happiness, sadness, anger, surprise, disgust, tiredness") through the presentation by the robot's interactional partners of "stimuli," at levels of intensity that will

[14] See http://www.ai.mit.edu/projects/sociable/overview.html (last accessed November 7, 2005).

FIGURE 13.3. Cynthia Breazeal with Kismet © Donna Coveney/MIT.

engender appropriate responses and avoid "distress."[15] A premise of the design is that both Kismet and its human interlocutors learn over the course of an encounter, in a trajectory aimed at mutual adjustment and increasingly appropriate forms of engagement.

Castañeda reminds us to locate "purportedly general claims about the child in particular discursive, cultural, and geopolitical contexts" (2002: 5). Among other things, the figure of the child in Euro-American imaginaries carries with it a developmental trajectory, a becoming made up of inevitable stages and unfulfilled potentialities, that in the case of Kismet simultaneously authorizes the continuation of the project and accounts for its incompleteness. Both Cog and Kismet are represented through an extensive corpus of media renderings – stories, photographs, and, in Kismet's case, QuickTime videos available on the MIT Web site. Pictured from the "waist" up, Cog appears in media photos as freestanding if not mobile, and Kismet's Web site offers a series of recorded "interactions" between Kismet and Breazeal as well as between Kismet and selected other human partners. Like other conventional documentary productions, these representations are framed and narrated in ways that

---

[15] For an extended interview with Breazeal regarding the project, see Menzel and D'Aluisio (2000: 66–71).

instruct the viewer in what to see. Sitting between the documentary film and the genre of the system demonstration or demo, the videos create a record that can be reliably repeated and reviewed in what becomes a form of eternal ethnographic present. These reenactments thereby imply that the capacities they record have an ongoing existence – that they are themselves robust and repeatable and that like any other living creatures Cog and Kismet's agencies are not only ongoing but also continuing to develop and unfold.

### THE HUMANLIKE MACHINE AS A FETISHIZED OBJECT

In their contribution to the animation of objects, narratives of the human-like machine rely on two recurring lacunae, one historical and one future oriented. Historically, devices made to perform at particular moments, as a contingent outcome of extensive networks and intensive hours of human labor, are rendered eternally and autonomously operational through the intercession of various representational media (demonstration videos, technical reports, media accounts, and Web sites).[16] The existence of such documents creates an archival record of the existence of humanlike artifacts, an existence reiterated through extended networks of further citation. Prospectively, the efficacies demonstrated are narrated as portents of developing capacities, from which the rest of human capabilities will logically and inevitably follow. Together these rhetorical leaps conjure into existence an imaginative landscape increasingly populated by "socially intelligent" artifacts, approaching closer and closer approximation to things that both think and feel like you and me. Through these modes of erasure of human labors and nonhuman alignments, the autonomous artifact is brought into being.

In a series of recent writings (2002a, 2002b, 2007) Fox Keller considers the ways in which automata, among other devices, have been taken to validate mechanical–cybernetic accounts of biology. The machine in this paradigm is naturalized, so that its development can be construed as evidence for that which it is taken to replicate. This move, in turn,

---

[16] When asked in an interview in 2000 how many person hours it had taken to develop Kismet, Breazeal replied (in a way suggestive of the shared ancestry and technical investments made in Cog and Kismet): "Oh God, I don't even want to think about it ... There's tons of infrastructure code that isn't specifically for this robot. Code to specifically run Kismet is probably two full-time people working for 2.5 years. The total size of all the software tools we have developed to support our computation environment is huge" (Menzel and D'Aluisio 2000: 66).

is based in a natural scientific paradigm of models, inspired by naturally occurring phenomena, which are then offered as experimental test beds from which explanatory theories regarding those phenomena can be generated. In "Booting up Baby" (in press), Keller points to what she names "the apparently circular trajectory" (ibid.: 253) involved in the logics of the Sociable Machines project, insofar as it materializes current discourses in developmental psychology and then represents itself as an independent testbed in which to assess their adequacy. Keller raises more specific concerns premised on the possible realization of the promises of the project, involving, for example, the implementation of humanoid robot caregivers. My own concern is less that robotic visions will be realized (though real money will be diverted from other projects and spent on them) than that the discourses and imaginaries that inspire them will retrench, rather than challenge and hold open for contest, received conceptions of humanness. As Keller concludes: "If there is a disturbing circularity in the expectations for robotic simulations of human development, and if I am right in suggesting that the same problem arises in the use of computer simulations [in physics, biology, etc.], then the issue becomes a more general one" (ibid.: 255).

Pursuing a quite different line of analysis in a discussion of the "apparent irrationality" of the worship of fetishes and idols as social others, anthropologist Alfred Gell follows religious scholars in proposing that it is precisely the fact that taking things as human is strange that gives the practices their distinctive character and religious efficacy or their "enchantment" (1998: 123). He goes on to consider how it is that people can simultaneously know that entities are categorically different from persons and at the same time attribute social agency to them. The key, he argues, is to locate the latter not in any necessary physical attributes (such as inanimate thing versus incarnate person) but in social relations: "it does not matter, in ascribing 'social agent' status, what a thing (or a person) 'is' in itself; what matters is where it stands in a network of social relations" (ibid.: 123). The resonance of this observation with claims for artificial intelligence and robotics, however, warrants closer scrutiny. On one hand, the latter share the rejection of material essentialism identified by Gell, seeing silicon and electrical circuitry as an alternative to flesh and blood. In this respect Gell's argument regarding social agency would seem to support the projects described above. A critical difference, however, lies in the extent to which the sciences of the artificial share the other central element of an anthropological theory of objects and agencies; that is, a radical relationality. Reading

AI discourses would seem to indicate that the project is less to displace an individualist conception of agency with a relational one so much as to displace the biological individual with a computational one. All else in traditional humanist understandings of the nature of agency seems unquestioned. How it might be otherwise – how the labors and contingencies of technological agencies might be recovered without a necessary loss of enchantment – is the topic of the following chapter.

# 14

# Demystifications and Reenchantments of the Humanlike Machine

> Since the outset of the discipline, anthropology has been signally preoc-
> cupied with a series of problems to do with ostensibly peculiar relations
> between persons and 'things' which somehow 'appear as', or do duty as,
> persons.
>
> (Gell 1998: 9)

As this epigraph from Alfred Gell suggests, the distinction of humans
and nonhumans marks a relation that has been extensively explored not
only by anthropologists but also by their research subjects, among other
ways through the fungibility of persons and things. My interest in this
book is to contribute to explorations of these "peculiar relations" at a particular site of contemporary cultural imaginaries, that is, the computing
sciences and arts. I have posited that the fascinations of artificial personhood for AI practitioners involve a kind of mimesis that works as a powerful disclosing agent for associated assumptions about the human.[1] In
this chapter I explore those assumptions through some specific encounters with contemporary humanlike machines, read through the lens of
recent developments in the anthropology of science and technology and
related fields.[2] Capacities for action are recast in these writings from

---

[1] Sherry Turkle (1984) was among the first to take up the broader question of the "aliveness" of computational artifacts and the workings of the computer as what she names
an "evocative object" for the human. I use the term *mimesis* here in the sense developed
by Michael Taussig, as "the faculty to copy, imitate, make models, explore difference,
yield into and become Other" (1993: xiii).

[2] More specifically, my aim in this chapter and the next is to identify the outlines of a figure
of humanness more consistent with conceptualizations currently under construction
within the fields of cultural anthropology (Downey and Dumit 1997; Gell 1998; Strathern

inherent capabilities to possibilities generated and reiterated through specific sociomaterial assemblages and enactments. These approaches shift the frame of reference from the autonomous human individual to arrangements that produce effective forms of agency within ramifying networks of social and material relations. Just how those networks are drawn and "cut" (Strathern 1996), and with what agential effects, is a practical, political, and aesthetic question, as well as a materially consequential one.

For scholars in the humanities and the social sciences, projects of artificial life in its various forms conjoin with ongoing reexamination of the tradition of liberal humanism and its figurings of persons, agency, and the like. This project of articulating the "posthuman" has been extensively described by Hayles (1999, 2002, 2005), who sees initiatives in the fields of situated robotics and artificial life as indicators of more profound shifts in the human sciences and in contemporary society. The position that I develop below intersects with that of Hayles but also differs in what I believe are critical (in both senses of that term) ways. I embrace Hayles's analysis of the history of the information sciences and the discursive disembodiment of mind and share her interest in the possibilities that computing affords for rethinking traditional conceptions of the human. But whereas Hayles anticipates resistance to projects in situated robotics and artificial life from those wedded to a conservative humanism (2005: 143), my own resistance to those projects is based on quite different grounds. I discuss these grounds in detail below, but in brief my concern is that, like their predecessors, these projects continue to restage the parochial and conservative forms of liberal humanism that in Hayles's reading they leave behind.

At the same time, my own analyses of initiatives in the design of humanlike machines have been concerned with resisting too easy elisions of difference at the human–computer interface. My approach has been to slow down discourses of the "smart" machine to attend closely to the practices through which purportedly intelligent and interactive artifacts are realized, including just what conceptions of intelligence and interaction are in play. The result of this is an enduring skepticism regarding the rhetorics of machine intelligence and an interest in

1999; Taussig 1993), science and technology studies (Casper 1994; Collins 1990; Cussins 1998; Haraway 1991, 1997; Latour 1993, 1999; Law and Mol 2002; Lenoir 2002), feminist theory (Barad 2003; Braidotti 1994, 2002; Butler 1993; Halberstam and Livingston 1995), and cultural studies (Balsamo 2000; Doyle 2003; Featherstone and Burrows 1995; Hayles 1999, 2002, 2005; Kember 2003).

demystifying the specific technologies and practices about which these discourses make their claims.

With the critique of the previous chapter in mind, I turn here to particular encounters with several of the most highly acclaimed realizations of the intelligent machine, the situated robots Cog and Kismet. In offering some different readings of these projects from those available in popular media representations, I hope to indicate how encounters at the human–computer interface could support more radical reworkings of the figures of both. This alternative is further elaborated through the case of an artifact sited more provocatively at the intersection of AI and new media art, performance artist Stelarc's *Prosthetic Head*.[3] My interrogation of the *Head* expands the unit of analysis to incorporate the ongoing labors of design practitioners, the unruly contingencies and material particularities of computational artifacts, and the artfully collusive performances that make up encounters at the human–computer interface.[4] In pursuing this line of research, I engage the body of scholarship that emphasizes the inseparability of the human from the artifactual and renders the relation as a more radically irreducible and intimate one. Taken together, these reflections are meant to contribute to the project that Taussig has named the demystification and reenchantment of lively things (1993: 1).

## MYSTIFICATIONS AND ENCHANTMENTS

A close consideration of humanlike machines suggests a radical inversion of the premises that inform AI and robotics projects, of even the most "situated" kind. Rather than flawed approximations of autonomous agency, we can take these artifacts as demonstrations that

---

[3] In her essay "Flesh and Metal: Reconfiguring the Mindbody in Virtual Environments" (2002), Hayles shifts her focus from AI and robotics to the computational arts, where she finds resources for a more radical rethinking of bodies, embodied experience, and the (post-)human. I share this assessment of where we might look for practices at the human–computer interface more aligned with recent critical reconceptualizations of persons and things.

[4] Hayles's discussion of the installation *Traces* is highly resonant with my argument here, in pointing to the designers' deliberate avoidance of effects that would obscure the particularities of the computational medium and their orientation to the interactions between persons and the VR environment. On her account, the designers turned problems that they encountered in getting a computationally generated avatar to exactly track the user's body into a lesson: "rather than regarding the avatar as a mirroring puppet, they think of it as a trace emerging from the borderlands created by the energetic body in motion. What was a tracking problem is thus tranformed into the possibility of creative play between user and avatar" (2002: 308–9).

agencies – whether robotic or human – might need to be conceptualized on very different grounds. It is at this point that recent critical writings on subjects, objects, and relations between them become relevant for rethinking interactions between humans and machines. In *Strange Encounters*, for example, Sara Ahmed develops a critique of the figure of "the stranger" by extending Marx's analysis of commodity fetishism (as the substitution of an enigmatic object for the social relations of labor) to include fantasy as well as materiality or a "fetishism of figures" (2000: 4). Among other moves, Ahmed argues, this form of fetishism involves cutting off a figure from the histories of its determination through particular, embodied encounters. The figure is treated as "having a nature," as being something that *is* and that has effects, rather than as an effect in itself. Ahmed's interest is not only in how such figures are produced but also in how they are put to work in particular times and places, including the labor that the fetishized figure conceals.

In an argument from a very different domain, but with strong resonances to Ahmed's, Gell (1998) has explored the "enchantment" of objects brought about through the masking of labors of production. Like Taussig, Gell starts from Walter Benjamin's proposal that mimetic practices, resulting in a plethora of images and simulacra, are based in a compulsion to imitate the world as a means of gaining access to it (see Gell 1998: 100; Taussig 1993: 20). Rejecting the idea of mimesis as a "primitive faculty" inherited from the past, Gell and Taussig adopt the category of mimesis as the more particular production of figures whose salient property is their resemblance to an original. They then use the concept to analyze a range of practices of magic and sorcery and their associated artifacts. Gell traces the history of this form of object enchantment back to Tylor, who, in *Primitive Culture* (1875), defined primitivism in terms of animism or the attribution of life and sensibility to inanimate things, as well as to Frazer (1900), Malinowski (1935), and Mauss (1902, 1954) in their studies of magic and the efficacy of objects in relations of exchange. Mauss's theories of exchange, in particular, consider how gifts act as extensions of persons and inspire Gell's theory of the agencies of art and of artifacts more generally. Artifacts are, by definition, Gell proposes, those objects taken to be instruments or outcomes of social agency. A found object like a stone, placed on a mantelpiece, becomes an art object and an artifact, indexing the agency of its finding and placement. At the same time, the enchanted object's effects are crucially tied to the indecipherability of prior social action in the resulting artifact.

It is through the specific materialities of the artifact, crucially, that its effects, and the absent presences on which they depend, are achieved.

Taussig (1993) takes as his focus what he characterizes as "the two-layered notion of mimesis that is involved [in Benjamin's analysis] – a copying or imitation, and a palpable, sensuous connection between the very body of the perceiver and the perceived" (1993: 21). From this he develops a critique of Frazer's typology of sympathetic magic into the two categories of "imitation" and "contact, " arguing that the two are always intertwined in practice. These observations call out the importance of the particular materialities of objects to their efficacy, however much the latter is also based in ephemeral and intangible imaginings. Indeed, by this analysis the two aspects – embodied, sensuous contact and magical efficacy – are inextricably intertwined.

Developed with respect to fetish figures made of wood, this analysis is richly suggestive for thinking about the computationally powered artifacts of contemporary AI and robotics. A more general characteristic of object fetishism in an age of commodity capitalism, the entanglement of sensuous corporeality and apprehension of the liveliness concealed within things has particular resonance in the case of humanlike machines. This despite the fact that the humanness assumed in discussions of the potential success (or the inevitable failure) of attempts to replicate the human machinically is typically stripped of its contingency, locatedness, historicity, and specific embodiments. If, in contrast, we take the human to be inseparable from our specifically situated social and material circumstances, the question shifts from "Will we be replicated?" to something more like "In what sociomaterial arrangements are we differentially implicated, and with what political and economic consequences?" This alerts us, in turn, to the possibility of encounters at the interface conceived very differently than as the meeting of a human and a machine, each figured as a self-standing entity possessed of preestablished capabilities. Rather, effective encounters at the computer interface are those moments of moving complicity between persons and things achieved through particular, dynamic materialities and extended socialities.

## DEMYSTIFICATIONS

To make the preceding argument more concrete, I return to the particular humanlike machines introduced above. I was able to experience my own encounters with the robots Cog and Kismet on a visit to the MIT AI lab in the fall of 2001. Cog, as the graduate student who led our tour explained apologetically, was inactive and had been so for some time. As there were no researchers actively working on its development, Cog was afflicted by a condition commonly known as "bit rot," or the degradation of code in the absence of ongoing maintenance of its compatibility with continually changing software and hardware environments (see Smith 1996: 203). We were, however, able to visit the inanimate Cog sitting in a corner of the lab. Although still an imposing figure of a robot, what struck me most powerfully about Cog was the remainder of its "body" not visible in media portrayals. The base of Cog's torso was a heavy cabinet from which came an extraordinarily thick sheaf of connecting cables, running centaurlike to a ceiling-high bank of processors that provided the computational power required to bring Cog to life. Seeing the robot "at home" in the lab, situated in this "backstage" environment, provided an opportunity to see as well the extended network of human labors and affiliated technologies that afford Cog its agency, rendered invisible in its typical media staging as Rod Brooks's singular creation and as an autonomous entity.[5]

Although Kismet was operational, in contrast to the interlocutors pictured in the Web site videos, none of our party was successful in eliciting coherent or intelligible behaviors from it. Framed as an autonomously affective entity, Kismet, like Cog, must be said to have failed in its encounters with my colleagues and me. But as in the case of Cog, there are more interesting and suggestive lessons to be learned from the difference between Kismet's demonstrated competencies and the Kismet that we encountered. Those lessons require that we reframe Kismet, like Cog, from an unreliable autonomous robot, to a collaborative achievement made possible through very particular, reiteratively developed and refined performances. The contrast between my own encounter with Kismet and that recorded on the demonstration videos makes clear the ways in which Kismet's affect is an effect not simply of the device itself but of Breazeal's trained reading of Kismet's actions and her extended history of labors with the machine. In the absence of Breazeal, correspondingly, Kismet's apparent randomness attests to the robot's reliance on the performative capabilities of its very particular "human caregiver."[6] Like all forms of agency, in other words, Cog and Kismet's capacities for action are created out of sociomaterial arrangements that

---

[5] For a closely related observation in a very different case, see Mialet's account of the extended corporeality of physicist Stephen Hawking (Mialet 2003).

[6] See http://www.ai.mit.edu/projects/sociable/overview.html (last accessed November 7, 2005). In an interview (Menzel and D'Aluisio 2000: 71), Breazeal responds to the suggestion that Kismet might be tuned specifically to her as an interactional partner with the hope that this is an early stage of the robot's development that will improve with time. One could argue, however, that this is the case with all beings both human and

instantiate histories of labor and more and less reliable, always contingent, future reenactments.

If humanlike robots comprise an other that mimes dominant cultural imaginaries of the human, a more literal doubling is materialized in performance artist Stelarc's *Prosthetic Head*.[7] The head is a three-dimensional graphical simulacrum of Stelarc's own, endowed with the capacity to take queries typed on a keyboard and to respond in automatically generated speech.[8] On exhibit at the InterAccess Gallery in Toronto in spring of 2003, the *Head* was displayed in larger than life-size dimensions on the wall of a darkened room, with no accompanying artifacts other than a pedestal holding a standard computer keyboard.[9] My visit to the gallery on March 29, 2003, was motivated by an interest in comparing the *Head* with previous attempts at conversational agents. I was delighted to discover that on that day the original Stelarc was also on hand, observing encounters with his digital doppelganger.[10] Our encounter, lasting over an hour and videotaped independently by my companion and by Stelarc himself, was augmented by Stelarc's

---

nonhuman, from the proverbial "two-year-old" child to the artifacts discussed throughout this book. In both cases, intelligibility is tied to increasingly intimate familiarity.

[7] See http://www.stelarc.va.com.au/prosthetichead/. The artist credits the following collaborators for the creation of the *Head*: Karen Marcelo, project coordination, system configuration, alicebot customization (http://karenmarcelo.org/); Sam Trychin, customization of 3D animation and text to speech software; Barrett Fox, 3D modelling and animation (http://www.barrettfox.com/); John Waters, system configuration and technical advice (http://www.shtech.net/); and Richard Wallace, creator of alicebot and AIML (http://alicebot.org/) (Stelarc 2004).

[8] It is an interesting feature of conversational agents like the *Head* that they make evident the greater contingency of competent machinic hearing than of speaking. Although automatic speech generation is a relatively mature and robust technology, speech recognition still requires prolonged "training" of machines to the particularities of individual voices. This affords an interesting contrast to human language learning, where comprehension is widely experienced to precede fluent expression.

[9] Stelarc reports that the database that informs the *Head* has since been purchased by the Australian National Gallery in Canberra, The Sherman Galleries in Sydney, and Gilbert Silvermann, an American collector in Detroit. After its exhibition at the InterAccess Gallery, the *Head* was installed as a four-meter-high display and exhibited at ACMI (The Australian Centre for the Moving Image) in Melbourne. (Stelarc, e-mail communication, August 22, 2005.)

[10] Taussig (1993), in a chapter titled "The Talking Machine," remarks on the fascination of European colonists with the fascination of "primitive" peoples with the former's technologies, "the white man's fascination with the Other's fascination with white man's magic" (207), including most dramatically the phonograph. He cites the number of accounts of "first contact" between native peoples and technologies, as retold by observing Europeans. On this analysis artifacts like the *Prosthetic Head*, and I would argue unfamiliar technologies more generally, are aimed at rendering us all as primitives as the creators of these machines look on with fascination.

FIGURE 14.1. The author in conversation with Stelarc's Prosthetic Head, Inter Access Gallery, Toronto, Canada 29 March 2003 (photograph courtesy of Andrew Clement).

responses to the *Head's* responses to my queries, as well as by his ongoing commentary on the *Head* and advice on how best to engage with it.

An encounter with Stelarc's *Head* affords further evidence for the collective and contingent nature of sociomaterial agencies. I offer one indicative exchange:

> Stelarc:  It also has a simple way of generating poetry on the fly, it
>           has a simple database with keywords, you can say, "recite a
>           poem" (pause)
> LS:       (types) "Recite a poem, please"
> Stelarc:  It'll, basically put together a bunch of words tha-
>                                           [
> Head:                               Your polite style is very nice.
>           Our breathing imploding breathing imploding,
>           City body electric system city excessive replicating,
>           And city city involuntary imploding. (Smiles)
> LS:       Oh, that was very nice! (laughs, glance to Stelarc, types)
>           "Very nice!"

Head:     Thanks, still Lucy.

LS:        (types) "Recite another one."

Head:     Bodies not the involuntary so exchanging,
             Absent inconsequential excessive perhaps city blurring,
             Pulsing system electric excessive obsessively. (Smiles)

LS:        (laughs) Yeah, right on.

Stelarc:  (laughs) And it does have some interesting kind of philo-
             sophical kind of data, and information,

LS         Yeah?

Stelarc:  and definitions, umm . . .

Obs:      Can it recite any philosophers, or commentators?

Stelarc:  Well for example if you ask it "What is reductionism"
             (laughter)

Stelarc:  That's one of it's favorite, my favorite, ah . . .

LS:        (types) "What is reductionism?"

Head:     Reductionism is the philosophy that all psychology reduces
             to biology, all biology to chemistry, chemistry to physics,
             physics to mathematical logic. Therefore, according to
             reductionism, I can understand you by logic alone without
             having a human brain.

Obs:      (laughs) What about emergent properties?

LS:        (types) "Do you believe in reductionism?"

Head:     Yes I believe in it. Do you?

LS:        (laughs, types) "I'm not sure."

Head:     Is there anything I can say to help you make up your mind?
             (Much laughter all around, including Stelarc)

LS:        (types) "Do yo" (backspaces to begin over)

Obs:      Why doesn't he have feelings?

LS:        (turns around to Obs) What?

Obs:      Why don't you have any feelings?

LS:        (types) "Do you have feelings?"

Head:     As a robot I do not have any human emotion. My appar-
             ent emotional responses are simply algorithms designed to
             make me easier to interact with.

LS:        (types) "Do you think robots should have emotions?"

Head:     That depends on what you mean by thinking.

This sequence is readable for some recurring characteristics of interactions with conversational software. In particular, near the beginning
is a moment that reveals a basic, and clearly consequential, difference

among the human and nonhuman participants in the encounter. I am referring to the *Head*'s "interruption," in its first turn, of Stelarc's account of its poetic abilities, indicative of its lack of any awareness of other events in the room around it. As I have elaborated in previous chapters, human–computer interactions occur at a relatively narrow point of intersection, that is, at just those moments when the human participant takes an action that changes the system's state (in this case, by hitting the return key on the keyboard). In contrast, human interactions invariably exceed what is made accountable in any direct sense. And it is this contingent horizon of possibly relevant phenomena, I want to propose, that effects interaction's open-endedness.[11]

I return to my exchange with Stelarc's *Head* shortly but want first to pursue for a moment the question of open-endedness and the cybernetic. In "Cybernetics and the Mangle" (2002), Andrew Pickering explores the resonance that he sees between the work of mid-twentieth-century British cyberneticists Hal Ashby, Stafford Beer, and Gordon Pask and Pickering's own theorizing of practice as "the emergent interplay of human and material agency" (ibid.: 414; see also Pickering 1995). He offers as one realization Ashby's homeostat, a device designed to achieve self-regulation through an iterative succession of autoreconfigurations – a process effecting what Pickering characterizes as a form of "liveliness." He writes: "I can't actually think of any prior example of a real machine that would randomly – *open-endedly*, as I would say – reconfigure itself in response to its inputs...It seems reasonable, then, to speak of the homeostat as having a kind of *agency* – it did things in the world that sprang, as it were, from inside itself, rather than having to be fully specified from outside in advance" (ibid.: 417, original emphasis).

I want to focus on the elision in this comment on Ashby's homeostat between randomness and open-endedness and also on the association

---

[11] In an article developed as a contribution to discussion of "awareness" within the field of CSCW, Heath et al. present a series of studies that make evident "the ways in which participants design activities to have others unobtrusively notice and discover actions and events which might otherwise pass unnoticed" (2002: 317). They make the important point that the mutuality of awareness does not necessarily involve a sameness or even symmetry among participants' orientations to an ongoing course of action: it is an orientation to the contingent possibility that something might become relevant that is crucial. It is the capacity for the latter, rather than any assumed sameness, that my use of "asymmetry" in the case of the human–machine interface is meant to reference. Heath et al. point out that "awareness" does not mean some form of general orientation through which relevant events are filtered but rather very particularly selective attention to an environment that, in turn, is highly differentiated. See also Pedersen and Sokoler (1997), Robertson (2002).

between agency and something that comes from "inside." First, what about the relation between randomness and open-endedness? Pickering here treats them as synonymous, though he concedes further on that in the case of the homeostat it is an open-endedness of a delimited kind, however large the space of possibilities. His idea of the mangle, in contrast, turns on a picture of agency as "indefinitely" open-ended.[12] The agency of the homeostat, moreover, was in an important sense a prespecified one; that is, "there was a principle of stability hard-wired in." In contrast, Pickering observes: "The mangle is in at least two ways on the wild side of the homeostat – involving indefinitely open-ended searches of spaces of agency, and with no fixed principle of assemblage" (ibid.: 418). This leads him to call for an exploration of differences as well as similarities between instantiations of sociomaterial agency, a point that I return to below. But Pickering concludes with a celebration of cybernetics as a radical alternative to the classical sciences: "While the latter seek to pin the world down in timeless representations, cybernetics directly thematizes the unpredictable liveliness of the world, and processes of open-ended becoming" (ibid.: 430).

My own much more skeptical reading of the cybernetic project hangs on contradictions between the legacy of behaviorism, teleology, and control engineering that I believe still sits at the core of its devices and aspirations and a sense of contingency and interactivity worthy of the name of "unpredictable liveliness" and "open-ended becoming."[13] To pursue these questions, I turn back to my encounter with Stelarc's *Head*. I was speaking of the *Head*'s (apparent) interruption of its progenitor, which in a moment of ironic serendipity takes the form of the *Head*'s complimentary remark regarding my own politeness. Rather than being read as rudeness, the *Head*'s action demonstrates its inability to perform the kind of competent interruption that rudeness requires, displacing a demonstration of social awareness with a mark of its machinic nature.[14] A second moment of mechanism revealed occurs when the *Head* responds to my compliment on its poetic abilities by addressing

---

[12] Pickering is excited by the possibility that a particular class of cybernetic machines (for example, Ashby's "Musicolor" device) can serve as instantiations of what he names "decentred becomings" (personal communication, November 8, 2005). The latter idea, as developed in his trope of "the mangle," is, I believe, deeply resonant with the forms of reconfiguration that I consider here and in Chapter 15. See Pickering (1995, 2002).

[13] On the history of cybernetics, including its universalizing and "closed world" rhetorics, see Bowker (1993), Edwards (1996).

[14] On the extraordinary competences involved in conversational turn-taking, see, for example, Sacks et al. (1978), Goodwin (1981).

me as "still Lucy." The installation at the InterAccess Gallery was configured with a pressure sensitive pad placed at the foot of the pedestal
on which the keyboard rested: it is the visitor's step onto the pad that
activates the software running the *Head*, effectively "waking it up" and
initiating a request for the visitor's name.[15] A standard feature of so-
called conversational agents, this salutation effects what Chesher (2004)
names an "avocation," a kind of interpolation of the prospective user–
participant into the configuration of the interface. In the case of the
*Head*, the three-dimensional corporeality of the encounter is enhanced
by the fact that, rather than sitting at a standard display screen, the
visitor stands opposite the *Head*, which in turn fills her field of view.
The activation of the *Head* software by the pressure-sensitive pad sets
up a spatial conjoining of *Head* and visitor in which both are entrained,
in other words, and which marks as well the temporal bounds of a
particular exchange. On the day of our encounter, however, the pressure pad was repeatedly failing to transmit, with the result that the
*Head* was liable to shut down and no longer respond to keyed input,
in a way that would be appropriate had its interlocutor walked away.
The fix for this bug was for the visitor to step off of the pad and
then step back onto it again. This interrupted the continuity, however,
with the result that the *Head* treated the ensuing exchange as a new
encounter, once again requesting a name. To draw attention to this
failure of recognition I introduced myself on reentering the dialogue
with the phrase "I'm still Lucy" and was named "still Lucy" from that
time on.[16]

Whereas breaches like this reveal the machinic limits of the *Head*'s
interactional competencies, other moments effect an uncanny sense
of presence and of generative spontaneity. The *Head*'s poetic abilities,
as Stelarc explains, are based on serendipitous juxtapositions from an

---

[15] The eyes of the *Head* when not activated are closed: the pressure on the pad initiates
its processes in much the same way that a touch of the space bar awakens a sleeping
laptop.

[16] Stelarc reports that in its subsequent installation at the The Australian Centre for the
Moving Image in Melbourne approximately 1,500 people went through the exhibition every day for five months, and the *Head* performed flawlessly (Stelarc, e-mail
communication, August 22, 2005). In any case, I cite this breakdown not as anything extraordinary or as diminishing of the *Head*'s success. On the contrary, I would
argue that in important respects it is moments like this which reveal the extraordinary
achievements of technical systems. In breaching the general invisibility of the infrastructure that would otherwise go unnoticed, they call our attention to other actors –
human and nonhuman – outside of the frame. I return to this question of framing below.

FIGURE 14.2. Prosthetic Head, San Franciso, Melbourne 2003, Programmers Karen Marcelo, Sam Trychin, 3-D models Barrett Fox, reprinted with permission from STELARC.

evocatively seeded database of "keywords." What is not available from the transcript is the singularly enchanting performance of these verses, effected through the cadence of the *Head*'s speech and the dynamic animation of its face, particularly the eyes and mouth. Special attention has been paid in the design of the *Head* to the eyeballs, teeth, and tongue, each of which are separate moving elements in the 3000-polygon mesh model of the artist's head from which the *Head* is constructed.[17] This brings us to the second issue raised by Pickering, regarding agency as action initiated "from inside." Pickering here invokes a contrast between things that achieve agency from within themselves or through external specifications. In his consideration of objects endowed with human (or superhuman) properties, Gell points out that mind can only ever be depicted suggestively, as that which is hidden "inside" an observable body. In the case of traditional idols, this is typically done through the introduction of some kind of opening or orifice, which designates an exterior–interior distinction to which the opening gives access. Eyes are the canonical example, as "the windows to the soul" (1998: 132, 136). In this sense mind and spirit are anthropologically symmetrical alternates, each standing for an indexically constituted mind–body contrast, an interior indicated by the surfaces of the body that enclose it. Gell observes: "There are thus two basic strategies for converting (conceptually) stocks and stones into quasi-persons in artifact-form. The first of these strategies consists of animating the idol by simply stipulating for it a role as a social other. The second consists of providing it with a homunculus, or space for a homunculus, or turning it into a homunculus within some larger entity" (1998: 133). Gell points to the primacy of vision and of the eyes in Hindu iconography, union coming from eye contact with the gods, as the "eyes of the god, which gaze at the devotee,

---

[17] See http://www.acmi.net.au/7E8A5C8E6F304A839116C3C74F81440C.htm.

mirror the action of the devotee, who gazes at the god" (1998: 119). Stelarc himself sees his project as a direct challenge to conceptions of consciousness, mind, intelligence, and the like as forms of mysterious interiority. In the context of prevailing figures of humanness, however, the desire to effect an uncanny liveliness for the *Head* inescapably suggests those very things.

The poetry that the head recites involves an ingenious use of the stored database of keywords strung together in ways that exploit the often deliberately nonlinear juxtapositions of poetry and the irrepressibly suggestive and meaningful nature of language. One result of this is the generation of what Stelarc characterizes as "alternate, intimate, involuntary experiences" for the *Head*'s interlocutors.[18] The flowing cadence of the *Head*'s recitation contributes to the sense of its artistry, with the result that its poetry generates laughter and delight from its listeners. Similarly, the exchange regarding the nature of "reductionism" reverberates with its reflexive relevance for the *Head* as speaker and comprises a moment of astonishingly coherent alignment effected by the well-established technique of matching certain key phrases ("I'm not sure") with associated responses ("Is there anything I say to help you make up your mind?").[19] What affords the liveliness of the exchange

---

[18] See http://www.stelarc.va.com.au/index2.html.

[19] The *Head* is based on the long-standing and widely circulating platform called ALICE. See http://www.alicebot.org/. (See Chapter 12.) Stelarc explains that the *Head*'s "general knowledge" is based on the ALICE database, which has had over five hundred contributors since 1995 when "Alice the Chatterbot" and AIML (the Artificial Intelligence Mark-up Language) was initiated by programmer Richard Wallace. The *Head*'s database has "inherited" much of this from ALICE but has also, since late 2002, been altered and extended, as Stelarc explains:

> in order to personalize the Head, to more express the artist's concerns and concepts. Not only in what it knows and how it says it but also that it develops some of its own "creative" capabilities. For example, the Head can make poetry-like sentences and song-like combinations of sounds (generated differently each time it is asked). Much of the Alice data-base is neutral information about the world, but some of it expresses the peculiar beliefs of the programmers. Often exposing particular American biases (the right to bear arms) and certain religious beliefs (a Christian God). Although much of this kind of data has been deleted or adjusted, occasionally the Head gives conflicting answers. It doesn't believe in God (me!) but it might still have embedded somewhere a response that contradicts this. So it is a fundamentally schizoid entity. (Aren't we all?) (Stelarc, e-mail communication, August 25, 2005)

This complex and inconsistent "inheritance," as Stelarc characterizes it, is part of what makes up the *Head* just as ours makes us.

is the simultaneous recognition of that alignment, of the creative pro-gramming labors that stand behind it, and of the ways in which it points, unwittingly, to a future relationship – of persuasive discussion – that we anticipate actually exceeds the *Head*'s capacity.[20] That mix of alignment and slippage, and the response that it evokes, is demonstrated most dramatically in the close of the sequence. The question "Do you think that robots should have emotions?" again explores the bounds of the *Head*'s self-reflective and humanlike capacities. But where the question anticipates an orientation to the problem of emotion, the *Head* disarm-ingly organizes its response around a prior problem – one moreover that is defining of the project of which the *Head* is a part – that of thought itself.

Reflecting on my afternoon with Stelarc and his *Head*, I am struck by the sense of collaborative performance involved, both within and beyond the gallery walls. Within the encounter all worked together to make the particular assemblage of exhibition space, persons, and arti-facts cohere into something if not always intelligible, at least interesting and worthwhile. As Kember characterizes the progeny of researchers in artificial life, "these novel agents do not so much evolve as coevolve in the dynamic interplay between observer and object, and they are more a facet of communication – the desire for life – than of computation – alife itself" (2003: 6). Stelarc is interested in what he describes as the "seductive couplings" that occur between the head and its interlocu-tors. He playfully proposes as well that the *Head* might serve a more useful purpose: of standing in for the artist in response to requests from the media, eager students, and the like. Framed as his virtual double, Stelarc's *Prosthetic Head* does effectively distribute the artist's agency. It does so not through any simple form of replication, however, but as an effect of complex and shifting assemblages of persons and things, specifically situated in time and place. It is to the question of differences *within* such assemblages that I now turn.

---

[20] Stelarc explains that because of the limitations of the AIML programming language, the *Head* is unable to increase its database from the conversations that it has. "It is programmed in stimulus–response modules. You anticipate the queries, you provide data for its responses" (Stelarc 2004). On Stelarc's view it is this inability to learn from its conversations that prevents the *Head* from being an artificial intelligence. At the same time "as its database increases the head will become more informed and less predictable in its responses. The head will appear to be more autonomous. The artist would then no longer be able to take full responsibility for what his head says" (Stelarc 2004).

## REENCHANTMENTS

These reflections on encounters at the human–computer interface are meant to contribute to an awakening of the "congealed life in the petrified objects" of AI and robotics (Taussig 1993: 1). Contrary to the apparent enlivening of objects promised by the sciences of the artificial, I want to propose that an investment in obscuring the performative foundations of persons and things instead works to deaden the resulting artifacts. To further emphasize these foundations of subject and objecthood, I turn to the question posed by Marilyn Strathern regarding the personification of objects. Strathern approaches the answer by asking a prior question; that is, in what respects might we understand the constitution of persons as a form of reflexive objectification?[21] She takes as her frame associated acts of separation and relation, as "it is through the separation of persons from one another that specific relations are created, and through relations that persons are defined . . . " (1999: 16). In her earlier studies of Melanesian personhood, Strathern introduces a distinction between "person" and "agent." The "person" is not a preexisting entity but an object of the regard of others and an objectification of the relations that constitute her. The "agent," in turn, is the one who acts with those relations as cause and reference – "with another in mind" (1988: 272–4).

The project of creating a humanlike machine requires that the phrase "with another in mind" be questioned more closely, however, than its colloquial sense would suggest. Standard readings within cognitive science would attempt a kind of literal mapping into a model of the mind of one actor of some model of the other. But the context of Strathern's statement suggests something else. The mind of the Hagener as Strathern recounts it is not an entity contained within the person but rather the enactment of an elaborate, and elaborating, history of social relationships implying specific agencies and consequences. It is impossible, on Strathern's account, to conceptualize Melanesian agency apart from those relations: agents are not the authors of their own acts, albeit that their actions are no less their own. This argument suggests that intentionality needs to be understood not as an attitude of mind located within the individual but as a field of socially and materially mediated relations within which persons act.

---

[21] Working within a very different intellectual tradition, social philosopher George Herbert Mead makes a related argument in his classic exploration *Mind, Self and Society* (1934).

These arguments reverberate with others in cultural anthropology as well, located at the interface not between humans and machines but at the moments when humans come into, and go out of, recognized social personhood. Casper (1994, 1998), Franklin (2000), Hogle (1999), Lock (2002), Thompson (Cussins 1998; Thompson 2005), and others concerned with the anthropology of birth and death have drawn our attention to the ways in which these transition zones at the edges of life provide poignant sites for the study of personhood and its problematics. In a moving analysis of neonatal intensive care, Middleton and Brown (2005) cite a physician who observes that at some point in the process of working to keep a premature baby alive it is the baby who, as the physician phrases it, "decides" its future. Read through the lens of Strathern's discussion of "cutting the network" (1996), this observation can be understood not as a statement of the infant's acquisition of autonomous agency but as a practical move in the enactment of the sociotechnical networks of which the infant is an integral part. The account by Middleton and Brown describes the ever-ramifying extensions to the network of neonatal intensive care that are now possible: as long as more and more human and nonhuman resources can be brought to bear, the infant body can, at least potentially, be sustained. Rather than reading the physician's statement to say that the infant at some point takes over the agency of this collective, we might read it as a statement that at some point the autonomy of the infant *must be posited* for the collective effort, and ramifying extensions to the network, to be cut. Constituting the infant's autonomous agency, in other words, makes it possible at least partially to disengage this morally and emotionally central – at once fragile and powerful – entity from its reliance on the wider human–nonhuman collective.

The sciences of the artificial operate in a cultural and historical frame that takes autonomous agency not as an effect of cutting the network, however, but as the precondition for participation in it. Given an ontology of separate things that need to be joined together, machines must in some sense be granted agency to be brought into relationship with us. Given a model of humanness as a set of separate components that need to be incorporated into a coherent whole, and the resulting individual as an entity that needs to be acculturated into a set of social relations, the projects of artificial intelligence make some kind of sense. But what if our starting place comprises configurations of always already interrelated, reiterated sociomaterial practices? What if we understand persons as entities achieved only through the ongoing enactment of separateness and always in relation with others? Rather than working to create autonomous objects that mimic Cartesian subjects, we might then undertake different kinds of design projects – projects discussed in the following chapter under the theme of human–machine reconfigurations.

# 15

# Reconfigurations

Agency is not an attribute but the ongoing reconfigurings of the world.
(Barad 2003: 818)

In this chapter I consider some new resources for thinking about, and acting within, the interface of persons and things. It is here, on the question of alternatives to information theoretic approaches to human–machine interactions, that I believe the ground has shifted most radically over the past twenty years. The shifts involve reconceptualizations of the social and the material and the boundary between them, with associated implications for practices of system design. The explorations are ongoing within relevant areas of cultural anthropology, science and technology studies, feminist theory, new media studies, and experiments in cooperative systems design, each of which is multiple and extensive in themselves and no one of which I can do full justice to here. I hope nonetheless to trace out enough of the lines of resonance that run through these fields of research and scholarship to indicate the fertility of the ground, specifically with respect to rethinking and creatively enacting the interface of humans and machines.

## EXCLUDED MIDDLES

It was the circular move of writing a cognitivist rationality onto machines and then claiming their status as models for the human that first provoked me to question the notion of intelligent, interactive artifacts. My concern then, as now, has to do with the implications of this move both for our notion of what machines are and also with ways

259

in which the premises and products of artificial intelligence research continue to restage traditional Euro-American assumptions about the nature of being human. In setting up my critique, however, I fell back into a familiar humanist stance, defending against what I saw as AI's attributions of (a certain version of) intelligence and interactivity to machines by effectively reclaiming (a different version of) those qualities for humans. Since then, I have struggled with the question of how to maintain the sense of human–machine difference that I developed in my analysis, while taking to heart the insights generated from subsequent thinking regarding the distributed and enacted character of agency, and the implications of such reconceptualizations for essentialist human–nonhuman divides.

Latour (1993: 77–8) usefully demarcates a "Middle Kingdom" with respect to human–nonhuman relations, within which he locates the space between simple translations from human to nonhuman, on the one hand, and a commitment to maintaining the distinctness and purity of those categories, on the other. Translation in the case of humans and machines involves practices through which capacities taken to be inherent in one are shifted to, or realized through, the other. In resisting the particular translations of intelligence and interactivity recommended by AI in the 1970s and 1980s, I turned to a kind of exercise of purification, attempting to maintain those qualities as exclusively human. I now believe that what we need is to, in Latour's words, "direct our attention simultaneously to the work of purification and the work of hybridization" (1993: 11) with respect to human–machine boundaries. This involves developing a discourse that recognizes the deeply mutual constitution of humans and artifacts, and the enacted nature of the boundaries between them, without at the same time losing distinguishing particularities within specific assemblages. Recognizing the interrelations of humans and machines, in other words, does not mean that there are no differences. The problem rather is how to understand the nature of difference differently.[1]

I want to wander about a bit in Latour's Middle Kingdom, then, in considering the question of agency in humans and machines. For those like Latour writing within the Actor Network framework and its

---

[1] Questions of difference have been most extensively considered within feminist and postcolonial scholarship. For some exemplary texts see Ahmed (1998, 2000); Ahmed et al. (2000); Bhabha (1994); Braidotti (1994, 2002); Castañeda (2002); Franklin, Lury, and Stacey (2000); Gupta and Ferguson (1997); Strathern (1999); Turnbull (2000); Verran (2001).

aftermath, agency is understood as a material-semiotic attribute not locatable in either humans or nonhumans.[2] Agency on this view is rather an effect or outcome, generated through specific configurations of human and nonhuman entities. Moreover, in a move echoing the Melanesian conception of personhood described by Strathern (see Chapter 14), the entities involved do not precede their incorporation into such configurations in any simple way but emerge through their participation in various networks of relations. In the words of Callon, the network of interest for Actor Network Theory (ANT) is "not a network connecting entities which are already there, but a network which configures ontologies. The agents, their dimensions, and what they are and do, all depend on the morphology of the relations in which they are involved" (1999: 185–6). ANT's call for a "generalized symmetry" in analyses of human and nonhuman contributions to social order performed a powerful intervention into sociological preoccupations with human agency, as the latter "[l]iberated from its containment in human entities... is dispersed through the networks" (Ashmore et al. 1994: 2). I return to the question of symmetry below. But I turn first to the rich body of empirical studies that have specified, elaborated, and deepened the senses in which human agency is only understandable once it is reentangled in the sociomaterial relations that the "modern constitution" (Latour 1993) has, since the seventeenth century, so exhaustingly attempted to take apart.

## MUTUAL CONSTITUTIONS

A growing corpus of studies of sites of sociomaterial practice over the past twenty years provide compelling empirical demonstrations of how capacities for action can be reconceived on foundations quite different from those of a humanist preoccupation with the individual actor living in a world of separate things. This body of work is too extensive to be comprehensively reviewed, but a few indicative examples can serve as illustration.

---

[2] The phrase *material-semiotic* was coined by Haraway (1991: 194–5) to indicate the ways in which the natural and the cultural, or the material and the meaningful, are inextricably intertwined. Although not cited in the early formulations of Actor Network Theory, the writings of Haraway and other feminist science studies scholars have since become increasingly central to writings "after" ANT. See, for example, the articles collected in Law and Mol (2002). I return to regenerative discussions of agency and difference within feminist scholarship below.

The question of human–nonhuman relations has been intensively explored within science studies. Pickering (1995) develops the metaphor of the "mangle" to create a performative account of knowledge practices, including centrally the construction of machines that "variously capture, seduce, download, recruit, enroll or materialize" human agency (ibid.: 7). Key to Pickering's analysis is time, the view that what he names *material agency* is always temporally emergent in practice, rather than fixed in either subjects or objects (see also Lynch, Livingston, and Garfinkel (1983)). Knorr-Cetina adopts a trope of "epistemic cultures" to think about laboratories as mutually shaping arrangements of scientists, instruments, objects, and practices aimed at the production of observably stabilized instantiations of "reality effects" (1999: 26–33). The notion of reconfiguration is central to her analysis as well, as the process through which subject/object relations are reworked. Considered over time, she argues, reconfigurations comprise what are commonly termed skills or expertise: "The alignments . . . work through the body of the scientist, but they also involve a drastically rearranged environment, a new life-world in which new agents ineract and move. When we ascribe skills to a person . . . the person acts as a symbol – a stand-in for the common life-world with objects, which, in the laboratory . . . is continually recreated" (219–20). Knorr Cetina's argument here has resonance as well with Lynch's (1991) formulation of "topical contextures" to indicate the inseparability of knowledge practices and the phenomenal fields of action that they at once constitute and inhabit, and with Ingold's (2000) analysis of skill not as an attribute of a body, but of a system of relations involving the artisan's presence in a specifically configured sociomaterial environment.

In his exploration of what he terms "professional vision," Charles Goodwin has carried out a series of studies focused on the sociomaterial interactions through which practitioners learn to see the phenomena that constitute the objects of their profession (C. Goodwin 1994, 1995a, 1997, 2003). A central argument is that these phenomena are not preexisting but are constituted as disciplinarily relevant objects through occasioned performances of competent seeing (see also Goodwin and Goodwin 1996, 1997). In looking at gestures and their objects, for example, Goodwin argues that the relation is a "symbiotic" one; that is, "a whole that is both different from, and greater than its parts, is constructed through the mutual interdependence of unlike elements" (2003: 20). Symbiotic gestures, Goodwin argues, are not referring to something outside of themselves: rather, the gesture's objects are integral components of the gesture itself (ibid.: 40, note 1). In the case of archaeologists "defining features" of relevance in a site of excavation, for example, Goodwin observes that a "feature" does not simply present itself but must be made visible through the embodied work of the archaeologist, including talk with colleagues, gestures, inscriptions in the dirt, and various forms of record keeping, mapping, and the like (see also Latour 1999: 58–61). In this way "a feature as a semiotic object...emerges as the product of both actual patterning in the soil being investigated, and the cultural categories and embodied practices used by archaeologists to make it visible as a particular kind of phenomenal object" (ibid.: 29). At the same time, the objects being defined and their categorization exist within a professional matrix of social and material accountability, subject to contest by the readings of others and by the objects themselves; for example, in the discovery of roots extending from what has been previously identified as a post mold, indicating instead the presence of a tree (ibid.: 30). Archaeological knowledge, on this analysis, comprises relations between particular culturally and historically constituted practices and their associated materials and tools. It is out of those relations, quite literally, that the objects of archeological knowledge and the identity of competent archeologist are co-constructed.

Although not concerned specifically with interactive machines, Goodwin's analysis provides further support for the wider argument against attributions of agency either to humans or to artifacts and gives us, in turn, a different way of understanding the problem of attributions of knowledge and agency to machines. The problem is less that we attribute agency to computational artifacts than that our language for talking about agency, whether for persons or artifacts, presupposes a field of discrete, self-standing entities.[3] As an alternative, we can take the interface not as an a priori or self-evident boundary between bodies and machines but as a relation enacted in particular settings and one, moreover, that shifts over time.

The shifting nature of body–machine boundaries is enacted quite literally in the case of technology-intensive medicine, and here again an instructive series of studies are available. Dawn Goodwin (2004) describes the practices through which patients in surgery are "transitioned" through anaesthetic states, a process involving the radical reconfiguration of their capacity for action; specifically, for the sustenance

---

[3] Latour makes a closely related argument, using the example of the gun. See Latour (1999: 179–80). See also Casper (1994), Law (1987).

of their own life support. Over the course of an anaesthesia, agencies involved in the maintenance of vital bodily functions are progressively delegated from the patient as an autonomously embodied entity to an intricately interconnected sociomaterial assemblage and then back again.[4] Through a series of cases, Goodwin demonstrates how the technologies of anaesthesia are joined to the patient's body, in ways that render the latter highly dependent and vulnerable but nonetheless intensely (albeit sometimes ambiguously) communicative. This joining is analyzed as a delicate choreography involving patients, medical practitioners, and machines.[5] Goodwin argues that questions of agency are crucial both to assess policy with respect to medical practice and to deepen our understanding of the dense sociotechnical arrangements that comprise much of contemporary medical activities and institutions.

In a related argument developed through the case of reproductive technoscience, Thompson (Cussins 1998; Thompson 2005) argues against the idea that medical interventions inherently objectify patients and thereby strip them of their agency. She observes that in the case of infertility clinics "the woman's objectification, naturalization, and bureaucratization involve her active participation and are managed by herself as crucially as by the practitioners, procedures, and instruments" (Cussins 1998: 167). Conversely, objectification does not inherently or necessarily lead to alienation, nor does it stand always in opposition to subjectivity or personhood. Among other things, the clinic relies on the possibility of separation (of egg and sperm from the bodies that produce them) without alienation. Cussins locates alienation not in objectification per se, but in the breakdown of synechdochal relations between parts and whole that make objectification of various forms into associated forms of agency. It is this process "of forging a functional zone of compatibility that maintains referential power between things of different kinds" that she names *ontological choreography* (ibid.: 192). Medical ethics and accountability, she argues, need to be founded

---

[4] The particular expertise of the anaesthetic practitioner on this account is to manage the often unruly contingencies of the unfolding course of anaesthesia through a combination of skillfully embodied techniques, reading of signs, professional judgments, and legitimating accounts, which together provide the grounds for practical action. See also Heath et al. 2002, Hirschauer 1991, Mort et al. 2005.

[5] The trope of "choreography" was introduced by Charis Thompson (Cussins 1998, Thompson 2005), whose work I return to below.

not in the figure of the rational, informed citizen but in the conditions for the maintenance of those crucial relations that configure identities and selves and that might allow them to be reconfigured in desired ways.

The assemblage of the pregnant woman has been the focus as well of Casper's research on experimental fetal surgery, where categories of the human and associated agencies take on a particular salience and urgency (1994, 1998). In the context of debates over abortion within the United States, the figuring of "fetal patients" has consequences that resonate not only within but also well beyond the walls of the surgery. In addressing this tricky political terrain, Casper calls for a methodological strategy aimed at "grounding the construction of social identities and subject positions in concrete practices, more specifically the practices through which fetal humanity, including agency, is socially and technologically shaped" (1994: 2). A central moral of Casper's story is that questions of agency are inseparable from the more extended frames of reference in which entities are entangled or, alternatively, that their separation is itself a strategically consequential act. I return to the question of frames below but note for the moment that Casper's analysis suggests in turn that the politics of fetal agency cannot be adequately debated without taking as our primary unit the woman *plus fetus, within* the context of the latter's contested material and symbolic status and its implications for actual women's lives.

Whereas fetal surgery would stand as among the most maximally invasive of medical procedures, a different sense of the fluidity of body–machine boundaries is provided by Prentice's ethnographic interviews with physicians engaged in its surgical opposite (2005). Minimally invasive or "keyhole" surgery, as it has developed over the past few decades, has involved a series of shifts in the gaze of the surgeon and attendant practitioners from the interior of the patient's body – formerly achieved through a correspondingly large incision – to views mediated first through microscopy and now through digital cameras and large screen monitors. Prentice finds that surgeons accustomed to operating within previous configurations of patient and instruments express a sense of disorientation when they are translated into the reconfigured sociotechnical network of video camera and monitor. One surgeon with whom Prentice speaks reports an experience not only of his gaze but also of his hands and entire body, effectively leaving the site of the patient's body and "going to work on the monitor" or image instead; a translation that he finds deeply alienating.[6] In contrast, Prentice found that surgeons who have performed minimally invasive surgery mediated by camera and monitor throughout their career report a very different phenomenal shift. Far from being alienated from the patient, they experience themselves as proprioceptively shifted more directly and proximally into the operative site, with the manipulative instruments serving as fully incorporated extensions of their own acting body.[7] As Prentice observes of these cases: "When the patient's body is distributed by technology, the surgeon's body reunites it through the circuit of his or her own body" (ibid.: 8). These differences suggest again that questions of alignment or dislocation, relation or alienation, are not immanent in human–machine boundaries or even, a priori, in particular human–machine configurations. Rather, they are effects lived and experienced within multifaceted subject–object assemblages.

The shifting boundaries of humans and machines and their consequences comprise the topic of another study of minimally invasive surgical practices by Aanestad (2003), who focuses on the labors performed by nurses and technicians in aligning the complex sociotechnical environment of the surgical theatre itself.[8] Her study follows the installation of multimedia communications technologies (cameras, microphones, and speakers) in a surgical operating theatre in ways intended not only to enable the surgery but also to facilitate communication with viewers outside, including with remotely located surgeons in training. Aanestad's analysis follows the course of shifting interdependencies in the surgical assemblage, as changes to existing arrangements necessitate further

---

[6] It is important to note that this is not a simple distinction between mediated and unmediated access. All of the surgeons with whom Prentice spoke in this study were experienced in keyhole or minimally invasive surgery. The surgeon who reported his sense of disorientation with the latest techniques had previously worked while looking through a microscopic eyepiece; the disruptive shift for him was from that to a video monitor more distal from both his own and the patient's body.

[7] This sense of the fluidity of body boundaries and their reconfigurability is resonant with Mol's findings (2002) regarding the ontologies of subjects, artifacts, and objects in medical practice.

[8] The question of visibility–invisibility and framing resonates throughout Aanestad's study, as nurses and technicians configure the theatre for transmission of the surgery to remote audiences in ways that center the surgeon and quite literally relegate their own work to the margins, outside the field of view. At the same time, this is not a simple story of power lost, as the technologies become available to them for appropriation in new ways, while their own role in the surgical process becomes more indispensable. On invisible work see Clement (1993), Shapin (1989), Star (1991), Suchman and Jordan (1989); on gendered (re-)appropriations of new technologies see Cherny and Weise (1996), Spender (1996), Terry and Calvert (1997), Wakeford (2000), Wolmark (1999).

changes in a process that she names the in situ work of "design in configuration" (2003: 2). She emphasizes that the agencies of the technologies involved do not exist before their incorporation into the network; for example, as questions of the adequacy of image and sound quality or shifts in the locus of control. Aanestad concludes that introducing telemedicine or other network technologies in such settings requires "open and evolutionary strategies, which are aimed at enrolling allies, rather than control-oriented, specification-driven strategies" (ibid.: 16). Her analysis makes clear how in such a setting the capacity for action is relational, dynamic, and collective rather than inherent in specific network elements and how the extension of the network in turn intensifies network dependencies.

Together these inquiries respecify sociomaterial agency from a capacity intrinsic to singular actors to an effect of practices that are multiply distributed and contingently enacted. Addressing similar questions, but from a position within feminist philosophy and science studies, physicist Karen Barad has proposed a form of materialist constructivism that she names "agential realism," through which realities are constructed out of specific apparatuses of sociomaterial "intra-action" (2003). Whereas the construct of interaction suggests two entities, given in advance, that come together and engage in some kind of exchange, *intra-action* underscores the sense in which subjects and objects emerge through their encounters with each other.[9]

More specifically, Barad locates technoscientific practices as critical sites for the emergence of new subjects and objects. Taking physics as a case in point, her project is to work through long-standing divisions between the virtual and the real, while simultaneously coming to grips with the ways in which materialities, as she puts it, "kick back" in response to our intra-actions with them (1998: 112; see also Knorr Cetina (1999), Pickering (1984, 1995), Traweek (1988)). Through her close readings of Niels Bohr, Barad insists that "object" and "agencies of observation" in his view form a nondualistic whole: it is that relational entity that comprises the objective "phenomenon" (1996: 170). In a position consistent with Haraway's adoption of the compound "material-semiotic," Barad takes concepts and their objects as mutually constitutive. Different "apparatuses of observation" enable different, always contingent, subject–object cuts that in turn enable measurement or other forms of

---

[9] Smith (1996) develops a kindred concept of "registration" to describe the partial effects of subject–object difference, generated through processes of engaged participation.

objectification, distinction, manipulation, and the like *within* the phenomenon. The relation is "ontologically primitive" (2003: 815), in other
words, or prior to its components; the latter come about only through
the "cut" effected through a particular apparatus of observation.

One implication of this view is a more radical understanding of
the sense in which "materiality is discursive (i.e., material phenomena are inseparable from the apparatuses of bodily production: matter
emerges out of and includes as part of its being the ongoing reconfiguring of boundaries), just as discursive practices are always already
material (i.e., they are ongoing material (re)configurings of the world)"
(Barad 2003: 822). This intimate co-constitution of configured materialities with configuring agencies clearly implies a very different understanding of the human–machine interface. Read in association with the
empirical investigations of complex sociomaterial sites described above,
"the interface" becomes the name for a category of contingently enacted
cuts occurring always *within* sociomaterial practices, that effect "person"
and "machines" as distinct entities, and that in turn enable particular
forms of subject–object intra-actions. At the same time, the singularity
of "the interface" explodes into a multiplicity of more and less closely
aligned, dynamically configured moments of encounter within sociomaterial configurations, objectified as persons and machines. It is the
differences effected *within* such configurations that I turn to next.

### DIFFERENCES WITHIN

The reconstructions of sociomaterial agency reviewed above are frequently summarized by the proposition that humans and artifacts are
*mutually constituted*. This premise of technoscience studies has been
tremendously valuable as a corrective to the entrenched Euro-American
view of humans and machines as autonomous, integral entities that
must somehow be brought back together and made to interact. But at
this point I think that the sense of mutual constitution warrants a closer
look. In particular, we are now in a position to elaborate that generative trope along at least two critical dimensions: first, in relation to the
dynamic and multiple forms of constitution that are evident in specific
sociomaterial assemblages and, second, in terms of questions of difference – and more particularly asymmetries – within those assemblages.

As the studies reviewed above and others like them have shown, the
constitution of humans and artifacts does not occur in any single time
and place, nor does it create fixed human–artifact relations or entities.

Rather, artifacts are produced, reproduced, and transformed through ongoing "labours of division," in Law's phrase (1996), that involve continuous work across particular occasions and multiple sites of use. This work of production and reproduction across time and space results in very diverse assemblages, involving participants with different histories, relations of familiarity or strangeness, and the like. As Mulcahy points out with respect to technologies (1999), it is their increasingly extensive distribution and the range of variations across user–machine pairings that render protocols, standards, instructions, and the like necessary to the successful production and reliable reproduction of human–artifact interactions. Empirical investigations of the workings of standards and other technologies aimed at the reproduction of sameness (including those that take the form of plans or instructions examined earlier in this book) provide ample evidence that the agencies of such artifacts do not inhere in the prescriptions themselves but rely on the skilled practices that bring them into alignment with a given case at hand.

Mutualities, moreover, are not necessarily symmetries. My own analysis suggests that persons and artifacts do not constitute each other *in the same way*.[10] In particular, I would argue that we need a rearticulation of asymmetry, or more impartially perhaps, dissymmetry, that somehow retains the recognition of hybrids, cyborgs, and quasi-objects made visible through technoscience studies, while simultaneously recovering certain subject–object positionings – even orderings – among persons and artifacts and their consequences. The emphasis in science and technology studies on symmetrical analysis and the agency of things arose from well-founded concerns to recover for the social sciences and humanities aspects of the lived world – for example, "facts of nature" and "technology" – previously excluded from consideration as proper sociological subjects. My project is clearly indebted to these efforts, which provide the reconceptualizations needed to move outside the frame of categorical purification and opposition between social and technical, person and artifact. My own engagement with these questions, however, came first in the context of technoscience and engineering, where the situation is in important respects reversed. Far from being excluded, "the

---

[10] As Pickering points out with respect to humans and nonhumans, "Semiotically, these things can be made equivalent; in practice they are not" (1995: 15). This notwithstanding the possibility of delegating humanlike actions to machines, or identifying machinelike actions within the activities of humans (see also Collins 1990).

technical" in regimes of research and development are centered, whereas "the social" is separated out and relegated to the margins. It is the privileged machine in this context that creates its marginalized human others.[11]

So what are the possibilities for recovering a sense of particular agencies of the human without at the same time reinstating essentialized human–machine differences? How might we reconceptualize the granting of agency in a way that at once locates the particular accountabilities of human actors, while recognizing their inseparability from the sociomaterial networks through which they are constituted? Analyses – including my own – that describe the active role of artifacts in the configuration of networks inevitably seem to imply other actors standing just offstage for whom technologies act as delegates, translators, mediators; that is, human engineers, designers, users, and so on. I want to suggest that the persistent presence of designers–users in technoscientific discourse is more than a recalcitrant residue of humanism: that it reflects a durable dissymmetry among human and nonhuman actors. The response to this observation is not, however, to cry "Aha, it really is the humans after all who are running the show." Rather, we need a story that can tie humans and nonhumans together without erasing the culturally and historically constituted differences among them. Those differences include the fact that, in the case of technological assemblages, persons just are those actants who configure material-semiotic networks, however much we may be simultaneously incorporated into and through them.[12] I want to keep in view as well the ways in which it matters when things travel across the human–artifact boundary, when objects are subjectified (e.g., machines made not actants but actors) and subjects objectified (e.g., practices made methods or knowledges made commodities).[13]

Applied to the question of agency, I have argued that in the case of the intelligent machine we are witnessing a reiteration of traditional humanist notions of agency, at the same time – even through – the

---

[11] I use "others" here in the sense nicely summarized by Lee and Brown as "all those entities and areas of inquiry that are rendered problematic by expansionist projects, be they formally political or theoretical" (1994: 773).

[12] Pickering (1995: 15) similarly poses the question of who does the "delegation" of agencies across actor networks.

[13] As Haraway (2003: 4) succinctly reminds us with respect to the machinic and animal, "the differences between even the most politically correct cyborg and an ordinary dog matter."

intra-actions of that notion with new computational media. In the remainder of this chapter I look to further experiments in configuring human–machine boundaries to explore the question of what other directions our relations with machines, both conceptually and practically, might take.

### REREADING THE HUMAN–MACHINE

I turn first to recent counterreadings of the humanlike machine, inspired by feminist discussions of materialities, subjectivities, and cyborg bodies. Like many, my attention was first drawn to these possibilities by Donna Haraway's "whip lashing" proposal (a phrase that she herself uses to describe those moments when a new idea comes along that turns one's head) that we should all prefer to be cyborgs than goddesses (1985/1991: 223). As Wolmark summarizes, in her discussion of the "Manifesto for Cyborgs": "The cyborg's propensity to disrupt boundaries and explore differently embodied subjectivities could ... be regarded as its most valuable characteristic, and it is undoubtedly one of the reasons for its continued usefulness in feminist and cultural theory" (1999: 6).[14] As feminist theorists trace a new path across the problematic terrain of how the sexed and gendered subject might be reconceived, they also provide us with resources for reconceptualizing the agential object. More specifically, feminist retheorizing of the body has been concerned to restore the dynamism emptied out of bodies by the mind–body split by moving through that split onto new terrain. In a similar way, feminist theorists suggest that we might find other grounds for recognizing the agential properties of the material than the operations of a transcendental intelligence over inert, mechanistically animated matter. As Butler famously puts it in *Bodies That Matter*: "What I would propose ... is a return to the notion of matter, not as site or surface, but as a process of materialization that stabilizes over time to produce the effect of boundary, fixity, and surface we call matter ... Crucially, then, [the construction of bodies] is neither a single act nor a causal process initiated by a subject and culminating in a set of fixed effects"

---

[14] At the same time, as Balsamo cautions, far from imploding the boundaries of human and machine, for most popular cyborg figures "Signs of human-ness and, alternatively, signs of machine-ness function not only as markers of the 'essences' of the dual natures of the hybrid, but also as signs of the inviolable opposition of human and machine. This is to say that cyborgs embody human characteristics that reinforce the difference between humans and machines" (2000: 149).

(1993: 9–10). Butler's argument that sexed and gendered bodies are materialized over time through the reiteration of norms is suggestive for a view of technology construction as a process of materialization through a reiteration of forms. Butler argues that "sex" is a dynamic materialization of always contested gender norms: similarly, we might understand "things" or objects as materializations of more and less contested, normative figurations of matter. Much as recognition and intelligibility are central to feminist conceptions of the subject, objects achieve recognition within a matrix of historically and culturally constituted familiar, intelligible possibilities. Technologies, like bodies, are both produced and destabilized in the course of these reiterations.

An early example of an alternative cyborgian embodiment is provided by Deirdre, the heroine of science fiction writer C. L. Moore's 1944 short story, "No Woman Born."[15] Deidre prefigures Haraway's challenge to the cultural imaginary of the goddess-turned-cyborg. Ambivalently positioned on the boundary of Cartesian and feminist imaginaries, the premise of Moore's story is that Deirdre, once an exquisitely beautiful and talented dancer, has been injured in a theater fire to the point that only her brain survives. As the brain of a *dancer*, however, Deirdre's brain is located by Moore in intimate relation to her body. As the story unfolds, it becomes clear that the restoration of Deirdre's agency is inseparably tied to the particularities of her rematerialization. We enter the story one year after the tragic fire, during which time Deirdre (Deirdre's brain?) has been painstakingly reembodied by Maltzer, a genius physician–scientist, assisted by a team of unnamed (but apparently greatly talented) sculptors and artists. The story that follows is effectively a set of variations around the theme of Deirdre's rematerialization, haunted by questions of memory, identity, recognition, transformation, and otherness. We approach these questions through the person of John Harris, Deirdre's former (human) agent and close friend, coming to see her for the first time following the accident. Torn by visions of, on one hand, the irrecoverable figure of Deirdre the human as he knew her and, on the other, culturally inspired imaginings of how the new, robotic Deirdre might be configured, Harris suffers agonies of anticipation in advance of their meeting. His anxieties are not allayed by the comments of her restorer Maltzer, in the anteroom of Deirdre's chambers: "It's not that she's – ugly – now ... Metal isn't ugly. And Deirdre ... well, you'll see.

---

[15] It is notable that this story appears in an anthology of science fiction short stories within which C. L. Moore is the only woman author.

I tell you, I can't see myself. I know the whole mechanism so well – it's just mechanics to me. Maybe she's – grotesque, I don't know" (1975: 67).

The Deirdre that Harris goes on to meet is less a replica than a new configuration, a reembodiment, of the Deirdre he remembers. In place of a face, she has a delicately modeled ovoid head with a kind of golden mask, in which a slit of aquamarine crystal occupies the place where her eyes would have been. And rather than a simulation of human skin over hinged metal joints, her body is made up of tiny golden coils, infinitely flexible, covered by a robe of very fine metal mesh, all of which she has learned to move with an extraordinary expressiveness and grace at once reminiscent of, and different from, her former dancer's body. As Harris struggles to come to terms with the neither–nor, both–and qualities of the new Deirdre, the story unfolds as a succession of reflections on the uncertainties of Deirdre's status, in relation to her former identity as Deirdre and to the rest of the human world. First, what is the relation of this new creature to "Deirdre" herself? Is "she" still alive? And what about the reembodied Deirdre's relation to her creator, Maltzer? Is she an extension of him, his property, or an autonomous being, animating the materials that he has provided with her own "unquenchable" essence? And is her essence that of the brain that survived or some irreducible spirit that animates her new body? In one of his more posthumanist moments, Harris muses, "She isn't human, but she isn't pure robot either. She's something somewhere between the two, and I think it's a mistake to try to guess just where, or what the outcome will be" (ibid.: 88). The story's pivotal question, on which the plot turns, is whether Deirdre is still human and, if not, whether the rematerialized Deirdre can survive given her singular otherness. Not surprisingly, this question remains unanswered at the story's end. But what Moore has achieved is to reframe the cyborg from its reiteratively human replicant form to something that dances elusively, and therefore suggestively, on the boundaries of old and new possibilities. Deirdre embodies the ambivalences of mid-twentieth-century technoscience, suggesting the possibilities for new configurations that are fabulous and expansive, while at the same time threatening the reassuring ground of normative categories on which our experiences of relationship, of knowing and being known, depend. Figured alternately as goddess, human, superhuman, and monster, Deirdre powerfully expresses the questions raised by new sociomaterial possibilities and their relations to old struggles around identity and difference.

More recently, Claudia Castañeda (2001) has written about the rematerialization of touch in contemporary robotic artificial intelligence.

Beginning from an understanding of touch as always semiotic and relational, and of signs as always entailing materialities, she takes up the
question of the skin and its materialization in the form of the robot
Cog (see Chapter 13).[16] Interactivity is framed by Cog's designers as the
litmus test of its competencies, with "the world" and with its human
counterparts. During Cog's early, awkward stage, its "skin" (described
as "an exquisitely sensitive piezo-electric membrane" in Dennett 1994:
139) is designed to serve as a protective device against contact, equipped
with the requisite sensors and alarms. Castañeda explores the premise
that Cog's embodiment, particularly its skin, is designed to change in
response to the robot's interactions over time. My skeptical reading of
the project falters on the question just how open the possibilities of
rematerialization are for Cog given the robot's origins in the historical
and cultural matrix of the Massachusetts Institute of Technology. But
Castañeda's hopeful reading points us to aspects of Cog that at least
signal the possibility of what she names a "feminist robotics" (2001:
233).

First, and most basically, Cog's design (at least on this telling) locates
touch as a way of knowing and being in the world. Second, Castañeda
suggests that Cog embodies a relational conception of the body, one
that extends beyond the boundaries of the skin and that is generated
through particular, changing combinations of materials and qualities.
And finally, as she puts it, Cog is "neither human nor anti-human, but
rather other-than-human" (ibid.: 232). As such, she argues that Cog's
reembodiment of the human in different terms generates the possibility,
in material form, of embodied alterity, a relation of difference that literally as well as figurally matters. Castañeda's interest, then, is in just what
kind of alterity is, or could be, embodied in the robot, which does not
take the human, normatively imagined, as the "origin and truth against
which the robot's value is always measured" (ibid.: 234).[17]

The question of how the robot could be other than second term to
the human aligns with feminist concerns regarding what Anne Balsamo
sums as "the systems of differentiation that make the body meaningful,"

---

[16] It is critical to Castañeda's reading of Cog that she relies on an account of Cog's conception offered by philosopher of mind Daniel Dennett (1994) rather than on accounts or
observations of the robot as implemented. This does not diminish the suggestive possibilities of her analysis, only the question of their realization within prevailing robotic
imaginaries.

[17] For another reflection on the robot's current and potential figurations, see Castañeda
and Suchman (in press).

most notably those of gender (1996: 21). Power works through binary opposites not in the simple sense that the first term holds power over the second but that their relative positionings – including, crucially, as opposites – enable their fundamental interrelatedness and the historically sedimented cuts that position them as separate categories to be obscured. In contrast, Judith Halberstam proposes that in her feminist conceptions: "The intelligent and female cyborg thinks gender, processes power, and converts a binary system of logic into a more intricate network" (1991: 454). Framed not as the importation of mind into matter, but as the rematerialization of bodies and subjectivities in ways that challenge familiar assumptions about the naturalness of normative forms robots, and cyborg figures more generally, become sites for change rather than just for further reiteration.

Feminist rereadings of the cyborg replace the binaries male–female, human–machine, and subject–object with the possibility of an open horizon of specific, historically and culturally constituted, sociomaterial relations. Crucially, these relations are still power differentiated but in ways that can be recovered, as distributions located in specific configurations. Although the cyborg since Haraway suggests generative new forms of analysis, however, to realize that promise requires shifting out from its popular figuring as a singular, albeit hybrid, entity. The latter inherits a problem that characterizes any strategy centered on a heroic (even monstrous or marginalized) figure; that is, it obscures the presence of distributed sociomaterialities in more quotidian sites of everyday life. Along with the dramatic possibilities of the feminist cyborg, we need to recover the ways in which more familiar bodies and subjectivities are being formed through contemporary interweavings of nature and artifice, for better and worse.[18] Put another way, now that the cyborg figure has done its work of alerting us to the political effects, shifting

---

[18] This includes, for example, the Silicon Valley workers identified by Sandoval (1995), who "know the pain of the union of machine and bodily tissue" as they assemble the components of new objects within old regimes of racially and ethnically based difference. Relatedly, Jain (1999) considers the multiple ways in which prostheses are wounding at the same time that they are enabling. In contrast to the easy promise of bodily augmentation, she observes, the fit of bodies and artifacts is often less seamless and more painful than the trope of the cyborg would suggest. Jain (2006) takes legal contests over injury as a public and consequential site for the exploration of attributions of agency across the person–artifact boundary, within the wider dynamics of American commodity culture. Subject to Jain's insightful analysis, normative debates over things and their social consequences provide evidence for how the worlds that we inhabit are configured and by whom. This question is further elaborated by Schull (2005, in press),

boundaries, and transformative possibilities in human–machine mixings, it is time to get on with investigation of particular configurations and their consequences. How then might we locate conditions for action and possibilities for intervention in the specificities of more mundane sociomaterial assemblages?

## DESIGN PRACTICES

Over the twenty years since the original publication of *Plans and Situated Actions*, new developments in professional practices of computer systems design have at least provided existence proofs of transformative possibilities. The emergence of increasingly distributed, networked computing during the late 1970s and early 1980s raised questions that clearly went beyond the limits of the human–machine interface narrowly construed to involve collective forms of computer use.[19] The turn to the social among computer scientists and information systems designers in the mid-1980s was accompanied by an intensification of interest among social researchers in the material grounds of sociality. Within ethnomethodology and conversation analysis, a growing awareness of the centrality of nonvocal activities (most obviously gaze and gesture) to the organization of face-to-face human interaction inspired a move toward the incorporation of materially based activity into the field of study. From Charles Goodwin's attention to the lighting of a cigarette in *Conversational Organization* (1981) to Goodwin and Goodwin's analyses of the interactional organization of eating and talk at a family dinner (1992), Heath's attention to the interactional enactment of patient pain (1986), and Schegloff's observations regarding the interactional effects of body "torque" (1998), interaction analysts increasingly recognized the interorganization of talk and other forms of embodied activity. Among

in her compelling account of the slippage between autonomy and automaticity in the case of human–machine couplings at the interface of video gambling machines.

[19] The phrase Computer-Supported Cooperative Work (CSCW) was coined by Irene Greif, then on the faculty in Computer Science and Electrical Engineering at MIT, to convene a small invited workshop in 1984. This led to a series of still ongoing biannual conferences, as well as events held in alternate years under the title of the European CSCW or ECSCW conferences. CSCW is now an established subfield within professional networks of research and development engaged with the design of computer-based systems and devices. The CSCW conferences and journal have been the primary site for both programmatic and empirically based discussion between researchers in the computing and social sciences and the venue for a rich corpus of technical explorations and ethnographically informed investigations of technology-intensive sites of social action.

those of us immersed in ethnomethodology and newly engaged with the enterprise of computer systems design, absence of attention to the social and material organization of relevant forms of practice – from following instructions in the operation of photocopier to maintaining the order of traffic in the air – was an obvious site for generative intervention. The corpus of studies is by now extensive and comprises an established resource in the repertoire of design for technology-intensive forms of practice across a range of settings.

A central argument of these studies is that the nature and relevance of environment, objects, and actions are reflexively constituted through the ongoing activities of their habitation, engagement, and recognition. In the context of administering organizations operating across widely distributed locales, moreover, many of the relevant objects materialize technologies of coordination and control – procedural instructions, schedules, protocols, and the like – that prescribe courses of action designed to be reliably reproduced or available for comparative assessment. Relevant artifacts include, for example, flight progress control strips (Hughes, Randall, and Shapiro 1993), airline schedules (Goodwin and Goodwin 1996; Suchman 1993b), and railway timetables (Heath and Luff 1992). The politics of such artifacts (as for any technologies) include relations between the sites and interests within which coordinative artifacts are generated and those of their use. Like the "plan" that forms a focal object for this book, such technologies presuppose an open horizon of sociomaterial practices that inevitably exceed their representational grasp. At the same time, those practices reflexively constitute themselves as implementations of the actions prescribed. As I discussed at length in Chapter 11, the frequent presence of multiple, often contradictory, agendas of workplace auditing, on the one hand, and the work required to enact an orderliness within the work, on the other, lead to various forms of both breakdown and creative resistance. Design for such settings is therefore an inherently ethical project (Robertson 2002: 300).

Whereas Computer-Supported Cooperative Work directs the attention of researchers and systems designers to the sociality of computer use, a second, intersecting research community has taken up the challenge of a more radically conceived interference in existing arrangements of professional systems design. Inspired initially by pilot projects in the Nordic countries, involving codevelopment of information systems among organized workers and politically astute computer scientists, the project of participatory design entered the awareness of North

American researchers in the 1980s.[20] The by-now extensive body of
research that has been conducted under the auspices of participatory
design by no means conforms to a single orthodoxy.[21] The guiding
commitment, however, is to rethinking critically the relations between
practices of professional design and the conditions and possibilities of
information systems in use. Central to this process is an attunement to
the politics of design, that is, an orientation to the inevitable interrelations of agendas of technological change and (re-)distributions of labor
with associated implications for both material and symbolic reward.

A common premise for both CSCW and participatory design, arising from their basis in empirical investigations of technologies-in-use
across a range of settings, is that design – the configuration of artifacts –
is not the exclusive province of professional practitioners. The necessity
and creativity of ongoing practices of design-in-use has by now been
extensively documented. Rather than a process that stops at the point
of hand-off from production to consumption, design is as an ongoing
process of (re-)production over time and across sites. Just what, then, is
the role of the professional designer? Although in no way obviating the
specific knowledges and material practices of the designer, the object of
design must shift. Rather than fixed objects that prescribe their use, artifacts – particularly computationally based devices – comprise a medium
or starting place elaborated in use. Rather than holding stable and separate the identities of "designer" and "user," the latter work as categories

---

[20] Invited by Irene Greif to act as Program Chair for CSCW 1988 and newly aware of activities in Scandinavia, I welcomed the opportunity to encourage this exchange through a
series of papers presented at the second annual CSCW conference in 1988. A more dedicated conference was convened in 1990 under the auspices of Computer Professionals
for Social Responsibility, with the title Participatory Design of Computer Systems or
PDC (see Schuler and Namioka 1993), and these conferences have continued biannu-
ally since. For founding volumes in this area see Bjerknes, Ehn, and Kyng (1987), Ehn
(1988), and for more recent collections see Greenbaum and Kyng (1991), Schuler and
Namioka (1993).

[21] Various of the ideas and design practices characteristic of participatory design have by
now made their way – more and less unscathed – into mainstream circulation under
the rubric of user-centered design. For thoughtful introductions see Carroll (2000);
Landauer (1995); Rogers, Sharp, and Preece (2002). At Xerox PARC during the 1990s I
and my colleagues characterized our approach as one of practice-based codesign. Our
aim in associating with these particular terms was not to stake out new terrain, but on
the contrary to avoid the inexorable slide toward what Verran has named "hardening
of the categories" that comes with the repetition (and initial captialization) of naming,
particularly in the context of competitive R&D. Our intent was to maintain the provi-
sionality and fluidity of our self-descriptions, while acknowledging our relations and
indebtedness to an extended research community.

describing persons differently positioned, at different moments, and/or with different histories and future investments in projects of technology development (see Suchman 1999, 2002a, 2002b).

## INHABITING THE INTERFACE

In her analysis of computer-based work, Susanne Bødker (1991) has discussed the shifting movement of the interface from object to connective medium. She observes that when unfamiliar, or at times of trouble, the interface itself becomes the work's object. At other times persons work, as she puts it, "through the interface," enacted as a transparent means of engagement with other objects of interest (for example, a text or an interchange with relevant others). As a case in point, we can consider the reflections of a civil engineer working at a CAD workstation (see also Henderson 1999; Suchman 2000). Although CAD might be held up as an exemplar of the abstract representation of concrete things, for the practicing engineer the story is more complex. Rather than stand in place of the specific locales – roadways, natural features, built environments, people, and politics – of a project, the CAD system connects the experienced engineer sitting at her worktable to those things, at the same time that they exceed the system's representational capacities. The engineer knows the project through a multiplicity of documents, discussions, extended excursions to the project site, embodied labors, and accountabilities: the textual, graphical, and symbolic inscriptions of the interface are read in relation to these heterogeneous forms of embodied knowing. Immersed in her work, the CAD interface becomes for the engineer a simulacrum of the site, not in the sense of a substitute for it but rather of a place in which to work with its own specific materialities, constraints, and possibilities. Like the symbiotic gesture described by Goodwin (2003), the CAD interface in use associates disparate elements both within and beyond its frame at the same time that those elements are essential to its intelligibility and efficacy.

Feminist film theorist Laura Marks describes what she calls "haptic visuality" as comprising "images that encourage a sympathy, intimacy and complicity between work and viewer" (2002: 3). She uses the term *work* in this context not with reference to a fetishized object resulting from cinematic practice but as an always only partially representable complex of social and material labors. Such works effect what Marks calls a "three-dimensional intimacy" among persons, images and their materiality, and the worlds to which the images connect. Those intimacies, in turn, dissolve the space between object and subject, evoking an embodied response that is more a form of inhabiting the cinematic work than a distanced appraisal of it. Central to such affective effects are the specific materialities of the medium. Marks observes that in the early days of cinema filmmakers demonstrated their fascination with the new medium's materialities as much as with its abstract representational power. Seen from this perspective, film is not a neutral conveyor of images, but rather the particular qualities of film stock are themselves an integral part of the imagery and imaginary created. It is not only the film's materialities, moreover, that this approach is aimed to recover but also "the rarely acknowledged workers who toil behind the scenes" (ibid.: 8). Viewing film is not then a matter of observer and image but an encounter among the efforts and effects of specifically situated persons and things.

Artist Heidi Tikka, in her work titled *Mother, Child*, offers an indicative case in point of a practice that plays with the multiplicity of materialities involved in so-called new or digital media. This work, which I had the opportunity to experience during its exhibition at the Art Gallery of Ontario in Toronto, Canada, in 2001, employs the shifting dynamics of installation, viewer–user, and onlookers, as well as the ambient environment of the exhibition space to invoke, and affectively evoke, an encounter between caregiver and infant. The piece does this not "in general" but always specifically: the caregiver is one particular visitor who enters the space of the installation and sits on a chair, and the infant is one particular infant (Tikka's son, recorded on digital video). A deliberate aspect of the piece is the heterogeneity of its forms: actual bodies and objects combine with projected images to comprise a hybrid of social and material elements. Together these elements create an interactive space characterized by a mix of predictability and contingency – a fragile stability – that affords the installation its affective kinship to the "real-world" encounter that it simulates. The three-dimensional image of a child that is projected – both technically and psychically – onto the soft cloth diaper that the viewer–user holds in her lap can be affected through her motions and orientation to it but dissolves as she stands and places the cloth back onto the chair. In this and other ways, the installation continually reminds us of, rather than conceals, its artifice. As Tikka herself comments, the piece is actually simpler (less reactive) in its composition than we experience it to be. The effects are created through the particular possibilities provided by an artful integration of persons, objects, spaces, fantasies, remembered experiences, and technologies to evoke and explore an emblematically human encounter but not to replicate it.

I would propose that in such projects the specific materialities of computing are under investigation, and reconfiguration, in forms that more radically challenge traditional imaginaries of the human than do the most ambitious projects in humanoid robotics. Central to this innovative approach is abandonment of the project of the "smart" machine endowed with capacities of recognition and autonomous action. Computational media artist Sha Xin Wei works with what he names "responsive media spaces" like the *Tgarden*, an installation populated by specially costumed participants instrumented with sensors, real-time tracking receivers, and media-synthesis generators. As Xin Wei describes it:

The TGarden software tracks gesture rather than recognizes gesture, because at no place in the software is there a 'model' that codes the gesture . . . The software does not infer what the player means by her gesture, it merely tracks the gesture and continuously synthesizes responses. So what we have done is to set aside entirely the problem of inferring human intent from behavior, or more generally from observables. Yet by providing and even thickening the sensuous response, we make fertile the substrate for agency. This approach remains agnostic as to whether movements are intentional; the responsive system simply does not need to know. (2002: 457)

More than conversation at the interface, it is creative assemblages like these that explore and elaborate the particular dynamic capacities that digital media afford and the ways that through them humans and machines can perform interesting new effects. Not only do these experiments promise innovations in our thinking about machines, but they open up as well the equally exciting prospect of alternate conceptualizations of what it means to be human. The person figured here is not an autonomous, rational actor but an unfolding, shifting biography of culturally and materially specific experiences, relations, and possibilities inflected by each next encounter – including the most normative and familiar – in uniquely particular ways.

Media scholar Chris Chesher (2004) has proposed a vocabulary of encounters with computer-based art that suggestively reworks information theoretic tropes at the interface. Although his proposal is applicable, I believe, to any example of human–computer interaction, Chesher starts from the premise that new media artists' noninstrumental applications of technology put the distinctiveness of computer-based forms into greater relief. From his consideration of new media art, Chesher proposes the concept of *avocation* to describe the arrangements and affordances through which persons are hailed to enter into a particular technological assemblage to become incorporated as integral actants in an associated form of sociomaterial agency. These include not only instrumental possibilities but also multiple and uncertain ways in which "new media art distracts and summons its users." *Invocation* involves those actions that define the terms of engagement written into the design script or discovered by the participating user, the calling up of events that effect changes to the assemblage. And finally, *evocation* describes the affective and effective material changes that result; transformations that in turn comprise the conditions of possibility for subsequent avocations. Together these terms articulate the distinctive dynamics of computing and the modes of engagement that it makes possible. The latter are characterized by what Chesher names a form of "managed indeterminacy," effected not only by databases and central processing units but crucially by "the peripherals that are in contact with materiality" that opens out from the boundaries of the machine narrowly construed. Offered in part as replacements for the more familiar terms *input*, *processing*, and *output*, these new "primitive technocultural formations" expand the space of interaction from the interface narrowly defined to the ambient environments and transformed and transformative subject–object relations that comprise the lived experience of technological practice.

Chesher's generative discussion of the distinguishing role of invocations in human–computer interactions provides a new basis on which to consider the forms of asymmetry that I described in *Plans and Situated Actions*. In particular, I identified as crucial what I characterized then as the machine's access to the activities of the user, limited specifically to those that changed its state. Working outside the bounds of AI's preoccupations with the agencies of the interactive machine, Chesher is less concerned with questions of human–machine symmetry than with the forms of invocation available and their evocative effects. For both analyses the question of invocation is central, but Chesher's framing helps to shift the focus from a preoccupation with whether the machine is like the human to a consideration of specific sociomaterial assemblages, their possibilities, and their consequences. New media artists, their works, and the persons whom the latter engage are configured together through these assemblages. Within that, difference becomes the basis for more than the repetition of relations of power, command and control, or obedient service.

## EXPANDING FRAMES AND ACCOUNTABLE CUTS

The past twenty years of scholarship in the humanities and social sciences have provided new resources for thinking through the interface of humans and machines. Reappropriation of the cyborg, as a figure whose boundaries encompass intimate joinings of the organic and inorganic, has provided a means of analyzing myriad reformations of bodies and artifacts, actual and imagined. Expanded out from the singular figure of the human–machine hybrid, the cyborg metaphor dissolves into a field of complex sociomaterial assemblages, currently under study within the social and computing sciences. From close readings of encounters at the interface of person and machine, through extended historical and comparative analyses of technology-intensive, distributed worksites, these reconceptualizations have opened a generative wave of new scholarship and practice.

Methodologically, this view of the nature of sociomaterial research objects has two profound consequences. First, it demands attention to the question of frames, of the boundary work through which a given entity is delineated as such. Beginning with the premise that discrete units of analysis are not given but made, we need to ask how any object of analysis – human or nonhuman or combination of the two – is called out as separate from the more extended networks of which it is part.[22] This work of cutting the network is, I have argued, a foundational move in the creation of sociomaterial assemblages as objects of analysis or intervention. In the case of the robot, or autonomous machine more generally (as in the case of the individual human as well), this work takes the form of modes of representation that systematically foreground certain sites, bodies, and agencies while placing others offstage. As I suggested in Chapter 14, this spatial attenuation of the relevant field of agencies is accompanied by the staging of performances repeatable over time through accounts and demonstrations that have themselves been congealed into modes of immutable mobility. Our task as analysts is then to expand the frame, to metaphorically zoom out to a wider view that at once acknowledges the magic of the effects created while

---

[22] This is what Law terms a *method assemblage* (2004: 14).

explicating the hidden labors and unruly contingencies that exceed its bounds.

At the same time, a full analysis needs to locate these entities and the sites and moments of their efficacy in still more extended spatial and temporal relations. Encounters at the interface invariably take place in settings incorporating multiple other persons, artifacts, and ongoing activities, all of which variously infuse and inform their course. Questions of scale in the social sciences have traditionally been conceived either as a matter of counting – how many more of these units of analysis are there – or of reformulation in more general terms. An alternative is to approach scale not as a matter of one to many, little to big, or specific to general but rather of extension in time and space. How far our analysis extends in its historical specificity and reach, or in following out lines of connection from a particular object or site to others, is invariably a practical matter. That is, it is a matter of cutting the network, of drawing a line that is in every case enacted rather than given. The relatively arbitrary or principled character of the cut is a matter not of its alignment with some independently existing ontology but of our ability to articulate its basis and its implications.

These methodological questions are not privileged issues for the social sciences but an endogenous aspect of every site of sociomaterial configuration. From the designer who must delineate the boundaries of system and user(s) to the surgeon's body reconfigured by telemetric vision or the nurse enrolled in redesign of an operating theatre, matters of joining and separation of human and nonhuman are everyday affairs. However entrenched through repetition or provisionally held together, these relations are enacted. The task for critical practice is to resist restaging of stories about autonomous human actors and discrete technical objects in favor of an orientation to capacities for action comprised of specific configurations of persons and things. To see the interface this way requires a shift in our unit of analysis, both temporally and spatially. Temporally, understanding a given arrangement of humans and artifacts requires locating that configuration within social histories and individual biographies for both persons and things. And it requires locating it as well within an always more extended network of relations, arbitrarily – however purposefully – cut through practical, analytical, and/or political acts of boundary making.

My concern in this book has been with the specific material-discursive apparatuses through which contemporary relations of humans and machines are rendered intelligible and made real. Karen Barad proposes

that "reality is sedimented out of the process of making the world intelligible through certain practices and not others" (1998: 105). Barad's agential realism reminds us that boundaries between humans and machines
are not naturally given but constructed in particular historical ways and
with particular social and material consequences. As Barad points out,
boundaries are necessary for the creation of meaning and, for that very
reason, are never innocent. Because the cuts implied in boundary making are always agentially positioned rather than naturally occurring, and
because boundaries have real consequences, "accountability is manda-
tory" (ibid.: 187). The accountability involved is not, however, a matter
of identifying authorship in any simple sense but rather a problem of
understanding the effects of particular assemblages and assessing the
distributions, for better and worse, that they perform. As Barad puts it:
"We are responsible for the world in which we live not because it is an
arbitrary construction of our choosing, but because it is sedimented out
of particular practices that we have a role in shaping" (ibid.: 102).

It is on this understanding of boundary making that I would propose that the price of recognizing the agency of artifacts need not be the
denial of our own. Now that the agencies of things are well established,
might we not bring the human out from behind the curtain, so to speak,
without disenchantment? This requires, among other things, that we
acknowledge the curtain's role. Agencies – and associated accountabilities – reside neither in us nor in our artifacts but in our intra-actions.
The question, following Barad, is how to configure assemblages in such
a way that we can intra-act responsibly and generatively with and
through them. The legacy of twentieth-century technoscience posits
autonomous agency as a primary apparatus for the identification of
humanness and takes as a goal the reiteration of that apparatus in the
project of configuring humanlike machines. Initiatives to develop a relational, performative account of sociomaterial phenomena indicate a different project. This project is based in recognition of the particularities of
bodies and artifacts, of the cultural–historical practices through which
human–machine differences are (re-)iteratively drawn, and of the possibilities for and politics of redistribution across the human–machine
boundary. Figured as interactions between humans and machines, the
question has been whether the latter are best treated as objects or might
one day successfully mimic the capacity of the autonomous human
subject. The alternative perspective suggested here takes persons and
machines as contingently stabilized through particular, more and less
durable, arrangements whose reiteration and/or reconfiguration is the

cultural and political project of design in which we are all continuously implicated. Responsibility on this view is met neither through control nor abdication but in ongoing practical, critical, and generative acts of engagement. The point in the end is not to assign agency either to persons or to things but to identify the materialization of subjects, objects, and the relations between them as an effect, more and less durable and contestable, of ongoing sociomaterial practices.

# References

Aanestad, Margunn (2003). The camera as an actor: Design-in-use of Tele-medicine Infrastructure in Surgery. *Computer Supported Cooperative Work* 12: 1–20.

Adam, Alison (1998). *Artificial knowing: Gender and the thinking machine.* New York: Routledge.

Agre, Philip (1995). Conceptions of the user in computer systems design. In P. Thomas (ed.)., *The social and interactional dimensions of human–computer inter-faces* (pp. 67–106). Cambridge, UK/New York: Cambridge University Press.

Agre, Philip (1997). *Computation and human experience.* New York: Cambridge University Press.

Agre, Philip, and Chapman, David (1987). Pengi: An implementation of a theory of activity. *Proceedings of AAAI* 87: 268–272.

Agre, Philip, and Chapman, David (1990). What are plans for? In Pattie Maes (ed.), *Designing autonomous agents: Theory and practice from biology to engineering and back* (pp. 17–34). Cambridge, MA: MIT Press. (Original version: Philip E. Agre and David Chapman, What are plans for?, A.I. Memo 1050a, *Artificial Intelligence Laboratory*, MIT, 1989.)

Ahmed, Sara (1998). *Differences that matter: Feminist theory and postmodernism.* Cambridge, UK: Cambridge University Press.

Ahmed, Sara (2000). *Strange encounters: Embodied others in post-coloniality.* London/New York: Routledge.

Ahmed, Sara, Kilby, Jane, Lury, Celia, McNeil, Maureen, and Skeggs, Beverly (2000). *Transformations: Thinking through feminism.* London/New York: Routledge.

Akrich, Madeleine (1992). The de-scription of technical objects. In W. Bijker and J. Law (eds.), *Shaping technology/building society* (pp. 205–224). Cambridge, MA: MIT Press.

Allen, James (1983). Recognizing intentions from natural language utterances. In M. Brady and R. Berwick (eds.), *Computational models of discourse* (Chapter 2). Cambridge, MA: MIT Press.

Allen, James (1984). Towards a general theory of action and time. *Artificial Intelligence* 23: 123–154.

Amerine, Ronald, and Bilmes, Jack (1990). Following instructions. In M. Lynch and S. Woolgar (eds.), *Representation in scientific practice* (pp. 323–335). Cambridge, MA: MIT Press.

Anderson, John, Boyle, C., and Reiser, B. (1985). Intelligent tutoring systems. *Science* 228: 456–462.

Anscombe, George (1957). *Intentions*. Oxford: Blackwell.

Appelt, Douglas (1985). Planning English referring expressions. *Artificial Intelligence* 26: 1–33.

Ashmore, Malcolm, Wooffitt, Robin, and Harding, Stella (1994). Humans and others: The concept of 'agency' and its attribution. *American Behavioral Scientist* 37(6): 733–738.

Atkinson, John, and Drew, Paul (1979). *Order in court: The organization of verbal interaction in judicial settings*. Atlantic Highlands, NJ: Humanities.

Austin, John L. (1962). *How to do things with words*. Oxford: Clarendon Press.

Balsamo, Anne (1996). *Technologies of the gendered body: Reading cyborg women*. Durham, NC: Duke University Press.

Balsamo, Anne (in press). *Designing culture: A work of the technological imagination*. Durham, NC: Duke University Press.

Bannon, Liam (1991). From human factors to human actors: The role of psychology and human–computer interaction studies in system design. In J. Greenbaum and M. Kyng (eds.), *Design at work: Cooperative design of computer systems* (pp. 25–44). Hillsdale, NJ: Erlbaum.

Banta, Martha (1993). *Taylored lives: Narrative productions in the age of Taylor, Veblen and Ford*. Chicago: University of Chicago Press.

Barad, Karen (1996). Meeting the universe halfway: Ambiguities, discontinuities, quantum subjects, and multiple positionings in feminism and physics. In L. H. Nelson and J. Nelson (eds.), *Feminism, science, and the philosophy of science: A dialog* (pp. 161–194). Norwell, MA: Kluwer.

Barad, Karen (1998). Getting real: Technoscientific practices and the materialization of reality. *Differences: A Journal of Feminist Cultural Studies* 10: 88–128.

Barad, Karen (2003). Posthumanist performativity: Toward an understanding of how matter comes to matter. *Signs: Journal of Women in Culture and Society* 28: 801–831.

Bardram, Jakob (1997). Plans as situated action: An activity theory approach to workflow systems. *Proceedings of ECSCW 97*, Lancaster, UK.

Barfield, Woodrow, and Caudell, Thomas (2000). *Fundamentals of wearable computers and augumented reality*. Mahwah, NJ: Erlbaum.

Barley, Stephen (1986). Technology as an occasion for structuring: Evidence from observations of CT scanners and the social order of radiology departments. *Administrative Science Quarterly* 31: 78–108.

Barley, Stephen, and Bechky, Beth (1993). In the back rooms of science: The work of technicians in science labs. *Work and Occupations* 21: 85–126.

Barley, Stephen, and Orr, Julian (eds.). (1997). *Between craft and science: Technical work in U.S. settings*. Ithaca, NY: Cornell University Press.

Barwise, Jon, and Perry, John (1985). *Situations and attitudes*. Cambridge, MA: MIT Press.

Bates, Elizabeth (1976). *Language and context: The acquisition of pragmatics.* New York: Academic Press.

Bates, Joseph (1994). The role of emotion in believable agents. *Communications of the ACM* 37: 122–125.

Beck, Eevi (1995). Changing documents/documenting changes: Using computers for collaborative writing over a distance. In S. Leigh Star (ed.), *Cultures of computing* (pp. 53–68). Oxford: Blackwell.

Beckman, Howard, and Frankel, Richard (1983). *Who hides the agenda: The impact of physician behavior on the collection of data.* Paper presented at the Fourth Annual SREPCIM Task Force on Interviewing, Washington, DC.

Beninger, James (1986). *The control revolution: Technological and economic origins of the information society.* Cambridge, MA: Harvard University Press.

Berg, Anna Jorunn (1994). A gendered socio-technical construction: The smart house. In D. Mackenzie and J. Wajcman (eds.), *The social shaping of technology* (pp. 301–313). Milton Keynes: Open University Press.

Berg, Marc (1997). *Rationalizing medical work decision-support techniques and medical practices.* Cambridge, MA: MIT Press.

Berg, Marc, and Timmermans, Stefan (2000). Order and their others: On the constitution of universalities in medical work. *Configurations* 8 (1): 31–61.

Berners-Lee, Tim, Hendler, James, and Lassila, Ora (2001). The Semantic Web. *Scientific American*, May: 36–43.

Berreman, Gerald (1966). Anemic and emetic analyses in social anthropology. *American Anthropologist* 68(2): 346–354.

Bhabha, Homi (1994). *The location of culture.* London: Routledge.

Birdwhistell, Raymond (1970). *Kinesics and context: Essays on body motion communication.* Philadelphia: University of Pennsylvania Press.

Bjerknes, Gro, Ehn, Pelle, and Kyng, Morten (eds.). (1987). *Computers and democracy: A Scandinavian challenge.* Aldershot, UK: Avebury.

Bleecker, Julian (1995). Urban crisis: Past, present and virtual. *Socialist Review* 24(1–2): 189–221.

Blomberg, Jeanette, Suchman, Lucy, and Trigg, Randall (1996). Reflections on a work-oriented design project. *Human–Computer Interaction* 11: 237–265.

Bloomfield, Brian (1991). The role of information systems in the UK National Health Service: Action at a distance and the fetish of calculation. *Social Studies of Science* 21: 701–734.

Blumer, Herbert (1969). *Symbolic interactionism.* Englewood Cliffs, NJ: Prentice Hall.

Bobrow, Daniel, Kaplan, Ron, Kay, Martin, Norman, Donald, Thompson, Henry, and Winograd, Terry (1977). GUS: A frame-driven dialogue system. *Artificial Intelligence* 8: 155–173.

Boden, Margaret (1973). The structure of intentions. *Journal of Theory of Social Behavior* 3: 23–46.

Bødker, Susanne (1991). *Through the interface: A human activity approach to user interface design.* Hillsdale, NJ: Erlbaum.

Bowers, John (2002). *Improvising machines: Ethnographically informed design for improvised electro-acoustic music.* Norwich, UK, and Stockholm, Sweden: University of East Anglia and Royal Institute of Technology.

Bowers, John, Button, Graham, and Sharrock, Wes (1995). Workflow from within and without. In H. Marmolin, Y. Sundblad, and K. Schmidt (eds.), *Fourth European Conference on Computer-Supported Cooperative Work* (pp. 51–66) Dordrecht: The Netherlands: Kluwer Academic Publishers.

Bowker, Geoffrey (1993). How to be universal: Some cybernetic strategies, 1943–1970. *Social Studies of Science* 23: 107–127.

Bowker, Geoffrey, and Star, Susan Leigh (1999). *Sorting things out: Classification and its consequences.* Cambridge, MA: MIT Press.

Brady, Michael, and Berwick, Robert (eds.) (1983). *Computational models of discourse.* Cambridge, MA: MIT Press.

Braidotti, Rosi (1994). *Nomadic subjects.* New York: Columbia University Press.

Braidotti, Rosi (2002). *Metamorphoses: Towards a materialist theory of becoming.* Cambridge, UK: Blackwell.

Brook, James, and Boal, Iain (eds.). (1995). *Resisting the virtual life: The culture and politics of information.* San Francisco: City Lights.

Brooks, Rodney (1999). *Cambrian intelligence: The early history of the new AI.* Cambridge, MA: MIT Press.

Brooks, Rodney (2002). *Flesh and machines: How robots will change us.* New York: Pantheon Books.

Brooks, Rodney, and Steels, Luc (1995). *The artificial life route to artificial intelligence: Building embodied, situated agents.* Hillsdale, NJ: Erlbaum.

Brown, Barry, Green, Nicola, and Harper, Richard (eds.). (2001). *Wireless world: Social and interactional implications of wireless technology.* London: Springer-Verlag.

Brown, John Seely, and Newman, Susan (1985). Issues in cognitive and social ergonomics: From our house to Bauhaus. *Human–Computer Interaction* 1: 359–391.

Brown, John Seely, Rubenstein, R., and Burton, R. (1976). *Reactive learning environment for computer assisted electronics instruction.* (BBN Report 3314). Cambridge, MA: Bolt Beranek and Newman, Inc.

Bruce, Bertram (1981). Natural communication between person and computer. In W. Lehnert and M. Ringle (eds.), *Strategies for natural language processing.* Hillsdale, NJ: Erlbaum.

Bruner, Jerome (1986). *Actual minds, possible worlds.* Cambridge, MA: Harvard University Press.

Burke, Julie (1982). *An analysis of intelligibility and practical activity.* Unpublished doctoral dissertation, University of Illinois at Urbana-Champaign.

Burton, Richard, and Brown, John Seely (1982). An investigation of computer coaching for informal learning activities. In D. Sleeman and J. S. Brown (eds.), *Intelligent tutoring systems* (pp. 79–98). London: Academic Press.

Butler, Judith (1993). *Bodies that matter: On the discursive limits of "sex."* New York: Routledge.

Button, Graham (1990). Going up a blind alley: Conflating conversation analysis and computational modeling. In P. Luff, N. Gilbert, and D. Frolich (eds.), *Computers and conversation* (pp. 67–90). London: Academic Press.

Button, Graham (1993). *Technology in working order: Studies of work, interaction, and technology.* London/New York: Routledge.

Button, Graham, Coulter, Jeff, Lee, John R., and Sharrock, Wes (1995). *Computers, minds, and conduct*. Cambridge, UK: Polity Press.

Callon, Michel (1999). Actor-network theory: The market test. In J. Law and J. Hassard (eds.), *Actor network theory and after* (pp. 181–195). Oxford: Blackwell.

Cambrosio, Alberto, and Keating, Peter (1995). *Exquisite specificity: The monoclonal antibody revolution*. New York: Oxford University Press.

Carbonell, Jaime (1971). *Mixed-intiative man–computer dialogues*. (Technical Report 1970). Cambridge, MA: Bolt Beranek and Newman, Inc.

Carey, Susan (1985). *Conceptual change in childhood*. Cambridge, MA: MIT Press.

Carroll, John M. (2003). Situated action in the zeitgeist of human–computer interaction. *The Journal of the Learning Sciences* 12 ( 2): 273–278.

Carroll, John M. (2000). *Making use: Scenario-based design of human–computer interactions*. Cambridge, MA: MIT Press.

Casper, Monica (1994). Reframing and grounding nonhuman agency: What makes a fetus an agent? *American Behavioral Scientist* 37: 839–856.

Casper, Monica (1998). *The making of the unborn patient: A social anatomy of fetal surgery*. New Brunswick, NJ: Rutgers University Press.

Cassell, Justine, Sullivan, Joseph, Prevost, Scott, and Churchill, Elizabeth (eds.). (1996). *Embodied conversational agents*. Cambridge, MA: MIT Press.

Castañeda, Claudia (2001). Robotic skin: The future of touch? In S. Ahmed and J. Stacey (eds.), *Thinking through the skin* (pp. 223–236). London: Routledge.

Castañeda, Claudia (2002). *Figurations: Child, bodies, worlds*. Durham, NC/London: Duke University Press.

Castañeda, Claudia, and Suchman, Lucy (forthcoming). Robot Visions. In Sharon Chamari Tabrizi (ed.), *Companions with Haraway. Thinking together.*

Chasin, Alexandra (1995). Class and its close relations: Identities among women, servants, and machines. In J. Halberstram and I. Livingston (eds.), *Posthuman bodies* (pp. 73–96). Bloomington: Indiana University Press.

Cherny, Lynn, and Reba Weise, Elizabeth (eds.). (1996). *Wired women: Gender and new realities in cyberspace*. Seattle, WA: Seal.

Chesher, Chris (2004). *Invocation, evocation and avocation in new media art*. Unpublished manuscript, University of Sydney, Australia.

Churchland, Paul (1984). *Matter and consciousness*. Cambridge, MA: MIT Press.

Clancey, William (1997). *Situated cognition: On human knowledge and computer representations*. Cambridge, UK: Cambridge University Press.

Clark, Andy (1997). *Being there: Putting brain, body, and world together again*. Cambridge, MA: MIT Press.

Clark, Andy (2001). *Mindware: An introduction to the philosophy of cognitive science*. New York: Oxford University Press.

Clark, Andy (2003). *Natural-born cyborgs: Minds, technologies, and the future of human intelligence*. Oxford/New York: Oxford University Press.

Clarke, Adele, and Fujimura, Joan (eds.). (1992). *The right tools for the job: At work in twentieth-century life sciences*. Princeton, NJ: Princeton University Press.

Clement, Andrew (1993). Looking for the designers: Transforming the 'invisible' infrastructure of computerized office work. *AI & Society* 7: 323–344.

Clement, Andrew (1994). Computing at work: Empowering action by 'low-level' users. *Communications of the ACM* 37: 53–63.

Clement, Andrew, and Van den Besselaar, Peter (1993). A retrospective look at PD projects. *Communications of the ACM* 36: 29–37.

*Cognitive Science* (1993). Volume 17, No. 1 Special Issue: Situated Action, pp. 1–117.

Cohen, John (1966). *Human robots in myth and science*. London: Allen and Unwin.

Cohen, Paul (n.d.). *Pragmatics, speaker-reference, and the modality of communication*. Unpublished manuscript, Laboratory for Artificial Intelligence, Fairchild Camera and Instrument Corp, Palo Alto, CA.

Cohen, Paul, and Perrault, C. Ray (1979). Elements of a plan-based theory of speech acts. *Cognitive Science* 3: 177–212.

Colby, Kenneth, Hilf, Franklin, Weber, Sylvia, and Kraemer, Helena (1972). Turing-like indistiguishability tests for the validation of a computer simulation of paranoid processes. *Artificial Intelligence* 3: 199–221.

Collins, Harry M. (1985). *Changing order: Replication and induction in scientific practice*. London / Beverly Hills: Sage.

Collins, Harry M. (1990). *Artificial experts: Social knowledge and intelligent machines*. Cambridge, MA: MIT Press.

Collins, Harry M., and Kusch, Martin (1998). *The shape of actions: What humans and machines can do*. Cambridge, MA: MIT Press.

Coombs, Michael, and Alty, James (1984). Expert systems: An alternative paradigm. *International Journal of Man–Machine Studies* 20: 21–43.

Cooper, Greg, and Bowers, John (1995). Representing the user: Notes on the disciplinary rhetoric of human–computer interaction. In P. Thomas (ed.), *Social and interactional dimensions of human–computer interfaces* (pp. 48–66). Cambridge, UK: Cambridge University Press.

Coulter, Jeff (1979). *The social construction of mind*. Totowa, NJ: Rowman & Littlefield.

Coulter, Jeff (1983). *Rethinking cognitive theory*. New York: St. Martin's Press.

Cowan, Ruth Schwartz (1983). *More work for mother: The ironies of household technology from the open hearth to the microwave*. New York: Basic Books.

Crist, Eileen (2000). *Images of animals: Anthropomorphism and animal mind*. Philadelphia: Temple University Press.

Crist, Eileen (2004). Can an insect speak?: The case of the honeybee dance. *Social Studies of Science* 34: 7–43.

Crutzen, Cecile (1005). Intelligent ambience between heaven and hell: A salvation? *Information, Communication Ethics and Society (ICES)* 4.

Cussins, Charis (1998). Ontological choreography: Agency for women patients in an infertility clinic. In M. Berg and A.-M. Mol (eds.), *Differences in medicine* (pp. 166–201). Durham, NC: Duke University Press.

de Certeau, Michel (1988). *The practice of everyday life*. Berkeley, CA: University of California Press.

de Laet, Marianne, and Mol, Annemarie (2000). The Zimbabwe bush pump: Mechanics of a fluid technology. *Social Studies of Science* 30: 225–263.

de La Mettrie, Julien Offray (1748 (1994)). *Man a machine and man a plant*. Trans. Richard A. Watson and Maya Rybaka. Indianapolis: Hackett Publishing Co., Inc.

Dehn, Doris, and van Mulken, Susanne (2000). The impact of animated inter-face agents: A review of empirical research. *International Journal of Human–Computer Studies* 52: 1–22.

Dennett, Daniel (1978). *Brainstorms.* Cambridge, MA: MIT Press.

Dennett, Daniel (1994). The practical requirements for making a conscious robot. *Philosophical Transactions of the Royal Society of London* A, 349: 133–146.

di Leonardo, Micaela (1998). *Exotics at home: Anthropologies, others, American modernities.* Chicago: University of Chicago Press.

Dourish, Paul (2001). *Where the action is: The foundations of embodied interaction.* Cambridge, MA: MIT Press.

Downey, Gary, and Dumit, Joseph (eds.). (1997). *Cyborgs and citadels: Anthropological interventions in emerging sciences and technologies.* Santa Fe, NM: School of American Research.

Doyle, Richard (1997). *On beyond living: Rhetorical transformations of the life sciences.* Stanford, CA: Stanford University Press.

Doyle, Richard (2003). *Wetwares: Experiments in postvital living.* Minneapolis: University of Minnesota Press.

Dreyfus, Hubert (ed.). (1982). *Husserl, intentionality and cognitive science.* Cambridge, MA: MIT Press.

Dreyfus, Hubert (1991). *Being-in-the-world: A commentary on Heidegger's being and time, division 1.* Cambridge, MA: MIT Press.

Dreyfus, Hubert (1992). *What computers still can't do.* Cambridge, MA: MIT Press.

Dror, Otniel (1999). Scientific image of emotion: Experience and technologies of inscription. *Configurations* 7: 355–401.

Dror, Otniel (2001). Counting the affects: Discoursing in numbers. *Social Research* 68 (2): 357–378.

Dumit, Joseph (2004). *Picturing personhood: Brain scans and biomedical identity.* Princeton, NJ: Princeton University Press.

Duncan, Starkey, Jr. (1974). On the structure of speaker–auditor interaction during speaking turns. *Language in Society* 3: 161–180.

Durkheim, Emile (1938). *The rules of the sociological method.* New York: The Free Press.

Edwards, Derek (1994). Imitation and artifice in apes, humans, and machines. *American Behavioral Scientist* 37: 754–772.

Edwards, Paul (1996). *The closed world: Computers and the politics of discourse in Cold War America.* Cambridge, MA: MIT Press.

Ehn, Pelle (1988). *Work-oriented design of computer artifacts.* Stockholm: Arbetslivscentrum.

Erickson, Frederick (1982). Money tree, lasagna bush, salt and pepper: Social construction of topical cohesion in a conversation among Italian-Americans. In D. Tannen (ed.), *Georgetown University roundtable on language and linguistics: Analyzing discourse: Text and talk.* Washington, DC: Georgetown University Press.

Erickson, Frederick (1982). *The counselor as gatekeeper.* New York: Academic Press.

Farrell, Robert, Anderson, John, and Reiser, Brian (1984). An interactive computer-based tutor for LISP. In *Proceedings of the Fourth National Conference on Artificial Intelligence,* 106–111. Menlo Park, Calif.: AAAI Press.

Featherstone, Mike, and Burrows, Roger (1995). *Cyberspace, cyberbodies, cyberpunk: Cultures of technological embodiment*. London: Sage.

Feitelson, J., and Stefik, Mark (1977). *A case study of reasoning in a genetics experiment*. (Heuristic Programming Project, Working Paper 77–18). Stanford, CA: Stanford University Press.

Fikes, Richard, and Nilsson, Neils (1971). STRIPS: A new approach to the application of theorem proving to problem solving. *Artificial Intelligence* 2: 189–205.

Fitter, Mike (1979). Towards more 'natural' interactive systems. *International Journal of Man–Machine Studies* 11: 339–349.

Fodor, Jerome (1983). *The modularity of mind*. Cambridge, MA: MIT Press.

Frankel, Richard (1984). From sentence to sequence: Understanding the medical encounter through microinteractional analysis. *Discourse Processes* 7: 135–170.

Franklin, Sarah (1995). Science as culture, cultures of science. *Annual Reviews of Anthropology* 24: 163–184.

Franklin, Sarah (2000). Life itself: Global nature and the genetic imaginary. In S. Franklin, C. Lury, and J. Stacey (eds.), *Global nature, global culture* (pp. 188–227). London: Sage.

Franklin, Sarah, and Ragone, Helen (eds.). (1998). *Reproducing reproduction: Kinship, power and technological innovation*. Philadelphia: University of Pennsylvania Press.

Franklin, Sarah, Lury, Celia, and Stacey, Jackie (2000). *Global nature, global culture*. London: Sage.

Frazer, James (1900). *The golden bough: A study in magic and religion*. London: Macmillan. (Reprinted 1980.)

Fujimura, Joan (1992). Crafting science: Standardized packages, boundary objects and "translation." In A. Pickering (ed.), *Science as practice and culture* (pp. 168–211). Chicago: University of Chicago Press.

Fujimura, Joan (1996). *Crafting science: A sociohistory of the quest for the genetics of cancer*. Cambridge, MA: Harvard University Press.

Galaty, James (1981). Models and metaphors: On the semiotic explanation of segmentary systems. In L. Holy and M. Stuchlik (eds.), *The structure of folk models* (pp. 63–92). New York: Academic Press.

Galison, Peter (1987). *How experiments end*. Chicago: University of Chicago Press.

Galison, Peter (1997). *Image and logic: A material culture of microphysics*. Chicago: University of Chicago Press.

Gardner, Howard (1985). *The mind's new science*. New York: Basic Books.

Garfinkel, Harold (1967). *Studies in ethnomethodology*. Englewood Cliffs, NJ: Prentice Hall.

Garfinkel, Harold (1972). Remarks on ethnomethodology. In J. Gumperz and D. Hymes (eds.), *Directions in sociolinguistics: The ethnography of communication* (pp. 301–324). New York: Holt, Rinehart & Winston.

Garfinkel, Harold (2002). *Ethnomethodology's programme: Working out Durkheim's aphorism*. Lanham, MD: Rowman & Littlefield Publishers. P. 23.

Garfinkel, Harold, Lynch, Michael, and Livingston, Eric (1981). The work of a discovering science construed with materials from the optically discovered pulsar. *Philosophy of the Social Sciences* 111: 131–159.

Garfinkel, Harold, and Rawls, Anne (2002). *Ethnomethodology's program: Working out Durkeim's aphorism*. Lanham, MD: Rowman & Littlefield.

Garfinkel, Harold, and Sacks, Harvey (1970). On formal structures of practical actions. In J. McKinney and E. Tiryakian (eds.), *Theoretical sociology: Perspectives and development* (pp. 337–366). New York: Appleton Century Crofts.

Geertz, Clifford (1973). *The interpretation of cultures*. New York: Basic Books.

Gell, Alfred (1998). *Art and agency: An anthropological theory*. Oxford: Oxford University Press.

Gilbert, Nigel, and Heath, Christian (eds.). (1985). *Social action and artificial intelligence*. Aldershot, Hampshire, UK/Brookfield, VT: Gower.

Gladwin, Thomas (1964). Culture and logical process. In W. Goodenough (ed.), *Explorations in cultural anthropology* (pp. 167–177). New York: McGraw–Hill.

Gladwin, Thomas (1970). *East is a big bird: Navigation and logic on Puluwat Atoll*. Cambridge, MA: Harvard University Press.

Goffman, Erving (1975). Replies and responses. *Language in Society* 5: 257–313.

Gonzalez, Jennifer (2000). Envisioning cyborg bodies: Notes from current research. In G. E. A. Kirkup (ed.), *The gendered cyborg* (pp. 58–73). New York/London: Routledge.

Goodwin, Charles (1981). *Conversational organization: Interaction between speakers and hearers*. New York: Academic Press.

Goodwin, Charles (1994). Professional vision. *American Anthropologist* 96: 606–633.

Goodwin, Charles (1995a). Seeing in depth. *Social Studies of Science* 25: 237–274.

Goodwin, Charles (1995b). Co-constructing meaning in conversations with an aphasic man. *Research on Language and Social Interaction* 28: 233–260.

Goodwin, Charles (1997). The blackness of black: Color categories as situated practice. In L. Resnick, R. Saljo, C. Pontecorvo, and B. Burge (eds.), *Discourse, tools and reasoning* (pp. 111–142). Berlin: Springer-Verlag.

Goodwin, Charles (2003). The body in action. In J. Coupland and R. Gwyn (eds.), *Discourse, the body and identity* (pp. 19–42). NY: Palgrave/Macmillan.

Goodwin, Charles, and Goodwin, Marjorie Harness (1992). Context, activity and participation. In P. Lauer and A. di Luzio (eds.), *The contextualization of language* (pp. 77–99). Amsterdam: Benjamins.

Goodwin, Charles, and Goodwin, Marjorie Harness (1996). Seeing as situated activity: Formulating planes. In Y. Engestrom and D. Middleton (eds.), *Cognition and communication at work* (pp. 61–95). Cambridge, UK: Cambridge University Press.

Goodwin, Charles, and Goodwin, Marjorie Harness (1997). Contested vision: The discursive constitution of Rodney King. In B.-L. Gunnarsson, P. Linell, and B. Nordberg (eds.), *The construction of professional discourse* (pp. 292–316). New York: Longman.

Goodwin, Dawn (2004). *Acting in anaesthesia: Agency, participation, and legitimation*. Unpublished doctoral dissertation, Lancaster University.

Goodwin, Marjorie Harness (1980). Processes of mutual monitoring implicated in the production of description sequences. *Sociological Inquiry* 50: 303–317.

Grand, Steve (2003). *Growing up with Lucy: How to build an android in twenty easy steps*. London: Weidenfeld & Nicolson.

Green, Nicola (2002). On the move: Technology, mobility, and the mediation of social time and space. *The Information Society* 18: 281–292.

Greenbaum, Joan, and Kyng, Morten (1991) (eds.). *Design at work: Cooperative design of computer systems* (pp. x, 294). Hillsdale, NJ: Erlbaum.

Gregory, Judith (2000). *Sorcerer's apprentice: Creating the electronic health record, re-inventing medical records and patient care.* Unpublished doctoral dissertation, Department of Communications, University of California, San Diego.

Grice, H. P. (1975). Logic and conversation. In P. Cole and J. Morgan (eds.), *Syntax and semantics: Vol 3. Speech acts* (pp. 41–58). New York: Academic Press.

Grint, Keith, and Woolgar, Steve (1997). *The machine at work: Technology, work, and organization.* Cambridge, UK/Malden, MA: Polity.

Grosz, Barbara (1981). Focusing and description in natural language dialogues. In A. Joshi, B. Webber, and I. Sag (eds.). *Elements of discourse understanding.* Cambridge, UK: Cambridge University Press.

Grosz, Elizabeth (1994). *Volatile bodies: Toward a corporeal feminism.* Bloomington: Indiana University Press.

Grudin, Jonathan (1990). The computer reaches out: The historical continuity of interface design. In J. C. Chew and J. Whiteside (eds.), *Proceedings of the ACM CHI 90 Conference on Human Factors in Computing Systems*, New York: ACM Press, pp. 261–268.

Gumperz, John (1982a). *Discourse strategies.* Cambridge, UK: Cambridge University Press.

Gumperz, John (1982b). The linguistic bases of communicative competence. In D. Tannen (ed.)., *Georgetown University roundtable on language and linguistics: Analyzing discourse: Text and talk* (pp. 323–334). Washington, DC: Georgetown University Press.

Gumperz, John, and Tannen, Deborah (1979). Individual and social differences in language use. In C. Fillmore et al. (eds.), *Individual differences in language ability and language behavior.* New York: Academic Press.

Gupta, Akhil, and Ferguson, James (1997). *Anthropological locations: Boundaries and grounds of a field science.* Berkeley: University of California.

Halberstam, Judith (1991). Automating gender: Postmodern feminism in the age of the intelligent machines. *Feminist Studies* 17: 439–460.

Halberstam, Judith, and Livingston, Ira (eds.). (1995). *Posthuman bodies.* Bloomington/Indianapolis: Indiana University.

Hales, Mike (1994). Where are designers? Styles of design practice, objects of design, and views of users in CSCW. In D. Rosenberg and C. Hutchison (eds.), *Design issues in CSCW* (pp. 151–177). New York: Springer-Verlag.

Haraway, Donna (1985/1991). Manifesto for cyborgs: Science, technology and socialist feminisim in the 1980s. In *Simians, cyborgs, and women: The reinvention of nature.* New York: Routledge. (Originally published in *Socialist Review* (1985) 80: 65–108.)

Haraway, Donna (1991). *Simians, cyborgs, and women: The reinvention of nature.* New York: Routledge.

Haraway, Donna (1997). *Modest _Witness @Second_Millenium.FemaleMan_Meets_ OncoMouse*™*: Feminism and Technoscience.* New York: Routledge.

Haraway, Donna (2003). *The companion species manifesto: Dogs, people and significant others.* Chicago: Prickly Paradigm Press.

Harding, Sandra (1986). *The science question in feminism*. Ithaca, NY: Cornell University Press.

Harding, Sandra (1991). *Whose science? Whose knowledge?: Thinking from women's lives*. Ithaca, NY: Cornell University Press.

Hayes, Patrick (1981). A construction-specific approach to focused interaction in flexible parsing. In *Proceedings of the Nineteenth Annual Meeting of the Association for Computational Linguistics* (pp. 149–152). Stanford, CA: Stanford University Press.

Hayes, Patrick, and Reddy, Raj (1983). Steps toward graceful interaction in spoken and written man–machine communication. *International Journal of Man–Machine Studies* 19: 231–284.

Hayles, N. Katherine (1999). *How we became posthuman: Virtual bodies in cybernetics, literature, and informatics*. Chicago, IL: University of Chicago Press.

Hayles, N. Katherine (2002). Flesh and metal: Reconfiguring the mindbody in virtual environments. *Configurations* 10: 297–320.

Hayles, N. Katherine (2005). Computing the human. *Theory, Culture & Society* 22: 131–151.

Heap, James (1980). Description in ethnomethodology. *Human Studies* 3: 87–106.

Heath, Christian (1986). *Body movement and speech in medical interaction*. Cambridge, UK/New York: Cambridge University Press.

Heath, Christian, and Luff, Paul (1992). Collaboration and control: Crisis management and multimedia technology in London Undergound line control rooms. *Computer-Supported Cooperative Work* 1(1): 69–94.

Heath, Christian, and Luff, Paul (2000). *Technology in action*. Cambridge, UK. Cambridge University Press.

Heath, Christian, Svensson, Marcus, Hindmarsh, Jon, Luff, Paul, and Vom Lehn, Dirk (2002). Configuring awareness. *Computer-Supported Cooperative Work* 11: 317–347.

Hedberg, Sara Reese (2000). After desktop computing: A progress report on smart environments research. *IEEE Intelligent Systems and Their Applications* 15: 7–9.

Helmreich, Stefan (1998). *Silicon second nature: Culturing artificial life in a digital world*. Berkeley: University of California Press.

Henderson, Kathryn (1999). *On line and on paper: Visual representations, visual culture, and computer graphics in design engineering*. Cambridge, MA: MIT Press.

Hendrix, Gary (1977). Human engineering for applied natural language processing. In *Proceedings of the Fifth International Joint Conference on Artificial Intelligence* (pp. 183–191). Cambridge, MA: MIT Press.

Heritage, John (1984). *Garfinkel and ethnomethodology*. Cambridge, UK: Polity Press.

Hirschauer, Stefan (1991). The manufacture of bodies in surgery. *Social Studies of Science* 21(2): 279–319.

Hirsh, Haym (1999). Roomservice, AI-style. *IEEE Intelligent Systems and Their Applications* March/April: 8–10.

Hogle, Linda (1999). *Recovering the nation's body: Cultural memory, medicine, and the politics of redemption*. New Brunswick, NJ: Rutgers University Press.

Hughes, John, Randall, David, and Shapiro, Dan (1993). From ethnographic record to system design: Some experiences from the field. *Computer-Supported Cooperative Work* 1: 123–141.

Hutchins, Edwin (1983). Understanding Micronesian navigation. In D. Gertner and A. Stevens (eds.), *Mental models* (pp. 191–225). Hillsdale, NJ: Erlbaum.

Hutchins, Edwin (1995). *Cognition in the wild*. Cambridge, MA: MIT Press.

Hymes, Dell H. (1974). *Reinventing anthropology*. New York: Random House.

Ingold, Tim (2000). *The perception of the environment: Essays in livelihood, dwelling and skill*. London/New York: Routledge.

Ito, Mimi, Okabe, Daisuke, and Matsuda, Misa (2005). *Personal, portable, pedestrian: Mobile phones in Japanese life*. Cambridge, MA: MIT Press.

Jain, Sarah (1999). The prosthetic imagination: Enabling and disabling the prosthesis trope. *Science, Technology and Human Values* 24: 31–54.

Jain, Sarah (2006). *Injury: The politics of product design and safety law in the United States*. Princeton, NJ: Princeton University Press.

Jefferson, Gail (1972). Side sequences. In D. Sudnow (ed.), *Studies in social interaction* (pp. 294–338). New York: Free Press.

Jefferson, Gail (1983). *Issues in the transcription of naturally occurring talk: Caricature versus capturing pronunciational particulars*. (Tilburg Papers in Language and Literature, no. 34). Amsterdam, The Netherlands: Tilburg University.

Jeremijenko, Natalie (2004). If things can talk, what do they say? In N. Waldrip-Fruin and P. Harrigan (eds.), *First person: New media as story, performance, and game* (pp. 262–287). Cambridge, MA: MIT Press.

Jordan, Brigitte, and Fuller, Nancy (1975). On the non-fatal nature of trouble sense-making and sense-managing in Lingua Franca talk. *Semiotica* 13: 1–31.

Jordan, Kathleen, and Lynch, Michael (1992). The sociology of a genetic engineering technique: Ritual and rationality in the performance of the 'plasmid prep.' In A. Clarke and J. Fujimura (eds.), *The right tools for the job: At work in twentieth-century life sciences* (pp. 77–114). Princeton, NJ: Princeton University Press.

Joshi, Arvon, Webber, Bonnie, and Sag, Ivan (eds.) (1981). *Elements of discourse understanding*. Cambridge, UK: Cambridge University Press.

Kantrowitz, Barbara (1994, January 17). The butlers of the digital age will be just a keystroke away. *Newsweek*, p. 58.

Keller, Evelyn Fox (2002a). *Making sense of life: Explaining biological development with models, metaphors and machines*. Cambridge, MA: Harvard University Press.

Keller, Evelyn Fox (2002b). Marrying the premodern to the postmodern: Computers and organisms after WWII. In D. Tofts, A. Jonson, and A. Cavallaro (eds.), *Prefiguring cyberculture* (pp. 52–65). Cambridge, MA: MIT Press.

Keller, Evelyn Fox (2007). Booting up baby. In J. Riskin (ed.), *The Sistine gap*. Stanford, CA: Stanford University Press.

Kember, Sarah (1998). *Virtual anxiety: Photography, new technologies and subjectivity*. Manchester: Manchester University Press.

Kember, Sarah (2003). *Cyberfeminism and artificial life*. London/New York: Routledge.

Kirby, Vicki (1997). *Telling flesh: The substance of the corporeal*. New York: Routledge.

Knorr Cetina, Karin (1999). *Epistemic cultures: How the sciences make knowledge.* Cambridge, MA: Harvard University Press.

Knorr Cetina, Karin, and Mulkay, Michael (eds.). (1983). *Science observed: Perspectives on the social study of science.* London: Sage.

Knorr, Karin (1981). *The manufacture of knowledge: An essay on the constructivist and contextual nature of science.* Oxford/New York: Pergamon.

Koschmann, Timothy (ed.). (2003). Plans and situated actions: A retro-review. Books & Ideas, *Journal of the Learning Sciences* 12(2): 257–306.

Kubrick, Stanley, and Clarke, Arthur C. (1968). *2001: A Space Odyssey.*

Landauer, Thomas (1995). *The trouble with computers: Usefulness, usability, and productivity.* Cambridge, MA: MIT Press.

Latour, Bruno (1986). Visualization and cognition: Thinking with eyes and hands. *Knowledge and Society* 6: 1–40.

Latour, Bruno (1987). *Science in action: How to follow scientists and engineers through society.* Cambridge, MA: Harvard University Press.

Latour, Bruno (1988). *The pasteurization of France.* Cambridge, MA: Harvard University Press.

Latour, Bruno (1992). Where are the missing masses: The sociology of a few mundane artifacts. In W. Bijker and J. Law (eds.), *Shaping technology/building society* (pp. 225–258). Cambridge, MA: MIT Press.

Latour, Bruno (1993). *We have never been modern.* Cambridge, MA: Harvard University Press.

Latour, Bruno (1999). *Pandora's hope: Essays on the reality of science studies.* Cambridge, MA: Harvard University Press.

Latour, Bruno, and Woolgar, Steve (1979). *Laboratory life: The social construction of scientific facts.* Beverly Hills: Sage.

Lave, Jean (1988). *Cognition in practice: Mind, mathematics, and culture in everyday life.* Cambridge/New York: Cambridge University Press.

Law, John (1987). Technology and heterogeneous engineering: The case of Portuguese expansion. In W. Bijker, T. Hughes, and T. Pinch (eds.), *The social construction of technological systems* (pp. 111–134). Cambridge, MA: MIT Press.

Law, John (1994). *Organizing modernity.* Oxford, UK/Cambridge, MA: Blackwell.

Law, John (1996). Organizing accountabilities: Ontology and the mode of accounting. In R. Munro and J. Mouritsen (eds.), *Accountability: Power, ethos and the technologies of managing* (pp. 283–306). London: International Thomas Business Press.

Law, John (2002). *Aircraft stories: Decentering the object in technoscience.* Durham, NC/London: Duke University Press.

Law, John (2004). *After method: Mess in social science research.* London/New York: Routledge.

Law, John, and Mol, Annemarie (eds.) (2002). *Complexities: Social studies of knowledge practices.* Durham, NC/London: Duke University Press.

Lee, Nick, and Brown, Steve (1994). Otherness and the actor network: The undiscovered continent. *American Behavioral Scientist* 37: 772–790.

Lenoir, Tim (2002). Embracing the posthuman. *Configurations* 10: 203–220.

Levinson, Stephen (1983). *Pragmatics.* Cambridge, UK: Cambridge University Press.

Lewis, David (1972). *We, the navigators.* Honolulu: University Press of Hawaii.

Lieberman, Henry (1997). Autonomous interface agents. *Proceedings of the ACM CHI 97 Conference on human factors in computing systems* (pp. 67–74). New York: ACM Press.

Lock, Margaret M. (2002). *Twice dead: Organ transplants and the reinvention of death.* Berkeley: University of California Press.

London, Bob, and Clancey, William (1982). Plan recognition strategies in student modeling: Prediction and description. *Proceedings of the Second National Conference on Artificial Intelligence*, 335–338. Menlo Park, Calif.: AAAI Press.

Luff, Paul, Gilbert, Nigel, and Frohlich, David (eds.). (1990). *Computers and conversation.* London/San Diego: Academic Press.

Luff, Paul, Hindmarsh, Jon, and Heath, Christian (eds.). (2000). *Workplace studies: Recovering work practice and informing system design.* Cambridge, UK: Cambridge University Press.

Lynch, Michael (1982). Technical work and critical enquiry: Investigation in a scientific laboratory. *Social Studies of Science* 12: 499–533.

Lynch, Michael (1985a). *Art and artifact in laboratory science: A study of shop work and shop talk in a research laboratory.* London/Boston: Routledge & Kegan Paul.

Lynch, Michael (1985b). Discipline and the material form of images: An analysis of scientific visibility. *Social Studies of Science* 15: 37–66.

Lynch, Michael (1988). The externalized retina: Selection and mathematization in the visual documentation of objects in the life sciences. *Human Studies* 11: 201–234.

Lynch, Michael (1991a). Laboratory space and the technological domplex: An investigation of topical contextures. *Science in Context* 4: 51–78.

Lynch, Michael (1991b). Ordinary and scientific measurement as ethnomethodological phenomena. In G. Button (ed.), *Ethnomethodology and the human sciences* (pp. 77–108). Cambridge, UK: Cambridge University Press.

Lynch, Michael (1993). *Scientific practice and ordinary action: Ethnomethodology and social studies of science.* Cambridge, UK/New York: Cambridge University Press.

Lynch, Michael (2001). Ethnomethodology and the logic of practice. In T. Schatzki, K. K. Cetina, and E. Von Savigny (eds.), *The practice turn in contemporary theory* (pp. 131–148). London/New York: Routledge.

Lynch, Michael, and Jordan, Kathleen (1995). Instructed action in, of, and as molecular biology. *Human Studies* 18: 227–244.

Lynch, Michael, and Jordan, Kathleen (2000). Patents, promotions and protocols: Mapping and claiming scientific territory. *Mind, Culture & Activity* 7: 124–146.

Lynch, Michael, Livingston, Eric, and Garfinkel, Harold (1983). Temporal order in laboratory work. In K. Knorr and M. Mulkay (eds.), *Science observed* (pp. 205–238). London: Sage.

Lynch, Michael, and Woolgar, Steve (eds.). (1990). *Representation in scientific practice.* Cambridge, MA: MIT Press.

Macbeth, Douglas (1996). The discovery of situated worlds: Analytic commitments, or moral orders? *Human Studies* 19: 267–287.

MacKay, D. (1962). The use of behavioral language to refer to mechanical processes. *British Journal of Philosophical Science* 13: 89–103.

Malinowski, Bronislaw (1935). *Coral gardens and their magic*. London: Allen & Unwin.

Mann, Steve, and Niedzviecki, Hal (2001). *Cyborg: Digital destiny and human possibility in the age of the wearable computer*. Doubleday Canada.

Marcus, George (1995). Ethnograpy in/of the world system: The emergence of multi-sited ethnography. *Annual Reviews of Anthropology* 24: 95–117.

Marcus, George (ed.). (1999). *Critical anthropology now: Unexpected contexts, shifting constituencies, changing agendas*. Santa Fe, NM: School of American Research.

Marcus, George, and Fischer, Michael (1986). *Anthropology as cultural critique: An experimental moment in the human sciences*. Chicago: University of Chicago Press.

Marks, Laura U. (2002). *Touch: Sensuous theory and multisensory media*. Minneapolis: University of Minnesota Press.

Markussen, Randi (1995). Constructing easiness – Historical perspectives on work, computerization, and women. In S. L. Star (ed.), *Cultures of computing* (pp. 158–180). Oxford: Blackwell.

Mauss, Marcel (1902). *A general theory of magic*. New York: Norton.

Mauss, Marcel (1954). *The gift*. London: Cohen & West.

McCorduck, Pamela (1979). *Machines who think*. San Francisco, CA: W.H. Freeman.

McDermott, Ray (1976). *Kids make sense: An ethnographic account of the itneractional management of success and failure in one first-grade classroom*. Unpublished doctoral dissertation, Stanford University.

M'charek, Amade (2005). *The Human genome diversity project: An ethnography of scientific practice*. Cambridge, UK: Cambridge University Press.

McNeil, Maureen (ed.) (1987). *Gender and expertise*. London: Free Association Books.

Mead, George H. (1934). *Mind, self and society from the standpoint of a social behaviorist*. Chicago: University of Chicago Press.

Menzel, Peter, and D'Aluisio, Faith (2000). *Robo sapiens*. Cambridge, MA: MIT Press.

Merritt, Marilyn (1977). On questions following questions in service encounters. *Language in Society* 5: 315–357.

Mialet, Helene (2003). Reading Hawking's presence: An interview with a self-effacing man. *Critical Inquiry* 29: 571–598.

Middleton, David, and Brown, Steven (2005). Net-working on a neonatl intensive care unit: The baby as a virtual object. In B. Czarniiawska and T. Hernes (eds.), *Actor-network theory and organizing* (pp. 307–328). Copenhagen: Copenhagen Business School Press.

Miller, George A., Galanter, Eugene, and Pribram, Karl H. (1960). *Plans and the structure of behavior*. New York: Holt, Rinehart and Winston.

Mills, C. Wright (1940). Situated actions and vocabularies of motive. *American Sociological Review* 5: 904–913.

Mol, Annemarie (2002). *The body multiple: Ontology in medical practice*. Durham, NC: Duke University Press.

Moore, C. L. (1975). No woman born. In T. Scortia and G. Zebrowski (eds.), *Human-machines: An anthology of stories about cyborgs* (pp. 63–118). New York: Vintage.

Mort, Maggie, Goodwin, Dawn, Smith, Andrew, and Pope, Catherine (2005). Safe asleep? Human–machine relations in medical practice. *Social Science & Medicine* 61: 2027–2037.

Mulcahy, Dianne (1999). Working bodies and representations: Tales from a training field. *Science, Technology and Human Values* 24: 80–104.

Newman, Susan (1998). Here, there, and nowhere at all: Distribution, negotiation, and virtuality in postmodern ethnography and engineering. *Knowledge and Society* 11: 235–267.

Newell, Allen, and Simon, Herbert (1972). *Human problem solving.* Englewood Cliffs, NJ: Prentice Hall.

Nickerson, Ray (1976). On conversational interaction with computers. In *Proccedings of ACM SIGGRAPH* workshop, October 14–15, pp. 101–113, Pittsburgh, PA.

Nilsson, Neils (1973). *A hierarchical robot planning and execution system.* (Technical Note 76). Menlo Park, CA: SRI Artificial Intelligence Center.

Noble, David (1984). *Forces of production.* New York/Oxford: Oxford University Press.

Oberquelle, Horst, Kupka, I., and Maass, S. (1983). A view of human–machine communication and cooperation. *International Journal of Man–Machine Studies* 19: 309–333.

Ochs, Eleanor (1979). Planned and unplanned discourse. In T. Givon (ed.), *Syntax and semantics: Vol. 12. Discourse and syntax* (pp. 51–78). New York: Academic Press.

Orr, Julian (1996). *Talking about machines: An ethnography of a modern job.* Ithaca, NY: ILR Press.

Oudshoorn, Nelly, and Pinch, Trevor (eds.). (2003). *How users matter: The co-construction of users and technologies.* Cambridge, MA: MIT Press.

Peachey, D., and McCalla, G. (1986). Using planning techniques in intelligent tutoring systems. *International Journal of Man–Machine Studies* 24: 77–98.

Pedersen, Elin Rønby, and Sokoler, Thomas (1997). AROMA – Abstract representation of mediated presence supporting mutual awareness. *Proceedings of the ACM CHI 97 Conference on Human Factors in Computing Systems* (pp. 51–58). New York: ACM Press.

Peirce, Charles (1933). In C. Hartshorne and P. Weiss (eds.), *Collected papers* (Vol. 11). Cambridge, MA: Harvard University Press.

Picard, Rosalind (1997). *Affective computing.* Cambridge, MA: MIT Press.

Pickering, Andrew (1984). *Constructing quarks: A sociological history of particle physics.* Edinburgh: Edinburgh University Press.

Pickering, Andrew (ed.). (1992). *Science as practice and culture.* Chicago/London: University of Chicago Press.

Pickering, Andrew (1995). *The mangle of practice: Time, agency and science.* Chicago: University of Chicago Press.

Pickering, Andrew (2002). Cybernetics and the mangle. *Social Studies of Science* 32: 413–438.

Piller, Charles (2001, May 13). A step toward creating thoughtful machines. *Greenwich Times*, A8.

Prentice, Rachel (2005). *Swimming in the joint: Surgery, technology, perception.* Unpublished manuscript.

Price, Janet, and Shildrick, Magrit (eds.). (1999). *Feminist theory and the body: A reader.* Edinburgh: Edinburgh University Press.

Pylyshyn, Zenon (1974). Minds, machines and phenomenology: Some reflections on Dreyfus' *What Computers Can't Do. Cognition* 3: 57–77.

Pylyshyn, Zenon (1984). *Computation and cognition.* Cambridge, MA: MIT Press.

Rawls, Anne (1996). Durkheim's epistemology: The neglected argument. *American Journal of Sociology* 102(2): 430–482.

Rawls, Anne (2002). Editor's introduction. In *Ethnomethodology's programme: Working out Durkheim's aphorism.* Lanham, MD: Rowman & Littlefield Publishers. Pp. 1–76.

Reid, Roddey, and Traweek, Sharon (eds.). (2000). *Doing Science + Culture: How cultural and interdisciplinary studies are changing the way we look at science and medicine.* New York: Routledge.

Riecken, Douglas (1994). A conversation with Marvin Minsky about agents. *Communications of the ACM* 37: 23–29.

Risan, Lars (1997). *Artificial life: A technoscience leaving modernity? An anthropology of subjects and objects.* Retrieved August 10, 2005, from http://anthrobase. com/Txt/R/Risan_L_05.htm.

Riskin, Jessica (2003a). The defecating duck, or, the ambiguous origins of artificial life. *Critical Inquiry* 20: 599–633.

Riskin, Jessica (2003b). Eighteenth century wetware. Representations 83: 97–125.

Riskin, Jessica (ed.). (2007). *The Sistine gap: Essays in the history and philosophy of artificial life.* Chicago: University of Chicago Press.

Robertson, Toni (2002). The public availability of actions and artefacts. *Computer-Supported Cooperative Work* 11: 299–316.

Rogers, Yvonne, Sharp, Helen, and Preece, Jennifer (2002). *Interaction design: Beyond human–computer interaction.* New York: Wiley.

Rubin, Andrea (1980). A theoretical taxonomy of the differences between oral and written langue. In R. Spiro et al. (eds.), *Theoretical issues in reading comprehension.* Hillsdale, NJ: Erlbaum.

Sacerdoti, Earl (1975). The nonlinear nature of plans. In *Proceedings of the Fourth International Joint Conference on Artificial Intelligence.*

Sacerdoti, Earl (1977). *A structure for plans and behavior.* New York: Elsevier.

Sack, Warren (1997). Artificial human nature. *Design Issues* 13: 55–64.

Sacks, Harvey (1963). On sociological description. *Berkeley Journal of Sociology* 8: 1–16.

Sacks, Harvey (1974). An analysis of the course of a joke's telling in converstion. In R. Bauman and J. Scherzer (eds.), *Explorations in the ethnography of speaking* (pp. 337–353). Cambridge, UK: Cambridge University Press.

Sacks, Harvey, Schegloff, Emanuel, and Jefferson, Gail (1978). A simplest systematics for the organization of turn-taking in conversation. In J. Schenkein (ed.), *Studies in the organization of conversational interaction* (pp. 7–55). New York: Academic Press.

Sandoval, Chela (1999). New sciences: Cyborg feminism and the methodology of the oppressed. In J. Wolmark (ed.), *Cybersexualities* (pp. 247–263). Edinburgh: Edinburgh University Press.

Sawyer, R. Keith (2003). *Improvised dialogues: Emergence and creativity in conversation*. Westport, CT: Ablex.

Schaffer, Simon (1999). Enlightened automata. In W. Clark, J. Golinski, and S. Shaffer (eds.), *The sciences in enlightened Europe* (pp. 126–165). Chicago: University of Chicago Press.

Schank, Robert, and Abelson, R. (1977). Scripts, plans and knowledge. In P. Johson-Laird and P. Wason (eds.), *Thinking: Readings in cognitive science*. Cambridge, UK: Cambridge University Press.

Scheflen, Albert (1974). *How behavior means*. Garden City, NY: Anchor Press.

Schegloff, Emanuel (1972). Sequencing in conversational openings. In J. Gumperz and D. Hymes (eds.)., *Directions in sociolinguistics: The ethnography of communication* (pp. 346–380). New York: Academic Press.

Schegloff, Emanuel (1982). Discourse as an interactional achievement: Some uses of "uh huh" and other things that come between sentences. In D. Tannen (ed.), *Georgetown University roundtable on language and linguistics: Analyzing discourse and talk* (pp. 71–93). Washington, DC: Georgetown University Press.

Schegloff, Emanuel (1998). Body torque. *Social Research* 65: 535–596.

Schegloff, Emanuel, and Sacks, Harvey (1973). Opening up closings. *Semiotica* 7: 289–327.

Schiebinger, Londa (ed.). (2000). *Feminism & the body*. Oxford: Oxford University Press.

Schmidt, C., Sridharan, N., and Goodson, J. (1978). The plan recognition problem. *Artificial Intelligence* 11: 45–83.

Schmidt, Kjeld, and Wagner, Ina (2004). Ordering systems: Coordinative practices and artifacts in architectural design and planning. *Computer-Supported Cooperative Work* 13: 349–408.

Schuler, Douglas, and Namioka, Aki (eds.). (1993). *Participatory design: Principles and practices*. Hillsdale, NJ: Erlbaum.

Schull, Natasha (2005). Digital gambling: The coincidence of desire and design. *ANNALS of the American Academy of Political and Social Science* 597: 65–81.

Schull, Natasha (in press). *Machine life: Control and compulsion in Las Vegas*. Princeton, NJ: Princeton University Press.

Schutz, Alfred (1962). *Collected papers I: The problem of social reality*. The Hague: Martinus Nijhoff.

Searle, John (1969). *Speech acts: An essay in the philosophy of language*. Cambridge, UK: Cambridge University Press.

Searle, John (1979). *Expression and meaning*. Cambridge, UK: Cambridge University Press.

Searle, John (1980). The intentionality of intention and action. *Cognitive Science* 4: 47–70.

Sengers, Phoebe (2004). *The autonomous agency of STS: Boundary crossings between STS and artificial intelligence*. Unpublished manuscript. (Submitted to *Social Studies of Science*.)

Shapin, Steve (1989). The invisible technician. *American Scientist* 77: 553–563.

Shapin, Steven, and Schaffer, Simon (1985). *Leviathan and the air-pump: Hobbes, Boyle, and the experimental life*. Princeton, NJ: Princeton University Press.

Sharrock, Wes, and Button, Graham (2003). Plans and situated actions ten years on. *The Journal of the Learning Sciences* 12(2): 259–264.

Shrager, Jeff and Finin, Tom (1982). An expert system that volunteers advice. *Proceedings of the Second National Conference on Artificial Intelligence*, 339–340. Menlo Park, Calif.: AAAI Press.

Sidner, Candace (1979). *Towards a computational theory of definite anaphora comprehension in English discourse*. (Technical Report TR-537). Cambridge, MA: MIT AI Laboratory.

Simon, Herbert (1969). *The sciences of the artificial*. Cambridge, MA: MIT Press.

Singleton, Vicky (1998). Stabilizing instabilities: The laboratory in the UK Cervical Screening Program. In M. Berg and A. Mol (eds.), *Differences in medicine* (pp. 86–104). Durham, NC: Duke University Press.

Smith, Brian Cantwell (1996). *On the origin of objects*. Cambridge, MA: MIT Press.

Smith, Dorothy E. (1987). *The everyday world as problematic: A feminist sociology*. Toronto: University of Toronto Press.

Spender, Dale (1996). *Nattering on the net: Women, power and cyberspace*. Toronto: Garamond.

Standage, Tom (2002). *The Turk: The life and times of the famous eighteenth-century chess-playing machine*. New York: Walker & Co.

Star, Susan Leigh (1989a). *Regions of the mind: Brain research and the quest for scientific certainty*. Stanford, CA: Stanford University Press.

Star, Susan Leigh (1989b). Layered space, formal representations and long distance control: The politics of information. *Fundamenta Scientiae* 10: 125–155.

Star, Susan Leigh (1991). Invisible work and silenced dialogues in knowledge representation. In I. Eriksson, B. Kitchenham, and K. Tijdens (eds.), *Women, work and computerization* (pp. 81–92). Amsterdam: North Holland.

Star, Susan Leigh (ed.). (1995). *The cultures of computing*. Oxford, UK/Cambridge, MA: Blackwell.

Star, Susan Leigh, and Griesemer, James (1989). Institutional ecology, 'translations' and boundary objects: Amateurs and professionals in Berkeley's Museum of Vertebrate Zoology. *Social Studies of Science* 19: 387–420.

Stelarc (2004). *Prosthetic head: Intelligence, awareness and agency*. Unpublished manuscript, University of Melbourne.

Stich, Stephen (1983). *From folk psychology to cognitive science*. Cambridge, MA: MIT Press.

Strathern, Marilyn (1988). *The gender of the gift: Problems with women and problems with society in Melanesia*. Berkeley: University of California Press.

Strathern, Marilyn (1992). *Reproducing the future: Essays on anthropology, kinship, and the new reproductive technologies*. New York: Routledge.

Strathern, Marilyn (1996). Cutting the network. *Journal of the Royal Anthropological Institute* 2: 517–535.

Strathern, Marilyn (1999). *Property, substance, and effect: Anthropological essays on persons and things*. London/New Brunswick, NJ: Athlone Press.

Strathern, Marilyn (ed.). (2000). *Audit cultures: Anthropological studies in accountability, ethics, and the academy*. London/New York: Routledge.

Streeck, Jurgen (1980). Speech acts in interaction: A critique of Searle. *Discourse Processes* 3: 133–154.

Suchman, Lucy (1982). *Toward a sociology of human–machine interaction: Pragmatics of instruction following.* (CIS Working Paper, Xerox Palo Alto Research Center). Palo Alto, CA: Author.

Suchman, Lucy (1987). *Plans and situated actions: The problem of human–machine communication.* New York: Cambridge University Press.

Suchman, Lucy (1993a). Response to Vera and Simon's 'Situated action: A symbolic interpretation.' *Cognitive Science* 17(1): 71–76.

Suchman, Lucy (1993b). Technologies of accountability: On lizards and airplanes. In G. Button (ed.), *Technology in working order* (pp. 113–126). London: Routledge.

Suchman, Lucy (1994a). Working relations of technology production and use. *Computer-Supported Cooperative Work* 2: 21–39.

Suchman, Lucy (1994b). Do categories have politics? The language-action perspective reconsidered. *Computer-Supported Cooperative Work* 2: 177–190.

Suchman, Lucy (1995). Making work visible. *Communications of the ACM* 38(9): 56–64.

Suchman, Lucy (1999). Working relations of technology production and use. In D. Mackenzie and J. Wajcman (eds.), *The social shaping of technology, 2nd ed.* (pp. 258–268). Buckingham, UK/Philadelphia: Open University Press.

Suchman, Lucy (2000). Embodied practices of engineering work. *Mind, Culture & Activity* 7: 4–18.

Suchman, Lucy (2001). Building bridges: Practice-based ethnographies of contemporary technology. In M. Schiffer (ed.), *Anthropological perspectives on technology* (pp. 163–177). Albuquerque: University of New Mexico Press.

Suchman, Lucy (2002a). Located accountabilities in technology production. *Scandinavian Journal of Information Systems* 14: 91–105.

Suchman, Lucy (2002b). Practice-based design: Notes from the hyper-developed world. *The Information Society* 18: 1–6.

Suchman, Lucy (2003). Writing and reading: A response to comments on plans and situated actions: The problem of human–machine communication. *The Journal of the Learning Sciences* 12 (2): 299–306.

Suchman, Lucy (2005). Affiliative objects. *Organisation* 12(3): 379–399.

Suchman, Lucy, Blomberg, Jeanette, Orr, Julian, and Trigg, Randall (1999). Reconstructing technologies as social practice. *American Behavioral Scientist* 43: 392–408.

Suchman, Lucy, and Jordan, Brigitte (1989). Computerization and women's knowledge. In K. Tijdens, M. Jennings, I. Wagner, and M. Weggelaar (eds.), *Women, work and computerization* (pp. 153–160). Amsterdam: North Holland. (Reprinted in P. Agre and D. Schuler (eds.) (1997). *Reinventing technology, rediscovering community: Critical explorations in computing as a social practice* (pp. 97–105). Greenwich, CT: Ablex.)

Suchman, Lucy, Trigg, Randall, and Blomberg, Jeanette (2002). Working artefacts: Ethnomethods of the prototype. *British Journal of Sociology* 53: 163–179.

Taussig, Michael (1993). *Mimesis and alterity: A particular history of the senses.* London: Routledge.

Terry, Jennifer, and Calvert, Melodie (eds.). (1997). *Processed lives: Gender and technology in everyday life.* London/New York: Routledge.

Thomas, Frank, and Johnston, Ollie (1981). *Disney animation: The illusion of life.* New York: Abbeville.

Thomas, Peter J. (1995). *The social and interactional dimensions of human–computer interfaces.* Cambridge, UK: Cambridge University Press.

Thompson, Charis (2005). *Making parents: The ontological choreography of reproductive technologies.* Cambridge, MA: MIT Press.

Timmermans, Stefan (1999). *Sudden death and the myth of CPR.* Philadelphia, PA: Temple University Press.

Timmermans, Stefan, and Berg, Marc (1997). Standardization in action: Achieving local universality through medical protocols. *Social Studies of Science* 27: 273–305.

Timmermans, Stefan, and Berg, Marc (2003). *The gold standard: The challenge of evidence-based medicine and standardization in health care.* Philadelphia, PA: Temple University Press.

Traweek, Sharon (1988). *Beamtimes and lifetimes: The world of high energy physicists.* Cambridge, MA: Harvard University Press.

Trigg, Randall, Blomberg, Jeanette, and Suchman, Lucy (1999). Moving document collections online. In *Proceedings of the Sixth European Conference on Computer Supported Cooperative Work (ECSCW):* (pp. 331–350). Copenhagen: Kluwer Academic Press.

Turing, Alan (1950). Computing machinery and intelligence. *Mind* 59(236): 433–461.

Turkle, Sherry (1984). *The second self: Computers and the human spirit.* New York: Simon & Schuster.

Turkle, Sherry (1995). *Life on the screen: Identity in the age of the Internet.* New York/Toronto: Simon & Schuster.

Turnbull, David (1990). *Mapping the world in the mind: A case study of the unwritten knowledge of the micronesian navigators.* Deakin University School of Humanities. Geelong: Deakin University Press.

Turnbull, David (1993). *Maps are territories, science is an atlas: A portfolio of exhibits.* Chicago: University of Chicago Press.

Turnbull, David (2000). *Masons, tricksters and cartographers: Comparative studies in the sociology of scientific and indigenous knowledge.* Amsterdam: Harwood Academic.

Turner, Ralph (1962). Words, utterances and activities. In *Ethnomethodology: Selected readings* (pp. 197–215). Harmondsworth, Middlesex: Penguin.

Tylor, Edward (1875). *Primitive culture.* London: Murray.

Varela, Francisco, Thompson, Evan, and Rosch, Eleanor (1991). *The embodied mind: Cognitive science and human experience.* Cambridge, MA: MIT Press.

Vera, Alonso (2003). By the seat of our pants: The evolution of research on cognition and action. *The Journal of the Learning Sciences* 12(2): 279–284.

Vera, Alonso, and Simon, Herbert (1993). Situated action: A symbolic interpretation. *Cognitive Science* 17(1): 7–48.

Verran, Helen (1998). Re-imagining land ownership in Australia. *Postcolonial Studies* 1: 237–254.

Verran, Helen (2001). *Science and an African logic.* Chicago: University of Chicago Press.

Viseu, Ana (2003). Simulation and augmentation: Issues of wearable computers. *Ethics and Information Technology* 5: 17–26.

Viseu, Ana (2005). *Augmented bodies: The visions and realities of wearable computers.* Unpublished doctoral dissertation, Ontario Institute for Studies in Education, University of Toronto.

Wakeford, Nina (2000). Gender and the landscapes of computing in an Internet cafe. In G. Kirkup, L. Janes, K. Woodward, and F. Hovenden (eds.), *The gendered cyborg* (pp. 291–304). London/New York: Routledge.

Watt, W. C. (1968). Habitability. *American Documentation* 19(3): 338–351.

Wei, Sha Xin (2002). Resistance is fertile: Gesture and agency in the field of responsive media. *Configurations* 10: 439–472.

Weizenbaum, Joseph (1983). ELIZA: A computer program for the study of natural language communication between man and machine. *Communications of the ACM, 25th Anniversary Issue* 29(1): 23–27. (Reprinted from *Communications of the ACM* 26(1): 36–45, January 1966).

Wells, Gordon (2003). Lesson plans and situated learning-and-teaching. *The Journal of the Learning Sciences* 12(2): 265–272.

Wenger, Etienne (1987). *Artificial intelligence and tutoring systems: Computational and cognitive approaches to the communication of knowledge.* Los Altos, CA: Morgan Kaufmann.

Wilkinson, Barry (1983). *The shopfloor politics of new technology.* London: Heinemann.

Wilson, Thomas (1970). Conceptions of interaction and forms of sociological explanation. *American Sociological Review* 35: 697–709.

Winograd, Terry, and Flores, Fernando (1986). *Understanding computers and cognition: A new foundation for design.* Norwood, NJ: Ablex.

Wise, J. Macgregor (1998). Intelligent agency. *Cultural Studies* 12: 410–428.

Wodehouse, P. G. (1999/1923). *The inimitable Jeeves.* Harmondsworth, UK: Penguin.

Wolmark, Jenny (ed.). (1999). *Cybersexualities: A reader on feminist theory, cyborgs and cyberspace.* Edinburgh: Edinburgh University Press.

Wood, Gaby (2002). *Living dolls: A magical history of the quest for mechanical life.* London: Faber & Faber.

Woolf, Beverly and McDonald, David (1983). Human–computer discourse in the design of a PASCAL tutor. *Proceedings of the ACM CHI 83 Conference on Human Factors in Computing Systems* (pp. 230–234). New York: ACM Press.

Woolgar, Steve (1991). Configuring the user: The case of usability trials. In J. Law (ed.), *A sociology of monsters: Essays on power, technology and domination.* London: Routledge.

Yates, JoAnne (1989). *Control through communication: The rise of system in American management.* Baltimore: Johns Hopkins University Press.

Zimmerman, Donald (1970). The practicalities of rule use. In J. Douglas (ed.)., *Understanding everyday life* (pp. 221–238). Chicago, IL: Aldine.

Zuboff, Shoshana (1988). *In the age of the smart machine: The future of work and power.* New York: Basic Books.

# Index